RETHINKING THE UNTHINKABLE

RETHINKING THE UNTHINKABLE
New Directions for Nuclear Arms Control

Edited by
Ivo H. Daalder
and
Terry Terriff

LONDON AND NEW YORK

First published in 1993 by
FRANK CASS & CO. LTD.

This edition published 2013 by Routledge
2 Park Square, Milton Park, Abingdon, Oxon OX14 4RN
711 Third Avenue, New York, NY 10017

Routledge is an imprint of the Taylor & Francis Group, an informa business

First issued in paperback 2016

Library of Congress Cataloging-in-Publication Data
Applied for.

British Library Cataloguing in Publication Data

Rethinking the Unthinkable:
New Directions for Nuclear Arms Control
I. Daalder, Ivo H. II. Terriff, Terry
327.1

This group of studies first appeared in a special issue on 'Rethinking the Unthinkable: New Directions for Nuclear Arms Control' in *Arms Control: Contemporary Security Policy*, Vol. 14, No. 1 (April 1993), published by Frank Cass & Co. Ltd.

ISBN: 978-0-714-64518-6 (hbk)
ISBN: 978-1-138-98539-1 (pbk)

CONTENTS

Introduction

TERRY TERRIFF and IVO H. DAALDER

The signing of the START-II Treaty on 3 January 1993 heralded the end of an era. Since the late 1960s the United States and the former Soviet Union have engaged in a series of laborious arms control negotiations that, though establishing some useful parameters for the management of the strategic nuclear relationship, did little to lessen concerns about each other's nuclear capabilities. Each feared that the other was seeking a strategic nuclear edge that could be exploited to its political, if not military, advantage. The main agenda of superpower arms control talks was to limit, and then reduce, the excessive build-up of strategic nuclear capacity and eliminate some of the more destabilizing components such as land-based ballistic missiles carrying multiple independently targetable warheads (MIRVs). But neither side trusted the other sufficiently to agree to limitations that would accomplish the goals of this agenda. As a consequence, the arms control agreements that the two nuclear superpowers were able to conclude only marginally eased strategic concerns and political tensions.

START II at last represents success. The United States and Russia have agreed to reduce their strategic nuclear arsenals by about two-thirds, from current levels of around 11,000–12,000 warheads to about 3,000–3,500 by 2003 at the latest. Perhaps most significant is that the agreement achieves the vital goal of eliminating MIRVed land-based missiles, long regarded as the most threatening and destabilizing component of the respective nuclear arsenals. But START II leaves some important issues unresolved, since it includes no requirements for the dismantlement of warheads, the verification of such dismantlement or the placement of fissile material under safeguards. The implementation of the treaty also is not yet assured, for this depends, first, on Ukraine ratifying the START-I Treaty and, second, on overcoming the considerable opposition to START II that exists in Russia. Nonetheless, once implemented, the START-II Treaty will complete at least the main elements of the superpower arms control agenda of the past quarter century.

The sweeping and deep reductions of START II were made possible by the end of the Cold War, which has brought a profound transformation of the relations between the United States and the former

Soviet Union. The political and strategic hostility and competition that characterized much of the Cold War has abated and been replaced by tractable and even co-operative behaviour. This climate is conducive to radical arms control, as represented by the deep cuts of START II. Washington no longer perceives the independent states of the former Soviet Union as much of a threat to the United States and its Western allies, and Moscow sees the West not as a source of threat but of political and economic assistance. With the relaxation of tensions, the United States and Russia have recognized that mutual security can be best achieved not through antagonism and competition but through mutual restraint and co-operation. Thus, in providing the coda to a generation of arms control efforts, START II has codified the end of the Cold War.

But does the successful conclusion of the START series of negotiations, and the arms control agenda they represented, mean the end of nuclear arms control? The political and strategic environment in which the superpowers pursued their nuclear competition and arms control negotiations no longer exists. New political and strategic realities are emerging. The end of the Cold War and the concomitant political and strategic transformation of the international system opens up new opportunities and brings new dangers. Amongst the dangers is the threat posed by the spread of ballistic missile and nuclear weapons technology. Amongst the opportunities is the possibility of further US-Russian co-operation in nuclear arms control efforts, both to reduce still further their respective arsenals and to strengthen the norm of nuclear non-proliferation. The changing nature of the US-Russian relationship and the international environment raise some fundamental questions about the future of nuclear arms control:

- What are the long-term objectives of nuclear arms control?
- Should further reductions beyond START II be made in the nuclear arsenals of the United States and Russia?
- Does nuclear arms control have other roles to play in the US-Russian nuclear relationship?
- Should nuclear arms control be extended to include the United Kingdom, France and the People's Republic of China?
- How do we manage the promise and problem of strategic defences?
- How do we manage the spread of ballistic missiles and nuclear weapons?
- Are there new ways of conceptualizing and addressing the problems posed by nuclear weapons?

In 1992 the Center for International and Security Studies at Maryland

(CISSM), supported by a grant from the W. Alton Jones Foundation, initiated the *Project on Rethinking Arms Control*. The aim of the project is to foster the reconceptualization of arms control in a manner that makes it more relevant to present day realities. The project has sponsored the presentation of papers presenting new and provocative proposals for the future direction of arms control at workshops attended by policy analysts, journalists, leading academics, and US government officials. Several of these presentations dealt with nuclear arms control. These have been revised and updated, and are published in this special issue of *Arms Control*. They include the contributions by Michael Brown, Ivo Daalder, William Durch, Lisbeth Gronlund, John Hawes, Lora Lumpe, and George Quester. Further articles exploring provocative or alternative approaches to nuclear arms control have been contributed by Alexei Arbatov, Michael Clarke, and Jonathan Dean.

In a short introduction it is not possible to capture fully the nature and scope of the analyses presented here. However, three central themes can be identified as undergirding the various analyses. The first concerns the potential for further positive bilateral efforts in nuclear arms control in the wake of START II. The START treaties may have been the culmination of a bilateral nuclear arms control agenda pursued by the United States and the former Soviet Union since the late 1960s, but it hardly signifies the end of bilateral nuclear arms control. Much more can be accomplished. The readiness of the United States and Russia to undertake radical cuts in their nuclear arsenals in START II underscores that a fundamental change in thinking about the role of nuclear weapons in warfare is taking place. The question is no longer how much is needed for deterrence, but how little is needed for deterrence and what is needed for mutual security. Opportunities exist for the United States and Russia to consolidate and deepen the progress made with the START treaties, both through further reductions and innovative arms control measures designed not just to reduce and restructure residual forces, but to create more transparency in, and place greater restrictions on, the development of nuclear weapons technology. An opportunity also exists for the bilateral nuclear arms control process to be expanded to encompass the other nuclear states.

The second theme concerns the past discontinuity between the nuclear policies of the nuclear states and the global attempt to limit the spread of nuclear weapons. As signatories to the nuclear Non-Proliferation Treaty (NPT), the United States, the Soviet Union, Great Britain, and, lately, France and China, in effect undertook to negotiate in good faith the end of the nuclear arms race in return for the promise of the non-nuclear states not to acquire nuclear weapons. The reality has been quite different; since 1970, when the NPT came into effect, the nuclear powers, with United States and Soviet Union in the lead, have sought to constrain the spread of nuclear weapons at the same time that they increased by several fold their own nuclear arsenals. During the Cold War, the contradiction between the policies of the nuclear powers toward the possession of their own nuclear weapons and their policies toward others possessing nuclear weapons could be overlooked. In the post-Cold War era this contradiction can no longer be avoided; it may not be possible to isolate politically the nuclear policies of the nuclear states from the nuclear behaviour, whether real or potential, of non-nuclear states. Not everyone agrees that there is a political link between the nuclear behaviour of the nuclear states and the spread of nuclear weapons. One view expressly rejects such political linkage. But a common motif running through much of the analyses is that the behaviour of the nuclear states likely will establish the political context for the future course of global nuclear arms control. Positive actions by the nuclear states to undertake more comprehensive bilateral or multilateral nuclear arms control measures can provide the foundation for the development of more inclusive international nuclear arms control regimes and enhanced international security.

The third theme concerns the need to consider new approaches to managing the spread of nuclear weapons technology. Past nuclear arms control efforts have focused on restricting the transfer of nuclear and nuclear-related technologies. Iraq's surprisingly extensive covert nuclear programme demonstrates the limits to this approach. Far too much of present-day technology can be used for legitimate peaceful purposes as well as for nuclear weapons development. As more and more states seek to develop their economies through the transfer of advanced technology, export controls are likely to become even more porous. What is needed is a re-examination and reconceptualization of the problem, and, from this, the development of innovative arms control approaches to manage the spread of nuclear weapons.

These themes underpin and interweave the analyses that follow. They show that the time has come to begin rethinking the unthinkable – not to see how a nuclear war could or should be fought, as Herman Kahn admonished more than 30 years ago, but to end the nuclear menace while still preserving security for all. The essays in this volume may not provide the final answer, but they begin where one should, by asking the right questions.

Nuclear Arms Control: Finishing the Cold War Agenda

IVO H. DAALDER and TERRY TERRIFF

The START-II Treaty signed by US President George Bush and Russian President Boris Yeltsin on 3 January 1993 caps a quarter-century of strategic nuclear arms control. Since November 1969, when formal talks first began, the course of negotiations between the two nuclear powers acted as a bellwether of the state of their political and military relations. It took three years to negotiate the SALT-I agreements, which marked the heyday of *détente*. Growing doubts about *détente* stalled negotiations on a follow-on agreement for six years. The 1980s failed to produce any strategic arms agreement, reflecting in part the deteriorating US-Soviet relations in the early years of the decade. The START-I Treaty was finally signed on 31 July 1991, after nine years of negotiations. At the time, it was widely regarded as the last arms control accord of its kind.[1] However, within 18 months a follow-on agreement had been negotiated cutting US and Russian forces by two-thirds, to 3,000–3,500 on each side.

What promulgated the acceleration of nuclear arms control in the early 1990s was the fundamental change in the Soviet Union that emerged following Mikhail Gorbachev's accession to power in 1985. Nothing underscored this change in the security environment more dramatically than the August 1991 coup in Moscow. Its failure signalled not only the end of communism in Europe, but also the end of the Russian empire that was the USSR. In the weeks following the failed putsch, communism was banned throughout the vast Soviet territories, and power shifted from Moscow to the capitals of the 15 Soviet republics. In December, the Soviet Union was disbanded, the Commonwealth of Independent States (CIS) was created, and Mikhail Gorbachev, the father of *perestroika* and *glasnost*, was forced to resign as the last President of the USSR.

These rapid and historic events dramatically altered the course of American nuclear diplomacy. For a quarter-century strategic nuclear arms control negotiations had concentrated on managing the nuclear competition. In the aftermath of the failed coup, the primary concern became to ensure continued, effective and centralized control over the vast Soviet nuclear stockpile. Particularly worrisome was the fact that this arsenal, which consisted of some 27,000 nuclear weapons, was spread out over much of the former Union.[2] The disintegration of the Soviet Union and the rising conflict over territory, resources, and power within it posed two specific dangers. One danger was the prospect of nuclear weapons falling into the wrong hands at a time when the possibility of civil war could not be excluded – what then-US Secretary of State James Baker termed the threat of a 'Yugoslavia with nukes'.[3] The other danger was the potential for instantaneous nuclear proliferation as command and control over nuclear weapons shifted from Moscow to the republics – what one commentator termed the threat of 'nuclear weapons acquiring more states'.[4]

The Bush administration sought to deal with these twin dangers of 'loose nukes' and instantaneous nuclear proliferation by pursuing a three-part strategy consisting of: (i) encouraging central control over nuclear weapons, preferably by removing all weapons from non-Russian republics; (ii) offering incentives for further reductions by proposing drastic, unilateral and reciprocal cuts; and (iii) providing technical and financial assistance to ensure the secure control, safe transportation and storage, and sound disablement and eventual dismantlement of nuclear weapons.

On balance, the Bush administration moved deftly to respond to the dangers posed by the disintegration of a nuclear superpower. Whether forced by circumstances and pressures from within or as a result of a fundamental strategic reassessment, the administration's actions in the wake of the Moscow coup effectively demonstrated the degree to which nuclear diplomacy in the post-Soviet world had been transformed. The objective had become ensuring secure command and control over the former Soviet Union's nuclear forces, not searching for some abstract notion of crisis stability. The speed of implementation became more important than ensuring effective verification. Residual nuclear force levels on the US side could be drastically reduced. And long-winded, tedious and often competitive formal negotiations were replaced by co-operative efforts to determine reciprocal obligations.

Although the administration effectively completed the Cold War nuclear arms control agenda, it did little to push that agenda into the post-Cold War era. The articles in this volume will address the issues that such an agenda might contain. Here, we review the developments in nuclear arms control during the 18 months separating the Moscow coup and the signing of START II, months in which the arms race was thrown into reverse and the Cold War arms control agenda essentially completed. This sets the stage for rethinking the unthinkable in regard to nuclear weapons and arms control undertaking in the remaining papers of this volume.

The Imperative of Centralized Control

Among the more alarming consequences of the failed August coup was the threat of instantaneous nuclear proliferation that might result from the disintegration of the Soviet Union. Although Soviet authorities had taken some steps to remove nuclear weapons from politically volatile regions in the Caucuses and the Baltics, strategic and tactical nuclear weapons remained widely dispersed throughout the Union. The rush to independence by Soviet republics in the aftermath of the coup threatened to make instant nuclear powers of those newly independent states on whose territory nuclear forces were based. According to the START Treaty's memorandum of understanding, more than 20 deployment, production and other strategic nuclear sites were located outside Russia. Of the actual weapons covered by the treaty, 72 SS-25 missiles were deployed in Belarus, 104 SS-18 missiles and 40 Bear-H bombers were deployed in Kazakhstan, and 46 SS-24 missiles, 130 SS-19 missiles, 14 Bear-H, and 16 Blackjack bombers were deployed in Ukraine. More than 3,000 tactical nuclear weapons were similarly deployed with army, air defence, air force and navy units stationed outside Russia. All remaining nuclear forces were deployed in Russia.[5]

Preventing instantaneous nuclear proliferation became a principal concern of American nuclear diplomacy. When, in early September 1991, Secretary of State Baker set out the key principles that would guide US-Soviet policy following the coup, he warned that the United States did 'not want to see the transformation that's taking place in the Soviet Union either create or add to the problems of nuclear proliferation'. He also expressed the US preference 'that it would be probably on balance best if not necessarily [nuclear weapons] ended up all in one republic, but that they ended up under one central command authority'.[6]

With the disintegration of the Soviet Union all but a fact in December 1991, Baker travelled to Moscow, Minsk, Alma-Ata and Kiev to seek reassurance on these points from the leaders of the four new states with nuclear weapons on their soil. In his discussions, the four assured Baker that they would maintain existing arsenals in a safe, secure and responsible manner and under reliable control by a single collective authority. All four leaders also pledged that they would join the nuclear Non-Proliferation Treaty (NPT), with the three non-Russian states agreeing to join as non-nuclear powers and submit their nuclear facilities to international safeguards administered by the International Atomic Energy Agency (IAEA).[7]

Some of these commitments were reiterated in agreements signed by these and other members of the new Commonwealth of Independent

States. Thus, in the Alma-Ata agreement of 23 December 1991, Belarus, Kazakhstan, and Ukraine agreed to remove all non-strategic forces to Russian facilities by 1 July 1992, for eventual dismantlement. Belarus and Ukraine also declared that they would join the NPT and conclude safeguards agreements with the IAEA. Noticeably absent from this provision was a commitment by Kazakhstan to do the same. In addition, the four countries undertook commitments not to transfer nuclear weapons or other explosive devices and technologies or in any other way encourage or assist a state not possessing nuclear weapons in acquiring them.[8] In the Minsk agreement on strategic forces of 30 December 1991, the CIS members declared the 'need for joint command of strategic forces and for maintaining unified control of nuclear weapons of mass destruction'. Any decision on the use of nuclear weapons would be made by the Russian President 'in agreement with' Belarus, Kazakhstan and Ukraine, and 'in consultation with' the other CIS member states. Finally, Ukraine agreed to remove all strategic forces from its territory by 1994.[9]

Welcome as these formal statements were, they did not consist of binding agreements that the United States or other members of the international community could enforce. As it turned out, the greatest problem was posed by the agreements affecting the strategic weapons on the territory of the three non-Russian states. The vehicle for implementing the commitments on strategic nuclear arms became the START-I Treaty. In the Alma-Ata agreement of December 1991, the four new states on whose territory nuclear forces covered by the treaty were based pledged to submit the START-I Treaty for ratification to their parliaments.[10] Following discussions with US officials in January 1992, the three non-Russian states further agreed that all strategic forces on their territory would be eliminated as part of implementing the treaty.[11]

A formula to implement these commitments was proposed by Moscow in which Russia would ratify the START-I Treaty, the other three states would seek parliamentary approval of it, and all four states would conclude a quadripartite agreement that would give Russia the right to implement the treaty as far as facilities, inspection provisions, and forces on non-Russian territory were concerned. In February 1992, the United States indicated that it could accept this approach.[12]

In March, however, Ukrainian President Leonid Kravchuk challenged the Russian approach to the ratification of START I when he announced that Kiev had halted the transfer of tactical nuclear weapons to Russia.[13] The ostensible reason for the decision related to Kiev's desire to verify the dismantlement of weapons that had been transferred and the withdrawal of all tactical weapons from non-Russian republics was in fact completed in May 1992, two months ahead of schedule.[14] However, the announcement highlighted an aspect of Ukrainian policy that until then had not been clear: while Kiev had agreed to a joint *command* of nuclear weapons on its soil, and this would not change, to its mind Ukraine *owned* the weapon systems themselves.[15] Such reasoning called into question not only Ukraine's pledge to sign the NPT as a non-nuclear weapons state, but also whether a US-Russian agreement affecting the former Soviet Union's strategic forces would *legally* apply to forces based in Ukraine (or, for that matter, in Kazakhstan or Belarus).[16] Moreover, to admit that these were Ukrainian (or Kazakh or Belarussian) strategic forces was to admit that these countries were nuclear-weapons states – something Washington was striving to avoid.

Although the United States had no objections to granting the three non-Russian states a role in the START-I ratification process that was consistent with their newly gained sovereignty, it insisted that the treaty itself remain a bilateral undertaking.[17] Publicly, Moscow continued to maintain that as the sole legal successor to the Soviet Union, Russia should be the bilateral partner of the United States.[18] In contrast, Ukraine and Kazakhstan (which, like Ukraine, insisted that it would retain ownership over some of the nuclear missiles on its soil so long as Russia, China, and the United States deployed missiles)[19] demanded to be co-equal treaty partners with Russia.[20]

The stalemate among the four new states on how to ratify START I forced the Bush administration to become actively involved in the discussions among the four states. Whereas previously the United States had encouraged the new states to devise among themselves an acceptable formula for ratifying START I, by late March 1992 Washington took a pro-active stance by directly suggesting what approaches it would find both reasonable and acceptable.[21] Weeks of intensive negotiations resulted in the four states and the United States signing a protocol to the START-I Treaty that legally settled the matter. Concluded in Lisbon on 23 May 1992, the protocol identifies the four states as the bilateral treaty partner of the United States; includes a commitment by Belarus, Kazakhstan and Ukraine to sign the NPT as non-nuclear-weapons states 'in the shortest possible time'; and requires the four states to make the necessary arrangements to implement the treaty's provisions.[22] In separate letters by the Presidents of Belarus, Kazakhstan and Ukraine to President Bush, each country also committed itself to the complete elimination of nuclear weapons, including strategic offensive arms, located on its territory within the seven-year implementation period of the treaty.[23]

While agreement to the protocol and the separate letters from the three non-Russian states to the United States should have effectively settled the issue, problems arose in the ratification of these commitments. Kazakhstan ratified the START-I Treaty, including the Lisbon protocol, in July 1992, although it did not sign or ratify the NPT. The US Senate ratified the treaty in October. In Russia, conservatives, joined by nationalist forces, mounted a vigorous campaign in an effort to block ratification in part to embarrass President Yeltsin and in part to express their displeasure with the deal reached by Presidents Bush and Yeltsin in June 1992 on further arms reductions.[24] In addition, many legislators believed that implementation of the treaty would have to await ratification of START I and the NPT by Belarus, Kazakhstan and Ukraine as well as agreement among the four former Soviet republics on the procedures of implementing START I. In November, the Russian parliament ratified the treaty, but conditioned its entry into force on the three other states ratifying the NPT and agreeing to procedures of implementation.[25]

The greatest obstacle to the entry into force of the START-I Treaty has been Ukraine. (Belarus, which must also ratify the treaty, is expected to do so once Ukraine does.)[26] Since the summer 1992, there has been growing opposition to the elimination of nuclear weapons on Ukrainian soil and a consequent hardening of the government's position on this issue in negotiations with Russia and the United States. President Kravchuk, who continues to assert that Ukraine will achieve non-nuclear status,[27] set forth the problem in a news conference in November 1992:

> We must not link the ratification of START to conditions of some sort, but we have to go before Parliament with specific proposals. In order for Ukraine to complete its disarmament, we must have some material benefit and fixed guarantees for its security. If these two arguments are presented to deputies, I am sure they will vote in favour of the agreement.[28]

These conditions moved the Ukrainian government towards the position of the nationalist opposition movement Rukh, which has long argued that Ukraine should retain the weapons, or at least get financial recompense for divesting itself of the systems on its soil.[29]

The Ukrainian position was designed to achieve three objectives.[30] First, to obtain assurances from the nuclear powers, and especially from the United States and Russia, that Ukraine will never be the target of attack by nuclear or non-nuclear weapons. Second, to get financial aid to offset the cost of removing the nuclear warheads and dismantling the ballistic missiles located on Ukrainian soil. Some Ukrainian officials have indicated that this cost could be as much as $1.5 billion.[31] And third, to receive a share in any proceeds that would result from selling highly enriched uranium, collected from dismantled nuclear warheads, for eventual use as fuel for nuclear power plants in the West.

Both Russia and the United States have moved to address these conditions. Andrei Kokoshin, the Russian First Deputy Minister of Defence, has indicated that Russia, in principle, would be willing to ensure that Ukraine would get a share of any income generated by selling highly enriched uranium to the West. Russia also made clear that it was willing to discuss the costs of dismantling the nuclear systems.[32] Finally, in January 1993 President Yeltsin told his Ukrainian counterpart that Russia 'gives a guarantee to preserve and safeguard the integrity of Ukraine and its borders and defend it from nuclear attack'.[33]

For its part, the United States has sought to encourage Ukraine with a combination of carrots and sticks. While visiting Ukraine in late November 1992, Senators Sam Nunn and Richard Lugar indicated that the United States would be willing to offer Ukraine $100 to $150 million to cover the cost of dismantling the nuclear weapons systems and storage silos. They added that the United States would also buy weapons-grade uranium recovered from dismantled warheads provided that Russia had reached an agreement with Ukraine, Belarus and Kazakhstan on how to share the proceeds. The senators warned leaders in Kiev, however, that 'relations between our two countries, the pattern of cooperation and investment by the private sector depend on Ukraine keeping its commitment'.[34] In December, President Bush sent a letter to President Kravchuk indicating that the United States would provide Ukraine with $175 million for the disabling and dismantling of nuclear weapons on its soil. At the same time, the letter stated that the funds would only be available once Ukraine ratified the START-I Treaty and had acceded to the NPT as a non-nuclear weapon state.[35]

The question of formal security guarantees was addressed in a meeting between US and Ukrainian negotiators in early January 1993 in Washington. During the discussions, the United States shared the text of a statement it was willing to issue once Ukraine had fulfilled its START and NPT commitments. The statement would commit the United States to seek immediate assistance from the UN Security Council if Ukraine were the object of or threatened by nuclear aggression. This is similar to the statement the United States issued to all NPT signatories following the completion of the treaty in 1968. At the end of the bilateral discussions, the State Department also issued a statement saying that 'Ukraine's security as a non-nuclear state, integrated within

European security structures, is an important matter for the United States'.[36]

The Bush administration indicated that the United States was not about to engage in a bargaining session with Ukraine over the conditions for Kiev fulfilling its commitments. No guarantees, investment or co-operation would be forthcoming until the Ukrainian parliament ratified the START-I Treaty and the NPT.[37] The Clinton administration is unlikely to change this position. Having gotten about as much as it could hope for, Kiev is likely to ratify its commitments in 1993. Once this step has been taken, one of the main dangers resulting from the break-up of the USSR – the prospect of instantaneous nuclear proliferation – will have been resolved. In so doing, one of the three goals set by the Bush administration in the aftermath of the Moscow coup would be fulfilled.

The Imperative of Nuclear Reductions

Among the more immediate issues raised by the failed August coup was the growing concern about the degree of control over the Soviet nuclear arsenal. This concern was heightened by reports surfacing in the immediate aftermath of the coup that the nuclear 'football' containing the electronic codes for transmitting launch orders had been taken away from the Soviet President, raising serious questions about the state of control over Soviet strategic nuclear forces.[38] In an effort to downplay this, the Bush administration released intelligence information indicating that during the coup Soviet nuclear commanders had taken precautionary steps to ensure effective control over strategic forces.[39]

The same sense of confidence was absent, however, with respect to control over *tactical* nuclear weapons, some 15,000–17,000 of which were deployed in all Soviet republics outside the Baltics and the Caucuses. Secretary of Defense Richard Cheney noted in late August, for instance, that 'tactical nuclear weapons are much more widely dispersed than strategic systems. Will they still be controlled from the center? Or will they come under the control of the respective republic governments?'[40] These questions reflected issues raised by an interagency committee inside the Bush administration that for months had been studying the question of nuclear command and control within the Soviet Union. Even before the coup, the committee had concluded that tactical nuclear weapons posed the gravest risk.[41]

The threat of a loss of control over tactical nuclear weapons topped Baker's agenda when he travelled to Moscow in early September 1991. In talks with Soviet officials, Baker suggested possible steps Moscow might take to counter the threat – including withdrawing nuclear weapons from places of potential or present conflict, removing from operational units older weapons lacking or having only primitive fail-safe devices, and concentrating tactical weapons on as few bases as possible to enhance their security.[42] He also sought a commitment from Moscow that it would match any unilateral US reductions in tactical nuclear weapons that Washington might announce in the future.[43]

In Moscow, Baker appeared to preach to the converted. The new Soviet Defence Minister, General Yevgeny Shaposhnikov, told Baker that keeping track of tactical weapons was difficult, particularly at times of chaos. The new Chief of the Soviet General Staff, General Vladimir Lobov, urged Baker to agree to negotiate the elimination of US and Soviet tactical nuclear weapons, in part because 'they are deployed across the vast territory of Europe, which is a risk, especially in the unstable political situation that took shape in the Balkans, on a part of Soviet territory, and in Germany'.[44]

In another reflection of these concerns, President Bush ordered the Pentagon in late August to develop new initiatives on nuclear weapons designed to provide the Soviet Union with incentives to consolidate and reduce their tactical nuclear stockpile. Working in customary secrecy, the Pentagon and other top administration officials developed a bold plan 'to step down the thermonuclear ladder', as the US Chairman of the Joint Chiefs of Staff, General Colin Powell, would later put it.[45] The initiative, which was announced by President Bush in an address to the nation on 27 September 1991, included the following steps, which, though undertaken unilaterally, the US asked the Soviet Union to match:[46]

- elimination of all ground-based tactical nuclear missile warheads and artillery shells;
- removal of tactical nuclear weapons from surface ships and attack submarines, destroying some and consolidating the remainder;
- standing down from alert all strategic bombers and those ICBMs scheduled for elimination under START;
- cancellation of the mobile MX missile, the mobile portion of the Midgetman programme, and the short-range attack missile.

President Gorbachev responded to the US initiatives on 5 October by matching the unilateral US moves and, in some cases, extending them to other areas.[47] Specifically, Gorbachev's response included:

- elimination of ground-based tactical nuclear weapons;

- removal of tactical nuclear weapons from naval vessels (destroying some) and a proposal for their elimination on a reciprocal basis;
- a proposal to remove tactical nuclear bombs and missiles from active air force units;
- standing down from alert all strategic bombers and those ICBMs to be eliminated under START, and confining rail-mobile missiles to their garrisons;
- halting development of MIRVed mobile missiles, the follow-on SS-25 missile, and the short-range attack missile and freezing the deployment of rail-mobile ICBMs;
- a unilateral cut of 1,000 warheads below START levels and a proposal for reciprocal cuts of 50 per cent post-START levels;
- a reciprocal ban on fissile material production and a one-year moratorium on nuclear testing to encourage agreement on a complete test ban.

The positive Soviet response to the Bush initiative signalled the emergence of a new era in arms control. Quite apart from the inherent significance of these steps, four factors in Bush's initiatives stood out as powerful evidence of the transformation of the nuclear arms control agenda.

First, the initiative underscored an emerging shift in American thinking about the role of nuclear weapons in a post-Cold War era marked by the ascendancy of true reformers in Moscow and the discrediting of the old line as a result of the failed coup. This shift was apparent in the decision to stand down from alert all strategic bombers, which signalled to Moscow that the United States no longer feared a bolt-out-of-the-blue attack.[48] But it was most obviously present in the unilateral elimination of all ground-based tactical nuclear weapons, which had long been the key to US extended deterrence policy in Europe and North East Asia.[49] With the disappearance of the Soviet military threat, ground-based nuclear weapons had become a liability rather than an asset. The same was true with regard to sea-based tactical nuclear weapons, with the US navy finally accepting the wisdom of removing these uncontrollable weapons from sea.[50] At the same time, the shift in thinking was not extended to its logical conclusion – air-based tactical nuclear weapons, even if at sharply reduced levels, would remain in Europe (though not in South Korea) to 'provide an essential political and military link between the European and the North American members of the Alliance,' as NATO's new strategic concept put it.[51]

Second, the fact that the administration concentrated its unilateral reductions in the tactical nuclear area, while leaving strategic forces largely untouched, underscored the degree to which the United States was concerned about a loss of control over these smaller weapons. The initiative accordingly emphasized the idea that fewer weapons posed fewer problems for control. In addition, the initiative was clearly geared to creating incentives for consolidating and eliminating Soviet weapons, both to reduce command and control problems and to remove nuclear weapons as a source of friction in the emerging power struggle among the Soviet republics. As Paul Wolfowitz, the US Under Secretary for Defense, stated, the 'real agenda is to get rid of 10,000 to 17,000 tactical nuclear weapons in the Soviet Union which nobody needs'. He also said that the United States was appealing to 'anyone who has any power to take a decision' in the Soviet Union to agree to their destruction.[52] For this reason, US officials travelling to Moscow in early October to explain the Bush initiative insisted that representatives of the four Soviet republics with strategic arms on their territory be included in the discussions.[53]

Third, the administration emphasized that speed was of the essence. Reciprocal, unilateral steps became the new arms control game. This represented a fundamental shift in US policy, as Cheney emphasized: 'We clearly, in moving unilaterally, have taken a different approach than I would have advocated even a few months ago.'[54] The reasons for the new approach were twofold. Previous arms control experience suggested that negotiations could end up delaying agreement on the required steps, thus undermining the US goal of achieving the rapid consolidation and elimination of Soviet tactical weapons. Arms control by example had the advantage of achieving immediate results.[55] In addition, Soviet disarray put the onus on Washington for breaking the internal deadlock in Moscow. As a State Department official explained, 'We know from them that tactical nukes are a political problem for them, given the changing political makeup. The president's proposal gives them the political cover to do what they want to do anyway.'[56]

Finally, in emphasizing speed over negotiations, the administration deliberately decided to forgo verifying agreed undertakings, and to rely instead on an exchange of information about how the commitments were being implemented.[57] Cheney offered four reasons for this omission, citing the START-I Treaty as a framework for monitoring tactical weapons cuts, the new degree of openness in Soviet society, the engagement of the republics in the arms control dialogue, and the dire straits of the Soviet economy – all of which suggested that the likelihood of cheating had been drastically reduced.[58] A fifth and more likely reason – the increasing US reluctance to allow Soviet and other foreign inspectors to check US facilities and capabilities that had become apparent in previous nuclear, chemical and conventional arms control negotiations – remained unstated. Whatever the reason, however, verification – long the bone of contention in arms control negotiations – was clearly becoming less important in an era of growing trust between Moscow and Washington.

The extent to which political change in the Soviet Union was forcing a transformation of the nuclear arms control agenda was underscored by a new round of unilateral and reciprocal measures proposed in late January 1992, after the USSR had formally ceased to exist. In back-to-back statements, President Bush and Russian President Yeltsin proposed significant additional reductions in strategic nuclear arms, announced the termination of almost all nuclear modernization programmes, and suggested new areas of co-operation.[59]

Bush's proposals focused narrowly on strategic arms. They included halting the B-2 bomber programme after 20 aircraft had been procured, cancelling the Midgetman missile programme, terminating the advanced cruise missile, and ending production of the W-88 warhead for the Trident D5 missile. The President further proposed that, in exchange for a mutual ban on land-based MIRVed missiles, the United States would eliminate all MX missiles, reduce the number of warheads on all the remaining 500 Minuteman missiles to one, cut the number of SLBM warheads by one-third from the level planned under START, and dedicate 'a substantial portion' of its strategic bombers to conventional use. According to General Powell, if Russia and the other CIS states were to accept this proposal, US strategic forces would be cut by about 50 per cent from post-START levels, to 4,700 warheads overall.[60]

Yeltsin's statements were more wide-ranging, covering not only nuclear but also conventional, chemical and biological weapons and arms control. Regarding the former, Yeltsin committed Russia to all the steps enunciated by Gorbachev the previous October and added some significant initiatives on his own. Among the more noteworthy of these were:

- an end to production of the Bear and Blackjack strategic bombers and of existing types of ALCMs and SLCMs;
- a proposal to reduce strategic offensive warheads to 2,000–2,500 on each side;
- a suggestion to create an international agency to ensure the reduction of nuclear weapons and placing gradually under its control the entire nuclear fuel cycle of all countries;
- a proposal to create a global defence system for the world community based on a reorientation of the US Strategic Defense Initiative and Russian defence technology.

Yeltsin's statements were followed two weeks later by even more far-reaching proposals put forward by Russian Foreign Minister Andrei Kozyrev to the UN Conference on Disarmament in Geneva. In his speech, Kozyrev reiterated an earlier proposal to end the targeting of each other's territory; suggested the adoption of a 'zero alert status' for nuclear forces by removing warheads from ICBMs, bombs and cruise missiles from bombers, and SLBMs from missile-carrying submarines, which would remain in port; proposed that the five nuclear powers exchange data on the number and type of nuclear weapons, the amount of fissile material in them, and the installations for their production, storage, and destruction; and recommended that countries take a new look at earlier ideas to place control over nuclear weapons under an international organization like the United Nations.[61]

These various US and Russian proposals highlighted the fundamental shift in nuclear arms control that had emerged after the Moscow coup in August 1991. Unilateral, though co-ordinated, public announcements, coupled with ministerial-level talks, replaced the competitive negotiating game. Agreements would no longer be formalized in treaty language drafted by international lawyers talented in rendering simple steps and obligations in convoluted and obscure language. Instead, an exchange of letters, or an agreed short document spelling out reciprocal obligations would suffice.[62] Formal verification provisions, other than those already accepted under START-I and other agreements, would be noticeably absent. Most remarkable, however, was the new strategic question guiding arms control negotiations; rather than asking 'How much is enough', both sides began to ask 'How low can we go?'

In ministerial talks between Baker and Kozyrev in the months following the Bush–Yeltsin initiatives, the United States and Russia sought to arrive at a common answer to this question. Though more amicable, collegial and co-operative than in previous years, these discussions still underscored a number of differences. First, there was disagreement on the mix of reductions. The United States insisted not only on deMIRVing all land-based missiles, but also on retaining multiple warheads on its sea-based missiles, though it was willing to reduce these from the present eight warheads per missile to between four and six. Since Russia had long emphasized its land-based missile capability and the United States its sea-based missile force, Moscow insisted that deMIRVing apply to all missiles, whether land- or sea-based.[63]

Second, the two sides differed on the scope of any post-START reductions. The Pentagon, in particular, made it clear that the Bush-proposed reductions to 4,700 warheads on the US side were as low as the United States could go and rejected any notion of going down to the 2,000–2,500 level proposed by the Russians. Thus, Secretary

Cheney argued that his 'basic instinct is [that] there's a level there that we want to hold at', in part because any further reductions would cut into the US SLBM force: 'It's important to preserve an adequate level in terms of the numbers of submarines we have. I think that's stabilizing, not destabilizing.'[64] Although the argument was in many ways debatable since the United States could maintain the planned number of 18 Trident submarines and still reduce much further by removing warheads from its SLBM force, the Pentagon's insistence on the 4,700 warhead level posed a major obstacle to reaching agreement with Russia on any post-START-I reductions.

The differences on the magnitude of any reductions were resolved during the Washington summit meeting between Presidents Bush and Yeltsin in June 1992. There it was decided that reductions would take place in two phases, with the final phase limiting US and Russian forces to 3,000–3,500 weapons each. President Yeltsin broke the deadlock by proposing that the overall limit consist of a range rather than a fixed number, which would allow Russia to come closer to its target of 2,500 weapons. At the same time, the upper boundary was set by dividing differences between the US preference for 4,700 weapons and Russia's for 2,500 weapons.[65]

Under the June 1992 joint understanding, the United States and Russia agreed that within the seven period following entry into force of the START-I Treaty they would reduce their strategic forces to no more than:

- an overall total number of warheads for each between 3,800 and 4,250;
- 1,200 MIRVed ICBM warheads;
- 650 heavy ICBM warheads; and
- 2,160 SLBM warheads.

In a second phase, to be completed by the year 2003 (or by the end of the year 2000 if the United States could contribute to the financing of the destruction or elimination of strategic offensive arms in Russia), the United States and Russia would:

- reduce their warheads to between 3,000 and 3,500 each;
- eliminate all MIRVed ICBMs; and
- reduce SLBM warheads to no more than 1,750.[66]

The accord further provided for counting nuclear heavy bombers according to the actual number of nuclear weapons they are equipped to carry, and for excluding from the overall count up to 100 heavy bombers that were never equipped to carry nuclear ALCMs and were reoriented to conventional roles.

The intention of the two countries was to translate Washington agreement promptly into a short treaty document. However, quick progress proved elusive. Negotiations were delayed, first, by Russia's belated response to the initial US draft proposal, which had been prepared and submitted to the Russians by July 1992.[67] Second, by late summer the US side had come to a virtual halt as a result of the presidential election campaign and Secretary Baker's resignation from the State Department to run the campaign from the White House. As a consequence, Acting Secretary of State Lawrence Eagleburger and Russian Foreign Minister Andrei Kozyrev did not meet until late September to begin serious discussions on the treaty language.[68]

By that time, it was clear that the Russian government faced an uphill domestic battle on finalizing the treaty. The reaction among Russian hard-liners and nationalists to the June 1992 joint understanding had been highly negative. There was a general sense that the agreement represented yet one more instance of Russia bowing to American wishes. Opposition to the joint understanding therefore soon became a rallying cry of those who rejected the Yeltsin government's overall approach to foreign as well as economic policy.

Opposition also centered around two specific issues.[69] One related to Yeltsin's proposal of a range limit rather than an equal ceiling. The Russian president's explanation of this proposal – that Russia was 'departing from the ominous parity where each country was exerting every effort to stay in line, which has led Russia, for instance, having half of its population living below the poverty line'[70] – proved particularly irksome, for it implied that Russia could no longer afford to retain the strategic parity that the Soviet Union had for so long sought to acquire and maintain. Second, there was the specific issue of the Russian land-based strategic forces in general and the SS-18 missiles in particular. This back-bone of the Russian strategic forces would be eliminated under the agreement, even though the traditional US strength in sea-based missiles would only be reduced. Again, this aspect of the agreement was viewed by many in Russia as favouring the United States at the expense of Russia.

The discussions between US and Russian negotiators reflected these concerns. Specifically, four issues proved particularly nettlesome. First, there was disagreement over whether Russia should have to destroy the silos for the SS-18 missiles, all of which were to be reduced under START II. The joint understanding called for the agreed reductions to be carried out by eliminating missile launchers using START-I procedures. Russia requested that it instead be allowed to modify the SS-18 silos for use of single-warhead missiles that it would be allowed to retain under the treaty. With its failing economy, Moscow wanted to save the expense of destroying these silos and building new ones. Washington was unwilling to accept such a change, fearing that the retention of these silos would give Russia the potential to place large missiles back into these silos covertly and break out of the treaty.[71]

Second, the two countries disagreed about whether Russia could retain its SS-19 missiles. Under START-I procedures, which were to apply to START II, the downloading of an individual ballistic missile by more than four warheads to achieve agreed reductions was prohibited. Adherence to START-I rules would therefore commit Russia to eliminating the six-warhead SS-19 missiles as well as the ten-warhead SS-18 and SS-24 missiles. Again for economic reasons, Moscow wanted to retain all 170 of its SS-19s by removing five warheads to meet the START-II ban on multiple warhead ICBMs. US officials balked at this demand. They worried that Russia might later be able to remount warheads on the missiles without being discovered by inspectors.[72]

Third, there was disagreement about how to count B-1 bombers under the treaty once they had been oriented to conventional roles. The United States indicated that it was likely to assign all its B-1 bombers to conventional roles and none would therefore count under the terms of the treaty.[73] However, the Pentagon wanted to reserve the right to reorient the bombers to a nuclear role after the B-52 bombers were retired. Russia objected to this US demand for flexibility and insisted that if B-1 bombers could be reoriented to a nuclear role, every one should be counted against the warhead limits established by the treaty.[74]

Finally, the two sides were at odds over whether Russia should be allowed to inspect the US B-2 bomber. The START-II framework agreed in Washington, unlike the START-I Treaty, limited bomber weapons to the actual number for which each bomber is equipped. The new counting rules, however, necessitated intrusive Russian inspection of the B-2 to determine how many weapons each actually carried. During the START-I negotiations the United States had managed to exclude the B-2 from intrusive inspection in order to protect its technological secrets, and it was still not disposed to permit Russian access to the aircraft.[75]

The common thread throughout these issues was concern about how deep reductions could be verified. This reflected in large part a continuity of old thinking in both Washington and Moscow. Despite the more collegial and co-operative atmosphere in which the treaty was being negotiated, each side clearly harboured lingering suspicions about the motives of the other. For Russia, the concern focused on getting adequate assurances that the American bomber capability would be strictly limited. For the United States, it reflected the continuing need for adequate monitoring of missiles and launchers to protect against Russian cheating.

What is surprising is that in the US case, the fear that Moscow could break out of the agreed limitations by deploying missiles in SS-18 silos and/or warheads on the SS-19 missile did not extend to concern about the disposition of weapons and missiles to be reduced by the agreement, both of which could be stored rather than deployed. When the US Senate had ratified START I, it had added a condition stating that

> in connection with any further agreement reducing strategic offensive arms, the President shall seek an appropriate arrangement . . . to monitor (A) the numbers of nuclear stockpile weapons on the territory of the parties to this Treaty; and (B) the location and inventory of facilities . . . capable of producing or processing significant quantities of fissile materials.[76]

But the Bush administration remained adamantly opposed to seeking adequate arrangements.

Aside from believing that the negotiation of such arrangements would delay completion of the START-II Treaty, the administration's opposition was based on three concerns. First, it believed that any monitoring or verification regime would have to be reciprocal. But as Robert Gallucci, assistant secretary of state for politico-military affairs, told Congress, the administration would be unwilling to accept or propose a monitoring scheme that would compromise 'US security interests and the statutory requirements of the Atomic Energy Act of 1954 for the protection of nuclear weapons design information'.[77] Second, the administration believed that 'any verification measures that would be consistent with US – or Russian – requirements for protection of nuclear weapons design information would be woefully inadequate to ensure that all weapons or facilities were declared'.[78] And third, Gallucci maintained that, though an agreed formula for monitoring declared weapons and facilities could be devised, the additional measures needed to monitor undeclared weapons and facilities would be exceedingly intrusive, expensive and complex, and would not be sufficient to ensure full compliance.[79]

Once the US presidential elections had run its course in early November 1992 and President Bush had reconciled himself to his stunning defeat, an intense round of diplomacy ensued in order to finalize the START-II agreement before the new Clinton administration would take office. Presidents Bush and Yeltsin made a series of telephone calls and letters, and Acting Secretary Eagleburger and Foreign Minister Kozyrev met in Stockholm and Geneva to work out a final compromise.[80] In the end, agreement was reached in Geneva on 29 December 1992, paving the way for the signing of the START-II Treaty by Presidents Bush and Yeltsin on 3 January 1993 in Moscow.[81]

In the final days of negotiations, each country made significant compromises leading to the successful outcome. First, although the missile silos for the 154 SS-18 missiles that are to be reduced under START I have to be dismantled, Russia will be permitted to convert 105 of the 154 remaining silos for the use of smaller missiles under START II. In return, Russia agreed to eliminate all SS-18 missiles, which it had not been required to do under the START-I Treaty. Second, while START-I rules limit the number of warheads that can be removed to achieve agreed reductions to four per missiles, under START II Russia is allowed to keep 90 SS-19 missiles by removing five warheads to comply with the agreement's ban on MIRVed ICBM warheads. Third, each side can orient to conventional roles up to 100 bombers that have never been equipped with ALCMs, provided that they are observably different from bombers with nuclear roles, based separately from bombers with nuclear roles, no nuclear weapons are stored at their bases, and the aircraft and crews undergo no training for nuclear missions. These bombers will continue to count under START I, but will be subject to START-II limitations only if they are again reoriented to nuclear roles. Such a re-orientation will be limited to one time only. Finally, START II will limit the number of bomber weapons to the actual number for which bombers are equipped. The inspection regimen for heavy bombers was amended to allow Russia a one-time inspection of the B-2.

The sense of urgency with which the United States pursued the final negotiations stemmed in part from the Bush administration's concern about its place in history and in part from uncertainties about the success of Russian political and economic reforms. Amongst US officials there was some concern that Russia would be increasingly less able to reach an agreement. Yeltsin's authority had been eroded early in December 1992 by a struggle with Russia's conservative-dominated parliament, in which he had to sacrifice his primary architect of reform and acting prime minister, Yegor Gaidar. Yeltsin's increasingly tenuous political situation raised the prospect that he would be susceptible to political pressure to move back toward the older conservative policies of the former authoritarian regime. Clearly, Bush administration officials recognized that it was better to make hard compromises to reach an agreement with Yeltsin than to risk delay, which could only increase the chance that Yeltsin might be swayed from his nuclear policies or be replaced by a Russian leader with a less favourable attitude toward the West.

The shared urgency that Russia brought to the final negotiations may have reflected similar concerns. Achieving significant military reductions to reduce the drain of military spending on the Russian economy was a central component of Yeltsin's economic reform programme. With his reform programme under attack from Russian conservatives, Yeltsin needed to consolidate the gains made on reducing strategic nuclear arms lest they be blocked down the road. Yeltsin also may have hoped that signing such a historic arms reduction treaty as START II might provide him with a much needed boost to his image at home. At the same time, it was clear Yeltsin would face an uphill battle in getting the parliament to go along with the final treaty.[82]

That the United States and Russia could bridge their differences despite their lingering concerns about verification reflects the degree to which nuclear arms control deliberations have changed in just a very few months. The scope of discussions as well as their nature underscored how truly radical a transformation of nuclear diplomacy has occurred. Perhaps nothing underscores this new trend more than the cooperative steps, in terms of financial and technical assistance by the United States to Russia and the other CIS states, that have been taken in the months since the Moscow coup.

The Emergence of Co-operative Denuclearization

The concern about a loss of control over the Soviet nuclear arsenal that had resulted in the bold unilateral reductions announced by the United States was also manifested in a second major departure from traditional American diplomacy – the provision of direct technical and financial assistance in the denuclearization process. Even before the August coup, US and Soviet officials had been worried about the security of the Soviet stockpile. Since early 1991, a US interagency committee had studied the matter in detail, and in early August General Powell received a letter from his Soviet counterpart suggesting that nuclear security be added to the regular military-to-military talks in which both sides had been engaged in.[83]

The failed coup, however, propelled this issue to the top of the agenda. In his 27 September 1991 initiative, President Bush suggested three areas of co-operation:

> First, we should explore joint technical cooperation on the safe and environmentally responsible storage, transportation, dismantling, and destruction of nuclear warheads. Second, we should discuss existing arrangements for the physical security and safety of nuclear weapons and how these might be enhanced. And third,

> we should discuss nuclear command and control arrangements, and how these might be improved to provide more protection against the unauthorized or accidental use of nuclear weapons.[84]

In his response, President Gorbachev announced his readiness to engage in a dialogue with the United States on these issues.[85]

During their meeting in Madrid at the opening of the Mideast peace conference in late October 1991, Presidents Bush and Gorbachev agreed to establish two working groups, including one group that would examine how to implement their initiatives while discussing modalities of nuclear weapons safety, dismantlement and control.[86] The first meeting of the working group on safety, security, and dismantlement (SSD) took place in Washington in November and included representatives of the four republics with strategic weapons on their soil. According to Bartholomew, the United States 'made a major push for the Soviets to disable and to consolidate in secure locations the widely dispersed tactical nuclear weapons'.[87] The United States also briefed the Soviet participants on the particulars of American safety, security and command and control arrangements, on how weapons could be disabled quickly, and on the dismantlement methods used by the United States. Unfortunately, however, the Soviet participants did not reciprocate. According to Bartholomew, there 'was a general reluctance to engage with us across the board, or to describe their systems and procedures in the detail that we described ours'.[88]

The greatest failure of the November SSD meeting, however, was a lack of real urgency on the part of the Bush administration in dealing with the nuclear issue. While discussions of sensitive matters were of course needed and desirable, nothing concrete was being done to consolidate the Soviet nuclear stockpile and implement the tactical nuclear weapons initiatives of Bush and Gorbachev. Frustrated by this lack of progress, the US Congress moved to spur the administration along.[89] In late November 1991, Congress voted to amend the Arms Export Control Act in order to allocate $400 million of Defense Department funds to assist in the destruction of Soviet nuclear and chemical weapons (as well as $100 million for humanitarian assistance).[90]

It took the overwhelming Ukrainian vote for independence on 1 December 1991, however, to convince the Bush administration of the need to take concrete steps in dealing with the nuclear danger posed by the disintegration of the Soviet Union. In a speech at Princeton University on 12 December 1991, Secretary Baker made three points in regard to nuclear issues.[91] First, he stressed the necessity of avoiding the emergence of new nuclear weapons states as a result of the Soviet transformation. Second, he announced that the SSD talks that had begun in

November would be accelerated. Third, he declared that the administration was prepared to draw on the $400 million appropriated by Congress to assist in the destruction of Soviet weapons of mass destruction. Baker received commitments from all four leaders of the republics with nuclear forces on their soil on the first point when he travelled days later to the Soviet Union.[92] The other issues were addressed subsequent to his trip.

In late December, President Bush wrote the presidents of the four new states proposing to send a US delegation 'to discuss practical steps on nuclear safety, security, disabling, and destruction, as well as controls to prevent proliferation'.[93] The delegation would also discuss how the US could assist in these efforts. The proposed agenda for the SSD talks included: command and control; safety, security, disabling and accelerated destruction of tactical nuclear weapons; START, CFE, and NPT obligations; and export controls, including arms transfers.

The American delegation travelled to the four capitals in mid-January and generally found a co-operative audience.[94] The delegation was reassured about the security of command and control arrangements, which remained physically in the hands of the Russian president and the head of the CIS armed forces, General Shaposhnikov. The main problem the US delegation confronted concerned the pace of dismantlement efforts inside Russia and the degree and scope of possible US assistance in this process. According to Bartholomew, the Russians believed that it would be difficult to meet the schedule outlined by Gorbachev earlier to dismantle all weapons by the year 2000. The problem they confronted was not the destruction process itself, but rather the absence of storage facilities for recovered plutonium and enriched uranium.[95] Russian officials suggested that the $400 million appropriated by Congress be used to construct such facilities.[96] Rather than endorsing the suggestion to construct these elaborate facilities, the Bush administration proposed a number of alternative and cheaper ways to store the recovered materials.[97] At the same time, the administration did not consider the option of storing fissile materials recovered from dismantled weapons under either international or joint supervision, an option suggested both by the Russians themselves and by the IAEA.[98]

In mid-February 1992, Secretary Baker travelled to Moscow prepared to settle this and other questions. He carried with him seven proposals dealing with the transportation, storage, disablement and dismantlement of nuclear warheads. These included information on: US warhead storage containers, fissile material containers, special rail cars and kevlar 'bullet-proof' blankets for warhead protection during transit; nuclear accident response planning; an accounting system for inventory management; and civil use of fissile materials.[99] Baker proposed that these items, as well as the question of long-term storage of recovered fissile materials, be discussed in subsequent meetings by US and Russian experts.[100]

In early March, a 67-person US SSD team, led by William Burns, the former Director of the Arms Control and Disarmament Agency, travelled to Russia to discuss these various items with its Russian counterparts. During these meetings, the Russians agreed to make available to the United States engineering diagrams on special containers and rail cars the Russians used for transporting weapons to determine whether it might be cheaper to build additional containers and rail cars than to convert US equipment to Russian use, as the United States had initially proposed. Based on information provided by Russian officials, the United States believed that some 45,000 containers were needed to transport weapons and fissile materials in a safe and secure manner. Building these to Russian rather than American specifications was believed to be both cheaper and quicker.[101]

As a result of the March SSD talks, in April 1992 the United States was able to certify Russia, Ukraine and Belarus as being committed to the courses of actions prescribed in the Soviet Nuclear Risk Reduction legislation passed by Congress in November 1991, thus releasing funds for assisting in the nuclear safety, security and dismantlement process.[102] This was followed by the signing of an agreement during the June summit in Washington to provide the legal basis for furnishing assistance to Russia under the act.[103]

The United States moved quickly to reach agreement with Russia on safety and security measures proposed by Baker to help speed the dismantlement of nuclear warheads. General Burns, testifying before the Senate Foreign Relations Committee in July 1992, was able to report that agreement had been reached on the following measures: the United States would produce 10,000 storage containers by December 1995 for the transport and storage of fissile material removed from dismantled Russian warheads, at an expected to cost of about $50 million; the United States had transferred 200 kevlar blankets to be used to protect nuclear weapon containers from small arms fire during transit, with a further 250 such armoured blankets to be produced and delivered by the spring of 1993, at an anticipated cost of about $5 million; and the United would transfer over 1,000 pieces of accident response equipment, at an estimated cost of $10 million.[104]

Burns also testified that a SSD team would visit Ukraine, Belarus and Kazakhstan in August and September to initiate discussions on how best to apply available funds to ensure the dismantlement of nuclear weapons in their territories. Discussions had already begun with Ukraine on control and accounting procedures for fissile material. Burns estimated that 'several tens of millions' of dollars would be required to establish initial projects to help these three states disassemble nuclear armaments on their soil.[105] The first results of these efforts consisted of agreements between the United States and Belarus to assist Minsk in developing better export laws and to provide Belarus with equipment to ensure safety of personnel during the transportation of nuclear weapons. The United States pledged $1 million and $5 million respectively for these efforts.[106] Washington agreed to a similar package to Ukraine, as well as financial help to set up government-to-government communication links.[107] Finally, in December 1992 President Bush pledged $175 to help Ukraine in dismantling weapons on its territory, provided Kiev fulfilled its START I and NPT commitments.[108]

Burns also informed the committee that some European allies had all made, or were in the process of making commitments to offer Russia assistance in dismantling its nuclear weapons.[109] But he also pointed out that 'If we tallied all the requests made, and the costs that our analysis showed, the amount would exceed the $400 million.'[110] Progress on implementing the SSD programme was going sufficiently quickly that he expected to have committed all of the $400 million within the next 60 to 90 days. An inescapable conclusion of his testimony was that the $400 million allocated by the Nunn–Lugar Act would not meet the needs of the evolving programme. Accordingly, Congress voted in October 1992 to allocate a further $400 million of Defense Department Funds to assist the former Soviet Republics with dismantling their weapons of mass destruction.[111]

In the months since the passage of the Freedom of Support Act, which doubled the total funds available to assist the former Soviet republics, Washington and Moscow pressed ahead to address Russia's need for storage facilities for the long-term storage of fissile material. In reciprocal visits, US and Russian design teams shared information about the type of facility Russia wanted and how to co-operate in the design of such a facility. In July, the United States had indicated that it would reserve up to $150 million at the request of Russia for the construction of such a storage facility.[112] The two countries took the first step in this direction on 6 October 1992, when they signed an agreement for the United States to provide $15 million in technical assistance to the Russian Ministry of Atomic Energy to support the design of a fissile storage facility. According to a Pentagon spokesman, under the agreement, 'the Department of Defense may provide technical assistance in such areas as development of design requirements and criteria for the proposed storage facility'.[113] In January 1993, the Russian Foreign Minister declared that US and Russian officials had agreed on the design of the facilities.[114]

As of January 1993, the United States had allocated about one-quarter of the $800 million available to assist the former Soviet republics in dismantling weapons of mass destruction.[115] These funds consist of the following: $50 million for fissile material containers; $35 million to set up international science centres in Moscow and Kiev to employ nuclear scientists on peaceful research projects; $25 million to assist in destroying chemical weapons; $25 million for accident response equipment; $20 million for modification of railway cars; $15 million for designing fissile material storage facilities; $15 million for material control and fissile material accounting; $5 million for kevlar armoured blankets; $2.4 million for government-to-government communication links; $2 million for export control development; and $10 million to assess the feasibility of other proposals.

In addition, the Bush administration announced in early September that it had taken the innovative step of making a deal with Russia to buy at least 500 metric tons of highly enriched uranium over 20 years, at a cost of several billions of dollars. This extraordinary arrangement, which was expected to be signed by the end of 1992, called for the US Department of Energy to buy no less than 10 metric tons annually for the first five years, and no less than 30 metric tons annually for the next 15 years. The idea was pursued by a number of American companies, which saw the potential for making considerable profit from diluting the fissile material recovered from Russian warheads and then selling it as fuel for nuclear power reactors. It was the administration that took the lead, however, seeing the deal as a way to reduce the risks of nuclear accidents, theft or the sale of the material to states with nuclear ambitions, to provide an infusion of money for the shaky Russian economy, and to speed the disarmament of Russia.[116]

Conclusions

This overview of American nuclear diplomacy since the failed Moscow coup in August 1991 demonstrates that while the nuclear arms control agenda has been unalterably transformed by the disintegration of the Soviet Union, some old habits die hard. It is true that the Bush administration should be credited with a degree of boldness in its vision of where it wanted to go in the nuclear realm. It effectively seized the moment, particularly in late September 1991, to take steps to eliminate weapons that had grown increasingly obsolete and whose deployment was slowly becoming politically untenable. In so doing, it provided the fragile leadership in the Kremlin the political cover necessary to take actions to secure effective control over the widely dispersed arsenal of thousands of tactical nuclear weapons. In addition, by embarking on the new road of arms control by example, the administration clearly demonstrated that the United States no longer feared the Soviet Union in the way it once did. Relaxing the alert status of strategic bombers, slashing modernization programmes, and proposing deeper cuts in strategic forces – all these steps manifested the changing political climate and the new military conclusions that could be drawn from it.

At the same time, there remained instances where the vision was more bold in appearance than reality. Three instances stand out. First, while eliminating ground-based tactical nuclear weapons and removing tactical weapons from sea, the Bush administration, this time supported by some important European allies, insisted on maintaining a residual air-based nuclear force in the conviction that nuclear weapons embodied the shared interests of the two sides of the Atlantic. This is old thinking, plain and simple. At a time of an overwhelming, offensively structured and forward-deployed Soviet military threat to Western Europe, American nuclear weapons on the continent were a welcome symbol of the US commitment to distant allies in the nuclear age. In the post-Soviet world, such symbols are outdated. Imparting values to nuclear weapons that they do not possess – not merely symbols, but the embodiment of the transatlantic link – is potentially dangerous and may become self-fulfilling.

Second, if in the tactical nuclear area the Pentagon and the Bush administration displayed a relative clarity of vision and a certain degree of boldness, in the strategic nuclear area they evidently continued to view the post-Cold War world through Cold War glasses. The commitment under START II to reduce US forces to 3,500 warheads still leaves a force equal to that deployed by the United States at the dawn of the strategic arms control era in the late 1960s. But for the Soviet build-up, that force sufficed then, a time not long after both sides had stood at the brink of nuclear war. In the present world, with a demonstrated willingness in Moscow to reduce forces to just about any level the United States desires, is it not in the US interest to seek a level of strategic forces that is considerably lower than 3,500?[117]

Finally, there is the strange case of verification. Throughout the Cold War, the United States insisted on adequate and effective verification as the condition for arms control. This insistence became the hallmark of the Reagan administration, as intrusive on-site inspections were demanded for nuclear forces in Europe, confidence- and security-building measures, strategic arms reductions, chemical weapons, and conventional force negotiations. The sincerity of this insistence was put in doubt, however, when, following Mikhail Gorbachev's coming to power, the Soviet Union accepted the principle of on-site inspections on a reciprocal basis. In the endgame of each of these arms control negotiations, it was the Soviet Union that held out for more intrusion and the United States that resisted. Under the Bush administration, the United States began to rely on a Russian free press and data exchanges, having more confidence in Russian compliance than in its ability to safeguard a few black programmes. To the administration, the costs of granting access outweighed the benefits from gaining it.

This turn-about conveys a narrow approach to the benefits of verification, focused singly on the likelihood of cheating. But verification is beneficial not just because it can detect or deter cheating; it has many other benefits as well. Verification is crucial to transparency, which is the source of information about all kinds of activities and thus a critical confidence builder. It may also help reassure third parties, which, as the case of Ukraine demonstrates, promotes security for all. Finally, verification adds legitimacy to agreed undertakings, assuring not only parties to agreements, but also non-parties that commitments are abided by. In these and other ways, verification is a tool for building security, not a threat to maintaining it.[118]

The transformation of American nuclear diplomacy has been far-reaching, indeed. Steps taken to date would have been unimaginable a few years ago. But this is only the beginning, not the end of the road. Nuclear stockpiles remain vast in size, with little if any idea concerning the purpose for which they are maintained at this or any other level. Fortunately, we now know that the road to arms control need not be tortuous, tedious, or time-consuming. Reciprocal unilateral measures, followed by simple, formal agreements setting out the terms and the manner in which these will be verified, point the way to more far-reaching steps in the future.

ACKNOWLEDGEMENTS

This article is a revised and updated version of a chapter by Ivo H. Daalder, which first appeared in Hans Binnendijk and Mary Locke (eds.), *The Diplomatic Record, 1991–1992* (Boulder, CO: Westview Press, 1992). Material included in this version is used with permission.

NOTES

1. See, for example, Michael Gordon, 'The Last Arms Accord?', *New York Times*, 16 July 1991, pp. A1, A9; and R. Jeffrey Smith, 'Comprehensive Arms Pact May be Last of its Kind', *Washington Post*, 18 July 1991, p. A29.
2. For details, see Robert S. Norris and William M. Arkin, 'Nuclear Notebook: Where the Weapons Are', *Bulletin of Atomic Scientists*, Vol. 47, No. 11 (Nov. 1991), pp. 48–9; and Robert S. Norris, 'The Soviet Nuclear Archipelago', *Arms Control Today*, Vol. 21, No. 10 (Dec. 1991), pp. 24–31.
3. Cited in Dunbar Lockwood, '"Commonwealth" Leaders Pledge Arms Cuts, Central Control', *Arms Control Today*, Vol. 21, No. 1 (Dec. 1991), p. 25.
4. Harlan Jencks, 'As Empires Rot, Nuclear Civil War?', *New York Times*, 14 April 1990, p. A23.
5. *Treaty Between the United States of America and the Union of Soviet Socialist Republics on the Reduction and Limitation of Strategic Offensive Arms* (Washington, DC: Arms Control and Disarmament Agency, 1991), pp. 150ff; 'Soviet Strategic Nuclear Weapons Outside the Russian Republic', *Arms Control Today*, Vol. 21, No. 10 (Dec. 1991), p. 29; and Norris, 'The Soviet Nuclear Archipelago', p. 25.
6. Quoted in Thomas Friedman, 'US Hoping Moscow Can Retain Control of Soviets' Nuclear Arms', *New York Times*, 5 Sept. 1991, pp. A1, A12.
7. David Hoffman, 'Quick Recognition Seen for Former Soviet States', *Washington Post*, 20 Dec. 1991, pp. A35, A39. See also Thomas Friedman, 'US to Delay Post-Soviet Recognition', *New York Times*, 20 Dec. 1991, p. A10.
8. 'Agreement on Joint Measures on Nuclear Weapons', Pravda, 23 Dec. 1991, p. 2, reprinted in Foreign Broadcasting Information Services (FBIS) *JPRS Report–Proliferation*, 16 Jan. 1992, pp. 35–6.
9. 'Text of Strategic Forces Agreement', Tass, 31 Dec. 1991, reprinted in FBIS, *JPRS Report–Arms Control*, 30 Jan. 1992, p. 23.
10. 'Agreement on Joint Measures on Nuclear Weapons', ref. 8.
11. See Thomas Friedman, 'US Says 4 Soviet Republics Vow To Carry Out Nuclear-Arms Cuts', *New York Times*, 19 Dec. 1991, pp. A1, A14; 'Prepared Statement by Reginald Bartholomew', in US Congress, Senate, *Assisting the Build-Down of the Former Soviet Military Establishment*, Hearing before the Committee on Armed Services, 102d Cong., 2d Sess., Feb. 1992, p. 17. (Hereafter 'Bartholomew Statement.')
12. Ibid; and Secretary of State Baker's statement before the House Appropriations Committee on 24 February, as quoted in *Arms Control Reporter*, 1992, p. 611.B.724.
13. Serge Schmemann, 'Ukraine Halting A-Arms Shift to Russia', *New York Times*, 13 March 1992, p. A3.
14. Don Oberdorfer, 'Ukraine Shifts Nuclear Arms to Russia', *Washington Post*, 8 May 1992, p. A19.
15. Since March 1992, Ukraine has been adamant that the weapons on its territory are under Kiev's 'administrative control', a claim that has clearly had a negative impact on Russian-Ukrainian relations. See, for example, Celestine Bohlen, 'Russia and Partners Meet, But Unity Still Eludes Them', *New York Times*, 23 Jan. 1993, p. 2.
16. See also US Congress, Senate, *Trip Report: A Visit to the Commonwealth of Independent States*, Report to the Committee on Armed Services by Senators Sam Nunn, Richard Lugar, John Warner and Jeff Bingeman, 102d Cong., 2d Sess., 10 March 1992, p. 12.
17. 'Testimony of Secretary of State Baker before the Senate Foreign Relations Committee', *Federal News Services*, 9 April 1992, p. 12–1.
18. See John Lloyd, 'Russia Brushes CIS Partners Aside on START Treaty', *Financial Times*, 18–19 April 1992, p. 2.
19. See, for example, Fred Hiatt, 'Commonwealth Faces Unstable Future', *Washington Post*, 22 March 1992, pp. A1, A30.
20. Associated Press, 'Nuclear Weapons Talks Up in the Air', *Washington Times*, 12 April 1992, p. A13.

21. George Leopold, 'US Raises Urgency Level on START', *Defense News*, 20 April 1992, p. 10.
22. *Protocol to the Treaty Between the United States of America and the Union of Soviet Socialist Republics on the Reduction and Limitation of Strategic Offensive Arms*, Lisbon, 23 May 1992.
23. The letters are reprinted in *Arms Control Today*, Vol. 22, No. 5 (June 1992), pp. 35-6.
24. See, for example, Yuriy Glukov, 'START Protocol Called "Unilateral Disarmament"', FBIS, *Daily Report–Central Eurasia*, 1 June 1992, p. 3; and Michael Dobbs and Fred Hiatt, 'Russian Politics Imperiling Arms Cuts', *Washington Post*, 31 Oct. 1992, pp. A17, A20.
25. 'Text of Supreme Soviet's START-I Ratification', *Rossiyskaya Gazeta*, 21 Nov. 1992, p. 5, reprinted in FBIS, *Daily Report–Central Eurasia*, 24 Nov. 1992.
26. A schedule for the withdrawal of nuclear missiles from Belarus to Russia, to be completed by 30 December 1994, was drawn up and approved on the instruction of the Belarussian Supreme Council Chairman in October 1992. See 'Belarus Approves Schedule for Withdrawal of Nuclear Missiles', FBIS, *Daily Report–Central Eurasia*, 27 Oct. 1992, p. 3.
27. See, for example, 'Kravchuk to Liquidate Weapons "With Pleasure",' *Agence France Press*, 7 July 1992 reprinted in FBIS, *Daily Report–Central Eurasia*, 8 July 1992, p. 2; and Eleanor Randolph, 'Ukraine Supports Treaty Cutting Strategic Arms', *Washington Post*, 2 Jan. 1993, pp. A13-14.
28. Quoted in Serge Schmemann, 'Ukraine May Slow Arms Pact Unless West Sends More Aid', *New York Times*, 13 Nov. 1992. See also Serge Schmemann, 'Ukraine Finds Nuclear Arms Bring a Measure of Respect', *New York Times*, 7 Jan. 1993, pp. A1, A12.
29. See, for example, Yuriy Kostenko, 'Ukraine's Nuclear Weapons: Good or Evil', *Golos Ukrainy*, 29 Aug. 1992, p. 6, reprinted in FBIS, *JPRS Report-Arms Control*, 27 Sept. 1992, pp. 23–6; and Crystia Freeland, 'Ukraine Having Second Thoughts About Giving Up Nuclear Weapons', *Washington Post*, 6 Nov. 1992.
30. See 'Ukraine Delays on Treaties', *Washington Post*, 16 Dec. 1992, A36; and Don Oberdorfer, 'Administration Rejects Ukrainian Appeal on START I Ratification', *Washington Post*, 7 Jan. 1993, p. A27.
31. See Celestine Bohlen, 'Ukraine, Stumbling Block at End of Nuclear Race', *New York Times*, 1 Jan. 1993, p. A10.
32. See Serge Schmemann, 'Ukraine Asks Aid for Its Arms Curbs', *New York Times*, 13 Nov. 1992, p. A10; and 'Russia, Ukraine to discuss cost of dismantling arms', *The Globe and Mail*, 6 Jan. 1993 (Toronto, Canada).
33. Quoted in Margaret Shapiro, 'Ukraine Gets Defence Offer From Yeltsin', *Washington Post*, 16 Jan. 1993, pp. A14, A18.
34. Quoted in Stephanie Simon, 'US will pay to Destroy Arms if Ukraine backs START Treaty', *Ottawa Citizen*, 24 Nov. 1992. See also Fred Hiatt, 'US May Buy Soviet Uranium', *Washington Post*, 24 Nov. 1992, p. A17.
35. Don Oberdorfer, 'Bush Offers $175 Million for Nonnuclear Ukraine',*Washington Post*, 10 Dec. 1992.
36. Don Oberdorfer, 'Bush Details Assurances for Security of Ukraine', *Washington Post*, 9 Jan. 1993, p. A18.
37. Oberdorfer, 'Administration Rejects Ukrainian Appeal on START I Ratification'.
38. See David Remnick, '"I Want to Breath the Air of Freedom in Moscow",' *Washington Post*, 23 Aug. 1991, p. A25; Patrick Tyler, 'Troubling Question of Coup: Whose Finger Was on Soviet Nuclear Trigger?', *New York Times*, 24 Aug. 1991, p. 9; Bill Gertz, 'Soviet Nuclear Arsenal Watched', *Washington Times*, 27 Aug. 1991, p. 8; Fred Hiatt, 'Soviet Official Questions Nuclear Arsenal's Security', *Washington Post*, 28 Aug. 1991, pp. A1, A18; John J. Fialka, 'Soviet Chaos Upends Strategies for Averting Nuclear Miscalculation', *Wall Street Journal*, 20 Aug. 1991, p. 1; Douglas Waller, 'Nuclear Codes and the Coup: Weapons in the Wrong Hands?' *Newsweek*, 2

Sept. 1991, p. 57; and Michael D. Lemonick, 'What About the Nukes?' *Time*, 9 Sept. 1991, p. 45.

39. See, for example, the comments of Secretary Cheney and Brent Scowcroft on NBC's *Meet the Press* and CBS's *Face the Nation* on 25 Aug. 1991, as reported in Jessica Lee, 'US Didn't Fear Nuclear Threat', *USA Today*, 26 Aug. 1991, p. 3. See also Barton Gellman, 'General Withdrew Missiles to Shelters During Coup', *Washington Post*, 28 Aug. 1991, p. A18. It should be noted that, despite reassurances to the contrary in the immediate aftermath of the coup, subsequent analysis of intelligence data indicated that Soviet nuclear forces had in fact gone on a higher state of alert during the crises. See Bill Gertz, 'US Missed Soviet Nuke Alert in Coup', *Washington Times*, 12 May 1992, p. A1.
40. Quoted in John Lancaster and Barton Gellman, 'Citing Soviet Strife, Cheney Resists Cuts', *Washington Post*, 30 Aug. 1991, p. A32.
41. See Strobe Talbott, 'Towards a Safer World', *Time*, 7 Oct. 1991, p. 20.
42. William Beecher, 'US to Seek Talks on Control of Soviet Nuclear Arms', *Minneapolis Star-Tribune*, 6 Sept. 1991, p. 7.
43. David Hoffman, 'US, Soviets Sign Afghan Arms Halt', *Washington Post*, 14 Sept. 1991, p. A1.
44. Quoted in Serge Schmemann, 'Soviets Hail US Arms Plan and Signal their Own Cuts', *New York Times*, 29 Sept. 1991. Shaposhnikov's comments were cited in 'Can We Trust the Russians to Go Along?', *Newsweek*, 7 Oct. 1991, p. 22.
45. 'Press Briefing by Secretary of Defense Richard Cheney and Chairman of the Joint Chiefs of Staff Colin Powell', *Defense Issues*, 28 Sept. 1991, p. 4. For background to the initiative, see also John Yang, 'Bush Plan Emerged After Failed Coup', *Washington Post*, 28 Aug. 1991, p. A23; and Andrew Rosenthal, 'Back-Porch Plotting and Secret Meetings Leading to Arms Cut Denouement', *New York Times*, 29 Sept. 1991, p. 14.
46. 'Remarks by President Bush on Reducing US and Soviet Nuclear Weapons', *New York Times*, 28 Sept. 1991, p. 4.
47. 'Gorbachev's Remarks on Nuclear Arms Cuts', *New York Times*, 6 Oct. 1991, p. 12.
48. See, for example, R. Jeffrey Smith, 'Initiative Affects Least Useful Weapons', *Washington Post*, 28 Sept. 1991, pp. A1, A22.
49. For a detailed examination of this issue in the European context, see Ivo H. Daalder, *The Nature and Practice of Flexible Response: NATO Strategy and Theater Nuclear Forces since 1967* (New York: Columbia University Press, 1991).
50. This step had first been proposed by Paul Nitze in the early 1960s. As the Reagan administration's chief arms control adviser, Nitze had again pressed the idea in the late 1980s, but to no avail. See Michael Gordon, 'Nitze Suggests A-Arms Trims For the US and Soviet Navies', *International Herald Tribune*, 7 April 1988, pp. 1–2. See also Ivo H. Daalder and Tim Zimmermann, 'Banning Nuclear Weapons at Sea: A Neglected Strategy', *Arms Control Today*, Vol. 18, No. 9 (Nov. 1988), pp. 17–23.
51. 'The Alliance's New Strategic Concept' (Brussels: NATO Information Services, 7 Nov. 1991), p. 15. General Powell justified the retention of air-based weapons in Europe in similar terms and also pointed out that 'the increased capability associated with conventional weaponry in recent years has to some extent inclined us in the direction of getting rid of tactical nuclear weapons. We can now do conventionally much more efficiently things we thought we could only do with tactical nuclear weapons'. See 'Press Briefing by Secretary Cheney and General Powell', p. 8. For arguments to the contrary, see Ivo H. Daalder, 'Abolish Tactical Warheads', *New York Times*, 10 Sept. 1991, p. A19; and Ivo H. Daalder, 'Nuclear Weapons in Europe – Why Zero Is Better', *Arms Control Today*, Vol. 23, No. 1 (Jan./Feb. 1993).
52. Quoted by Neil Buckley and Lionel Barber, 'Moscow Will Act on N-Arms', *Financial Times*, 1 Oct. 1991, p. 1. See also David Hoffman, 'Bush Attempting to Capitalize on Major Changes in Moscow', *Washington Post*, 28 Sept. 1991, p. A19.
53. See 'Bartholomew Statement', p. 14.
54. 'Briefing by Secretary Cheney and General Powell', p. 9. However, the extent of

Cheney's acquiescence to the new approach was put in doubt when, a day later, he said that if Moscow did not reciprocate, 'then obviously there are certain steps we've taken we could reverse. We can put the bomber force back on alert, we can redeploy our sea-based tactical nuclear systems', thus putting into doubt the unilateral nature of at least some of the announced measures. See 'This Week with David Brinkley', *Reuters*, 29 Sept. 1991, p. 1.

55. See, for example, Richard Perle, 'Bush's Jump Start', *New York Times*, 30 Sept. 1991, p. A17; and R. Jeffrey Smith, 'Cutting Arms Unilaterally: A Different Approach for a New Era', *Washington Post*, 29 Sept. 1991, pp. A33, A37.
56. Quoted in 'Will Bush's Plan Work?' *Newsweek*, 7 Oct. 1991, p. 25. See also Doyle McManus and Michael Parks, 'At Summit Arms Discussions, It Will Be a Whole New Ballgame', *Los Angeles Times*, 28 Oct. 1991, p. A4.
57. In a statement released the day after the president's announcement, the Pentagon argued that with respect to 'the SNF and naval systems, we do not envision any formal verification regime, although we are willing to discuss possible confidence building measures with the Soviets. It will also be very important to use the increased openness that currently exists between the US and the new Soviet leadership to further enhance the transparency of both sides' actions.' US Department of Defense, 'Fact Sheet on the Strategic Arms Reduction Treaty', 28 Sept. 1991, p. 2. This approach was acceptable to the Soviet Union. See, for example, the statement by Soviet Deputy Foreign Minister Aleksey Obukov in *Moskovskiye Novosti*, 27 Oct. 1991, p. 12, reprinted in FBIS, *JPRS Report–Proliferation*, 11 Dec. 1991, p. 13; and Michael Parks, 'Leaders Approve Ways to Verify Arms Cutbacks', *Los Angeles Times*, 30 Oct. 1991, p. A1.
58. 'Press Briefing by Secretary Cheney and General Powell', p. 9. See also Michael Gordon, 'A New Era: Trust Without Verification', *New York Times*, 29 Sept. 1991, p. 12.
59. For President Bush's proposal, see his State of the Union Address in *New York Times*, 29 Jan. 1992, p. A16. Yeltsin's proposals were contained in three statements: 'Russia's Policy in the Field of Arms Limitation and Reduction', Speech on Moscow Television, 29 Jan. 1992, in United Nations, Conference on Disarmament, CD/1123, 31 Jan. 1992; 'Statement by President Yeltsin before the United Nations Security Council', 31 Jan. 1992, excerpted in *New York Times*, 1 Feb. 1992, p. 5; and 'Letter by President Yeltsin to UN Secretary-General Boutros Boutros Ghali', *Rossiyskaya Gazetta*, 31 Jan. 1992, pp. 1, 3, reprinted in FBIS, *JPRS Report–Arms Control*, 3 March 1992, pp. 16–20.
60. Of the 4,700 warheads, Powell indicated that 500 would be deployed on ICBMs, 2,300 on SLBMs, and 1,900 on bombers. Of the latter, 800 would be START accountable. See 'Briefing on the FY1993 Budget for Defense Programmes', Department of Defense, *Reuters*, 29 Jan. 1992, p. 6.
61. See UN Conference on Disarmament, *CD/PV.611*, 12 Feb. 1992, p. 4.
62. On these new modalities, see the statements by Secretary Baker in Thomas Friedman, 'US and Russia See New Arms Accord for a July Summit', *New York Times*, 19 Feb. 1992, pp. A1, A6; David Hoffman, 'US, Russia Seek to Create Missile Warning Site', *Washington Post*, 19 Feb. 1992, p. A24.
63. See Barry Schweid, 'Russian: Deal Possible on Multiple Warheads', *Philadelphia Inquirer*, 11 March 1992, p. 4.
64. Quoted in Kathy Sawyer, 'Cheney Dismisses Yeltsin Offer on Bigger Arms Cuts', *Washington Post*, 3 Feb. 1992, p. A5. See also the statements by Cheney and Powell in 'US Defense Chief Skeptical on Yeltsin's Proposals for Strategic Weapons Cut', *Aviation Week & Space Technology*, 10 Feb. 1992, p. 21; and by General George Butler, Commander of US Strategic Command, in 'Former Soviets Continue to Modernize Nuclear Forces–SAC Chief', *Defense Daily*, 9 April 1992, p. 53.
65. Don Oberdorfer and R. Jeffrey Smith, 'Bush, Yeltsin Agree on Massive Nuclear Cuts', *Washington Post*, 17 June 1992, pp. A1, A30.
66. 'Joint Understanding' (Washington, DC: The White House, Office of the Press Secretary, 17 June 1992), p. 1.

67. 'Strategic Arms Reduction Treaty II Chronology', US Arms Control and Disarmament Agency, *Fact Sheet*, 6 Jan. 1993, p. 1.
68. See John Goshko and Jackson Diehl, 'New Arms Cuts Readied', *Washington Post*, 27 Sept. 1992, pp. A27, A30.
69. See, for example, Fred Hiatt, 'Russian Conservatives Hit Yeltsin Arms Cuts', *Washington Post*, 19 June 1992, p. A33; 'Arms Accord With US "Cannot Be Ratified",' FBIS, *Daily Report–Central Eurasia*, 8 July 1992, p. 2; Boris Surikov, 'Opinion: Disarm, But Intelligently', *Pravda*, 21 July 1992, p. 7, reprinted in FBIS, *JPRS Report–Arms Control*, 17 Aug. 1992, pp. 20–2; P. Belov, 'Missiles in SDI Sauce: Will We See the Day when our Parliament gives Bush a Standing Ovation?', *Komsomolskaya Pravda*, 20 Aug. 1992, p. 3, reprinted in FBIS, *JPRS Report– Arms Control*, 11 Sept. 1992, pp. 10–12; Victor Litovkin, 'Russians split over arms cut', *WE/Mir*, 27 Aug. 1992, p. 1; and George Leopold, 'Russian Military Could Hamper START', *Defense News*, 7–13 Sept. 1992, pp. 1, 76
70. 'Excerpts from Bush-Yeltsin Conference', *New York Times*, 17 June 1992, p. A10.
71. See Thomas Friedman, 'US-Russian Accord On Arms Hits Snag', *New York Times*, 15 Oct. 1992, p. A13.
72. Ibid.; Michael Wines, 'Bush and Yeltsin in Talks to Gain A-Arms Accord', *New York Times*, 8 Dec. 1992, p. A7; and Elaine Sciolino, 'US and Russia Fail to Narrow Gap on Arms Cuts', *New York Times*, 14 Dec. 1992, p. A9.
73. See 'Defense Department Briefing', *Federal News Services*, 18 June 1992, p. 14–1.
74. See Michael Gordon, 'Bush and Yeltsin May Meet in January', *New York Times*, 25 Dec. 1992, p. A20.
75. See Ivo H. Daalder, 'START II: A Grand Finale', *Arms Control Brief*, Vol. 1, No. 3 (January 1993) p. 2.
76. Resolution of ratification, printed in *Congressional Record–Senate*, 1 Oct. 1992, p. S15958.
77. Robert L. Gallucci, 'Disposing of Nuclear Weapons in the Former Soviet Union', prepared statement of before the Senate Foreign Relations Committee, reprinted in *Dispatch*, 10 Aug. 1992, p. 633.
78. Ibid.
79. For arguments to the contrary, see, for example, US Congress, Senate, *The START Treaty*, Report of the Committee on Foreign Relations, 102d Cong., 2d Sess., 18 Sept. 1992, pp. 69–72; Spurgeon M. Keeny Jr. and Wolfgang K.H. Panofsky, 'Controlling Nuclear Warheads and Materials: Steps Toward a Comprehensive Regime', *Arms Control Today*, Vol. 22, No. 1 (Jan./Feb. 1992), pp. 3–9; and Christopher Paine and Thomas B. Cochran, 'Kiev Conference: Verified Warhead Controls', *Arms Control Today*, Vol. 22, No. 1 (Jan./Feb. 1992), pp. 15–17.
80. Ann Devroy and R. Jeffrey Smith, 'Bush Phones Yeltsin to Try to "Wrap Up" START II Treaty', *Washington Post*, 8 Dec. 1992, p. A12; Don Oberdorfer, 'US and Russia Try to Finalize Arms Cut Pact', *Washington Post*, 14 Dec. 1992, p. A14; Don Oberdorfer, 'Strategic Arms Pact Almost Ready to Sign', *Washington Post*, 23 Dec. 1992, p. A20; and Alan Elsner, 'Eagleburger Optimistic on START', *Washington Post*, 28 Dec. 1992, p. A9.
81. See Elaine Sciolino, 'US and Russia Agree on Atomic-Arms Pact Slashing Arsenals and the Risk of Attack', *New York Times*, 30 Dec. 1992, pp. A1, A6.
82. See, for example, Clinton O'Brien, 'Russian Hard-Liners set High Hurdle for START II', *Washington Times*, 12 Jan. 1992, p. A8.
83. See Talbott, 'Towards a Safer World', p. 20; and Associated Press, 'State of Soviet Weapons Unclear', *Washington Times*, 28 Aug. 1991, p. A8.
84. 'Remarks by President Bush on reducing US and Soviet Nuclear Weapons', p. 4.
85. 'Gorbachev Remarks on Nuclear Arms Cuts', p. 12.
86. Parks, 'Leaders Approve Ways to Verify Arms Cutbacks', p. A1.
87. 'Bartholomew Statement', p. 14.
88. Ibid.
89. See Sam Nunn and Richard Lugar, 'Dismantling the Soviet Arsenal', *Washington*

Post, 22 Nov. 1991, p. A25; and Les Aspin, *Memorandum on Legislation to Reduce the Soviet Nuclear Threat* (Washington, DC: House Committee on Armed Services, 2 Dec. 1991).

90. The amendment, known as the 'Soviet Nuclear Threat Reduction Act of 1991', is reprinted in *Arm Control Reporter*, 1991, p. 611.E-3.27. See also Don Oberdorfer, 'First Aid for Moscow: The Senate's Foreign Policy Rescue', *Washington Post*, 1 Dec. 1991, p. C2.
91. James Baker, 'America and the Collapse of the Soviet Empire: What Has To Be Done', Address at Princeton University, 12 Dec. 1991.
92. Hoffman, 'Quick Recognition Seen for Former Soviet States'.
93. 'Bartholomew Statement', p. 15.
94. For details, see ibid., pp. 15ff.
95. 'Bartholomew Statement', p. 16.
96. See William Broad, 'Soviets Say Arms Scuttling Will Take 10 Years', *New York Times*, 18 Dec. 1991, p. A20; Stanislav Kondrashov, 'Dollars for Nuclear Disarmament Seek Employment in CIS States', *Izvestiya* 25 Jan. 1992, p. 5, reprinted in FBIS, *Daily Report-Central Eurasia*, 29 Jan. 1992; Fred Hiatt, 'A-Arms Chief Says Russia Needs Help', *Washington Post*, 5 Feb. 1992, p. A22.
97. 'Bartholomew Statement', p. 16.
98. See R. Jeffrey Smith, 'Soviets Suggest Giving US Keys to Nuclear Sites', *Washington Post*, 19 Dec. 1991, p. A42; 'IAEA Seeks to Guard Soviet A-Fuel', *Washington Post*, 16 Jan. 1992, p. A22; and Hiatt, 'A-Arms Chief Says Russia Needs Help'. For an interesting proposal along these lines, see the letter by Charles N. Van Doren and Ambassador Roland Timerbaev in *Arms Control Today*, Vol. 22, No. 3 (April 1992), pp. 17, 25.
99. Congress, Senate, *Trip Report*, pp. 10–11. Baker also presented a plan to address the 'brain-drain' problem, involving the establishment in Moscow of a US-German-Russian financed international centre for employing weapons scientists in non-weapons related work. Thomas Friedman, 'Baker and Yeltsin Agree on US Aid in Scrapping Arms', *New York Times*, 18 Feb. 1992, pp. A1, A6; and David Hoffman, 'Ex-Soviet Scientists To Get Aid', *Washington Post*, 18 Feb. 1992, pp. A1, A10.
100. See *Arms Control Reporter*, 1992, p. 602.B.216.
101. 'Opening Statement of the Honorable William F. Burns', House Armed Services Committee, 26 March 1992.
102. 'Certification Pursuant to the Soviet Nuclear Risk Reduction Legislation', US State Department, 8 April 1992. The certification of Kazakhstan was sent to Congress in July 1992. See Dunbar Lockwood, 'Plans for US Aid for Russian Warhead Dismantlement Detailed', *Arms Control Today*, Vol. 22, No. 6 (July/Aug. 1992), p. 32.
103. See *Agreement Between the United States of America and the Russian Federation Concerning the Safe and Secure Transportation, Storage and Destruction of Weapons and the Prevention of Weapons Proliferation*, Washington, 17 June 1992.
104. See Testimony of General William Burns before the Senate Foreign Relations Committee, *Hearing on US Plans and Programs Regarding Weapons Dismantlement in the Former Soviet Union*, 27 July 1992, pp. 3–4 (hereafter 'Burns Testimony'). See also *Russian Nuclear Weapons: Implementation of the Soviet Nuclear Threat Reduction Act of 1991*, Prepared Statement of Frank C. Conahan before the Senate Committee on Foreign Relations, 27 July 1992, GAO/T-NSIA-92-47 (Washington, DC: US General Accounting Office, 1992); and Lockwood, 'Plans for US Aid to Russian Warhead Dismantlement Detailed', pp. 27, 32.
105. 'Burns Testimony', p. 5,
106. 'Belarus, US Agree to Dismantle Nuclear Weapons', ITAR-TASS, 23 Oct. 1992, reprinted in FBIS, *JPRS Report–Arms Control*, 28 Oct. 1992, p. 21.
107. 'US Security Aid to the Former Soviet Union', *Arms Control Today*, Vol. 22, No. 10 (Dec. 1992), p. 32.
108. Oberdorfer, 'Bush Offers $175 Million for Nonnuclear Ukraine'.
109. Allied commitments to date include: DM10 million provided by Germany in in-kind

assistance; $75 million over a four-year period provided by France to assist in establishing a surveillance system for nuclear waste storage facilities, in programmes to safeguard against nuclear accident, and in processing fissile materials recovered from weapons into reactor fuel; and the delivery of 250 nuclear weapons containers and 20 nuclear weapons transport vehicles by Britain. See Dieter Seher, 'Help for Nuclear Disarmament', *Berliner Zeitung*, 20 Oct. 1992, p. 4, reprinted in FBIS, *JPRS Report–Arms Control*, 28 Oct. 1992, pp. 22-3; 'France to Help Dismantle Russia's Nuclear Arsenal', *News from France*, 20 Nov. 1992, p. 2; and 'British aid to Russia', *Trust & Verify*, No. 33 (Nov. 1992), p. 2.

110. 'Burns Testimony', p. 2.
111. US Congress, House, *Freedom Support Act*, Conference Report, 102d Cong., 2d Sess. 1 Oct. 1992, p. 23.
112. 'Burns Testimony', p. 3.
113. Quoted in 'US to Aid Russia On Nuclear Storage', *Washington Post*, 7 October 1992, p. A22.
114. Randolph, 'Ukraine Supports Treaty Cutting Strategic Arms', p. A13.
115. 'US Security Aid to the Former Soviet Union', *Arms Control Today*. See also Peter Grier, 'US Efforts to Aid Ex-USSR in Disarming Bogs Down', *Christian Science Monitor*, 13 Jan. 1992, p. 1.
116. See William J. Broad, 'From Soviet Warheads to US Reactor Fuel', *New York Times*, 6 Sept. 1992, sec. IV, p. 4.
117. For arguments why it is, see Michael Brown, 'The End of Nuclear Arms Control'; Ivo H. Daalder, 'Stepping Down the Thermonuclear Ladder: How Low Can We Go?'; and Jonathan Dean, 'Comprehensive Control over Nuclear Weapons', all in this volume.
118. On this point see Lisbeth Gronlund, 'From Nuclear Deterrence to Reassurance', in this volume.

The 'End' of Nuclear Arms Control

MICHAEL E. BROWN

Since the end of the Cold War, several important steps have been taken to reconfigure the nuclear forces deployed in the United States and the former Soviet Union. These steps include: the signing of the Strategic Arms Reduction Treaty (START I) in July 1991; US President George Bush's unilateral cuts in tactical and strategic nuclear forces, announced in late September 1991; Soviet President Mikhail Gorbachev's unilateral cuts in tactical and strategic arms, announced in early October 1991; Bush's arms cuts and arms reduction proposals of late January 1992; Russian President Boris Yeltsin's cuts and proposals, which followed the next day; the transfer to Russia of all Soviet tactical nuclear weapons stationed outside Russia, a process completed in the first five months of 1992; the written commitments by Ukraine, Kazakhstan and Belarus to give up the strategic nuclear weapons stationed on their territory; and the signing of the START-II agreement in January 1993.[1]

If all these agreements and unilateral initiatives are fully implemented, the nuclear balance will be transformed in important respects. First, Washington and Moscow have pledged to reduce their strategic and tactical nuclear arsenals from a combined total of almost 47,000 weapons to some 13,500 weapons, a reduction of over 70 per cent. Many of the 33,500 weapons that are to be removed from the arsenals of the two countries are to be destroyed, not stored. Second, decisions to reduce ballistic missile warhead deployments and to eliminate multiple-warhead ICBMs, in conjunction with the continued commitment on both sides to retain survivable retaliatory forces, will significantly reduce first-strike capabilities and first-strike incentives in a foreign policy crisis or military confrontation, should one occur. In short, crisis stability will be enhanced. Third, several decisions that have been made – including to reduce strategic arsenals, to take large numbers of strategic forces off alert, to establish single commands for strategic forces, and to take most tactical nuclear weapons away from operational commands and move them to central storage – will make it much more difficult for renegade military officers to launch unauthorized attacks. Fourth, weapons modernization efforts have been significantly curtailed. In a series of unprecedented moves, Washington and Moscow have agreed to terminate over a dozen ICBM, bomber, and cruise missile programmes.[2] The qualitative dimension of the nuclear arms race has therefore been dampened.

Although a great deal was accomplished in 1991 and 1992, much remains to be done on the nuclear arms control front. There is widespread agreement in the arms control community that several steps should be taken in the short run.[3] First, the START treaties should be ratified by all of the relevant parties – including Kazakhstan, Ukraine, and Belarus in the case of START I – and implementation of thier provisions should begin as soon as possible. Second, unilateral initiatives and informal agreements should be transformed into legally-binding treaties. Formal treaties are less likely to be misinterpreted or violated than informal commitments and understandings. Third, implementation of these agreements should be accelerated. It is not at all clear, for example, why the United States and Russia will need between seven and ten years to implement the terms of the START-II agreement. Fourth, existing agreements on offensive forces could and should be extended. In addition to eliminating all ground-launched tactical nuclear weapons, for example, the United States and Russia could eliminate all sea-based tactical weapons as well. Agreements on strategic forces should be extended to include provisions that call for dismantlement of missile warheads and gravity bombs. The dismantlement process for both tactical and strategic weapons should be subjected to outside inspection. It is in the West's interest to ensure that all Soviet weapons are accounted for, that all weapons scheduled for dismantlement are actually dismantled, and that all fissile material taken from weapons is stored in a safe and secure manner.

There is a great deal of disagreement, however, when it comes to defining the long-term objectives of the nuclear arms control process. Four main positions have been staked out in the policy debate. First, some believe that Washington and Moscow should each retain several thousand nuclear weapons – that is, massive nuclear arsenals. One finds supporters of this view in both capitals.[4] Second, some believe that Washington and Moscow should adopt minimum deterrence strategies and deploy nuclear forces that number no more than a few dozen or a few hundred weapons.[5] Third, some believe that national nuclear forces should be abolished, but that a small nuclear force under international control should be retained to reinforce strategic stability.[6] Finally, many believe that the long-term goal of the arms control process should be nothing less than complete nuclear disarmament. This position has been articulated by policy analysts as well as government officials such as Mikhail Gorbachev, Boris Yeltsin and Rajiv Gandhi.[7]

The purpose of this paper is to assess the advantages and disadvantages of these four options, and to determine what the long-term goal – or end – of the nuclear arms control process should be. I argue that, while all four of these proposals involve drawbacks and risks, the best course of action for policy-makers in Washington and Moscow would be to move toward adoption of minimum deterrence strategies and deployment of nuclear arsenals consisting of 200–500 weapons. However, it will be difficult to move in this direction, given the strong inclination in both capitals to retain arsenals that contain thousands of nuclear weapons.

Before we can come to a decision about long-term options for nuclear arms control, we need to understand the impact nuclear weapons have had on international security since 1945. We also need to have a clear understanding of what our overarching objectives are. This study consequently begins with an examination of the role nuclear weapons have played and can be expected to play in international politics. It then proceeds with a discussion of our basic objectives in the arms control enterprise. This provides a useful point of departure for an assessment of the four arms control options outlined above.

Nuclear Weapons and International Politics

What impact have nuclear weapons had on international security since 1945? What impact will they have on international security in the future? There are three main schools of thought on these questions: some believe that nuclear weapons have detrimental effects on international security; some believe that nuclear weapons have little impact on international security; and some believe that nuclear weapons make the world a safer place.

One school of thought contends, in essence, that nuclear weapons are bad.[8] According to this line of thinking, nuclear weapons have made the world a more dangerous place because they have failed to stop conventional wars from breaking out, failed to ensure that conventional wars will stay conventional, and have made the costs of all-out wars astronomical. Not only have conventional wars broken out in many parts of the world since 1945, some of these wars have involved nuclear powers: non-nuclear states have challenged nuclear powers in the Falklands and elsewhere; the United States and the Soviet Union fought proxy wars in Korea, Vietnam, the Middle East and Nicaragua; the Soviet Union and China almost went to war over border disputes in the late 1960s. The existence of nuclear deterrents, it is said, does not prevent nuclear states from engaging in hostilities, even with other nuclear states. If conventional wars are still common and escalation is still possible – implicit or explicit nuclear threats were made during Cold War crises in Korea, Berlin, Cuba and the Middle East – then nuclear weapons have done little good and they have the potential to do grievous harm. The probability of war is still high and the consequences of all-out war are many orders of magnitude greater than they were in the pre-nuclear age. In addition, it is said that the costs of defence preparations are higher than they were in the pre-nuclear age because of the costs of the qualitative and quantitative nuclear arms races. Not surprisingly, those who subscribe to this point of view believe that nuclear arsenals should be reduced and eventually eliminated.

A second school of thought holds that nuclear weapons are irrelevant.[9] According to this line of reasoning, nuclear weapons have not had a significant impact on international stability one way or the other. It is certainly true that there have been no great power wars in Europe since 1945 despite the existence for several decades of two heavily-armed, adversarial blocs on the continent. But this 'long peace' is not attributed to the existence of nuclear arsenals on both sides of the European divide. Rather, it is said that great power war was discouraged by several other factors, including: the memory of World War II, a highly destructive but largely conventional war; recognition on both sides that escalation to all-out conventional war would be difficult to control; recognition on the Soviet side that the American military-industrial war machine was formidable; contentment on both sides with the status quo; the existence of a risk-averse ideology in Moscow; and a general trend away from war in the industrialized world. Those who subscribe to this point of view are largely agnostic on the question of nuclear arms control. They contend that, although nuclear weapons have done little good, they are likely to do little harm because all-out wars have become a thing of the past. Getting rid of nuclear weapons would not undermine international security; nor would it make the world a substantially safer place. Spending money on essentially irrelevant weapons is held to be 'profoundly foolish', however, the implication being that existing nuclear arsenals should be allowed to wither away.[10]

A third and final school of thought maintains that nuclear weapons are good.[11] According to this line of thinking, nuclear weapons have enhanced international security. More specifically, they have discouraged the great powers from going to war with each other. Nuclear weapons have done this, it is said, by making the costs and risks of war great and by making these costs and risks hard to misperceive. In conventional confrontations, national leaders often delude themselves about the military capabilities of their adversaries, engage in wishful thinking, and conclude that wars can be won at acceptable costs. In a nuclear confrontation, it is hard for leaders to delude themselves about their adversary's capabilities and about the likely outcome of an all-out war; this outcome will be sudden, incontrovertible and devastating. In addition, it is said that nuclear weapons make territory and military-industrial assets less important from the perspective of national security or the balance of power; states consequently have less incentive to embark on campaigns of conquest. It is also said that nuclear weapons make conquest harder. Since defenders value their freedom more than attackers value the gains of conquest, defenders can be expected to use nuclear weapons if necessary. Finally, it is said that nuclear weapons make imbalances of power and changes in alliances less important; states are consequently less likely to engage in the kinds of corrective balancing actions that could lead to war. In short, it is said that nuclear weapons make aggression less attractive, deterrence more effective, and war less likely. For these reasons, those who subscribe to this point of view believe that, while some nuclear arms cuts might make sense – to enhance stability or save money – complete nuclear disarmament is a bad idea. Some go further, believing that nuclear proliferation could stabilize potentially dangerous regional imbalances.

In my opinion, all three schools of thought are flawed. Those who believe that nuclear weapons are bad are correct to point out that conventional wars – even conventional wars involving nuclear powers – have taken place on a number of occasions since 1945. But it does not follow that nuclear deterrence has failed to have *any* effect on the occurrence of war over the course of the last several decades. The fact that two heavily-armed, antagonistic blocs faced each other in Europe and did not go to war is significant. That the Soviet Union and China did not go to war in the face of an array of historical, territorial, political and ideological grievances is equally important. If nuclear weapons played a role in keeping these two confrontations from escalating into all-out conventional wars – as I believe they did – then our cost-benefit calculations about the value of nuclear weapons should change.

Those who believe that nuclear weapons are irrelevant underestimate the differences between all-out conventional war and all-out nuclear war. As Robert Jervis has argued, conventional wars have indeed been horrifying, but their consequences pale in comparison to what we would experience in a nuclear holocaust. In World War II, leaders could imagine that their countries would survive, even emerge intact, if their armies were victorious on the battlefield; the United States, of course, ultimately emerged relatively unscathed from the war. Because victory was conceivable, states were willing to aggress. In an all-out nuclear war, victory would be inconceivable. Nuclear arsenals thereby reinforce stability.[12] This is not to say that nuclear deterrence was by itself responsible for the 'long peace' Europe experienced after World War II, only that it was an important part of the equation.

Those who believe that nuclear deterrence is a stabilizing influence in world politics have failed to develop a rigorous framework for distinguishing between 'good' proliferation and 'bad' proliferation. Taken to its logical conclusion, their argument would hold that every state in the international system should be encouraged to acquire nuclear deterrent capabilities. No serious analyst takes this position, however. Where, then, should we draw the line? What kind of states in what kind of situations should be encouraged to acquire nuclear deterrent capabilities? Answers to these questions are needed before we can accept the argument that nuclear deterrence is a blessing and nuclear proliferation is to be welcomed.

Under what conditions are nuclear weapons dangerous? Under what conditions are they propitious? Although development of a comprehensive analytical framework is beyond the scope of this paper, five factors should guide our thinking on these questions.

First, much depends on the character of the leaders in the states in question. As Stephen Van Evera has argued, nuclear deterrence can be safe and effective if the leaders of the states involved in the deterrent relationship are intelligent, rational, content with the status quo, and risk-averse. However, nuclear relationships can be volatile and dangerous if the leaders in question are stupid, irrational, aggressive, and casualty-insensitive.[13]

Second, much depends on the stability of the states in question. Nuclear deterrence is more likely to be safe and effective if the governments involved in the deterrent relationship are stable and not vulnerable to political intrigue; external adversaries might be tempted to take advantage of such instability and attack during times of political confusion. Nuclear deterrence can also be undermined if one of the states in the relationship is being subjected to secessionist pressures or is involved in a civil war; neighbouring, adversarial states often become parties to such conflicts.

Third, much depends on the strategic circumstances of the states in question. It might be hard to establish a stable deterrent relationship, for example, if the states in question are already involved in an arms race; both sides would rush to acquire nuclear weapons, and the side that did so first would have a strong incentive to use its weapons and prevent the other side from deploying a secure, retaliatory capability. Similarly, it might be difficult to establish a stable deterrent relationship if the states in question have outstanding border disputes or territorial grievances against one another, or if they are already engaged in actual military hostilities.

Fourth, much depends on technology. For all the well-known reasons, the existence of secure, retaliatory capabilities on both sides enhances stability; the absence of such capabilities on either side is potentially problematic. Since the chances of two or more adversarial states deploying comparable retaliatory capabilities at precisely the same time are infinitesimal, much depends on whether or not the first to acquire such capabilities is a status quo power or an aggressor.

Fifth and last, much depends on whether or not we have to negotiate the transition from a non-nuclear world to a nuclear world, or *vice versa*.[14] For example, nuclear deterrence might be well and good, but it does not follow that injecting nuclear weapons into a non-nuclear situation will enhance stability: sudden, massive changes in balances of power always generate instabilities and, as noted earlier, nuclear deployments could generate particularly powerful preventive incentives. Alternatively, nuclear deterrence might be vile and dangerous, but it does not follow that trying to eliminate nuclear weapons will improve matters. States in a denuclearized world would be tempted to hide a few weapons or re-build nuclear arsenals in an attempt to dominate the international balance of power. A denuclearized world would not be the same as or as safe as a truly non-nuclear world – that is, one with no knowledge of nuclear weapons.[15]

The Objectives of Arms Control

Although people disagree about the role nuclear weapons have played and should play in world politics, it is nonetheless possible to identify several goals that most people would accept as our broad policy objectives.[16]

What should we try to accomplish through the arms control process? The answer to this question was best enunciated in the early 1960s by the first generation of arms control theorists: Hedley Bull, Donald Brennan, Thomas Schelling and Morton Halperin.[17] Reducing their complex arguments to a few simple guidelines, they argued that arms control has three primary objectives: (i) to reduce the probability of war; (ii) to reduce the consequences of war, should war break out; and (iii) to reduce the costs of military preparations.

In order to reduce the probability of war, one should take steps to reduce incentives for aggression, for preventive attack, or for pre-emptive attack. One should also take steps to minimize the possibility of unauthorized nuclear attacks being launched or accidental nuclear attacks leading to inadvertant escalation. Nuclear proliferation is problematic because, as discussed above, it could proceed in ways that make war more likely. Finally and more generally, it is important to keep in mind that we have a compelling interest in reducing the probability of both nuclear and conventional wars breaking out. In order to reduce the consequences of the wars that do break out, one should endeavour to reduce destructive capabilities and to minimize collateral damage from military attacks. One should also endeavour to dampen incentives for intra-war escalation and to develop ways of terminating wars quickly.

It might be difficult to realize all of these objectives at the same time. It is possible, for example, that the prospect of conventional wars escalating into nuclear wars makes conventional wars less likely. If this is true, then eliminating nuclear weapons – which would make nuclear wars less likely – would make conventional wars more likely. It is also possible that the prospect of horrifyingly destructive nuclear wars might keep leaders from starting nuclear wars in the first place. If this is true, then reducing nuclear arsenals to very low levels might make nuclear wars more likely. Since decisions about arms control will be made by national leaders, it is also important to look at the arms control process from the standpoint of national interests. American leaders, for example, will want to reduce the possibility that the United States will be attacked with nuclear weapons. This will be a concern as long as: hostile (or potentially hostile) powers have nuclear weapons; unauthorized attacks can be launched from foreign soil; and renegade regimes or terrorists have a chance of acquiring nuclear weapons and the means to deliver them. American leaders will also want to ensure that, whenever an arms control agreement is entered into, the chances of strategically significant cheating taking place or an of adversary breaking out of the agreement are miniscule, if not non-existent.

Long-term Options for Nuclear Arms Control

With these considerations in mind, we can proceed with an assessment of the four long-term nuclear arms control options outlined earlier: (i) retaining massive nuclear arsenals; (ii) adopting minimum deterrence postures; (iii) abolishing national nuclear forces, but retaining a small nuclear force under international control; and (iv) eliminating nuclear weapons altogether. In assessing these options, we need to take into account their desirability – that is, the impact they would have on the probability of war, the consequences of war, and the costs of military preparations – as well as their feasibility.

Retaining Massive Nuclear Arsenals

Those who favour retention of large nuclear arsenals in the United States and Russia argue, first of all, that the arsenals envisioned by military planners in Washington and Moscow are substantially smaller than those currently deployed. As of late 1992, the US strategic arsenal consisted of approximately 10,000 deployed weapons; the Russian arsenal consisted of approximately 7,500 weapons; and Ukraine, Kazakhstan and Belarus fielded an additional 3,000 weapons. If the START agreements are fully implemented, the United States will reduce its strategic arsenal to just under 3,500 weapons; Russia will deploy roughly 3,000 weapons; and the other three republics of the former Soviet Union will oversee the elimination of all the strategic weapons currently deployed on their territory. In addition, the United States plans to reduce its inventory of tactical nuclear weapons from 5,750 to 2,500. All Soviet tactical nuclear weapons have been moved to Russia and the number of weapons in the inventory will be reduced from an estimated 17,000 to perhaps 4,000. In sum, by the year 2003 at the latest, strategic and tactical nuclear arsenals in the United States and the former Soviet Union will be reduced by over 70 per cent.

Those who support the retention of large arsenals also point out that steps are being taken to enhance the stability of the forces that are to be retained. The START-II agreement mandates deep cuts in ballistic missile warhead deployments and, more importantly, the elimination of all multiple-warhead ICBMs. Implementation of these measures, in conjunction with continued commitments on both sides to retain survivable retaliatory forces, will significantly reduce first-strike capabilities and first-strike incentives, thereby enhancing crisis stability. Steps are also being taken to stengthen command and control arrangements, which will make it harder for renegade military officers to launch unauthorized attacks. These steps include: reducing overall force levels, which will make the force structure more manageable; taking large numbers of strategic forces off alert; establishing single commands in the United States and Russia for strategic forces; and taking most tactical nuclear weapons away from operational commands and moving them to central storage. These are all welcome developments. It is good that nuclear arsenals are being reduced to take new political conditions into account, that the stability of the nuclear balance is improving, and that command and control arrangements are being strengthened. But these developments, however encouraging they may be, do not constitute a case for retaining large nuclear arsenals. To do this, one must argue that this option has decisive advantages over other options.

The case for retaining large nuclear arsenals rests on five main contentions.[18] First, it is said that large nuclear forces deter better than small nuclear forces because they would clearly annihilate any attacker. Second, large forces provide several counterforce options, which, it is said, are more credible than threats to attack an adversary's cities. Small forces, on the other hand, are said to provide decision-makers with few targeting options, and no counterforce options. Third, it is said that large forces are better from a national security standpoint because cheating and attempts to break out of agreements by deploying additional forces are less likely to have a significant impact on the nuclear balance. Fourth, it is said that retaining large forces ensures that new nuclear powers or nuclear-armed terrorists will still face overwhelming retaliation if they engage in nuclear blackmail. Fifth, it is argued that the United States needs to retain a massive nuclear arsenal in case a resurgent, expansionist regime comes to power in Moscow. This 'insurance policy' would provide capabilities for extended deterrence, should it be needed again in the future.

All of these arguments are weak. First, although it is true that large arsenals could inflict tremendous damage on the society of an attacker, much smaller arsenals could also inflict unacceptable levels of damage. The prospect of a retaliatory attack consisting of a few dozen, let alone a few hundred, nuclear weapons would deter any responsible leader from embarking on a campaign of aggression. Living with tens of thousands of nuclear weapons for decades has, perhaps, blinded us to this fact. Second, setting aside the question of whether or not counterforce options enhance deterrence, it is simply not true that small nuclear arsenals leave decision makers with few targeting options and that they can only be used in attacks against cities. Retaliatory forces consisting of a few hundred weapons could effectively attack a wide variety of conventional and military-industrial targets, including those dedicated to supporting ground, naval, and air operations. There is more to counterforce than attacking an adversary's nuclear assets: small nuclear arsenals would have impressive, flexible counter-military capabilities.[19] Third, large forces do provide more insurance against cheating and break-out problems, but it is hard to imagine national leaders entering into *any* agreement that failed to address these problems effectively. Better verification is the appropriate response to these concerns. Fourth, the United States and Russia do not need thousands of nuclear weapons to deal with the threats posed by potential proliferators or nuclear terrorists. New nuclear states will not be able to deploy large arsenals quickly; established arsenals consisting of even a few hundred weapons will be awesome in comparison. If proliferators try to deploy large forces, established powers will have years to build up their own forces in response. If they desire to do so, established nuclear powers will be able to retain a substantial margin of superiority over most new nuclear powers.[20] Nuclear terrorists might not be deterrable and, if they are, the threat of conventional retaliation might be more credible than nuclear retaliation. Even in cases where the threat of nuclear retaliation gives terrorists pause, massive arsenals will add little to one's credibility. Arsenals consisting of dozens or hundreds of weapons would be more than adequate. Fifth, if one is worried about the possibility of a hostile, expansionist regime seizing power in Moscow, why would one want to take steps that will leave thousands of nuclear weapons in Russia? It would make more sense, from a Western perspective, to reduce nuclear forces on both sides now, while congenial leaders are in power in the Kremlin. Although a hard-line regime could abrogate force reduction agreements and embark on an nuclear arms build-up, it would pay a high political and economic price if it went down this path. It would have strong incentives to uphold existing international commitments, whatever they might be. If a hard-line regime began to build up Russian conventional forces, the West would not necessarily have to rely on extended nuclear deterrence in response. Russian conventional forces are currently in complete disarray; Western conventional forces are far more capable, even though they are being reduced. The West could respond to a conventional build-up with a conventional build-up of its own. Given its vastly superior industrial and technological base, it has the capacity to stay several steps ahead of any Russian military surge. And if needed, an effective nuclear backstop could be provided by a small but flexible American strategic nuclear arsenal. In short, the extended deterrence problem does not exist now and appears to be manageable in the future.

In addition to having few unique advantages, large nuclear arsenals have several important disadvantages. First, if the United States and Russia retain massive arsenals, nuclear proliferation will be harder to control. To be sure, some leaders in some threshold states will be inclined to deploy nuclear weapons in any event, but others might be influenced by the behaviour of established nuclear states. More specifically, leaders in Ukraine, Kazakhstan and Belarus will be more inclined to rescind their denuclearization pledges if Russia retains massive nuclear forces. If any of these republics decides to become a nuclear power, Germany, Japan, South Korea, Taiwan and other non-nuclear states might reconsider their non-nuclear pledges. Those who believe that nuclear proliferation is good might not be unduly alarmed by this prospect, but there is no denying that developments of this type would take international security into uncharted territory. Second, although the key to maintaining effective command and control over nuclear forces is maintaining the integrity of civil-military relations and the relevant military organizations, large forces are inherently more difficult to control than smaller forces. If one is worried about the possibility of an unauthorized attack being launched by renegade military officers, as many in the West are, then one should be uneasy about pursuing a policy that will leave thousands of nuclear warheads in the hands of a Russian military that is experiencing political, economic and social trauma.[21] Third, retaining massive nuclear arsenals will ensure that the consequences of an all-out war, should one occur, will remain cataclysmic. Fourth, retaining nuclear arsenals will keep the costs of military preparations high. Although force levels are being cut sharply, current plans call for the United States and Russia to retain thousands of nuclear weapons each. If these levels are to be maintained over time, new delivery systems, bombs and warheads will have to be developed, produced, and deployed as old systems wear out. Procurement of sophisticated systems such as these is always an expensive proposition, especially when large numbers of weapons are involved. Large force structures also incur high operating and support costs.

In short, the arguments for retaining massive nuclear arsenals are not compelling.

Adopting Minimum Deterrence

Before we can discuss the advantages and disadvantages of minimum deterrence, we need to have a clear understanding of what it is. For years, nuclear strategy in the United States and Russia has been based on two main propositions. First, it is believed that threats to attack cities in the early stages of a conflict are not credible; one must therefore be able to attack the military forces of the adversary. This has come to mean having the capability to attack the adversary's strategic nuclear force structure in a systematic way.[22] Second, it is believed that one must also have the capability to destroy an adversary's society, even after absorbing an attack designed to blunt one's retaliatory capabilities. In the 1960s, for example, American war planners believed that the United States had to have the capability to kill up to 25 per cent of the Soviet population and destroy 50 per cent of Soviet industrial capacity. These nuclear counterforce and assured destruction requirements ultimately led to the deployment of massive nuclear arsenals in both the United States and the former Soviet Union.

Some maintain that with START II mandating cuts in US and Russian strategic forces to no more than 3,000–3,500 weapons, the two countries are beginning to embrace minimum deterrence.[23] I would argue, to the contrary, that a shift to minimum deterrence involves more than lowering force levels: it involves changing the strategic assumptions that guide and shape policy. To date, the assumptions guiding American and Russian policy have not changed: each side still believes that it is important to deploy massive nuclear counterforce and assured destruction capabilities. What has changed are calculations about the level of forces needed to fulfil these demanding requirements.

A minimum deterrence strategy would have to be based on five main principles. First, it would be based on the contention that, although having counterforce capabilities is important, one does not have to define 'counterforce' in the narrow way it has been defined in the past. That is, one does not have to define it in terms of having a robust capability to attack an adversary's entire strategic nuclear force structure. Instead, one should have the ability to inflict a substantial amount of damage on an adversary's military infrastructure, focusing in particular on power projection capbilities.[24] Second, although it is important to have the capability to inflict substantial amounts of damage on an adversary's society, one does not need 'assured destruction' capabilities, as defined in the 1960s, unless one is dealing with a totalitarian state bent on expansion and conquest. Given the end of the Cold War, the dissolution of the Warsaw Pact, the break-up of the Soviet Union, and the beginnings of democratization in Russia and many of the other republics of the former Soviet Union, the United States can substantially lower its targeting requirements in this area. As noted earlier, the prospect of a retaliatory attack consisting of a few dozen, let alone a few hundred, nuclear weapons would deter any responsible leader from international adverturism. Third, force levels should be set high enough to ensure that strategically significant cheating could not occur. Similarly, force levels should be high enough to ensure that neither side would be tempted to break out of an arms control agreement by building up its arsenal. Determinations about force levels will therefore be strongly influenced by the intrusiveness of the verification measures the two sides are willing to implement: the better the verification, the lower the force levels. Fourth, force levels should be high enough to ensure that new nuclear states will not be able to acquire comparable capabilities in short order. This will give established nuclear states an opportunity to maintain a margin of superiority over new nuclear states, should they be inclined to do so for political reasons. Fifth, American force levels should be high enough to convince allied governments that the American nuclear umbrella is not being withdrawn. If allies came to this conclusion, they would have an incentive to develop nuclear weapon capabilities of their own. Although some believe that nuclear proliferation need not be dangerous, this development would, as noted earlier, take international security into uncharted territory.

What are the implications of these requirements for force levels? A recent study has persuasively argued that an arsenal containing 300–500 strategic weapons would generate a retaliatory force of 200 weapons that would be able to inflict extensive damage on an adversary's conventional military and military-industrial infrastructure.[25] Since many military-industrial targets are co-located with cities and since a force of this size would have a strategic reserve, this arsenal would also be able inflict tremendous damage on an adversary's society. A force of several hundred weapons, therefore, would satisfy the first two of the five requirements outlined above.

How low can we go? The requirement to prevent strategically significant cheating from taking place is one limiting factor. If arsenals are reduced to a few hundred weapons per side, political and military leaders will want to ensure that no more than a few dozen weapons could be surreptitiously stored or deployed by a potential adversary. Given current verification agreements and capabilities, this should be within the realm of the possible. If arsenals are reduced to just a few dozen weapons per side, however, then the two sides would want to make sure that no more than a handful of weapons could be surreptitiously stored or deployed. This is a much more demanding task, and would require the two sides to agree to even more intrusive and extensive verification procedures. Given current verification arrangements, therefore, each side should retain a minimum of a few hundred weapons. Similarly, reducing arsenals to a few dozen weapons per side would make it more difficult for established nuclear states to counter the efforts of new nuclear powers, and it would probably lead America's allies to question the value of the US nuclear umbrella. For these reasons, therefore, reducing forces to a few dozen weapons per side would be problematic. Force structures containing 200–500 weapons would be more appropriate.[26]

Adopting minimum deterrence strategies and reducing nuclear forces to 200–500 nuclear weapons per side would enhance both international and national – that is, American and Russian – security. This argument is based on five main contentions. First, deploying smaller nuclear forces would reduce the probability of a nuclear war taking place while continuing to discourage conventional wars between and among the great powers. More specifically, reducing nuclear forces would reduce first-strike incentives because a state would have to use almost all of its available weapons if it wanted to attack an adversary's nuclear forces. If one has an arsenal of 3,000 strategic weapons, for example, one could assign two weapons to each of several hundred ICBM silos, ten weapons to each of several bomber bases, a handful of weapons to each main submarine base, and still have a substantial strategic reserve. If one has an arsenal of 200–500 strategic weapons, on the other hand, it would be badly depleted in an attack that involved targeting two weapons to each of 100 ICBM silos and ten weapons to each of ten bomber bases. An attacker foolish enough to do this would be left with little strategic reserve, which it might need for attacks on conventional forces or for intra-war bargaining. In short, reducing nuclear arsenals to 200–500 weapons per side would make large-scale attacks on an adversary's strategic force structure counter-productive.[27] Reducing nuclear arsenals to these levels would necessitate a shift to a different targeting strategy, the non-nuclear counterforce strategy outlined above. Taking strategic nuclear counterforce out of the deterrence equation would stabilize the strategic balance: neither side would have to worry about large-scale attacks on its strategic forces in a crisis; pre-emptive instabilities would therefore be dampened.

Second, deploying smaller nuclear forces would reduce the probability of an unauthorized attack being launched by renegade military officers. As noted earlier, the key to maintaining effective command and control over nuclear forces is maintaining the political and institutional integrity of the relevant organizations, but small forces are inherently easier to control than large forces. Given the collapse of the military in the former Soviet Union – which has not yet spread to the Strategic Rocket Forces, but could do so at any time – reducing nuclear arsenals and reducing the risk of unauthorized attacks would enhance Western security.

Third, deploying smaller nuclear forces would put the international community in a better position to deal with the break-up of Russia, should this come to pass. If Russia and the Russian military begin to fragment, it will be easier to maintain command and control over nuclear forces – or dismantle them altogether – if they number in the hundreds rather than the thousands. Although it seems unlikely at this juncture that Russia will break up, no one can guarantee that this will not happen. Fourth, deploying smaller nuclear forces in the United States and Russia would dampen proliferation incentives in Ukraine, Kazakhstan, Belarus, and perhaps elsewhere. As noted earlier, some leaders in some states will be inclined to deploy nuclear weapons in any event, but international non-proliferation efforts will be strengthened – as will the hand of those in threshold states who favor adopting or retaining a non-nuclear status – if American and Russian forces are slashed to very low levels. Plans to deploy thousands of strategic and tactical nuclear weapons in Russia, on the other hand, will inevitably make Ukraine more inclined to possess nuclear capabilities. For obvious reasons, the establishment of a Ukrainian nuclear arsenal would have a detrimental effect on Russian national security. It would have a detrimental effect on American national security if long-range delivery systems were involved, if Russia decided to build up its own nuclear forces in response, or if other states began to rethink their non-proliferation pledges. Fifth, relying on smaller nuclear arsenals would reduce the costs of defence preparations. Although research and development of new systems would continue, production costs would be reduced because production runs would be shorter. Operating and support costs would also be reduced.

Minimum deterrence has its critics, including those who favour retaining large arsenals as well as those who favour more radical disarmament regimes. Those who favour large arsenals oppose the idea of instituting additional deep cuts for several reasons. More specifically, they believe: that smaller arsenals would be easier to destroy in a first strike; that smaller arsenals would provide political and military leaders with few targeting options and only counter-city options; that smaller arsenals would be more susceptible to cheating and break-out attempts; and that smaller arsenals would be unable to provide the extended deterrence capabilities that the West still needs.[28]

These criticisms are on the whole easy to refute. For starters, it is easy to devise highly survivable force structures containing 200–500 strategic weapons, provided that one's potential adversary has comparable forces. The United States, for example, could deploy a balanced triad consisting of: twelve Trident submarines, each equipped with sixteen single-warhead SLBMs (for a total of 192 warheads); 100 single-warhead ICBM deployed in silos, on road-mobile platforms, or both; sixteen B-2 bombers, each equipped with four gravity bombs or short-range attack missiles, and sixteen B-52 bombers, each equipped with four air-launched cruise missiles (giving the air-breathing leg of the triad a total of 128 deployed weapons). This 420-weapon force would be highly survivable, and it would have highly flexible capabilities against conventional military or military-industrial targets. Other complaints about small nuclear forces – that they give leaders few targeting options, that they could only be used in attacks on cities, that they would leave one vulnerable to cheating and break-out attempts – have already been addressed. In short, small nuclear forces would provide highly credible and highly flexible deterrence capabilities.

A more powerful critique of minimum deterrence comes from disarmament advocates.[29] They point out, first of all, that reducing American and Russian forces would not eliminate proliferation incentives. Many states are driven by strategic or political considerations of their own. Others, India being the most notable example, see the existing non-proliferation regime as inherently discriminatory: these states will not give up the nuclear option until declared nuclear weapon states give up all of their weapons, not just most of them. Disarmament advocates argue that the existing non-proliferation regime will be impossible to sustain in the long run if some states remain committed to keeping nuclear weapons. Second, disarmament advocates point out that reducing nuclear forces would not eliminate the threat posed by unauthorized attacks. If this is a genuine problem, the only way to keep nuclear weapons out of the hands of renegade officers is to keep them out of everyone's hands; that is, to eliminate nuclear forces altogether. Third, disarmament advocates insist that reducing nuclear arsenals from a few thousand to a few hundred weapons per side would not reduce the consequences of an all-out nuclear war to acceptable levels: millions of people would die and societies would be obliterated in a war involving several hundred powerful nuclear weapons. Finally, disarmament advocates note that even small nuclear forces will be expensive to operate and maintain. Some savings will materialize, to be sure, but infrastructure costs will not go away.

These are legitimate criticisms. Whether or not these drawbacks are outweighed by the contributions national nuclear forces make to international peace and security depends on the view one has of the role nuclear weapons play in international politics. If one believes that the existence of nuclear arsenals helps to keep the great powers from starting conventional wars with each other – as I do – then the benefits of retaining national nuclear forces outweigh the costs of doing so. If one believes that nuclear weapons play no such role, then the costs of retaining national nuclear forces outweigh the benefits of keeping them. This is a question over which reasonable men and women disagree.

One final issue has to be addressed: whether or not going down the path of deep reductions in nuclear forces is technically and politically feasible. There would seem to be few technical barriers to the adoption of minimum deterrence strategies and the deployment of small nuclear arsenals. As discussed earlier, it should be easy to devise force structures that are highly survivable, and it should be possible to address concerns about cheating.

The issue of strategic defences is more troublesome but still manageable. Both the United States and Russia are interested in deploying more robust defences against ballistic missile attacks from potential proliferators and terrorists; the United States is also interested in guarding against the possibility of unauthorized attacks involving Russian strategic forces. Some strategic defence proposals on the American side, for example, call for deployment of 700–1,200 ground-based launchers complemented by a constellation of 1,000 or more space-based Brilliant Pebbles interceptors. Obviously, if offensive forces were reduced to 200–500 weapons per side, deployment of such a system would undermine the credibility of Russia's retaliatory capability. If offensive forces are to be reduced to these levels, therefore, defensive deployments will have to be limited to around 100 ground-based launchers per side. Limiting defensive deployments in this way would not compromise American and Russian national security. The best way to reduce the risks of unauthorized attacks, for example, is to reduce long-range nuclear forces to very low levels.[30] The best way to deal with the proliferation problem is to strengthen controls on ballistic missile and nuclear proliferation. This will be difficult to do, however, if the United States and Russia retain massive arsenals of ballistic missiles armed with nuclear weapons. Ballistic missile defences would not provide complete protection against new nuclear states or terrorists in any event: nuclear weapons could be smuggled into the United States or Russia, or carried on cruise missiles.

The political feasibility of this option is more problematic. Hard liners in Moscow oppose the START-II cuts; the idea of reducing forces by another factor of ten will make them absolutely apoplectic.[31] If the United States wants to move down this path, it should take advantage of the fact that congenial leaders are currently in power in Moscow. In addition, it should do what it can to neutralize the hard-line opposition in Moscow. More specifically, it should make some unilateral cuts while engaging in discussions with Russian leaders about setting substantially lower force levels. This would send an important political signal to those in Russia who feel that their country is crumbling militarily, becoming vulnerable to the West, and being forced to live in a world run from Washington. It would demonstrate that the United States is also disarming, that the United States is not dictating the terms of the disarmament process, and that the United States is also giving up some of the accoutrements of superpower status.

Britain, France and China constitute another political hurdle. Each of these countries deploys several hundred strategic and tactical nuclear weapons.[32] The United States and Russia will not be inclined to reduce their arsenals to 200–500 weapons per side unless significant reductions are made in British, French and Chinese forces as well. To date, British, French and Chinese leaders have indicated that they are not yet ready to participate in the arms reduction process. They argue that, although deep cuts are to be made in American and Russian nuclear forces, the nuclear superpowers still plan to field five to ten times as many nuclear weapons as Britain, France and China. This arithmetic has led officials in these three countries to argue that they should not and will not join the arms reduction process until the United States and Russia reduce their forces much more. Chinese officials have insisted that the United States and Russia must reduce their forces to China's level before Beijing will contemplate cuts of its own.[33]

One way to finesse this problem would be for the United States and Russia to begin reducing their strategic arsenals to 1,000 weapons each. They could do this without compromising their military security or political position with respect to the three medium-sized nuclear powers. They could then approach Britain, France, and China about devising a framework for 'Big Five' nuclear arms reductions. If the United States and Russia reduce their strategic forces to 1,000 weapons each, if relations between Russia and the West continue to develop in a constructive manner, and if European security problems between the great powers remain manageable, Britain and France might be willing to entertain the idea of making some cuts in their own forces. They could, for example, simply reduce the number of warheads deployed on their SLBMs; they would thereby reduce overall deployment levels while retaining highly survivable forces. China is more problematic, because its strategic forces do not lend themselves as easily to cuts and because the Chinese leadership appears to be particularly stubborn on this issue. It might be possible to ignore China, though, because most of its nuclear weapons are wedded to intermediate-range rather than intercontinental delivery systems. Chinese participation would not be essential, therefore, if the discussion was limited to strategic systems.[34]

In short, there are good arguments for adopting minimum deterrence strategies and reducing nuclear forces substantially. This option is no panacea, however, and it might not be possible to move very far in this direction given the deep attachment many in Washington and Moscow have to large nuclear arsenals.

Establishing an International Nuclear Force

The idea of eliminating national nuclear forces and establishing international control over nuclear weapon capabilities has a long history. In 1946, the United States proposed that states currently manufacturing atomic bombs should stop doing so and that an international agency be established to ensure that this was taking place. This agency would have the authority to inspect any atomic energy facility anywhere in the world in order to determine that nuclear weapons were not being made by any state. Once it was clear that an effective system of inspections and sanctions was in place, the United States proposed to dispose of all the atomic bombs (a total of nine) then in its arsenal.[35]

The Soviet Union objected to the American plan on several grounds.[36] First, the Soviet Union argued that because its atomic programme was not as advanced as that of the United States, Washington's proposals would place Moscow at a disadvantage. The Soviet Union would have to stop work on the bomb and open its facilities to international inspection before the United States dismantled its arsenal; if the United States reneged on the deal, Moscow would be even farther behind in the arms race. Second, the Soviet Union objected to the highly intrusive inspections the American proposal called for. As far as Moscow was concerned, these inspections would allow the West to learn too much about Soviet military capabilities and would thus compromise Soviet security. Third, the Soviet Union objected to the American proposal for international sanctions against violators of the agreement. The United States wanted decisions about sanctions to be determined by a majority vote of the United Nations (UN) Security Council. The Soviet Union feared that the Security Council would be dominated by the United States and its allies; it therefore wanted to retain its veto over such decisions.

In the 1990s these obstacles are not as formidable as they once were: strategic assymetries no longer exist because the United States and Russia have nuclear parity; the two sides have accepted the idea of incorporating highly intrusive inspections into both nuclear and conventional arms control agreements; and the two powers have adopted a much more cooperative stance in the United Nations. This has led some analysts to revive the idea of establishing international control over nuclear weapon capabilities.[37] Two main proposals have been put forward. The first calls for the elimination of all national nuclear forces and the establishment of a small international force that would be used to deter states from aggressing and to punish states that try to deploy nuclear forces of their own. The second, more modest proposal calls for the elimination of all national nuclear forces and the creation of a small international stockpile of weapons that would simply serve as a hedge against cheating or attempts to break out of the denuclearization agreement.

The case for establishing an international deterrent force is based on the contention that the benefits of nuclear deterrence would be preserved while the costs and risks associated with nuclear deterrence would be significantly reduced. More specifically, it is believed that an international nuclear force would promote international peace and stability by deterring aggression: because states would have only conventional weaponry at their disposal, they would have to bend to the will of the international community. At the same time, because nuclear weapons would be taken out of the hands of national leaders, it is assumed that the probability of a nuclear war taking place would be reduced, that the consequences of any nuclear attack would be limited, that the costs of nuclear armaments programmes would be reduced to very low levels, that the dangers posed by unauthorized attacks would be reduced, and that the risks posed by nuclear proliferation would be dramatically reduced.

Upon closer examination, however, this option has serious limitations. First, one assumes that decisions to use nuclear weapons would be made by the UN Security Council, but it is not clear how these decisions would be reached. Allowing the five permanent members of the Security Council to retain their veto rights would mean that nuclear threats could not be employed when they would be needed most: when great powers become involved in hostilities or when they seek nuclear capabilities of their own. Any attempt to take away the veto rights of the five permanent memebers of the Security Council would undoubtedly be resisted. Decision-making rules would be problematic even if the veto problem could be overcome; if a simple majority could authorize a nuclear attack, then any majority on the Security Council could coerce others; if twelve or thirteen votes out of fifteen are needed, then any small coalition could stymie international action. Putting such power in the hands of the Security Council would lead, in any event, for calls to overhaul Security Council membership: Germany, Japan, India and others would want to become permanent members of the Council, and expansion of the Council might consequently be necessary.

A second problem is that, unless the United Nation's conventional military forces are greater than those of any potential coalition of renegades, it would be hard ensure that its international nuclear force will stay under international control. If UN conventional forces are weak, renegade states might be able to seize its nuclear forces. If the international nuclear force includes land-based systems such as ICBMs and bombers, then it will be particularly vulnerable to seizure unless UN conventional forces are formidable. Even if the international force relies exclusively on submarines, bases will be needed somewhere. These bases will be vulnerable to seizure unless UN naval forces are formidable and UN intelligence capabilities – which would provide warning of an impending attack – are highly sophisticated. Put another way, for an international deterrent force to be secure, the United Nations would need to have conventional military capabilities almost comparable to those of a world government. But, if UN conventional forces are strong enough to deal with any potential coalition of adversaries, it is not clear why the United Nations would need nuclear forces as well: it could use its superior conventional forces to stop wars and stop states from trying to acquire national nuclear forces.

Preserving effective command and control presents a third problem. In a world with only one nuclear force, it would be vitally important to ensure that the commanders of the force remain loyal to the United Nations. Fourth and last, even if these procedural and technical problems can be resolved, the existence of an international nuclear force would probably not deter states from aggressing or trying to develop nuclear arsenals of their own. Nuclear deterrence works when nuclear weapons are in the hands of states, because those who are attacked will use all of the weapons at their disposal to defend themselves; the threat of nuclear retaliation is therefore credible. The United Nations would not have as much at stake in a conflict and would therefore be less likely to cross the nuclear threshold. The UN's nuclear threats would consequently have little credibility.

A more modest proposal for international nuclear forces calls for the elimination of all national nuclear arsenals and the creation of a small international nuclear stockpile that would serve as a hedge against cheating or attempts to break out of denuclearization commitments. This proposal is based on the assumption that complete nuclear disarmament is a good idea. The validity of this assumption is the focus of the next section of this article.

Eliminating Nuclear Weapons

The idea of complete nuclear disarmament also has a long history. Most of the proposals that have been made over the years share some common elements.[38] Most nuclear disarmament proposals begin by recommending that all nuclear powers should pledge not to use nuclear weapons first in a crisis or war, that all nuclear powers should stop testing nuclear weapons and undertake to sign a comprehensive test ban treaty, and that all nuclear powers should stop developing and producing nuclear weapons and delivery systems for these weapons. Production of weapons-grade fissile material should also stop; all uranium enrichment and plutonium production and reprocessing plants should be shut down. Once all production records have been examined and all nuclear weapons have been inventoried, the process of dismantling the weapons themselves would begin. The fissile material taken from these weapons, along with the rest of the weapons-grade material in the production pipeline, would be placed under international control. The entire process would be subjected to stringent international inspections, including challenge inspections of declared and suspect sites. Some believe that, to strengthen these efforts, the international community should make an explicit commitment to use military force against any state that tries to keep or acquire nuclear weapons. Some also believe that nuclear disarmament should be followed by conventional disarmament and, ultimately, dismantlement of national military organizations and conversion of all defence industries to civilian applications.

The arguments made in favour of complete nuclear disarmament are fairly straightforward. Eliminating nuclear weapons, it is said, would reduce the probability of a nuclear war taking place to zero: states would not be able to start nuclear wars; unauthorized nuclear attacks and accidental launches would no longer be a concern. The consequences of an all-out war would be significantly reduced. Less money would be spent on military activities.[39] Non-proliferation efforts would be strengthened because the disarmament regime would be non-discriminatory. Looked at from the standpoint of national security, states would be more secure because they would not face the prospect of being devastated by a nuclear attack. The United States, for example, would be virtually invulnerable for the first time since 1954, when the Soviet Union first unveiled an intercontinental-range bomber capable of carrying nuclear weapons.

Is complete nuclear disarmament possible? One obstacle is strategic. Many states believe they need nuclear weapons for national defence: Britain and France believe they need to retain nuclear weapons to hedge against the possibility of a hard-line regime in Moscow launching a conventional arms build-up they would be unable to match; many Ukrainians would like to offset Russia's conventional military superiority by keeping the nuclear weapons currently on Ukrainian territory; Russia, for its part, worries about large numbers of Chinese soldiers pouring across the still-disputed Russian-Chinese border; India feels that it needs nuclear weapons to counteract Chinese conventional superiority; Pakistan feels that it needs nuclear weapons to offset Indian conventional superiority; and Israel feels that it needs nuclear weapons to counteract Arab conventional superiority.[40]

States will be disinclined to scrap their nuclear arsenals so long as formidable threats to national security are seen to exist. These threat perceptions will not go away as long as people organize themselves into political entities called states, as long as states arm themselves to protect and advance their interests, and as long as some states are capable of aggressing against others. In other words, threat perceptions will lead some states to embrace nuclear weapons as long as military security has to be provided at the national rather than international level. International organizations are not yet ready or able to guarantee national security, as many in Bosnia have recently discovered.

A second obstacle is political. Many people in many countries believe that having nuclear weapons enhances a state's influence, position and status in international affairs. Many in Russia, for example, believe that keeping large numbers of nuclear weapons is important because this is the only way Russia can still claim to be a superpower. Many in Ukraine, Kazakhstan and Belarus believe that keeping the nuclear weapons currently deployed on their territory is important because it gives them leverage in negotiations with other countries over economic, financial and technical assistance; it also gives them a higher place in the international pecking order than they otherwise would have. Many people in India believe that developing a nuclear arsenal (or maintaining a nuclear option) is a way of being taken seriously as a world power; Britain and France, they argue, are treated as great powers mainly because they are nuclear powers.

The political value of nuclear weapons would be reduced if the United States, Russia, Britain and France reduced their nuclear arsenals to very low levels. This would not eliminate political incentives to have or acquire nuclear weapons, but it would dampen them. Another option would be to make Japan and Germany permanent members of the UN Security Council, demonstrating that one does not need to be a nuclear power to be taken seriously as a world power. In fact, the international community could let it be known that any state that crosses the nuclear threshold and acquires nuclear weapons will be denied a seat on the Security Council. India could be offered a permanent seat if it gives up its nuclear option and opens up all of its nuclear facilities to international inspections. These are only palliatives, however. The heart of the problem is a catch-22: states will want to have nuclear weapons as long as they are seen to have political value, and they will have political value as long as states possess them.

A third obstacle to complete nuclear disarmament is technical. Tremendous amounts of weapons-grade fissile material have been produced in many countries since 1945, and untold numbers of bombs and warheads have been produced, dismantled, recycled and redeployed. International inspectors might not be able to determine how much fissile material now exists, how many bombs and warheads exist, and where this material and these weapons are. Some are of the opinion that a completely accurate, global inventory of fissile material and nuclear weaponry can no longer be taken; states will be able to cheat – and they will be under great pressure to cheat, because they will expect others to do so – if an agreement on complete nuclear disarmament is put into effect. Others believe that a vigorous system of inspections and controls might eventually address this problem.

One way to minimize concerns about cheating, as noted earlier, would be to keep a small stockpile of weapons under international control; this reserve force, it is said, would serve as a hedge against cheating or attempts to break out of denuclearization agreements. The existence of such a stockpile would accomplish nothing, however, unless it contributed to the international community's ability to deter would-be proliferators from crossing the threshold. It would do so only if there was an expectation that it might be used. As discussed earlier, it would be difficult for the international community to threaten would-be proliferators with nuclear attack: a broadly-based consensus to attack with nuclear weapons would be difficult, if not impossible, to reach; if great powers retained veto rights on the UN Security Council, they could stymie international action against them. If the would-be proliferator was a weaker power, the international community would not need nuclear weapons: it could deter or attack with conventional forces. In addition, all of the basing, safety, and command and control problems noted earlier would have to be overcome. In short, an international stockpile would not address the concerns states would have about cheating because its credibility as a deterrent would be suspect. States will want to have their own stockpiles of weapons unless and until the cheating problem can be completely set aside.

If these obstacles can be overcome, would complete nuclear disarmament be desirable? In my opinion, nuclear disarmament will be dangerous as long as people organize themselves into political entities called states, as long as states can arm themselves with conventional weapons, as long as states are capable of aggressing against others, and as long as military security has to be provided at the national rather than international level. That is, nuclear disarmament will be dangerous until international politics is transformed and the system of states that currently exists is replaced by a system dominated by a central authority capable of maintaining international order.

This argument is based on two main propositions. First, I believe that, if the conditions outlined earlier in this paper are met, nuclear deterrence makes conventional wars less likely. Many disagree. This debate is for the moment unresolvable. Second, I feel that nuclear disarmament would not eliminate the nuclear threat from world politics, it would only transform it – probably for the worse. If states are still capable of arming themselves with conventional weapons and going to war, many will be tempted to build and use nuclear weapons if things go badly on the battlefield. Two (or more) combatants could engage in a nuclear arms race, a race that would unfold under the worst possible circumstances: when tensions and emotions are high and restraints are few. Once they acquire nuclear capabilities, warring states would have strong incentives to use them, either in preventive attacks against the nuclear facilities of others or on the battlefield. If powerful states – Russia and China, for example – are the combatants in question, outsiders, even if banded together under the umbrella of the United Nations, would probably be unable to stop this renuclearization process from unfolding.[41] Ironically, the probability of nuclear weapons being used in a denuclearized world could be quite high – higher perhaps than in a world in which a few powers possess small but survivable nuclear forces.

It would not be enough, therefore, to eliminate nuclear arsenals from the face of the Earth. It would not be enough to dispose of nuclear infrastructures and civilian nuclear facilities. It would not be enough to eradicate conventional armaments. As long as people organize themselves into states and as long as these states have the capacity to wage war, conventional rearmament can lead to nuclear rearmament. For the foreseeable future, the world will have to live with nuclear risks of one kind or another. The risks associated with a denuclearized world could be particularly grave.

These risks are relative, of course. If some nuclear states begin to break up – Russia, China, India, and Pakistan being possible candidates – and command and control in these countries begins to fall apart, then complete nuclear disarmament will become an increasingly attractive – though still highly problematic – option.

Conclusions

Many policy-makers in Washington and Moscow are deeply attached to the idea of retaining massive nuclear arsenals. This is unfortunate because American and Russian national security would be enhanced by bold steps to reduce nuclear inventories to much lower levels. First, the two nuclear superpowers should reduce their arsenals to 1,000 weapons each. Then, if Britain, France and China are willing to participate in the arms reduction process – which they should be encouraged to do – the United States and Russia should adopt minimum deterrence strategies and force structures containing 200–500 weapons each. Taking these steps would further stabilize the nuclear balance, reduce the chances of unauthorized attacks being launched, dampen nuclear proliferation and save all concerned a great deal of money in the long run.

It will not be easy for policy-makers in Washington, Moscow, London, Paris and Beijing to take these steps. A heightened awareness of the main dangers of the new era – unauthorized attacks and nuclear proliferation – will have to be developed. Obsolete ideas about the value of massive nuclear arsenals will have to be discarded. New nuclear strategies will have to be refined and implemented. New force structures will have to be designed. Entrenched bureaucratic interests in the military and in nuclear weapons laboratories will have to be overcome. Pressing domestic problems will have to be set aside, at least momentarily, while time is spent resolving arcane strategic questions and pushing ahead with delicate international negotiations. That said, no issue is more important than maintaining the nuclear balance. One hopes that leaders in Washington and Moscow, in particular, will address these strategic challenges and take advantage of the strategic opportunities currently before them.

ACKNOWLEDGEMENTS

The author would like to acknowledge the constructive comments he received on his presentations at: a Stanley Foundation conference on 'US Defense Priorities', Annapolis, March 1992; an Australian National University conference on 'Arms Control in the post-Cold War Era', Canberra and Perth, June 1992; a workshop of the Project on Rethinking Arms Control, sponsored by the Center for International and Security Studies at Maryland, September 1992; a seminar at the Center for Science and International Affairs, Harvard University, November 1992; and a United Nations Institute for Disarmament Research conference on 'The Future of Nuclear Deterrence', Paris, December 1992. In particular, he would like to thank Ivo H. Daalder for his help in shaping this article, and Naomi Mobed for her research assistance.

NOTES

1. For more details, see *Treaty Between the United States of America and the Union of Soviet Socialist Republics on the Reduction and Limitation of Strategic Offensive Arms*, signed on 31 July 1991; 'US Disarmament Initiatives', and 'Soviet Disarmament Initiatives', both in *Survival*, Vol. 33, No. 6 (Nov./Dec. 1991), pp. 567–70; 'President George Bush's State of the Union Address', and 'Russian Arms Control Initiatives', both in *Survival*, Vol. 34, No. 2 (Summer 1992), pp. 121–24; 'Protocol to the Treaty Between the United States of America and the Union of Soviet Socialist Republics on the Reduction and Limitation of Strategic Offensive Arms', *Survival*, Vol. 34, No. 3 (Autumn 1992), pp. 136–37; and 'Treaty between the United States of America and the Russian Federation on Further Reduction and Limitation of Strategic Offensive Arms' (Washington, DC: Arms Control and Disarmament Agency, Jan. 1993). For an overview of these developments, see Ivo H. Daalder and Terry Terriff, 'Nuclear Arms Control: Finishing the Cold War Agenda', in this volume.
2. In September 1991, Bush terminated development of mobile launchers for the MX ICBM and small ICBM, as well as development of the short-range attack missile (SRAM). In October, Gorbachev scrapped plans to build new rail-car launchers for ICBMs, a small/mobile ICBM, as well as development of a SRAM. In January 1992, Bush announced that he would stop production of the B-2 bomber, the advanced cruise missile, the MX ICBM, the small ICBM and new warheads for SLBMs. The

next day, Yeltsin announced that production of the Bear bomber, the Blackjack bomber, and existing air-launched and sea-launched cruise missiles would be terminated.

3. See, for example, Ivo Daalder, 'The Future of Arms Control', *Survival*, Vol. 34, No. 1 (Spring 1992), pp. 51–73; Steven E. Miller, 'Western Diplomacy and the Soviet Nuclear Legacy', *Survival*, Vol. 34, No. 3 (Autumn 1992), pp. 3–27.
4. The Bush administration opposed the idea of reducing US strategic forces below the 3,500 level specified in START II. Hard-liners in Moscow have opposed the START II cuts; the idea of making even deeper cuts in Russian nuclear forces is anathema. See Kathy Sawyer, 'Cheney Rejects Yeltsin Offer on Bigger Arms Cuts', *Washington Post*, 3 Feb. 1992; Peter Pringle, 'Doubts Raised in Moscow on Arms Deal', *The Independent* (London), 18 June 1992; Fred Hiatt, 'Russian Critics Call Arms Deal Betrayal', *International Herald Tribune*, 19 June 1992. Other analysts have also supported the idea of retaining very large nuclear arsenals, although much of this work was written before the break-up of the Soviet Union in December 1991. See Walter B. Slocombe, 'Strategic Stability in a Restructured World', *Survival*, Vol. 32, No. 4 (July/Aug. 1990), pp. 299–312; Walter B. Slocombe, 'The Continued Need for Extended Deterrence', *Washington Quarterly*, Vol. 14, No. 4 (Autumn 1991), pp. 157–72; Thomas C. Reed and Michael O. Wheeler, 'The Role of Nuclear Weapons in the New World Order', Report of a Study Group of the Strategic Air Command, 1991; Paul Nitze, 'Keep Nuclear Insurance', *Bulletin of the Atomic Scientists*, Vol. 48, No. 4 (May 1992), pp. 34–6. Also, see the review of the nuclear debate in Michael J. Mazarr, 'Nuclear Weapons After the Cold War', *Washington Quarterly*, Vol. 15, No. 3 (Summer 1992), pp. 185–201.
5. See, for example, Carl Kaysen, Robert S. McNamara, and George W. Rathjens, 'Nuclear Weapons After the Cold War', *Foreign Affairs*, Vol. 70, No. 4 (Fall 1991), pp. 95–112; Ivo H. Daalder, 'Stepping Down the Thermonuclear Ladder: How Low Can We Go?' in this volume; Stephen S. Rosenfeld, 'But Who Really Needs 3,000 Nuclear Warheads?', *International Herald Tribune*, 22 June 1992; 'New Nuclear Arithmetic', *International Herald Tribune*, 18 August 1992; and the views of Herbert York, cited in Keay Davidson, 'Experts Dare to Imagine a Nuke-Free US', *San Francisco Examiner*, 3 November 1991.
6. See William Epstein, 'And Now – The U.N. Century', *Bulletin of the Atomic Scientists*, Vol. 48, No. 4 (May 1992), pp. 22–3; Paul C. Warnke, 'Missionless Missiles', *Bulletin of the Atomic Scientists*, Vol. 48, No. 4 (May 1992), pp. 36–8; Daniel Ellsberg, 'Manhattan Project II', *Bulletin of the Atomic Scientists*, Vol. 48, No. 4 (May 1992), pp. 42–4. Many advocates of this position see international control of nuclear weapons as an interim step on the way to complete nuclear disarmament.
7. See, for example, Richard A. Falk, 'Nuclear Policy and World Order: Why Denuclearization?', in Burns H. Weston (ed.), *Toward Nuclear Disarmament and Global Security: A Search for Alternatives* (Boulder, CO: Westview, 1984), pp. 463–81; Richard J. Barnet, 'Twin Anachronisms: Nuclear Weapons and Militarism', *Bulletin of the Atomic Scientists*, Vol. 48, No. 4 (May 1992), pp. 26–7; Theodore B. Taylor, 'Just Unplug 'Em', *Bulletin of the Atomic Scientists*, Vol. 48, No. 4 (May 1992), pp. 27–8; Joseph Rotblat, 'Citizen Verification', *Bulletin of the Atomic Scientists*, Vol. 48, No. 4 (May 1992), pp. 18–20; Randall Forsberg, 'Keep Peace By Pooling Armies', *Bulletin of the Atomic Scientists*, Vol. 48, No. 4 (May 1992), pp. 41–2; Gar Alperovitz and Kai Bird, 'Dream of Total Disarmament Could Become Reality', *Los Angeles Times*, 12 Jan. 1992; Mikhail Gorbachev, 'To Enter the 21st Century Without Nuclear Weapons', 15 Jan. 1986; Yeltsin, 'Russian Arms Control Initiatives', p. 124; Rajiv Gandhi, 'World Free of Nuclear Arms', *India Perspectives* (July 1988), pp. 4–9; 'Final Statement of the Palme Commission on Disarmament and Security Issues', *Disarmament*, Vol. 13, No. 1 (1990), pp. 165–86.
8. Ibid.
9. See John Mueller, 'The Essential Irrelevance of Nuclear Weapons', *International Security*, Vol. 13, No. 2 (Fall 1988), pp. 56–79; Evan Luard, *War in International Society* (New Haven: Yale University Press, 1986), pp. 395–99.

10. See Mueller, 'Essential Irrelevance', pp. 78–9.
11. See Kenneth N. Waltz, *The Spread of Nuclear Weapons: More May Be Better*, Adelphi Paper 171 (London: International Institute for Strategic Studies, 1981); Robert Jervis, *The Meaning of the Nuclear Revolution: Statecraft and the Prospect of Armageddon* (Ithaca: Cornell University Press, 1989); John Mearsheimer, 'Back to the Future: Instability in Europe After the Cold War', *International Security*, Vol. 15, No. 1 (Summer 1990), pp. 5–56; Charles L. Glaser, *Analyzing Strategic Nuclear Policy* (Princeton: Princeton University Press, 1990), especially chapters 6, 10.
12. See Robert Jervis, 'The Political Effects of Nuclear Weapons', *International Security*, Vol. 13, No. 2 (Fall 1988), pp. 80–90.
13. See Stephen W. Van Evera, *Causes of War* (University of California at Berkeley, Ph.D. dissertation, 1984), pp. 704–21.
14. For a discussion of these transitional problems, see ibid.
15. The risks and dangers of a denuclearized world will be discussed in detail in a later section of this article.
16. Those who believe that nuclear weapons are 'evil' and that we are morally compelled to eliminate them would not accept these arguments. See Barnet, 'Twin Anachronisms'.
17. See Hedley Bull, *The Control of the Arms Race* (London: Weidenfeld and Nicolson, 1961); Donald G. Brennan, 'Setting and Goals of Arms Control', in Donald G. Brennan (ed.), *Arms Control, Disarmament, and National Security* (New York: George Braziller, 1961), pp. 19–42; Thomas C. Schelling and Morton H. Halperin, *Strategy and Arms Control* (New York: Twentieth Century Fund, 1961). Also, see Thomas C. Schelling, 'What Went Wrong With Arms Control?', *Foreign Affairs*, Vol. 64, No. 2 (Winter 1985-86), pp. 219–33.
18. See sources cited in note 4.
19. See Michael J. Mazarr, 'Military Targets for a Minimum Deterrent: After the Cold War, How Much is Enough?', *Journal of Strategic Studies*, Vol. 15, No. 2 (June 1992), pp. 147–71.
20. Established nuclear powers would have little trouble maintaining a margin of superiority over new nuclear powers in the developing world. However, all but the United States would be pressed to maintain a margin of superiority over Germany or Japan, should either of these economic powerhouses decide to field nuclear forces.
21. For an assessment of the state of the Russian military, see Christopher Donnelly, 'Evolutionary Problems in the Former Soviet Armed Forces', *Survival*, Vol. 34, No. 3 (Autumn 1992), pp. 28–42.
22. For an overview of developments in US nuclear strategy, see Desmond Ball and Robert C. Toth, 'Revising the SIOP: Taking War-Fighting to Dangerous Extremes', *International Security*, Vol. 14, No. 4 (Spring 1990), pp. 65–92.
23. See Joseph Fitchett, 'Nuclear Pact Sounds Knell For Old Ideas', *International Herald Tribune*, 18 June 1992; 'The World Bids Farewell to Its Balance of Terror', *The Independent* (London), 17 June 1992.
24. One would have to be careful to set modest parameters for this counterforce requirement. There are many conventional military facilities in Russia, for example, and many of these targets are big; conventional forces are often spread out over wide areas. I am indebted to Alexei Arbatov for emphasizing the importance of this point.
25. See Mazarr, 'Military Targets'.
26. The vast majority of these weapons should be strategic weapons. It might be necessary for the United States to deploy small numbers of air-launched tactical nuclear weapons in Western Europe to reassure its allies about the dependability of the US nuclear deterrent, even though strategic weapons could perform the same military functions. All ground-launched tactical nuclear weapons are scheduled for dismantlement, and all sea-based tactical nuclear weapons should be scrapped.
27. If force levels are set at 3,000–3,500 weapons per side, one could reduce incentives for large-scale counterforce attacks by deploying 1,000–1,500 single-warhead ICBMs in silos (or on mobile platforms) and by deploying strategic bombers at dozens of

bases. In all probability, though, neither side will deploy more than 500–800 single-warhead ICBMs or deploy bombers at more than a few bases under a START II regime. Although it is possible in theory further to stabilize the balance even if arsenals contain thousands of weapons, neither side is likely to take these steps because of the costs involved.

28. See note 4. Also see Alexei Arbatov, 'The Debate on Minimal Nuclear Deterrence', paper presented at a conference organized by the United Nations Institute for Disarmament Research, Paris, 10–11 December 1992.
29. See sources cited in note 7.
30. See William Durch, 'Rethinking Strategic Ballistic Missile Defences', in this volume.
31. I am indebted to Rose Gottemoeller and Steve Miller for stressing the importance of this point. For more details on views in Russia, see George Leopold, 'Russian Military May Hamper START', *Defense News*, 7–13 September 1992, pp. 1, 76; Dunbar Lockwood, 'The Penchant for Peace', *Bulletin of the Atomic Scientists*, Vol. 48, No. 8 (October 1992), pp. 10–11, 45; Pringle, 'Doubts Raised'; Hiatt, 'Russian Critics'.
32. Although the information available in the public domain is sketchy, Britain's arsenal of strategic and tactical nuclear weapons probably consists of some 350–500 weapons; France's, 500–650 weapons; and China's, 250–400 weapons. For more details, see International Institute for Strategic Studies (IISS), *The Military Balance, 1992–1993* (London: IISS, October 1992), pp. 40–1, 143–7, 231–2, 236; Robert S. Norris, Richard W. Fieldhouse, Thomas B. Cochran, and William B. Arkin, 'Nuclear Weapons', in SIPRI Yearbook 1991 (Oxford: Oxford University Press, 1991), pp. 3–47; Richard Fieldhouse, 'China's Mixed Signals on Nuclear Weapons', *Bulletin of the Atomic Scientists*, Vol. 47, No. 4 (May 1991), pp. 37–42; Michael E. Brown, 'Recent and Future Developments in Nuclear Arsenals', paper presented at a United Nations Institute for Disarmament Research Conference, Paris, 10–11 December 1992, pp. 37–45.
33. See Nicholas D. Kristof, 'China Gives No Hint of Reciprocity', *International Herald Tribune*, 30 September 1991. Also, see Zhang Ping, 'State Lauds Disarming Proposals', *China Daily*, 31 Jan. 1992; cited in John Wilson Lewis and Hua Di, 'China's Ballistic Missile Programmes', *International Security*, Vol. 17, No. 2 (Fall 1992), p. 39. Also, see the comments by French President François Mitterrand and French Defence Minister Pierre Joxe, quoted in Giovanni de Briganti and Charles Miller, 'Allies Hail US Move to Cut Nuclear Arms From NATO Stock', *Defense News*, 7 Oct. 1991, p. 29.
34. It is believed that China deploys twelve SLBMs on one submarine, eight ICBMs, and a variety of intermediate-range ballistic missiles and nuclear-capable aircraft. See IISS, *The Military Balance, 1992–1993*, p. 236.
35. For more details, see Bernard G. Bechhoefer, *Postwar Negotiations for Arms Control* (Washington, DC: The Brookings Institution, 1961), pp. 27–82; Barton J. Bernstein, 'The Quest for Security: American Foreign Policy and International Control of Atomic Energy, 1942–1946', *Journal of American History*, Vol. 60, No. 4 (March 1974), pp. 1003–44; Richard G. Hewlett and Oscar E. Anderson, Jr., *A History of the United States Atomic Energy Commission*, Vol. 1, (University Park, Pa.: Pennsylvania State University Press, 1962), pp. 408–619; J. Robert Oppenheimer, 'International Control of Atomic Energy', *Foreign Affairs*, Vol. 26, No. 2 (January 1948), pp. 239–52; Coit D. Blacker and Gloria Duffy (eds.) *International Arms Control: Issues and Agreements* (Stanford: Stanford University Press, 1984), pp. 94–9.
36. Ibid.
37. See sources cited in note 6.
38. For a review of various nuclear disarmament proposals, see Blacker and Duffy, *International Arms Control*, pp. 94–112; Bechhoefer, *Postwar Negotiations*, pp. 521–60; Arthur H. Dean, *Test Ban and Disarmament: The Path of Negotiation* (New York: Harper and Row, 1966), pp. 63–80; John J. McCloy, 'Balance Sheet on Disarmament', *Foreign Affairs*, Vol. 40, No. 3 (April 1962), pp. 339–59. Also see sources cited in note 7.

39. This point is conditional. States could compensate for declining nuclear capabilities by building up conventional forces, which are generally more expensive than nuclear forces. They would not be able to do this, of course, if conventional disarmament measures were also part of the disarmament equation.
40. With the collapse of the Soviet conventional threat to Western Europe, the United States does not have to contend with significant conventional threat to its security and would be hard-pressed to justify possession of nuclear weapons on these grounds.
41. This process might take time, even years, but conventional wars in the past have lasted for distressingly long periods of time. In many cases, therefore, states would have enough time to rebuild their nuclear establishments and build nuclear weapons, a process that would be expedited by the knowledge they would retain about how to do these things.

Stepping Down the Thermonuclear Ladder: How Low Can We Go?

IVO H. DAALDER

In commenting upon President George Bush's nuclear weapons initiative of September 1991, the Chairman of the US Joint Chiefs of Staff, General Colin Powell, noted that the United States and the Soviet Union were beginning 'to step down the thermonuclear ladder' that both had ascended during 40 years of confrontation.[1] Since that time, the United States and Russia have agreed either formally or informally to: destroy ground-based non-strategic nuclear forces and remove those at sea to central storage sites on land; cancel virtually all strategic nuclear modernization programmes; end the 24-hour alert status of heavy bombers; and reduce their strategic offensive arms to 3,000–3,500 actual weapons within a decade.[2]

Following the implementation of these unilateral initiatives and bilateral agreements, how far down the thermonuclear ladder will the United States have gone? The previous administration believed that it had reached the very bottom. As Defense Secretary Richard Cheney told Congress in July 1992, the START-II limit of 3,500 strategic nuclear weapons represents the minimum number of forces the United States will need in the post-Soviet, post-Cold War world:

> The Joint Understanding [on START II] reflects our best judgment as to what strategic forces the United States requires to maintain an effective deterrent . . . Our analysis took account of the break-up of the Soviet Union, its reduced capabilities to project conventional power, and the further reductions in military potential promised by this agreement. It also reflected our assessment of the type of force structure that we would like to retain in a world without MIRVed ICBMs. These assessments of military requirements and alternative force structures informed our decisions on acceptable limits for the new agreement.[3]

The key US objective should therefore be to secure the implementation of the START-I and II agreements. The goal, Cheney argued, was 'to allow reality to catch up with what we have achieved as policy . . . [A] stable implementation of already agreed reductions, rather than talk of further reductions, will be the focus of our continuing discussions with the states of the former Soviet Union'.[4]

This paper challenges the prevailing assumption that the United States has reached the bottom of the thermonuclear ladder. Although it is important to focus diplomatic efforts on securing implementation of agreements that have already been negotiated, it is equally vital to begin thinking now about how low we can go down the ladder. There are at least two reasons why this is so. First, the time has come to reassess American nuclear weapons requirements in the post-Cold War era. While granting that the Bush administration had succeeded in negotiating major reductions in US and Russian nuclear forces, the analysis informing these agreements continued to rest on the criteria and assumptions that prevailed during the Cold War. This analysis is obsolete. What we need instead are criteria for US nuclear weapons requirements that are firmly grounded in the post-Cold War world. And these clearly differ from those that were employed when US-Soviet relations were highly confrontational.

A second and more fundamental reason to determine how low the United States can go relates to the changing US policy objectives in regard to nuclear weapons. In the past, US policy toward nuclear weapons was informed foremost by the need to deter an expansionist threat emanating from the Soviet Union. In the future, deterrence should take a back seat to the more urgent objective of reducing the likelihood of nuclear weapons being used. The threat of nuclear weapons use has increased in recent years both as a result of the disintegration of the Soviet Union and the consequent concerns about the safety and security of nuclear weapons and materials and because of the proliferation of nuclear technology more generally. Neither of these challenges can be addressed adequately through a strategy of deterrence or the traditional arms control policy derived from this strategy. Instead, the most effective way to reduce the likelihood of nuclear weapons use is to eliminate as many nuclear weapons as soon as possible. Therefore, determining the absolute minimum number of nuclear weapons the United States should retain becomes not just a useful intellectual exercise but a high priority.

In this paper, I suggest that the only remaining purpose of US nuclear weapons in the post-Cold War world is as a background insurance policy during a time of growing political uncertainty, particularly in Russia. For this purpose, the United States requires no more than 200 highly survivable nuclear weapons.[5] I further argue that in order to reduce the likelihood of nuclear weapons being used, the United States should adopt a concerted arms control strategy to move toward this level of forces by the end of the millennium. In addition to moving to much smaller forces, the focus of this strategy should be on the operational aspects of nuclear weapons, including in particular on their alert status and on the safety and security of the weapons that remain.

The Role of US Nuclear Weapons

One of the more remarkable aspects of the flurry of unilateral and bilateral nuclear weapons initiatives that separated the eighteen months between the failed Moscow coup in August 1991 and the signing of the START-II Treaty in January 1993 was that few opposed the notion of going down to 3,500 actual US weapons by the year 2000.[6] Only a few years ago, many who now support this two-third reduction in US strategic forces would have argued with vehemence that retaining around 10,000 weapons was absolutely vital to US security. Since the late 1980s, however, studies conducted in and outside the US government concluded that the United States should strive to limit strategic forces in a post-START environment to about 3,000 to 3,500 actual weapons.[7]

What is the basis for this apparent consensus? Central to nearly all arguments in favour of retaining somewhere around 3,000 weapons is the belief that such a force is need to deter a newly hostile Russian regime under all circumstances. A much smaller force would require a fundamental and, to most, an undesirable change in US nuclear strategy. In addition, advocates of maintaining this level of forces in the foreseeable future point to three subsidiary requirements for US nuclear forces: to extend deterrence to non-nuclear allies; to deal with the proliferation of weapons of mass destruction (WMD) in the Third World; and to maintain America's status as a superpower. I examine each of these arguments below.

Deterring the Russian Threat

Most non-governmental assessments of US strategic nuclear requirements in the post-Soviet age that conclude that 3,000 weapons represent a desirable minimum rely on the traditional calculus of 'military sufficiency' – that is the ability of US strategic forces to survive a massive Russian first strike and retaliate with devastating effectiveness.[8] The criteria for determining the minimum force levels for military sufficiency are the familiar ones employed by all strategic force-exchange models: the alert status of forces under attack, the number and types of surviving warheads, the required number of weapons to be held in reserve, the reliability and penetrability of surviving warheads, the levels of desired and expected damage, and the nature of the targets to be attacked.[9] The last of these generally continue to be the targets that have been held at risk for decades – nuclear forces, military and political leadership facilities, other military forces, and urban-industrial centres.[10]

The belief that 3,000 weapons could in the future meet the targeting requirements that just a few years ago required four times as many weapons anticipated or reflected the changes in nuclear targeting requirements that have evolved inside the Pentagon since 1989. Although US nuclear strategy remains guided by National Security Decision Directive 13, which was issued by President Ronald Reagan in November 1981, the number of targets to be covered has been steadily reduced from 12,000 targets in 1989 to 4,800 by the end of 1992.[11] This reduction in targets reflects political changes (with the dissolution of the Warsaw Pact and Soviet Union leading respectively to the elimination of non-Soviet and non-Russian targets), technical changes (with more accurate weapons reducing cross-targeting requirements), better information (with the opening up of Soviet/Russian society reducing the degree of uncertainty and the importance of political leadership targets), and arms control (with shrinking Soviet/Russian military capabilities reducing the number of aimpoints).

The important point to remember, however, is that despite these changes and reductions, the essential nature and means of US nuclear strategy, including its primary focus on the need to deter a hostile Russian adversary, has not changed in any fundamental respect. With few exceptions, Russian nuclear forces and military and political leadership facilities remain the principal targets of choice. Other than as a necessary withhold option, there is little sense that the traditional assured destruction criteria – the ability to destroy 50 per cent of industrial capacity and 25 per cent of the population – are at all important in considerations of strategy, force sizing and weapons requirements. As the US Congressional Budget Office noted in late 1991, the Bush administration 'apparently still believes – as do many military officials – that many thousands of targets must be held at risk with nuclear warheads to achieve deterrence'.[12]

Central to the belief that some 3,000 weapons are required to deter a potential Russian nuclear threat is the presumption that any further reductions would require a fundamental and undesirable change in strategy. This argument rests on the assumption that there is a breakpoint in US nuclear force requirements – that is, a point below which the United States would be unable to meet its deterrence requirements.[13]

Interestingly, this breakpoint seems to have shifted over the years. In

1990, General John Chain, then SAC's Commander-in-Chief, argued that he could support the anticipated START Treaty only if Congress funded the full complement of 132 B-2 bombers, maintaining that 'forty-nine hundred missile-carried warheads are not enough to destroy the Soviet Union'.[14] One year later, General Chain's successor, General George Butler, defended a post-START force with half the number of B-2s, arguing that 'we haven't hit that breakpoint yet as we have [already] modified target sets and requirements'. But START was as low as the United States could go; a 3,000-warhead limit 'would require different guidance because you couldn't cover today's target set'.[15] By 1992, when the START-II framework limiting US forces to 3,500 weapons had been agreed, General Powell could testify that parity was no longer important: 'We're not dueling . . . my warhead against your warhead. The question is, does the United States' force structure give us enough capability to deliver a devastating blow against any nuclear State that may choose to attack use?' The answer, according to Powell, was that 'with a US force structure of about 3,500 warheads . . . we have the capability to deter any actor in the other capital, no matter what he has at his disposal'.[16] Both General Powell and General Butler further maintained that any further reductions would call the ability to maintain a strategic nuclear triad into question and, with it, the continued effectiveness of the US deterrent.[17]

Clearly the breakpoint of US nuclear strategy has shifted downward as arms control has led to lower and lower US force levels. But who or what is to say that the breakpoint is really at 3,500 weapons other than the fact that US forces will now be limited at that level? At least one analysis that relies on the traditional methodology of military sufficiency has suggested that US forces could possibly be reduced to as low as 1,000 weapons without reaching the breakpoint.[18]

But perhaps the question should be not how low we can go without fundamentally changing US nuclear strategy but why retain that strategy at all. Why, indeed, continue to insist that the United States must be able to target Russian nuclear forces and leadership facilities? The traditional answer to this question has been that the credibility of deterrent threats is enhanced by holding at risk those targets the adversary is believed to value most.[19] Though few still believe that it is necessary to target Russian missile silos and mobile ICBM capabilities, many continue to favour targeting submarine and nuclear bomber bases, strategic command and control facilities, and the full panoply of Russian military capabilities, including war-supporting industries, in the belief that these are the targets that Russian leaders value most.[20]

These arguments in favour of the traditional American nuclear strategy have always been inherently unconvincing, even during the Cold War.[21] In the present political climate, however, they are fundamentally flawed for a number of reasons. First, the insistence on counter-nuclear targeting continues the schizophrenic policy the United States has pursued for years. US arms control policy has been guided for a quarter century by the belief that strategic stability would be enhanced if the vulnerability of both US *and* Soviet/Russian strategic forces was assured. At the same time, nuclear doctrine and weapons acquisition have focused on developing the means to threaten those very forces arms control has sought to render invulnerable. Clearly, US nuclear doctrine and weapons acquisition policy should now support rather than undermine US arms control and overall deterrence objectives – which depend on a secure second-strike force on *both* sides.

Second, the emphasis on leadership targeting, never very convincing, is now obsolete given the changes in Russian society. There no longer is a communist party to target. More importantly, it is more vital than ever to retain the option to communicate with those responsible for the conduct of war during an actual conflict. This option is the best, if not only, way to retain some modicum of hope that a nuclear war, once started, can be terminated short of complete destruction.

Finally, and most importantly, insistence on the continuing relevance of the traditional strategy perpetuates the dangerous adversarial character of US-Russian relations. It is important to base US policy on a clear understanding that Russia is not the Soviet Union and never again will be. Russia is a significantly smaller country with nowhere near the power of the former Soviet Union. Its military is in shambles, its economy is in need of a decades-long overhaul, and its people have tasted the fruits of freedom. Communism is a discredited ideology – at least in Europe and the former Soviet Union. Certainly, a reversal in the current situation is possible, perhaps even likely. An authoritarian leadership may come to power – but it would have neither the economic nor the military resources to pose a threat on the scale of the Soviet Union. Clearly, nuclear weapons in the hands of such a regime would be less desirable than in the hands of a Yeltsin. But this points to the need to seek further reductions in Russian weapons now, before it is too late. This may require the United States to reduce its forces, but that is a price well worth paying.

More fundamentally, the notion that the United States should maintain large numbers of nuclear weapons and target them according to traditional Cold War criteria lest things go wrong in Russia is inherently counter-productive and may even be dangerous. As Fred Iklé has argued, the failure to free nuclear strategy from Cold-War thinking perpetuates the accident-prone nature of nuclear postures placed on a hair-trigger and, worse, may have the makings of a self-fulfilling prophecy:

> the dangers inherent in this nuclear legacy will continue to create new tensions in the American-Russian relationship. Whenever one side modernizes elements of its strategic forces, the other side will find reason to worry. Military staffs on each side will continue to perform calculations to estimate whether the Other Side (who used to be The Enemy) could somehow launch a first strike without having to fear massive and certain retaliation . . . Such cold war imagery is likely to persist, like a genetic defect, long after the conflict itself has ended.[22]

To escape this legacy and the dangers it entails, it is necessary to abandon the strategies that dominated years of confrontation. As a first step, the United States should eliminate nuclear forces and leadership facilities from its targeting base. Continuing reliance on counter-nuclear and leadership targeting perpetuates the confrontational image of US-Russian relations at a time when this image no longer accords with reality, stimulates mutual fears, anxiety and suspicions about the other's motives when confidence and trust are within reach, and keeps nuclear forces in a high state of readiness that is prone to accidents. Second, as General Powell has indicated, the criterion of parity as a guide to force deployments no longer fulfils a useful function. What is important is that those forces one wants to retain are survivable and capable of reaching their intended targets, and that the nuclear command and control arrangements are secure.

With these changes it is possible to go much lower than the 3,500 weapons currently favoured. How low depends in part on whether Russia needs to be deterred and, if so, how; and in part on whether additional reasons – discussed below – exist for maintaining nuclear weapons. Today, it is not clear that the United States needs to maintain any nuclear weapons to deter Russia. The big uncertainty concerns tomorrow. Yeltsin's political position remains precarious and few can rule out the possibility of an adversarial regime coming to power in Moscow. US nuclear weapons could do little to prevent such an eventuality. But having some weapons as a form of insurance for just such a case may be necessary to remind the new regime of its own vulnerability.

How few weapons would suffice for such an insurance policy? Considering the character of nuclear weapons, the prospect of just a few weapons – tens rather than hundreds, and certainly not thousands – exploding on Russian soil would be a very stark reminder of the country's inescapable vulnerability. In the real world, populated with real people, the consequences of ten or twenty nuclear weapons exploding will be no less impressive than if hundreds or thousands of weapons were detonated.[23] Therefore, the deterrent effect of the knowledge that the United States possessed a survivable and deliverable stockpile of some 200 nuclear weapons would be sufficient even if the path of political reform in Russia were to be blocked by the advent of a more nationalistic and authoritarian leadership.

This being the case, are there other reasons why the United States should retain thousands of nuclear weapons? Some argue that extending deterrence to non-nuclear allies, dealing with the proliferation of weapons of mass destruction in the third world, and maintaining US status as a superpower are sufficient reasons of themselves to maintain a large nuclear inventory. An examination of these arguments demonstrates that none are persuasive.

Extending Deterrence to Allies

For 40 years the United States has justified its possession of nuclear weapons not just to deter an attack on itself but also to deter an attack on its allies. This extension of deterrence served US vital interests in two ways: it preserved the independence of important allies in Europe and the Far East; and it discouraged these same allies from acquiring nuclear weapons of their own. This policy has been largely successful. The independence and prosperity of all important allies was preserved and, with the exception of Britain and France, no allied country decided to build a nuclear weapon even though most possessed the technical ability to do so.

It clearly remains in the American interest to preserve the independence of, and discourage nuclear proliferation among, US allies.[24] What will be different in the future, however, is the fact that the only threats to allies that require the United States to extend its strategic deterrent will be nuclear. No ally currently faces a conventional threat from a major power. Should one appear in the future, conventional means will most likely suffice to defeat such a threat. Therefore, many of the dilemmas that confronted US extended deterrence policy in the past will be much less salient in the future.[25]

The future requirements for extended deterrence are to a large extent dependent on the nature of the nuclear threat to allies. One way to ease these requirements, therefore, is to reduce the nuclear risks posed to allies by reducing Russian nuclear forces through arms control. Any reduction in these forces entails a lesser nuclear risk to allies and thus a lesser dependence on the American nuclear commitment. Of course, so long as Russia maintains nuclear weapons and so long as its future political course remains uncertain, it is impossible to eliminate the nuclear risk to allies entirely. Given that there will remain a requirement for extended deterrence, how will this affect the size of US forces? Some clearly doubt that very low US force levels would suffice to reassure allies, even if Russian forces were similarly reduced.[26] These doubts rest on a belief that there is an inherent tension in US force requirements for central and extended deterrence, in that strategic forces dedicated to deterring an attack on allies would not be available for deterring an attack on the United States and vice versa.[27] This argument is based on dubious logic. The only difference between extended and central deterrence is that in the former case strategic forces may have to be used *before* the US homeland has come under direct nuclear attack. Weapons used for this purpose would therefore no longer be available for retaliation in case of a direct attack. However, if the number of US weapons used in retaliation to a nuclear attack on an ally did not exceed the number used in the initial Russian attack, the balance of US and Russian forces would remain the same, leaving the ability to deter a direct attack on the US homeland unaffected. Even by the traditional calculus of nuclear deterrence, therefore, there is no direct competition between the force requirements for central and extended deterrence of a nuclear attack.

There remains the question whether non-nuclear allies would continue to be reassured by the American commitment to their defence if that commitment was backed by only 200 weapons. There is every reason to believe that they would, if only because allied doubts never derived from the level of US forces, but rather, as Charles de Gaulle and Henry Kissinger were fond of reminding their fellow Europeans, from the fact of US vulnerability to nuclear retaliation – a fact that does not change so long as Russia has survivable nuclear weapons. Those allies that have so far abstained from acquiring nuclear weapons in the belief that the American nuclear umbrella offered them protection are unlikely to change their views now. If anything, the reverse might be the case, since the nuclear risk would have been reduced.

In short, neither the reassurance of allies nor the deterrence of adversaries should be affected by the level of US forces. The credibility of extended deterrence to allies and potential adversaries alike is a function foremost of American vulnerability to nuclear retaliation. This central fact will not change in the foreseeable future; neither will it be affected by how many or few nuclear weapons the United States maintains. Indeed, the purposes for which the United States extends its deterrent are likely to be served more by concerted efforts to reduce force levels to a minimum rather than maintaining artificially large forces in the name of extended deterrence. This becomes all the more evident when we examine the third argument for maintaining thousands of nuclear weapons.

Dealing with the Proliferation of Weapons of Mass Destruction

The demise of the Soviet Union and the war in the Persian Gulf have re-focused attention on the need to prevent the proliferation of weapons of mass destruction, particularly in the Third World. There is today a broad consensus that such proliferation, particularly of nuclear weapons, represents the primary threat to US and international security in the post-Cold War era.[28] The proliferation threat has also become an additional, and relatively recent, justification for maintaining a large and secure American nuclear arsenal. The Joint Chiefs of Staff, for example, argued in early 1991 that the 'reality of strategic nuclear arsenals will be with us for decades to come. Indeed, the number of nations with long-range nuclear weapons will very likely increase. Therefore, under even the most optimistic assumptions about the future of US-Soviet political relations, our nation requires a capable strategic Triad of survivable systems sufficient to deter any potential adversary'.[29]

The threat of WMD proliferation, and the role of US nuclear weapons in dealing with it, raises a number of related, yet distinct, issues. First, it is important to differentiate between nuclear and other weapons of mass destruction, principally chemical and biological weapons (CBW). While there appears to be a wide consensus that US nuclear weapons should have a role in deterring the proliferation and, especially, the use of nuclear weapons in the Third World, there is no such consensus on this issue with respect to CBW. Second, whatever the role of US nuclear weapons in preventing the proliferation and use of WMD, there remains the issue of the size and kind of US nuclear forces that are necessary to accomplish these objectives.

With few exceptions, official US statements on the role of US nuclear weapons in deterring WMD threats in the Third World focus on the nuclear threat, even though no one has ruled out the use of nuclear weapons in response to CBW use or even against an overwhelming conventional threat.[30] Thus Secretary Cheney stated in January 1992 that 'strategic nuclear forces will continue to play an essential role with respect to countries other than the Soviet Union [*sic*]. Nuclear weapons cannot be disinvented. Other countries – some of the them, like Iraq, hostile and irresponsible – threaten to acquire them. This requires us to maintain a secure retaliatory capability to deter their use'.[31] Some have gone further, suggesting, as the US Air Force did in April 1992, that the 'emphasis of the deterrence equation has been shifted from just deterring the use of nuclear weapons by the Soviet Union [*sic*] to deterring the *development or use* of nuclear weapons by other countries, as well'.[32]

Whether US nuclear weapons deter the development of nuclear weapons (other than by allies) is questionable – in fact, the opposite might be the case. Fearing US intervention, countries might decide that a nuclear deterrent provides the only means to safeguard their interests.[33] It is undeniable, however, that the existence of US nuclear weapons cannot but affect the calculations of others on whether or not to use nuclear weapons. For this reason, the possession of nuclear weapons by others provides the United States with a justification for maintaining at least some nuclear weapons as a residual deterrent capability.

Maintaining a residual deterrent force, however, does not imply that the United States should seek to deter the use of nuclear weapons by committing in advance to an in-kind retaliatory response. Not only is it unclear that such an a priori commitment would in fact deter the use of nuclear weapons given the uncertainties on what deters, especially in a Third World context,[34] but a non-nuclear response would be far preferable. For example, concerted collective action on the part of the international community (including the five permanent members of the UN Security Council) to punish and defeat any country using nuclear weapons, would demonstrate the futility not just of using but also of possessing nuclear weapons.[35] The United States, Russia and Great Britain are in fact committed to such action as part of UN Security Council Resolution 255 (1968). In September 1992, President Bush reiterated the US commitment to 'provide assistance in accordance with the Charter to any non-nuclear weapons state party to the NPT that is a victim of aggression or an object of a threat of aggression involving nuclear weapons'.[36]

How should these considerations be applied to the issue of chemical and biological weapons use? Some have argued that the United States should not exclude using nuclear weapons in case of CBW use. The Reed study argued that theatre nuclear weapons, in particular, could play a material role in deterring 'not-yet-nuclear states from a variety of chemical and biological attacks and threats on our allies, friends and forces abroad'.[37] The study proposed the creation of a 'Nuclear Expeditionary Force', which would consist of a 'handful' of nuclear weapons on alert and deployed on short-range aircraft, B-2 bombers or sea-launched cruise missiles, to deal with this and similar eventualities.[38]

There are a number of fundamental problems with this approach. First, the notion of a roving nuclear expeditionary force capable of an instantaneous response would accord nuclear weapons a role and symbolic importance that they never possessed even at the height of the Cold War, nor should they ever possess. Second, the credibility of a US nuclear response to CBW attack is, as Paul Nitze has suggested, in serious doubt.[39] The consequences of using nuclear weapons in these circumstances would also be severe, shattering the 45-year-old tradition of non-use that has become a central element of the nuclear age.[40]

Third, the wartime use of chemical and biological weapons is proscribed by international law under the Geneva Protocol of 1925. Now that the Chemical Weapons Convention has been completed, the United States will have renounced the option of in-kind retaliation in case of CBW use.[41] Rather than threatening or using nuclear weapons, which many states regard as immoral, if not illegitimate, a more appropriate response to the violation of international law would be for the United States and other states to commit to a collective response using the instruments available under the UN Charter, including the use of military force.

Finally, there are important reasons not to threaten or use nuclear weapons in response to CBW use. If the United States reserves the right to use nuclear weapons in these circumstances, other countries would have every reason to do the same, thus creating new incentives for nuclear proliferation. Moreover, the delegitimization of CBW has, with 125 countries having signed the Chemical Weapons Convention in January 1993, received the full backing from the international community. An a priori commitment to punish and defeat any country using CBW with collective action and doing so with conventional forces would clearly demonstrate the disutility of chemical and biological weapons and thus further encourage their delegitimization.

The threat posed by the proliferation of weapons of mass destruction is real and their use in the future cannot be excluded. But the appropriate US response is not to maintain large and flexible nuclear forces. Instead, the best response is to state unequivocally that the proliferation of weapons of mass destruction poses a threat to international peace and security and that their use will lead to collective military action on the part of the international community.[42] In addition, every attempt should be made to extend the delegitimization of weapons of mass destruction to nuclear weapons. That requires further and deep reductions in nuclear force levels, including those of the United States, not wielding the nuclear sword in the form of an 'expeditionary force' at every opportunity. At the same time, it must be recognized that so long as the United States possesses any nuclear weapons, their very existence will affect the decision by others on whether or not to use weapons of mass destruction. In this existential sense, even 200 US nuclear weapons will have a role in deterring the use of force by others.

Maintaining US Superpower Status

The final reason why some contend that the United States should maintain large nuclear forces is the idea that the number of nuclear weapons is an indicator of international stature. For over 45 years, the possession of nuclear weapons as well as the size of the total stockpile relative to that of others has been an important indicator of US and Soviet status not just as 'major' or even 'great' but as 'super' powers. Although the disintegration of the Soviet Union and the evisceration of Russia's economic and political bases have all but eliminated the notion of Russia as a 'super' power, some continue to maintain that overall nuclear force levels matter as indicators of international stature. Even President Yeltsin, speaking to officials at the Russian Ministry of Defence, maintained that 'it is no secret that Russia's status as a great power depends on its armed forces having nuclear weapons'.[43] The same notion pervades much of the discussion in the United States.[44]

How many nuclear weapons ensure a country's superpower status? Though no absolute numbers are given, those who favour retaining large forces argue that the United States should at least maintain parity with the strategic forces of the former Soviet Union as well as with the nuclear forces of all other powers combined.[45] This means that even if Russia were to reduce its forces to the level of all other nuclear powers, the United States should retain three-to-four times the Russian level to maintain its status as a superpower.

There are two problems with this argument. First, the fact that Russia today is no longer regarded as a superpower suggests that absolute levels of nuclear forces are not the sole ingredient of international status. Therefore, so long as the United States retains its pre-eminent political and economic position in the world, it will remain a superpower no matter how few nuclear weapons it deploys.[46] Second, accentuating the importance of nuclear weapons as an indicator of international status provides other countries with an incentive to acquire nuclear weapons. Is it really in the American interest to advertise the centrality of nuclear weapons to power in international affairs at a time when countries such as Germany, Japan and Argentina aspire to a greater role in, and increased responsibility for, preserving international security? Surely the United States has much to gain and very little to lose in arguing the opposite – that power and responsibility reside in the political and economic well-being of nations rather than in their nuclear status.

Two supplementary reasons for maintaining nuclear forces larger than those of other powers have also been given. First, in keeping with his long-standing concern about the post-nuclear-exchange balance of forces, Paul Nitze suggests that the United States 'should retain a strategic reserve that would be as large as the strategic arsenals of all other nuclear nations combined to prevent their domination in the aftermath of a US-Russian or comparable exchange'.[47] Although the notion that the United States will or should be concerned about anything after a nuclear exchange appears macabre to say the least, the concept of a strategic reserve force for this and other purposes is intellectually defensible. What is not defensible is the notion that such a force be several times larger than any other nuclear force. Any additional damage a third party could inflict on the United States after a nuclear exchange would surely be much less significant than the damage one or a dozen US weapons could inflict on a country that had not been subject to prior attack. Therefore, a reserve force of 10–20 weapons should suffice for such residual deterrence purposes.

Second, there is the argument, that if the United Sates 'moves from superpower to being an equal, others may decide to become equals as well'.[48] Although this notion might have some validity if one is talking about very low force levels of 10–20 weapons and, even more so, if forces have been reduced to zero, it is difficult to accept its validity if the United States maintained hundreds of weapons. As Michael Brown explains, few countries in the world could marshal the resources necessary to build up a force of hundreds of weapons and the United States will always have the ability to stay ahead of the few who do.[49] In addition, the whole notion of a US nuclear edge deterring the acquisition of nuclear weapons by others places an exaggerated importance on nuclear weapons as symbols of power and prestige and disregards other, more tangible reasons related to security perceptions that drives the demand for nuclear weapons. Moreover, to the extent that countries value nuclear weapons for power and prestige reasons, a concerted effort to devalue nuclear weapons by reducing force levels to an absolute minimum and emphasizing the general disutility of nuclear weapons as political and military instruments would be more likely to dissuade countries from going nuclear than a policy that advocates the prestige value of possessing nuclear weapons.[50]

In short, questions of international status should have no influence on determining how low the United States can go with respect to its nuclear forces. US power and prestige is above all derived from its economic, political and overall military power, not from the absolute or relative level of nuclear forces. Possessing 200 highly survivable nuclear weapons when others have reduced to similar or lower levels will be sufficient to meet US security objectives; the reductions themselves will have no impact on the status of the United States as a superpower.

Reducing the Likelihood of Nuclear Weapons Use – Why Less is Better

The discussion so far has suggested that the residual purposes for which the United States maintains nuclear weapons can be served by a force of some 200 highly survivable strategic weapons. But to say that 200 weapons may be sufficient is not the same as having demonstrated the need to go this low. Indeed, 3,000 weapons could also serve the residual US nuclear weapons requirements, and may do so with greater confidence, flexibility and credibility – all highly desirable characteristics of nuclear forces. So why not maintain 3,000 weapons? The answer can be found in the changing US policy objectives in regard to nuclear weapons, which, in the post-Cold War world, should be to reduce the likelihood of nuclear weapons ever being used. Deterrence, and thus the traditional criteria for sizing and structuring nuclear forces, will be one element of a concerted strategy to meet this objective. However, deterrence can no longer be the only or even the dominant element, since the principal threat of nuclear use is now effectively beyond deterrence.

That threat is a direct consequence of the break-up of the Soviet Union and the proliferation of nuclear technology more generally. In the past, decisions on the use of nuclear weapons were tightly controlled. Only five countries had openly declared that they possessed the means to make such a decision, and perhaps two others – India and Israel – were widely believed to be able to use nuclear weapons in short order should either decide to do so. In each case, however, the command and control over nuclear weapons was believed to be secure. Each country had devised elaborate systems to ensure not only that nuclear weapons would be used if appropriate political authorities so decided, but also that the weapons would *not* be used unless the decision was specifically to do so.[51]

The dissolution of the Soviet Union has called the security of nuclear command and control arrangements into question.[52] Particular concern focused on the safety and security of the 15,000 tactical or non-strategic nuclear weapons deployed across the territory of the former Soviet Union, not all of which contained the electronic safeguards – so-called permissive action links or PALs – against unauthorized use. None of the worst-case scenarios that were prominently talked about in the aftermath of the August 1991 coup in Moscow has yet come to pass; no weapons have been stolen, sold, or used. Indeed, tactical nuclear weapons were rapidly consolidated inside Russia and active US diplomacy, including financial and technical assistance, succeeded to prevent the worst, at least for now.[53]

The fact remains, however, that thousands of nuclear weapons are still deployed in Russia and, indeed, in Belarus, Kazakhstan and Ukraine. To date, there has been no formal, international agreement to dismantle any one of the estimated 27,000 nuclear weapons in the former Soviet arsenal, although some are being destroyed. The initiatives on non-strategic nuclear forces of the fall of 1991, under which the United States and Russia pledged to eliminate large parts of their respective stockpiles, were only unilateral commitments. Neither START I nor START II (nor, indeed, the INF Treaty that preceded both) requires the dismantlement of any nuclear weapon to be reduced. Therefore, even after all formal and informal agreements have been fully implemented, many thousands of nuclear weapons and many tons of fissile materials will remain stored in a variety of sites across Russia. Given the uncertain state of political developments inside the country and the not-inconceivable possibility that Russia will experience secessionist pressures from the autonomous republics that comprise the Federation, the possibility that nuclear weapons or materials may fall into the wrong hands therefore remains as real as before.

There is only one way to address this threat effectively and that is to eliminate as many nuclear weapons as quickly as possible and to ensure that those weapons that remain are safe and secure. Aside from continuing to provide financial and technical assistance, the United States must provide the necessary incentives for Russia to embark on this course. The best way to do this would be to eliminate the primary rationale for maintaining large numbers of Russian nuclear weapons, which is the continued deployment of large numbers of US nuclear weapons. Therefore, a concerted strategy to move to much smaller US forces will be the only effective way to get a firm and enduring grip on the dangers posed by the former Soviet nuclear arsenal.

A strategy to move to much lower US and Russian nuclear force levels will also serve wider nuclear non-proliferation goals. For reasons suggested earlier, a concerted effort to devalue the role of nuclear weapons in international politics should help to counter pressures in some countries to acquire them. This is particularly true if this effort leads not just to lower force levels, but also to non-discriminatory restrictions on nuclear weapons, including on their development, production and deployment. Such restrictions would effectively cap the nuclear capabilities of all countries (thus preventing any from trying to 'catch up' with the nuclear powers as the force levels come down). They would also clearly demonstrate the commitment of the nuclear powers to live up to their obligations under the nuclear Non-Proliferation Treaty (NPT) to reduce nuclear force levels. This is particularly important in view of the 1995 NPT review conference, at which the states parties must decide for how long to extend the NPT regime.

Of course, lower nuclear force levels and non-discriminatory restrictions will not of themselves eliminate nuclear proliferation in every instance. Some countries clearly desire nuclear weapons for reasons that are completely unrelated to the capabilities of the declared nuclear powers. But, again for reasons discussed earlier, this need not prevent the United States from going much lower, particularly if doing so mitigates proliferation pressures elsewhere.

In short, there are good reasons why the United States should go much lower down the thermonuclear ladder than it has so far. While there remains a residual need for deterrence, the thrust of US policy toward nuclear weapons should now be to reduce the likelihood of nuclear weapons ever being used. This means eliminating as many nuclear weapons as soon as possible, in particular Russian nuclear weapons. It also means adopting a vigorous and more positive nuclear non-proliferation strategy, including negotiating non-discriminatory restrictions on nuclear weapons to cap the nuclear capabilities of all countries.

Characteristics of a Nuclear Insurance Force

If the United States can and should reduce its forces to as low as 200 nuclear weapons, it is fair to ask why should it not go all the way to zero? It could be argued that if nuclear weapons did not exist today, the United States would be unlikely to acquire any. Indeed, as Les Aspin commented before becoming Secretary of Defense, in the past nuclear weapons 'were the great equalizer that enabled western capitals to deal with numerically larger Eastern Bloc forces . . . Nuclear weapons still serve the same purpose – as a great equalizer. But it is the United States that is now the potential equalizee.' Aspin concluded that 'if offered that magic wand to eradicate the existence and knowledge of nuclear weapons, we would very likely accept it'.[54] The problem, of course, is that no such magic wand currently exists. The road to zero is difficult because, unlike chemical and biological weapons, nuclear weapons are still regarded by many to have political and military utility. Therefore, so long as this remains the common perception, no country that currently has nuclear weapons is likely to give them up in the near future.

But this is no reason for the nuclear powers to reject efforts to move down to considerably lower numbers, including, in the US case, to a nuclear force of 200 weapons. Indeed, doing so would go a long way towards depreciating the role of nuclear weapons in international affairs,[55] and may even create the conditions necessary for moving down even further, including ultimately to zero.

What doctrinal considerations should guide a US force of 200 weapons and how should it be structured? One doctrinal issue concerns targeting. It has been suggested that a force of hundreds of weapons would necessarily be targeted at civilians. Reed and Wheeler, for example, argue that 'the concept of a minimum deterrent based upon a few hundred nuclear weapons or less is unrealistic. It is immoral to plan for a war which targets only civilians or cities *per se*, which is inherent in the minimum deterrent concept.'[56] There is no inherent reason why small nuclear forces should rely on a policy of targeting cities, however, even though that capability will exist so long as nuclear weapons do. Even with 200 weapons, the United States would retain the option to attack conventional military forces and/or critical industries.

A recent analysis by Michael Mazarr identified 110 major conventional force and 90 defence industry targets in Russia, the destruction of which would severely degrade Russian conventional force projection capabilities and virtually eliminate its defence industrial base. Fatalities would be in the tens of millions, with casualties many times higher.[57] To any rational leadership, destroying even a fraction of these targets would be akin to the 'disaster beyond history' McGeorge Bundy warned about a quarter-century ago in respect to ten weapons on ten cities.[58]

Another doctrinal consideration is when to resort to nuclear use. The time has certainly come for the United States to adopt a no-first-use policy. The Soviet conventional threat, which led the United States in the late 1940s to maintain the option to use nuclear weapons first, has clearly disappeared.[59] There is therefore no longer a need to threaten nuclear use in any circumstances other than a direct nuclear attack on the United States or its allies. As the experience of 'Desert Storm' has clearly demonstrated, the United States alone or in concert with others possesses the conventional forces necessary to inflict devastating punishment on, and effectively defeat, any potential aggressor that does not possess or use nuclear weapons.[60]

In addition to a no-first-policy, the time has also come to adopt what Bruce Blair has called a 'no-immediate-second-use' policy. As Blair argued in the mid-1980s,

> the justification for this policy is that nuclear decisionmaking should not be reduced to reflexes and brief drills but should instead be regarded as a careful deliberative exercise of national

> leadership that could take days or longer. A moment's reflection would suggest that a decision on nuclear retaliation should not be forced on officials before they have had a chance to assess actual damage, evaluate Soviet political and military objectives, define US security interests, and determine the role of nuclear weapons in promoting those interests. These matters cannot be given adequate consideration in a matter of minutes or hours.[61]

The literature on nuclear force planning has increasingly come to recognize the inherent dangers of basing strategic force postures and doctrinal guidance on the need to respond rapidly to attack.[62] Whatever justification might have existed during the Cold War for emphasizing the ability to respond promptly to an attack, no such requirement any longer exists. Instead, priority should in the future be placed on designing strategic forces in such a way that they are able to ride out an attack and retaliate only if and when national authorities, having had time to assess the situation, decide that this is desirable. In short, nuclear forces should be capable of what Ashton Carter has called 'dumb rideout': the 'ability to retaliate effectively should be independent of warning or other information, independent of what other forces in other basing modes are doing, and independent of time'.[63] It is this feature that allows for confidence in a strategy of no immediate second use.

Strategic bombers and missiles based at sea are most suited to fulfilling this criterion. Bombers have the benefit of being both slow-flying and recallable after launch. Their retaliatory nature resides in the hours rather than minutes necessary to reach their targets; their survivability rest on their being able to take off without having to be committed to attack. SLBMs at sea are the most survivable nuclear system, even during an actual nuclear conflict. A two-year evaluation of the strategic triad by the US General Accounting Office concluded that SLBMs have 'about the equal of speed and reliability of communications to ICBM silos. Contrary to conventional wisdom, SSBNs are in essentially constant communication with national command authorities'.[64] This means that their launch can be postponed until so ordered by national authorities. In contrast to bombers and SLBMs, ICBMs are neither particularly survivable nor can they be recalled after launch. Their chief characteristic – promptness and high accuracy – may have been suitable to a Cold War strategy, but today this is the opposite of what is needed. For these reasons, a nuclear insurance force should be composed of strategic bombers and missiles based on submarines. Land-based missiles should be eliminated.[65]

Bombers should be confined to carrying air-launched cruise missiles (ALCMs) to ensure that retaliatory strikes will reach their intended target. A total of 100 bombers, with one ALCM each, could be deployed at

25 bases throughout Russia and United States.[66] As for SLBMs, a first step to lower numbers would be to de-MIRV all 432 US missiles aboard 18 Trident submarines and all 456 missiles aboard 27 Typhoon and Delta IV and III submarines, so that each missile carries only one warhead. Subsequently, the number of missiles per submarine could be gradually reduced and the launch tubes filled with concrete. The 18 Trident submarines could carry six single-warhead missiles each, while the 27 Russian submarines would carry 4 missiles each.[67] In this way, US and Russian forces would be reduced to about 200 weapons each, without appreciably reducing the number of nuclear delivery systems below that currently envisaged under START II.

To enhance mutual reassurance about the safety and security of these forces, a number of operational changes should also be instituted. With respect to bomber weapons, both countries should agree to store the ALCMs separate from the bombers at sites that would be subject to portal and perimeter continuous monitoring. The sites should have direct communication links to the opposite capital, so that entry (and possible retrieval) would be instantaneously communicated. A similar procedure should be used for SLBM warheads aboard submarines that are in port. The warheads (and possibly the missiles as well) should be removed from the submarines and stored at sites that are subject to the same monitoring arrangements as the ALCM storage sites.

Three additional changes should be agreed for submarine-based weapons. First, both countries should agree to deploy no more than 24 warheads at sea at any one time. The remaining weapons should at all times be stored on land. Second, the United States and Russia should both operate their SLBMs at sea in a 'modified' alert posture, which is the normal alert status for US submarines leaving port. According to Bruce Blair, submarines on modified alert require at least 18 hours 'to complete the complex procedures – for instance, the removal of the flood plates from the launch tubes and the installation of vital electronic components into the fire control system – that enable them to assume a launch-ready disposition'.[68] The final operational change should be for the United States to follow Russia in equipping its SLBM warheads with PALs and agree to retain the electronic locks on the warheads even at sea. The US Navy's concern that interference with communication might prevent the launching of SLBMs at a time of war is no longer justified, even if it ever was. Instead, negative control of nuclear weapons (that is, the denial of unauthorized use) should now have clear priority over positive control (that is, the certainty of authorized use).[69]

A nuclear insurance force based on these characteristics would be invulnerable to pre-emptive attack, yet consistent with a policy of nuclear reassurance and residual deterrence.[70] Both countries would retain a sufficient number of nuclear weapons to inflict unacceptable damage and at least 24 of these weapons would be invulnerable to any conceivable nuclear or conventional attack. Equally important, by storing the bulk of weapons at monitored sites, the safety and security of remaining nuclear forces would be significantly enhanced.

An Arms Control Strategy for Nuclear Insurance

To suggest what a lower level of strategic nuclear forces should be is not the same as suggesting how we should get there from where we are today. The process of reducing forces to the desired level will be difficult to say the least. This is particularly true since the United States and the four former Soviet republics on whose territory strategic forces are based still deploy about 10,000 strategic weapons each.[71] Moreover, the START treaties have yet to enter into force, and when they do, full implementation will take between seven and ten years. It is therefore understandable that US policy-makers believe that finalizing and implementing these agreements should receive top priority, rendering any discussion of how much lower we can go of only theoretical interest.

At the same time, a careful analysis of nuclear weapons requirements in the future may have practical benefits. Such an analysis may highlight possible policy changes needed to rectify certain inadequacies in the agreements themselves. Current obstacles to implementing the START treaties include the reluctance of some non-Russian republics to ratify their promised non-nuclear status and the perception among some in Russia that the reductions mandated by the START-II agreement place undue burdens on Moscow.[72] There are also a number of inadequacies in the agreements themselves. For example, one glaring omission is the failure to require the actual elimination of those nuclear weapons and missiles that must be reduced to reach agreed levels. The implementation period of the agreements is also far too long, thus increasing the risk that adverse political developments in the former Soviet Union may pose a threat to agreed undertakings.

The earlier discussion of US nuclear weapons requirements suggests that these obstacles and inadequacies could be overcome if the United States acted on the notion, endorsed by General Powell amongst others, that the concept of strategic parity can be safely abandoned. Recall that General Powell defended the START-II agreement by stating that 'with a US force structure of about 3,500 warheads . . . we have the capability to deter any actor in the other capital no matter what he has at his disposal'.[73] This would be true even if the Russians had secretly hidden

20,000 single-warhead SS-25 missiles. It follows that the United States can safely reduce its strategic forces to 3,500 warheads *even if Russia does not follow suit immediately*. Washington could announce that it would unilaterally reduce its strategic forces to the START-II levels by removing those warheads and missiles that will be reduced from active service within a year. It could invite Moscow to inspect the residual forces to verify that reductions had indeed taken place. The United States could also place the weapons removed from active service in secure storage and invite Russia to monitor the sites on a permanent basis. Finally, though undertaking these steps unconditionally, the United States could ask Russia as well as Belarus, Kazakhstan and Ukraine to reciprocate the reductions within the same timeframe and institute similar inspection and monitoring arrangements on a bilateral basis with the United States.

The potential benefits of these unilateral steps are great, whereas the costs are few.[74] The most important benefit is that a clear American demonstration that the United States is not interested in exploiting Russian political weakness will strengthen those political forces in Russia and elsewhere that support the START-II agreement. The unilateral reductions and the offer to have Russia verify residual levels and monitor deactivated forces on a permanent basis will likely reassure those still suspicious of American intentions, thus increasing the likelihood of reciprocity. Reciprocity would bring additional benefits, most notably the effective denuclearization of the non-Russian republics as well as a two-third reduction in Russian forces within months rather than years.

The costs of taking these steps unilaterally would be marginal. The stability of the nuclear balance would be unaffected, as General Powell has pointed out. Fears that on-site inspections by Russia of US forces will compromise national security are also unfounded. Under the START-I Treaty, Russia will monitor residual force levels in ways identical to those suggested. As to the permanent monitoring of deactivated weapons, warheads could be stored in a manner that need not compromise vital design secrets yet provide confidence that no weapons can be removed without detection.[75] Finally, although it may be true that these arrangements will not guarantee a full accounting of all nuclear weapons, this is no reason to forgo monitoring altogether, as some US officials have suggested it should.[76]

Therefore, even if Russia were not immediately to reciprocate, little would be lost in terms of security. The United States would retain 3,500 modern, reliable, and survivable weapons that would be more than sufficient to deter any hostile act, even by a power possessing two-to-three times as many weapons. At the same time, if the past is any guide, Russia is very likely to reciprocate. As in the September 1991 unilateral initiative of President Bush in regard to non-strategic nuclear forces, the proposed course of action is likely to strengthen the forces of reform and reason inside Russia and effectively nullify the arguments of those who oppose the current course of nuclear reductions.

Once agreement on how past strategic arms treaties can best be implemented has been reached, the door would be open to consider still further reductions, ultimately to the level of 200 weapons suggested earlier. A comprehensive arms control strategy should aim to achieve this end-point in two phases by the year 2000, although the actual destruction of weapons will take more time. The strategy would combine bilateral negotiations between Russia and the United States, negotiations among all five declared nuclear powers, and multilateral negotiations.

In *Phase One*, to be completed by 1995:

- the international community would negotiate a comprehensive nuclear test ban (CTB) and a world-wide cut-off of fissile material production for weapons purposes; and
- the United States and Russia would negotiate further reductions in their strategic forces.

In moving towards a policy of nuclear insurance, the United States should seek to devalue or depreciate nuclear weapons as instruments of military and political power in international affairs. Central to this effort should be international agreements to ban nuclear testing and to halt the production of fissile materials for weapons purposes. Both agreements would place non-discriminatory restrictions on nuclear weapons capabilities of all countries and should therefore encourage wider adherence to international non-proliferation standards. More importantly, the agreements would effectively cap the nuclear weapons capabilities of actual proliferators and deny potential proliferators the ability to acquire such a capability. Both agreements are therefore critical to achieving reductions in US forces to very low levels.[77]

The United States, Russia and France have each declared a moratorium on nuclear testing until July 1993.[78] Neither China nor Britain has joined the moratorium, although Britain will effectively be prevented from testing at the US test site in Nevada.[79] While US law allows the United States to recommence testing for safety and reliability purposes, it will be limited to 15 tests over a three-year period, after which testing would be suspended indefinitely unless another nuclear power were to conduct a nuclear test.[80] The Clinton administration should seek to modify this testing programme in two ways. First, the United States should commit to complete negotiations of a CTB by the time of the 1995 NPT review conference. Second, if a number of safety and/or reliability tests are deemed politically or technically necessary before a CTB enters into force, then this right to testing should be granted to all nuclear powers, including Russia. This may require opening up the Nevada test site to Russia and perhaps France, as it has long been to the United Kingdom. Each country would be limited to the same number of tests – say, six over a two-year period – whereafter all agree to sign a comprehensive test ban treaty, which would be open for signature to all countries.

A second element of a concerted strategy to devalue nuclear weapons should be an international agreement banning the production of fissile materials for weapons purposes. In July 1992, the Bush administration announced a permanent halt to the production of plutonium and highly enriched uranium for weapons purposes, a policy that had been in effect since 1988.[81] The administration opposed formalizing this ban in an international treaty, however, arguing in part that US goals in regions like the Middle East and South Asia were more comprehensive, including a ban on fissile-material production facilities.[82] But the two need not be contradictory and can, in fact, complement each other, for example, by supplementing an international agreement to halt fissile material production for weapons purposes with regional agreements banning facilities capable of producing these materials in their entirety.[83]

Ultimately, the agreement could be extended to a ban on the production of fissile material for any purpose, but this would require France and Japan to forgo current plans to use plutonium for the production of nuclear energy and may require changing designs of reactors fuelling nuclear-powered submarines. As to the verification of such an agreement, the United States has studied this issue since the dawn of the nuclear age and included a ban in all its nuclear disarmament proposal of the 1950s and 1960s. The International Atomic Energy Agency also has long-standing experience in verifying the production of fissile materials under the safeguards agreements it has signed with most NPT member states.[84]

Finally, in the first phase of this nuclear arms control strategy, the United States and Russia should negotiate further reductions in their strategic nuclear forces. In order to enhance prospects for moving to a nuclear insurance force consisting of 200 weapons on each side, Washington and Moscow should agree to: eliminate all land-based missiles; de-MIRV all sea-based missiles; and reduce conventional and nuclear strategic bombers to 100 on each side, while limiting their weapons load to 200 ALCMs in total. These steps would reduce nuclear weapons inventories to about 650 weapons on each side: 200 weapons on strategic bombers and approximately 450 weapons on sea-based missiles. All weapons to be reduced under this proposal would eventually be dismantled. Until that time, the weapons should be disabled and placed in the storage sites containing weapons reduced in earlier stages, which should continue to be subject to permanent bilateral or international monitoring. Fissile materials recovered from dismantled warheads should be placed under international safeguard or, where possible, converted for use in civilian power reactors.

With a concerted effort on the part of the major powers, and decisive leadership by the United States, it should be possible to complete negotiations on the agreements proposed for phase one by 1995. This assumes, of course, that the United States adopts the underlying rationale of a nuclear insurance policy. On that assumption, the steps advocated are, with the exception in further US-Russian reductions, relatively straightforward. All have been part of the international nuclear arms control agenda for years, some even since the mid-1940s. In completing phase one, the United States, Russia, and the rest of the international community will have taken decisive steps towards reducing the nuclear danger still further, while clearly devaluing the role of nuclear weapons in general. This would therefore open the way towards phase two.

In *Phase Two*, to be completed by the year 2000:

- the international community would negotiate a world-wide ban on military ballistic missiles based on land with ranges greater than 100 km;
- the five declared nuclear powers would agree to de-MIRV all ballistic missiles; and
- the United States and Russia would limit their nuclear forces to approximately 200 weapons and place the bulk of them in monitored storage sites.

With the United States and Russia agreeing to eliminate their land-based ballistic missiles, the next step would be to begin negotiations on a global ban on all military ballistic missiles based on land with ranges greater than 100 km. The dangers of ballistic missile proliferation to international security have become increasingly apparent in recent years, as the war of the cities between Iran and Iraq and the SCUD attacks on Israel and Saudi Arabia demonstrated.[85] Rather than concentrating on the development of highly capable theatre and strategic ballistic missile defences, the appropriate response to this growing threat would be to seek a complete ban on such missiles on a world-wide basis. Having demonstrated by their own actions that land-based missiles have little military utility, the United States and Russia can together attempt to convince other countries that they should follow in Moscow's and Washington's footsteps. Although the practical details of verifying such a ban on land-based missiles will take some time to work out given the continuing desire and need of some to have access to space,[86] an agreement that land-based missiles for military purposes be banned would strengthen international security in general. Whether all countries (including China and, thus, India and Pakistan) would immediately sign on is perhaps doubtful, but the pressure of the US and Russian example would be more helpful than if both still deployed land-based missiles of their own.

The second element of phase two would consist of an agreement among the five declared nuclear powers to de-MIRV their ballistic missiles. Such an agreement would in practice affect only France and Great Britain, since China does not possess any MIRVed missiles and the United States and Russia would have de-MIRVed their SLBMs in the earlier phase. A de-MIRVing of French and British sea-based missiles would limit their nuclear forces to about 64 to 80 warheads, depending on the number of submarines each would deploy. If Britain were to produce a fourth submarine, as seems likely, it would deploy 64 warheads; the same would be true for France, unless it developed a fifth submarine, in which case it could deploy 80 warheads. Assuming that strategic missile defences were banned, forces of this size should suffice to perform the limited deterrent functions for which they have been developed.

Finally, assuming the first two elements had been agreed upon, it would be possible for the United States and Russia further to reduce their strategic forces. Both should agree to remove missiles from their submarines so that each deployed no more than 108 single-warhead SLBMs.[87] They should also agree to limit the number of warheads at sea to 24 at any one time and operate these SLBMs on a 'modified' alert. The remaining warheads would be placed in monitored storage sites. In addition, both countries should limit their nuclear air-delivered inventory to 100 ALCMs, all of which would be placed in monitored storage sites. The ALCM and SLBM warhead sites should be monitored electronically so that entry (and possible retrieval) was communicated instantly to the other side. Both would then be in a position to take necessary counter-action in case unexpected developments occurred. At the same time, neither side would be able to make preparations for use of these weapons without the other being informed well in advance.

This final phase of the proposed arms control strategy would bring all declared nuclear powers into the nuclear reductions process. France, Britain and China will have to make fundamental choices about the role of their nuclear weapons (as opposed to those of Russia and the United States) for the first time. None could claim that the two 'super' powers had not reduced their forces to sufficiently low levels and all would therefore be confronted directly by their rhetoric and promises of participation in the disarmament process that they made in the past. It may be that London, Paris and/or Beijing will refuse to play. But in that case, the onus would be on them for the first time to explain to the international community why nuclear disarmament is good for Washington and Moscow but not for them. Confronted with this political reality, as well as the concerted effort by the United States and Russia to emphasize the growing irrelevance of nuclear weapons as instruments of international power and status, Britain, France and China may find it difficult to oppose the course proposed here.

Conclusion

The end of the Cold War demands a radical reassessment of the role of nuclear weapons in international politics. To date, the major nuclear powers have begun a process that is slowly bringing them down the thermonuclear ladder both ascended, often with precious little thought, during 40 years of confrontation. Old habits of thinking may have convinced many that the United States and Russia are now approaching the very bottom of the ladder. But even after agreed commitments have been implemented, both countries will deploy nearly 7,000 strategic nuclear weapons, as well as thousands more non-strategic weapons. And this does not even account for the thousands of weapons that may be stored rather than destroyed as forces are reduced.

This paper has suggested that the United States and Russia can and must go further down the thermonuclear ladder, initially to perhaps as low as 200 weapons on each side. This conclusion is based on the belief that the only remaining role for nuclear weapons in the post-Cold War world is that of insurance – to remind whomever might think otherwise of their inescapable vulnerability to nuclear devastation.

Getting from here to there is by no means an easy task. The details of the phased arms control strategy make this clear. But success or failure will not be determined by these details; instead, success is possible only if we abandon old habits of thinking about nuclear weapons, deterrence, and arms control. The time to start is now.

ACKNOWLEDGEMENTS

I would like to thank participants at the workshop of the Project on Rethinking Arms Control for their comments on an earlier draft of this paper. I am particularly grateful to Bruce Blair, Michael Brown, Mac Destler, Daniel Ellsberg, Elisa Harris, John Hawes, George Quester and Tom Schelling, who prodded me to state the argument of this paper more clearly and forcefully.

NOTES

1. 'Department of Defense Press Briefing by Secretary of Defense Richard Cheney and General Colin Powell' (Washington, DC: Federal News Services, 28 Sept. 1991), 2–4.
2. These various initiatives were announced in a series of speeches by President Bush, then-President Gorbachev and President Yeltsin from September 1991 onwards. See 'Remarks by President Bush on Reducing US and Soviet Nuclear Weapons', *New York Times*, 28 Sept. 1991, p. 4; 'Gorbachev's Remarks on Nuclear Arms Cuts', *New York Times*, 6 Oct. 1991, p. 12; 'President Bush's State of the Union Address', *New York Times*, 29 Jan. 1992, p. A16; and 'Russia's Policy in the Field of Arms Limitation and Reduction', Statement by President Yeltsin, 28 Jan. 1992, reprinted in United Nations, General Assembly, *A/47/79*, 29 Jan. 1992. The initiatives on strategic nuclear forces culminated in the signing of the START-II Treaty on 3 January 1993. See 'Treaty between the United States of America and the Russian Federation on Further Reduction and Limitation of Strategic Offensive Arms' (Washington, DC: Arms Control and Disarmament Agency, Jan. 1993). For an overview of these developments, see Ivo H. Daalder and Terry Terriff, 'Nuclear Arms Control: Finishing the Cold War Agenda', in this volume.
3. 'Prepared Statement of Secretary of Defense Cheney before the Senate Armed Services Committee on the Strategic Arms Reduction Treaty', 28 July 1992, p. 10.
4. Ibid., pp. 9–10.
5. This paper focuses on evaluating US strategic nuclear force requirements. For reasons argued elsewhere, I believe the United States should seek to eliminate non-strategic nuclear forces on a global basis. See 'Abolish Tactical Warheads', *New York Times*, 10 Sept. 1991, p. A19; and 'Nuclear Weapons in Europe – Why Zero is Better', *Arms Control Today*, Vol. 23, No. 1 (Jan./Feb. 1993).
6. The only criticism I am aware of came, predictably, from Frank Gaffney. See Frank Gaffney, Jr., 'Finding Flaws in the Hastily Woven Fabric of START II', *Washington Times*, 6 Jan. 1993, p. G1.
7. See, for example, Michael May, George Bing and John Steinbruner, *Strategic Arms Reductions* (Washington, DC: Brookings Institution, 1988); Dean Wilkening, *A Future Targeting Doctrine for US Strategic Nuclear Forces* (Livermore, CA: Center for Technical Studies on Security, Energy and Arms Control, June 1991); Committee on International Security and Arms Control (CISAC), *The Future of the US-Soviet Nuclear Relationship* (Washington, DC: National Academy Press, 1991); Kurt Gottfried and Jonathan Dean, *Nuclear Security in a Transformed World* (Cambridge, MA: Union of Concerned Scientists, Sept. 1991); Linda L. Gaines, *START II: Thinking One Move Ahead* (Argonne, Ill: Argonne National Laboratory, Nov. 1991); Leon Sloss, 'US Strategic Forces After the Cold War: Policies and Strategies', *Washington Quarterly*, Vol. 14, No. 4 (Autumn 1991); Walter B. Slocombe, 'The Continued Need for Extended Deterrence', *Washington Quarterly*, Vol. 14, No. 4 (Autumn 1991); and Andrew J. Goodpaster, *Tighter Limits on Nuclear Arms: Issues and Opportunities for a New Era* (Washington, DC: The Atlantic Council of the United States, May 1992). A 1990 Department of Energy plan for future nuclear

weapons production requirements included an option of 3,000 weapons as a 'minimum' future force. See Jeffrey Smith and Thomas Lippman, 'DOE Plans Production of Nuclear Arms Until 2050', *Washington Post*, 15 July 1990, p. A9. The Strategic Advisory Group (SAG) of the Joint Strategic Target Planning Staff concluded that a level of forces 'in the 5,000 20% range' would be sufficient. See Thomas C. Reed, 'The Role of Nuclear Weapons in the New World Order', Briefing to General George L. Butler, 10 Oct. 1992, p. 12 (hereafter 'Reed Briefing'). For a more comprehensive justification of the SAG's views, see Thomas Reed and Michael Wheeler, *The Role of Nuclear Weapons in the New World Order* (Washington, DC: Dec. 1991), reprinted in US Congress, Senate, *Threat Assessment, Military Strategy, and Defense Planning*, Hearings before the Committee on Armed Services, 102d Cong., 2d Sess., Jan.–March 1992, pp. 156–213.

8. See note 7.
9. See William Arkin, 'How Much Isn't Enough?' paper prepared for a study on 'US Nuclear Weapons After the Cold War', Center for Strategic and International Studies, Sept. 1992, pp. 6–7. For an argument in favour of the continuing relevance of these traditional measures, see Paul Chrzanowski, *Impact of Reduced Nuclear Weapons Stockpile on Strategic Stability* (Livermore, CA: Center for Technical Studies on Security, Energy and Arms Control, March 1991), p. 2.
10. See US General Accounting Office, *Strategic Weapons: Nuclear Weapons Targeting Process* (Washington, DC: USGAO, Sept. 1991) for an overview of the traditional targeting process, including targeting categories.
11. Arkin, 'How Much Isn't Enough', p. 7. See also US General Accounting Office, *Strategic Weapons*, pp. 12–13; US Congress, Congressional Budget Office, *The START Treaty and Beyond* (Washington, DC: CBO, Oct. 1991), pp. 13–14; Reed Briefing, p. 11; Jeffrey Smith, 'US Expected to Reduce Number of Nuclear Targets', *Washington Post*, 19 April 1991, p. A17; Jeffrey Smith, 'US Trims List of Targets in Soviet Union', *Washington Post*, 21 July 1991, pp. A1, A29; and Melissa Healey, 'US Speeds Review of Nuclear-War Plan', *Los Angeles Times*, 4 Oct. 1991, p. A10.
12. CBO, *The START Treaty and Beyond*, p. 16.
13. See Arkin, 'How Much Isn't Enough?', pp. 3 ff.
14. Bruce Van Voorst, 'America's Doomsday Machine', *Time*, 16 July 1990, p. 19.
15. Cited in Arkin, 'How Much Isn't Enough?', p. 7.
16. Cited in US Congress, Senate, *The START Treaty*, Report of the Committee on Foreign Relations, 102d Cong., 2d Sess., 18 Sept. 1992, p. 51. It is perhaps noteworthy that Powell defended the 3,500 level even under a scenario under which Russia had secretly hidden 20,000 SS-25 missiles: 'I'm not sure what that truly does for them as long as we have very survivable systems at sea, for example. What would they do with these?'. Ibid.
17. See the statements of General Powell cited in US Congress, Senate, *Military Implications of the START I Treaty and the June 14, 1992 US/Russian Joint Understanding on Further Reductions in Strategic Offensive Arms*, report of the Committee on Armed Services, 102d Cong., 2d Sess., 18 Sept. 1992, pp. 22–3.
18. CISAC, *The Future of the US-Soviet Nuclear Relationship*, p. 30.
19. For a defence of this argument, see Brent Scowcroft (chairman) *Report of the President's Commission on Strategic Forces* (Washington, DC: Commission on Strategic Forces, April 1983), pp. 1–7. For a current argument to this effect, see Reed Briefing, pp. 13–15.
20. See, for example, Leon Sloss, *Rethinking Nuclear Employment Policy* (Livermore, CA: Center for Technical Studies on Security, Energy and Arms Control, January 1991); and Dean Wilkening, *A Future Targeting Doctrine for US Strategic Nuclear Forces*; Prepared Statement of Paul H. Nitze, in US Congress, Senate, *Threat Assessment, Military Strategy, and Defense Planning*, p. 108; Reed and Wheeler, *The Role of Nuclear Weapons*, p. 26; CISAC, *The Future of the US-Soviet Nuclear Relationship*, pp. 28–9; John Van Oudenaren, 'Nuclear Weapons in the 1990s and

Beyond', in Patrick Garrity and Steven A. Maaranen (eds.), *Nuclear Weapons in a Changing World* (New York: Plenum Press, 1992), p. 36; and Walter Slocombe, 'The Future of US Nuclear Weapons in a Restructured World', in ibid. p. 59.

21. See, for example, Robert Jervis, *The Illogic of American Nuclear Strategy* (Ithaca, NY: Cornell University Press, 1984); and Charles Glaser, *Analyzing Strategic Nuclear Policy* (Princeton, NJ: Princeton University Press, 1990).
22. Fred C. Iklé, 'Comrades in Arms: The Case for a Russian-American Defense Community', *National Interest*, No. 26 (Winter 1991/92), p. 25.
23. On this point, see also Carl Kaysen, Robert McNamara, and George Rathjens, 'Nuclear Weapons After the Cold War', *Foreign Affairs*, Vol. 70, No. 4 (Fall 1991), p. 105.
24. See Sloss, 'US Strategic Forces After the Cold War', p. 152; Slocombe, 'The Continued Need for Extended Deterrence'; Reed Briefing, p. 2; Prepared Statement of Keith B. Payne in U.S. Congress, Senate, *Threat Assessment, Military Strategy, and Defense Planning*, p. 108; and George H. Quester and Victor A. Utgoff, 'US Arms Reductions and Nuclear Nonproliferation: The Counterproductive Possibilities', *Washington Quarterly*, Vol. 16, No. 1 (Winter 1993), pp. 135–7.
25. On nuclear dilemmas of the past, see Ivo H. Daalder, *The Nature and Practice of Flexible Response: NATO Strategy and Theater Nuclear Forces since 1967* (New York: Columbia University Press, 1991).
26. See, for example, Reed and Wheeler, *The Role of Nuclear Weapons*, p. 21. Reed and Wheeler also argued that the size of the US arsenal matters in absolute ways in discouraging allied proliferation: 'If the American arsenal shrinks to the size of the arsenals of virtually all other states, it is doubtful that Germany and Japan can over time resist pressures to acquire similar capabilities'. Ibid. But it is absurd to think that the size of the *American* nuclear stockpile is what deters Germany or Japan from acquiring a deterrent force equal to that of France or Great Britain. If either had such ambitions, they would have embarked on this course long ago, particularly since the Soviet threat and the dubious credibility of the American nuclear umbrella, further discussed below, would have given them every incentive to do so.
27. The point was illustrated by Henry Kissinger in the late 1970s when he argued that the assignment of strategic forces (400 Polaris warheads) to cover targets threatening European allies would no longer be available for strategic deterrence: 'Thus in case of war we are likely to be strained either with respect to our strategic or with respect to our theater nuclear coverage.' Kissinger, 'Statement before the Committee on Foreign Relations on SALT II', 31 July 1979, reprinted in Kissinger, *For the Record* (Boston, MA: Little, Brown, 1981), p. 197.
28. See, for example, Les Aspin, *From Deterrence to Denuking: Dealing with Proliferation in the 1990s* (Washington, DC: House Armed Services Committee, 18 Feb. 1992).
29. Joint Chiefs of Staff, *1991 Joint Military Net Assessment* (Washington, DC: USDOD, March 1991), p. 2–8.
30. For example, the 1992 National Military Strategy states that the 'purpose of nuclear forces is deter the use of weapons of mass destruction and to serve as a hedge against the emergence of an overwhelming conventional threat'. Joint Chiefs of Staff, *National Military Strategy of the United States* (Washington, DC: USDOD, Jan. 1992), p. 13.
31. 'Statement of Secretary of Defense Richard Cheney on the FY1993 Budget for the Department of Defense', Senate Armed Services Committee, 31 Jan. 1992, p. 22.
32. 'Air Force Research, Development, Test, and Evaluation', Presentation to the House Appropriations Defense Subcommittee, 29 April 1992, p. 6, emphasis added. Cited in Arkin, 'How Much Isn't Enough?', p. 10. General George Butler similarly stated that a 'US nuclear deterrent force . . . encourages non-proliferation, albeit within limits bounded by rationality.' Statement by General George Butler before the House Armed Services Committee Defense Policy Panel, 8 April 1992, p. 5.
33. Indeed, the Indian Defence Minister is reported to have taken this lesson away from

the Gulf War: 'Don't fight the United States unless you have nuclear weapons.' Cited in Aspin, *From Deterrence to Denuking*, p. 6.

34. On this point, see Reed and Wheeler, *The Role of Nuclear Weapons*, p. 18.
35. On this issue, see Thomas C. Schelling, 'The Thirtieth Year', *Daedalus*, Vol. 120, No. 1 (Winter 1991), p. 27.
36. Speech by President Bush to the United Nations General Assembly, 21 Sept. 1992, p. 6.
37. Reed Briefing, p. 7. See also Reed and Wheeler, *The Role of Nuclear Weapons*, p. 19; and Quester and Utgoff, 'US Arms Reductions and Nonproliferation', pp. 133–4, 138. The need to deter the use of weapons of mass destruction in regional contingencies also pervades Keith Payne's reasoning for maintaining a large and flexible US nuclear force. See Prepared Statement of Payne.
38. Reed Briefing, p. 16.
39. Paul Nitze, 'Keeping Nuclear Insurance', *Bulletin of the Atomic Scientists*, Vol. 48, No. 4 (May 1992), p. 34.
40. On this point, see McGeorge Bundy, 'Nuclear Weapons and the Gulf', *Foreign Affairs*, Vol. 70, No. 4 (Fall 1991), pp. 83–94.
41. The United States unilaterally renounced the right to use biological weapons in 1969. Although it has reserved the right to retaliate with chemical weapons to chemical use, under the Chemical Weapons Convention the United States and other parties unconditionally renounce the use of chemical weapons.
42. The first element of such a statement was issued in January 1992 by the fifteen members of the UN Security Council. See 'Security Council Summit Declaration', *New York Times*, 1 Feb. 1992, p. 4.
43. Cited in George Leopold and Neil Munro, 'Russia Renews Nuclear Reliance', *Defense News*, 21 Dec. 1992, p. 20. See also Fred Hiatt, 'Russians Favoring Retention of Nuclear Deterrent', *Washington Post*, 25 Nov. 1992, pp. A1, A14.
44. For example, Keith Payne maintains that 'our nuclear arsenal is an important element in the broad perception of the United States and its status in the world'. See Prepared Statement of Payne, p. 120. Similarly, Thomas Reed claims that by maintaining a substantial nuclear force, the United States 'retains and reaffirms its status as the world's pre-eminent military, economic, and political power'. See Reed Briefing, p. 2. And General Butler contends that a 'US nuclear deterrent force is a key element in the pervasive international role we must continue to play well into the future'. See 'Statement by General Butler to the House Armed Services Committee', p. 5.
45. Prepared Statement of Payne, p. 120; Reed and Wheeler, *The Role of Nuclear Weapons*, p. 28; Nitze, 'Keep Nuclear Insurance', p. 34; and Sloss, 'US Strategic Forces After the Cold War', p. 153.
46. On the continuing American pre-eminence in the world, see Charles Krauthammer, 'The Unipolar Moment', *Foreign Affairs*, Vol. 70, No. 1 (America and the World 1990/91), pp. 23–33. On the nature of international power generally, and American pre-eminence specifically, see Joseph S. Nye, Jr., 'Soft Power,' *Foreign Policy*, No. 80 (Fall 1990), pp. 153–71.
47. Nitze, 'Keep Nuclear Insurance', p. 32. On Nitze's long-standing concern about the post-exchange nuclear balance of forces, see Nitze, *From Hiroshima to Glasnost: At the Center of Decision – A Memoir* (New York: Grove Weidenfeld, 1989), p. 248.
48. Reed briefing, p. 9. Note that the concept of 'moving from superpower to being an equal' stresses the importance of relative force levels in the definition of US superpower status. On this point, see also Quester and Utgoff, 'US Arms Reductions and Nonproliferation', pp. 131–3; and 'Why Zero Nukes Are Too Few' (Editorial), *New York Times*, 15 Aug. 1992, p. 18.
49. Michael Brown, 'The "End" of Nuclear Arms Control', in this volume, pp. 47–8.
50. On this point, see also Lewis Dunn and Frank Jenkins, 'Nuclear Arms Control in the Post-Cold War World', in Lewis Dunn and Sharon Squassoni (eds.), *Arms Control: What Next?* (Boulder, CO: Westview Press, 1992), p. 16.

51. In the case of India, this capability rests in the fact that New Delhi has not actually produced any weapons, although it could do so in short order. On the state of Indian weaponization, see Prepared Statement of Robert Gates in US Congress, Senate, *Threat Assessment, Military Strategy, and Defense Planning*, p. 19.
52. See, for example, Les Aspin, *A New Kind of Threat: Nuclear Weapons in an Uncertain Soviet Union* (Washington, DC: House Armed Services Committee, 12 Sept. 1991); Prepared Statements by Bruce Blair and Gennadi A. Pavlov before the European Affairs Subcommittee of the Senate Foreign Relations Committee, 24 Sept. 1991; Kurt M. Campbell, *et al., Soviet Nuclear Fission: Control of the Nuclear Arsenal in a Disintegrating Soviet Union*, CSIA Studies in International Security no. 1 (Cambridge, MA: Center for Science and International Affairs, Nov. 1991).
53. For an overview of these efforts, see Steven E. Miller, 'Western Diplomacy and the Soviet Nuclear Legacy', *Survival*, Vol. 34, No. 3, 1992; and Daalder and Terriff, 'Nuclear Arms Control', in this volume.
54. Aspin, *From Deterrence to Denuking*, p. 4.
55. For a discussion on this point, see Patrick Garrity, 'The Depreciation of Nuclear Weapons in International Politics: Possibilities, Limits and Uncertainties', *Journal of Strategic Studies*, Vol. 14, No. 4 (Dec. 1991), pp. 463–514. Elsewhere I have suggested that there is now the possibility to enter the 'post-nuclear' era, at least within a European context. See 'The Future of Arms Control', *Survival*, Vol. 34, No. 1 (Spring 1992), pp. 55–7.
56. Reed and Wheeler, *The Role of Nuclear Weapons*, p. 28. See also Slocombe, 'US Nuclear Weapons in a Restructured World', p. 58.
57. Michael Mazarr, 'Military Targets for Minimum Deterrence: After the Cold War, How Much is Enough?' *Journal of Strategic Studies*, Vol. 15, No. 2, 1992, pp. 162–4. The Congressional Budget Office has similarly concluded that several hundred warheads could 'target most Soviet petrochemical, electrical, metallurgical, and heavy-machinery industry; all major Soviet storage sites for ammunition, fuel, and other military supplies; all major tactical airfields; some troop concentrations; and all major Soviet transportation nodes and choke points en route to the European and Far Eastern theaters'. CBO, *The START Treaty and Beyond*, p. 21. See also CISAC, *The Future of the US-Soviet Nuclear Relationship*, appendix B. For an analysis of the effect on industry and civilian casualties of limited nuclear attacks against critical industries involving tens of weapons, see Frederic S. Nyland, 'Exemplary Industrial Targets for Controlled Conflict', in Desmond Ball and Jeffrey Richelson (eds.), *Strategic Nuclear Targeting* (Ithaca, NY: Cornell University Press, 1986), pp. 209–33.
58. McGeorge Bundy, 'To Cap the Volcano', *Foreign Affairs*, Vol. 48, No. 1 (Oct. 1969), p. 10.
59. As David Alan Rosenberg, the pre-eminent historian of American nuclear strategy, has argued, 'US planners initially chose in the late 1940s to make nuclear weapons the centerpiece of US defense policy, even before the Soviet Union acquired a nuclear capability, in order to meet the challenge of Soviet conventional superiority in Europe.' Rosenberg, 'Reality and Responsibility: Power and Process in the Making of United States Nuclear Strategy, 1945–68', *Journal of Strategic Studies*, Vol. 9, No. 1 (March 1986), p. 49.
60. On this point, see William J. Perry, 'Desert Storm and Deterrence', *Foreign Affairs*, Vol. 70, No. 4 (Fall 1991). This suggests, however, that the United States should maintain a conventional posture that is second to none. See George Quester, 'Multilateral Management of International Security: The Non-Proliferation Model', in this volume.
61. Bruce Blair, *Strategic Command and Control: Redefining the Nuclear Threat* (Washington, DC: Brookings Institution, 1985), pp. 288–9.
62. Bruce Blair's work on this subject has been pioneering. See especially Blair, *Strategic Command and Control*; Blair and John Steinbruner, *The Effects of Warning on Strategic Stability* (Washington, DC: Brookings Institution, 1991); and Blair, *The Logic of Accidental War* (Washington, DC: Brookings Institution, 1993). See also Ashton Carter, 'Emerging Themes in Nuclear Arms Control',

Daedalus, Vol. 120, No. 1 (Winter 1991), pp. 233–50; and Ashton Carter, William Perry and John Steinbruner, *A New Concept of Cooperative Security* (Washington, DC: Brookings Institution, 1992), pp. 11–20.

63. Carter, 'Emerging Themes in Nuclear Arms Control', p. 238.
64. US General Accounting Office, 'Unclassified Summary Statement on the GAO Triad Project', inserted in *Congressional Record – House*, 29 Sept. 1992, p. H9862.
65. For a similar conclusion, see US General Accounting Office, 'Unclassified Summary Statement on the GAO Triad Project', p. H9863; and Stansfield Turner, 'Land-Based Missiles Are Obsolete', *New York Times*, 29 Dec. 1992, p. A15.
66. These bombers could also be assigned conventional missions, therefore limiting the total inventory of strategic bombers to 100 aircraft on each side.
67. Alternatively, if the 14 Delta III submarines were to be phased out, the number of missiles on the remaining 13 boats could be limited to eight.
68. Bruce Blair, 'Beyond the Strategic Arms Reduction Treaty: Nuclear Alert Levels', in *Non-Proliferation and Arms Control: Issues and Options for the Clinton Administration* (Washington, DC: Ad Hoc Working Group on Non-Proliferation and Arms Control, Jan. 1993), pp. 6–7.
69. On this point, see also Bruce Blair, 'Strengthening Nuclear Safeguards Through Arms Control', in US Congress, House, *The Future of Arms Control: New Opportunities*, Report by the Congressional Research Services for the Subcommittee on Arms Control, International Security and Science of the Committee on Foreign Affairs, 102d Cong., 2d Sess., April 1992, pp. 93ff; and Carter, Perry, and Steinbruner, *A New Concept of Cooperative Security*, pp. 18–19.
70. Reductions to these low levels would, of course, require strict limits on air and missile defences, at least until such time that both countries are ready to abandon their residual deterrent capabilities. On this issue, see William Durch, 'Rethinking Strategic Ballistic Missile Defences', in this volume.
71. See 'Factfile: Past and Projected Strategic Nuclear Forces', *Arms Control Today*, Vol. 22, No. 6 (July/Aug. 1992), p. 36.
72. On these issues, see Alexei Arbatov, 'Russian Nuclear Disarmament: Prospects and Dilemmas', in this volume.
73. US Congress, Senate, *The START Treaty*, p. 51.
74. The idea of an early deactivation of US and Russian weapons on a bilateral (though not unilateral) basis has been advocated by others, including by some officials in the Bush administration, as has the concept of sequestering and monitoring of deactivated weapons on a reciprocal basis. See, for example, Carter, Perry, and Steinbruner, *A New Concept of Cooperative Security*, pp. 15–16; 'Statement by Cheney on START before the Senate Armed Services Committee', p. 9; Senator Joseph Biden, *On the Threshold of the New World Order* (Washington, DC: United States Senate, 1992), p. 34; and Arjun Makhijani and Katherine Yih, 'What to Do at Doomsday's End', *Washington Post*, 29 March 1992, p. C3.
75. The general manager of Pantex, the US nuclear weapons assembly and disassembly plant, has stated that 'Inspectors would be able to verify that weapons were coming in and going out . . . without compromising weapons design [secrets].' Quoted in Jeffrey Smith, 'Reporters Granted First Look at Texas Nuclear Weapons Facility', *Washington Post*, 14 Jan. 1993, p. A6.
76. See, for example, Robert Gallucci, 'Disposing of Nuclear Weapons in the Former Soviet Union', Prepared Statement to the Senate Foreign Relations Committee, 4 Aug. 1992, reprinted in *Dispatch*, Vol. 3, No. 32 (10 Aug. 1992), pp. 631–4.
77. A fissile material cut-off would, in particular, deny potential proliferators the ability to 'catch up' with the nuclear powers as the forces of the latter come down, a possibility that has led some to oppose deep cuts in US forces. See, for example, Quester and Utgoff, 'U.S. Arms Reducations and Nonproliferation', pp. 131–3; 'Why Zero Nukes Are Too Few', *New York Times*; and Reed and Wheeler, *The Role of Nuclear Weapons in the New World Order*, p. 21.
78. See Dunbar Lockwood, 'US Begins Testing Moratorium', *Arms Control Today*, Vol.

22, No. 8 (Oct. 1992), pp. 32, 40; Fred Hiatt, 'Russia Extends Test Ban', *Washington Post*, 14 Oct. 1992, p. A25; and Jacques Isnard, 'France Considering Suspending Nuclear Tests Until July 1993', *Le Monde*, 6 Nov. 1992, reprinted in Foreign Broadcasting Information Services (FBIS), *Daily Report – Western Europe*, 12 Nov. 1992, pp. 11–12.

79. British Prime Minister John Major has stated that 'we have no intention of carrying out new tests so long as the moratorium declared by the United States is in effect'. Aleksandr Krivopalov, 'Interview with British Prime Minister Major', *Izvestia*, 7 Nov. 1992, p. 7, reprinted in FBIS, *JPRS Report – Arms Control*, 27 Nov. 1992, p. 44.
80. For the text of the US law, see *Congressional Record – Senate*, 24 Sept. 1992, p. S14698.
81. 'Fact Sheet on Non-proliferation Initiative' (Washington. DC: The White House, Office of the Press Secretary, 13 July 1992), p. 1.
82. Interview with US government official, Washington, 23 Oct. 1992.
83. The two Koreas have already signed an agreement to this effect. See 'Declaration for a Non-Nuclear Korean Peninsula' (Washington, DC: Embassy of the Republic of Korea, 31 Dec. 1992).
84. For details on this issue, see Spurgeon Keeney and Wolfgang Panofsky, 'Controlling Nuclear Warheads and Materials', *Arms Control Today*, Vol. 22, No. 1 (Jan./Feb. 1992), pp. 7–9.
85. On this issue, see Janne E. Nolan, *Trappings of Power: Ballistic Missiles in the Third World* (Washington, DC: Brookings Institution, 1991); Aaron Karp, 'Controlling Ballistic Missile Proliferation', *Survival*, Vol. 33, No. 6 (Nov./Dec. 1991); and Martin Navias, *Ballistic Missile Proliferation in the Third World*, Adelphi Paper no. 252 (London: International Institute for Strategic Studies, 1990).
86. For some suggestion on how this might be done, see Lora Lumpe, 'Zero Ballistic Missiles and the Third World', in this volume.
87. If the United States were limited to six missiles per Trident, it could deploy 108 missiles. A limit of four missiles on 27 submarines would lead to the same force for Russia.

Russian Nuclear Disarmament: Problems and Prospects

ALEXEI G. ARBATOV

Developments within the USSR after 1985, which culminated in the failed coup of August 1991, have opened unexpected opportunities for a profound revision of the hostile relations between Moscow and the West, and in particular between Moscow and the United States. This was manifested in unprecedented unilateral nuclear weapons reductions and programme cancellations by both sides, and by new agreements on radical arms cuts in 1991–92. But, as history indicates, new opportunities simultaneously bring about new problems and sometimes new dangers. Disintegration of one of the two nuclear superpowers (which was as much the result of as the reason for the end of the Cold War) into a number of conflicting and unstable states; disarray in the governmental structures of the former USSR, including its armed forces; and deep economic crisis and domestic political collisions, erupting in some places into bloody violence, have created great uncertainties and potential threats.

Among the uncertainties related to arms control is the future of the START-I Treaty and the follow-on START-II Treaty. The commitment of Ukraine, Kazakhstan and Belarus to the co-implementation of START I, accepted in Lisbon in May 1992, is encouraging. Still, their ability to co-operate effectively on this matter will be put to hard tests in the near future. Dividing everything that for seven decades constituted the Soviet Union amongst fifteen new republics is painful and damaging in the areas of national entities and human ties, economy and finances, infrastructure and resources, cultural values, and communications. But the most threatening prospective division is that of the Soviet nuclear arsenal and its support and production infrastructure.

Now that all tactical nuclear weapons have been withdrawn to Russia, the strategic forces of the former USSR are the focal point of international concern. Of about 11,000 nuclear warheads in the nuclear arsenal of the former Soviet Union, less than one per cent is located in Belarus, 14 per cent in Ukraine, 13 per cent in Kazakhstan, and 73 per cent in Russia. If these forces are split amongst the republics, Ukraine and Kazakhstan would respectively become the third and fourth nuclear powers in the world, each superior to Britain, France and China taken together.

Finding a wise solution to the control of the strategic forces of the former Soviet Union is crucial for further strategic arms reductions. The prospect of a failure to maintain centralized control over these forces makes the rest of the world break out in a cold sweat, and not without reason. The security and physical safety of the intercontinental ballistic missiles (ICBMs) deployed outside Russia and the reliable prevention of unsanctioned launch or detonation would be diminished simply as a result of technical-economic factors. The nuclear postures and arms control attitudes of Britain, France and China likely would also be affected. Their reaction to the sudden emergence of Ukraine as the third greatest nuclear power, with more arms than they hold together, might very well be a rapid build-up of forces and rejection of limitations. However, the heaviest blow would be struck to the non-proliferation of nuclear missile weapons in the world. The chances of extending the term of the nuclear Non-Proliferation Treaty (NPT) at the conference scheduled for 1995 would be close to zero. If Ukraine can have them, then why not India, Pakistan, Iran, Iraq, Israel, let alone Germany and Japan?

Nuclear arms reductions beyond those established in START I and START II should be sought in the interest of international security. But the prospects for any such future reductions are intertwined, like the START-I and START-II treaties, with the prevention of the disintegration of the strategic forces of the former USSR. Neither is achievable without the other. In addition, the future of strategic arms control will depend on the evolution of strategic defence systems, policies of third nuclear powers, and nuclear and ballistic missile proliferation in the world.

Control of the Strategic Forces of the Former Soviet Union

Immediately after the creation of the Commonwealth of Independent States (CIS) in December 1991, the leaders of the four largest republics acted to address the nuclear issue. In the Alma-Ata Agreement, signed on 22 December 1991, they established joint strategic armed forces (later simply called strategic forces) to ensure the collective security of all CIS states.[1] In the subsequent Minsk Agreement, signed on 30 December 1991, they recognized the need for the joint command of strategic forces and for the maintenance of the unified control of nuclear weapons.[2] To this end, they created the Combined Strategic Forces Command. It was agreed that any decision to use nuclear weapons would be taken by the

President of Russia with the consensus of the heads of state of Belarus, Kazakhstan and Ukraine as well as in consultation with the heads of state of other CIS states.

At the 23 May 1992 meeting in Lisbon, the leaders of the four states and the United States signed a protocol to the START-I Treaty. This protocol committed the CIS states to 'make such arrangements among themselves as are required to implement the Treaty's limits and restrictions; to allow functioning of the verification provision of the Treaty . . . and to allocate costs'. The protocol also committed Belarus, Kazakhstan and Ukraine to adhere to the NPT as non-nuclear-weapons states in the 'shortest time possible'. In separate letters, the three countries further guaranteed the elimination of nuclear weapons on their soil within the seven-year implementation period of START I.[3]

For all the general political significance of these commitments, from a legal point of view they created some new uncertainties and more confusion. No dates were specified by which the three states had to join the NPT and some additional reservations were made, such as Kiev's demand that 'nuclear charge components' from dismantled weapons not be used to produce other weapons (a condition that is irrelevant to START I). Moreover, the date by which Ukraine is required to eliminate ballistic missiles on its territory was tied to the seven-year treaty implementation period, making the previous commitment to do this by the end of 1994 quite uncertain. Hasty initial arrangements on nuclear weapons and growing contradictions amongst the republics has led to significant strategic-political and legal confusion on the issue of CIS nuclear arms. Under the Alma-Ata and Minsk agreements, the Russian President was the only CIS leader to have technical control over the capability to launch strategic forces of the former Soviet Union, regardless of where they were deployed. But Ukraine does not recognize Russian ownership of strategic forces located on Ukrainian soil. Neither Russia nor the CIS Combined Strategic Forces Command, though responsible for their maintenance and launch, are capable of redeploying, withdrawing, dismantling or modernizing them with new systems without the permission of the Ukrainian government.

Leaving the situation as it currently stands, in the hope that the three smaller republics will, in accordance with the Lisbon Protocol, cooperate with the elimination of missiles on their territory within seven years of the implementation of START I, would be a very risky course of action. The future of the CIS is too unpredictable to rely on the present agreements. It is possible that, under the pressure of nationalistic forces on all sides, the CIS could disintegrate or Ukraine withdraw unilaterally much earlier than the missiles are eliminated. Moreover, internal economic and social calamities, violent collisions of national minorities with the predominant ethnic population in the republics (including Russia) or the rise of Islamic fundamentalism in Central Asia and Kazakhstan may lead to a change of leadership in some republics. A changing leadership could greatly affect relations amongst the CIS states and with outside states, and lead to a revision of their commitments – with unpredictable consequences for the nuclear question.

Since apportioning command and control of the nuclear forces in accordance with their geographical deployment would actually mean splitting strategic forces amongst the four republics, this option should be avoided at all costs. Adapting deployment to centralized control is the best, safest and most conducive solution for the security interests of both the CIS and the international community at large. In the present circumstances, due to the positions of republican leadership and CIS top military command, this can only be accomplished with US participation within a broader arms control framework. This coincides with the general thrust of US – Russian political relations and the end of the Cold War.

Further Reductions in Strategic Nuclear Forces

Starting in early 1992 Moscow and Washington began to exchange proposals for a follow-on agreement to START I. After a remarkable year during which both sides unilaterally stopped or cancelled a number of weapons programmes and proposed radical bilateral reductions, Russia and the United States signed the START-II Treaty on 3 January 1993.

START II achieves a breakthrough in the scale and scope of nuclear reductions. In two phases the sides will reduce their present arsenals of strategic nuclear warheads by about two-thirds. At the end of the first phase, to be complete seven years after START I enters into force, the aggregate number of warheads permitted each side will be cut to 3,800–4,200. Each will be further limited under this ceiling to 1,250 warheads on MIRVed ICBMs, of which only 650 may be on mounted on heavy ICBMs, and to 2,150 warheads on SLBMs. At the end of the second phase, which must be completed no later than 2003, the aggregate ceiling will be reduced to 3,000–3,500 warheads, MIRVed land-based missiles will be banned altogether and SLBM warheads will be limited to 1,700–1,750. Heavy bomber weapons will be counted according to their actual loading, and up to 100 bombers may be oriented to non-nuclear missions.

Although the treaty calls for deep cuts in the strategic offensive forces of both countries, President Boris Yeltsin's concessions on the road to agreement have been much the most significant. This has left him open to fierce attacks by Russian conservatives and nationalists. The major complaint by opponents to the treaty is Moscow's agreement to drastic cuts and eventual elimination of MIRVed ICBM warheads – traditionally the backbone of Soviet strategic offensive forces. After the end of the first phase, Russia probably will retain 65 heavy SS-18 MIRVed ICBMs (instead of 154 under START I) and 60 fixed/mobile MIRVed missiles (instead of 120–130 under START I). About 500 single warhead SS25 road-mobile ICBMs may be deployed by 1999. At this juncture, the share of ICBMs of the total Russian strategic forces will be 43–48 per cent by warheads (depending on counting rules), which is not much different from what was envisioned under START I (about 53 per cent). But at the end of the second phase of reductions Russia would face a hard dilemma because of the requirement to eliminate MIRVed ICBM warheads entirely while aggregate warhead ceilings remain relatively high. The essence of the Russian dilemma is whether radically to restructure the traditional composition of its strategic triad or to deploy single warhead ICBMs on a very large scale.

The best option would be to go for a radical restructuring of strategic forces and reduce the share of ICBMs by warhead from 53 per cent under START I (or 65 per cent of pre-START I levels) to only about 15 per cent. This calculation is based on the assumption that by 2003 Russia may at a bearable economic cost be able to deploy about 500 single warhead ballistic missiles, using some combination of mobile and fixed SS-25s, single warhead SS-19s, and/or a new generation of single warhead ICBMs. Depending on the counting rules, this force would constitute some 14–17 per cent of Russia's overall posture of 3,000–3,500 warheads.

This option almost certainly will not be supported by the CSFC, in which the leading role still belongs to the Strategic Rocket Forces. Adherence to traditional concepts of strategic stability and abiding concerns about the various problems with maintaining, operating and communicating with sea-based missile forces, means that the Russian military on strategic grounds will be quite dubious about placing too much reliance on SLBMs. The resulting balance, calculated by the strategic capabilities of the strategic offensive forces of each side if not by their numbers, would be shifted significantly in favour of the United States as compared to the START-I reductions. American strategic forces would have the potential to achieve a substantial advantage in counterforce and countervalue capabilities compared to Russian forces remaining under START II.

One way to make the deal more equitable and less vulnerable to right-wing attack in Russia would be to apply more stringent limitations on the United States within the guidelines of START II. One area of American strategic advantage is heavy bombers. Counting bomber weapons by the number of cruise missiles, short-range attack missiles, and gravity bombs carried by each aircraft is an improvement over START I, but it is not enough. To make the agreement more balanced, the commitment made by both sides in the fall of 1991 to take bombers off alert and put their weapons in storage should be codified by special agreement and additional inspection procedures. All bomber weapons should be placed in central facilities under mutual permanent monitoring or with provision for challenge inspections. In addition, continued negotiations should be carried out to reduce the arsenals of both countries even further, to about 2,500–2,700. This lower aggregate ceiling would permit Russia to deploy about 700–1,000 single warhead ICBMs and retain 6 Typhoon, 7 Delta-IV and 12 Delta-III class SSBNs, provided the SS-N-20 SLBMs on the Typhoons were downloaded from 10 to 6 warheads (an equivalent downloading of four warheads as the United States plans for its Trident-II missiles). Such a scheme would mean that the 700–1,000 single warhead ICBMs (in part deployed in silos and in part on mobile launchers) would constitute 35–37 per cent instead of 14–17 per cent of Russia's alert strategic forces, and at comparatively lower financial outlay.

To ensure that START II eventually is implemented, it is essential to get the bulk of the Russian military on board and to repel attacks by conservatives in Moscow. Thus additional US concessions to make the agreement more balanced and to reduce American counterforce and break-out capabilities are likely necessary. In particular, the number of Trident-II (D-5) SLBMs should be limited to those currently deployed on five existing Ohio-class SSBNs, with their deployment prohibited on the eight Ohio-class boats currently carrying the Trident-I (C-4) SLBM and the five Ohio-class SSBNs yet to be built. As an alternative, eight Ohio-class SSBNs could remain outfitted with Trident-I SLBMs and the remaining 10 boats with Trident-II missiles equipped with a MIRV bus system suitable for no more than four warheads each.

Important and complicated though it is, strategic offensive arms control is not the only area of Russian nuclear policy where Russia faces hard choices and difficult dilemmas. Another concerns strategic defenses, which may strongly affect the strategic balance and arms control process during the next decade or two.

Arms Control and Strategic Defences

For almost a decade Moscow adhered to a very tough stance on the issue of anti-ballistic missile (ABM) defence. In recent years, however, Moscow's attitude appears to have started to mellow. This became apparent in President Mikhail Gorbachev's response to the US initiatives on nuclear weapons reductions in October 1991. For the first time since 1983 the USSR agreed to discuss the prospects for the mutual development of non-nuclear defences against ballistic missiles. Russian President Yeltsin moved still further along this path in early 1992, when at the United Nations he proposed the creation of a joint ABM system in space for the defence of mankind against nuclear missiles.

Taking into account the importance of the issue, on which the whole future of the strategic balance and arms control depends, it is not surprising that the above changes have provoked great confusion and intense debate in Russia, the United States and other countries. The improved attitude in Moscow toward co-operation with the United States on strategic defence and space issues is motivated mainly by general political and economic considerations (and, most of all, an expectation of large contracts and transfer of technology). Without exception, all past attempts by proponents of ABM expansion to justify this policy on strategic and technical grounds have been unavailing. At the same time Russian authorities continue to insist on the importance of retaining the ABM Treaty, citing it as the only legally binding and long-term strategic arms control agreement between the two states that still has strong support in both the United States and Russia. As long as high levels of strategic nuclear offensive forces remain to serve as a sobering reminder of the peculiarity of US–Russian bilateral relations, the ABM Treaty will be valued as a barrier against unfavourable and extremely costly avenues of military-technological development. In formal negotiations or regular summits the Russian government is quite likely to display greater flexibility on the issue of ballistic missile defense. But any unilateral US decision to withdraw from the treaty and proceed with deployment would be perceived as evidence of a serious setback in Russian-American relations.

Provided the United States refrains from such unilateral action, negotiations on strategic defence and space problems should concentrate on three major sets of issues, which are coupled to three principle options regarding the future Russian force posture and possible solutions to the whole matter. These issues are: space sensors, expanded ground-based ABM systems, and space-based interceptors. The ban on development, testing and deployment of space-based sensors as ABM components and adjuncts, capable of substituting or supplementing ABM radars, has been a mute question as far as treaty compliance is concerned. The growing number of C^3I satellites, including optical and radio early-warning, detection, tracking and reconnaissance types, the absence of any definitions of prohibited and permitted parameters, and the virtual impossibility of verification in the absence of a fully co-operative regime, together make ensuring full compliance neither feasible nor sufficiently desirable. President Yeltsin's UN proposal, as officially clarified later, emphasized improvement and joint programmes in space warning and monitoring capabilities. The US response to this suggestion was quite positive. These systems will therefore certainly proliferate and improve until the year 2000 and beyond, regardless of the destiny of other ABM components. Neither side is likely to raise this issue with regard to compliance with the ABM Treaty.

A principal and obvious option, consisting of an 'historic compromise' between Moscow and Washington, is for an agreement to permit expansion of ground-based ABM interceptors and radars together with overt deployment of space-based sensors, while reinstating the prohibition on space-based interceptors (and anti-satellite systems) with the necessary definitions and verification provisions. To make this option more acceptable to the United States it need not be of indefinite duration, but may fix a deal for 5–10 years until the strategic and technical situation has been further clarified (including the trends in offensive reductions and nuclear/missile proliferation).

This option could be modified by either a narrow or broad variant. The narrow variant would consist basically of preserving the ABM Treaty intact (with the exception of space-based sensors) and concluding a protocol on permitted parameters of anti-tactical ballistic missile (ATBM) systems. This point appears to be the minimum common denominator amongst the various positions of the vast majority of partisans and opponents of the ABM Treaty both in Russia and the United States. An anti-tactical system is now an integral part of the Global Protection Against Limited Strikes (GPALS) programme in the United States and is pushed forward in universal ABM/air defence mode by Russian air-defence centres and industries. Such systems would provide the United States with a direct response to the only unquestionable contingency in sight: future Persian Gulf scenarios. If ATBM parameters are delineated liberally, this would also create a substantial collateral capability for the point-defence of high value facilities (such as command centres, ICBM silos and mobile launchers, nuclear power stations, chemical plants, oil refineries, etc.) against limited strategic missile strikes. ATBM systems could be available for US allies and would not destabilize the strategic nuclear balance on either bilateral or pentagonal planes. Thus such systems would not hinder current offensive strategic arms reductions and would even facilitate further reductions by increasing the survivability of ICBMs and command and control infrastructure against nuclear or conventional counterforce strikes.

Finally, ATBM systems would not be too expensive and divisive in funding allocation amongst the Russian armed services. ATBM development and deployment programmes also could help keep afloat some Russian R&D and industrial sectors. Development of ATBMS might further serve as a non-controversial testing ground for post-Cold War US-Russian defence co-operation. If successful, many fears and biases for such co-operation would be removed. If not, many illusions for joint programmes on strategic projects would be dropped in favour of traditional negotiated reductions and limitations.

However attractive, the narrow option may seem too restrictive for proponents of ballistic missile defence in the United States. ATBMs would not provide an effective, thin protection of US territory against unauthorized or provocative long-range missile strikes. A broader option might seem a better choice to defence supporters and could provide a fall-back for advocates of the ABM Treaty. The broader option would consist of increasing the number of legitimate ABM deployment areas (thus reversing the 1974 Protocol) in a package that permitted space-based sensors but prohibited space-based interceptors. Variations of this option have been advanced by Senators Sam Nunn, William Cohen, and others in the US Congress in 1990–91 both as a compromise within the United States and between the United States and the USSR. Although much less controversial than deployment of GPALS with space-based interceptors, this option might be quite difficult to negotiate. There are an abundance of reasons for such an assessment: asymmetric geostrategic requirements of the two sides; nuclear/nonnuclear issues of interceptor arming; reaction of third nuclear states; cost; potential interaction with strategic offensive arms reductions, INF Treaty and tactical nuclear withdrawals; and growing contradictions amongst CIS states, among other reasons.

It is not beyond reason to go so far as to speculate that, if the issue of the basic parameters of the ABM Treaty is reopened and some influential Russian ABM-related institutions enter the game, the two sides might swap positions for the fourth time. Then it may be Moscow that will insist on maximum relaxation of the quantitative and qualitative limitations of the treaty. The latter could refer to the ban on mobile land-based components, multiple and rapid-reload launchers, and ABM-capable components of the systems, which are not strategic ABM systems in and of themselves. Even should Russia for economic reasons not be capable of immediate deployments on a massive scale, it might want to lay the foundation for such a programme for future years and might make a number of decisions on resource allocation and programme management, which politically would be hard to reverse later.

The change of administration in the United States in January 1993 might provide an opportunity to implement the narrow option. This approach to ballistic missile defence would be much less controversial, more conducive to radical offensive arms reduction and more relevant to realistic tasks of ABM systems as a protection against Third World missiles in regional conflicts.

Minimum Deterrence and Arms Control

All the benign political changes of the past several years and the prospects of deep nuclear weapons reduction are encouraging politicians and strategic experts to think once again about the old idea of minimal (or finite) nuclear deterrence, including its contemporary meaning, requirements and feasibility. From the very beginning this concept was an intellectual compromise between, on the one hand, recognition of the absurdity and dangers of the enormous arsenals of nuclear overkill, acquired by the United States and USSR by the mid-1960s, and, on the other, a realization of the great political, strategic and technical obstacles on the way to complete nuclear disarmament. However, it seems that in the present debate, as before, too much emphasis is placed on the numbers of nuclear forces as a criterion of minimal or surplus deterrence. Numbers are only a function of other properties of the concept. In trying to formulate a new policy, based not on momentum but on rationality, the numbers have to be treated in only the last phase. A number of problems have to be solved first, and they are only indirectly addressed by partisans of different viewpoints. Meanwhile these problems have to be scrutinized head-on when for the first time in four decades the doctrine of minimum deterrence is being discussed in practical and not only theoretical terms.

Rather than how many nuclear weapons are needed, the primary question is what the tasks of minimal nuclear deterrent forces should be and, in this connection, what are their targets, methods of employment and expected effectiveness? Destroying population centres deliberately, as suggested by some experts, can be accomplished with small numbers of deliverable warheads, less complex employment plans (that is timing, co-ordination, strike options, and so on) and weapons with poor accuracy. In short, this strategy is very inexpensive. But it has obvious political and moral deficiencies, especially in times of cordial political relations and a growing partnership between former mortal rivals. It has to be kept in mind that in the 1950s the targeting of population *per se* was a matter of necessity because of inaccurate weapons, long flight-times and inadequate target intelligence. Population has not been targeted deliberately by either country for a long time, although enormous collateral fatalities were always expected from counterforce and counter-industrial strikes. To embrace openly a strategy of counter-population targeting as a matter of conscious political choice, with the destructiveness of contemporary weapons, would be quite a dubious proposition for any responsible state leader. Strategies of counterforce targeting also should be avoided. Such strategies underpinned the enormous growth of the superpower nuclear arsenals and undermined crisis stability. Thus any target list should avowedly exclude command and control centres, early warning capabilities and strategic forces, as well as population centres. Probably the rational minimal target list should include several dozen sites of defence production facilities and energy infrastructure.

Both sides could be tempted to adopt a launch-on-warning instead of a pure second-strike strategy, as this would permit a minimum deterrent posture based on a much smaller force and less robust command and control system. But reliance on launch-on-warning would greatly increase the risk of accidental nuclear war and require high alert rates clearly not conducive to relaxed political relations. Instead, to bolster strategic stability and underpin their improved political relations, both should adopt an unequivocal second-strike strategy. Further, they should seek to develop joint early warning systems and to ban outright offensive systems that threaten these capabilities.

Reductions in US and Russian nuclear arsenals to the levels of minimal deterrence would also inevitably bring the problem of third nuclear powers to the forefront of strategic policies. Nuclear third parties clearly have to join future arms control talks at some point. To do so undoubtedly would complicate further reductions, but this is not actually the biggest problem. The real issue is defining the strategic requirements of Russia and the United States in a multipolar nuclear balance. If the superpowers insist on the 'British naval paradigm' – having nuclear forces at least not smaller than those of all third powers taken together – third nuclear states would hardly join efforts to achieve further reductions. Instead, their programmes would drive the force levels of the superpowers upward from minimal deterrence. Solving the new problems of multipolar nuclear balances, in which political moves and alliance patterns may once again affect military capabilities, is a great challenge. The way this is addressed will define both the strategic prospects for achieving truly minimal deterrence and the feasibility of multilateral strategic arms control.

One possible solution for the United States and Russia may be to reduce their strategic offensive forces below the 3,000 warhead level by placing limits on combat ready warheads. This could be achieved by using technical means to 'decapitate' ICBMs while keeping them at combat status, and by lowering the patrol rate of SSBNs and off-loading their missiles when in port. Both countries could retain about 1,000 ballistic missiles as a prudent reserve and a margin of advantage over third nuclear states. But their combat-ready forces of alert ICBMs and non-reserve SSBNs might consist of only 500–600 warheads. Equal multilateral limits on combat ready warheads may become the principle of multilateral arms control involving third nuclear powers.

Further nuclear proliferation in the world might also have an impact on multilateral arms control. It could do so directly by raising the perceived strategic requirements of the third nuclear powers and even those of Russia and the United States. Greater targeting flexibility, sub-kiloton munitions, and new, cheaper strategic and tactical delivery systems may lead them away from the logic and force structures of minimal deterrence. Indirectly, proliferation could encourage the development and deployment of anti-ballistic missile systems by the nuclear powers, which would inadvertently affect their own strategic relations and force postures. Even now, implementation of START II, which would reduce forces to levels much higher than necessary for minimal deterrence, is conditioned by the Russian military on preserving the ABM Treaty. This is incompatible with the testing and deployment of an American limited ABM system such as GPALS, supposedly designed against proliferating missiles in the Third World. With the new Russian-US relationship, a much more effective policy to prevent nuclear proliferation has to be devised and joined by other nuclear powers. Otherwise nuclear weapons reduction beyond START II likely will be infeasible.

To implement deeper cuts through downloading and decapitation after the year 2000, Russia and the United States must greatly expand the regime of transparency, predictability and confidence-building with regard to their strategic forces. Amongst other elements, such a regime may include new verification procedures like tagging, perimeter monitoring of warhead storage, permanent or semi-permanent inspections at missile, bomber and SSBN bases, and larger quotas on challenge inspections to verify the number of missile warheads. The two sides should agree to build joint early warning systems and to exchange permanent representatives at central and local command centres. Stringent limitations on bomber and SSBN patrol rates and exercises, mobile missile deployments and strategic anti-submarine warfare in adjacent seas would provide additional confidence. Eventually other nuclear powers should join this regime.

Under the new political relations of Russia and the United States such an expanding regime is not needed for lack of trust, as before, but to bring about greater transparency and predictability in their strategic relationship. The purpose of the regime would be to transform gradually the conduct of the strategic relationship from the balancing of retaliatory capabilities against each other to the joint management of strategic stability at decreasing weapons numbers and alert levels.

NOTES

1. *Izvestia*, 23 Dec. 1991.
2. *Krasnaya Zvezda*, 31 Dec. 1991.
3. The protocol and letters are reprinted in *Arms Control Today*, Vol. 22, No. 5 (June 1992), pp. 34–6.

British and French Nuclear Forces after the Cold War

MICHAEL CLARKE

Deterrence in the Cold War was regarded as a well-understood system that provided the best balance of strategic virtues in a difficult situation. Whether or not this was really the case, it is clear that the post-Cold War world raises some fundamental questions about nuclear deterrence, particularly for Britain and France. Yet in the wake of the collapse of communism our attention has been so taken up with the ethnic and regional problems of the new world that consideration of nuclear weapons has been pushed firmly down the agenda. But if this is a comfortable position for nuclear planners in London and Paris – particularly after the fierce debates of the 1980s – it is not wise to assume that nuclear deterrence does not require as much rethinking as other aspects of defence policy.

This paper attempts to look at the forces and rationales that have underpinned deterrence thinking in Britain and France during the Cold War; the way such thinking has been affected by the new situation; and finally to indicate that there is a credible nuclear disarmament logic that can be followed either in whole or in part to the advantage of both countries and the international community as a whole. Taken together, Britain and France are only a small part of the global picture and have a limited capacity to affect nuclear politics for either good or ill; but the choices they presently face are in some ways more important than those of Russia or the United States, since their situation bears more closely on other nuclear or near-nuclear states in the world.

Deterrence in the Cold War

Nuclear Forces

Following the rounds of unilateral arms cuts among NATO members in response both to the progress of arms control and to the graduated collapse of the Warsaw Pact threat, British nuclear systems for the 1990s can be listed fairly easily. In 1992 the British strategic deterrent consisted of a four-boat force of Polaris nuclear submarines (the *Resolution* class) each capable of firing 16 Polaris missiles and each missile carrying 3 multiple re-entry vehicle (MRV) warheads. At any given time, one of the four submarines could be expected to be involved in an extended refit, leaving three for operations.[1] On some estimates, however, the number of operational boats has on some occasions fallen to two for prolonged periods and resulted in there being the bare minimum of one boat at sea during 1991.[2] It is also thought that Britain may have produced only a 2-MRV warhead, and only enough warheads to equip three full Polaris boats at any given time. Its total number of missiles may have been as low as 48, therefore, with a total of 96 warheads.[3]

For the future, Britain aims to maintain, however, a four-boat level of commitment to the strategic deterrent in the Trident successor to Polaris. Four *Vanguard* class Trident submarines are planned, the first of which was launched in 1992 and due to enter service in 1994–5. Firm orders for the fourth have now been placed. Each submarine will be capable of launching 16 Trident D5 MIRVed missiles, carrying up to 8 warheads each. The warhead numbers could be higher, since the original specifications for both the submarines and the missiles allow for greater warhead loadings. US Trident submarines, for example, carry 24 missiles, and multiple independently targetable re-entry vehicle (MIRV) warhead loadings of 10 per missile are believed possible. The British government has stated that each submarine will normally carry a maximum of 128 warheads (that is, 16 times 8). This, however, 'is a self-imposed maximum, not a rigid specification'. It reserves the right to revise the warhead loading in the light of strategic developments – in particular, the development of anti-ballistic missile systems.[4] If, however, the low estimates for Polaris boats are accurate, and are maintained for Trident, then it may be that only some 48 missiles will be maintained, carrying four rather than eight MIRV warheads each. This would yield a total of 192 strategic warheads.

At the sub-strategic level, Britain has announced – as part of NATO's gradual denuclearization – the scrapping of its Lance short-range missiles, its nuclear artillery, and its various maritime nuclear depth bombs. There will be no replacement for the Lance missile. It plans only to retain the air-delivered WE-177 free-fall bombs, the precise number of which is unknown. There is an official commitment to cut these by more than half. By 1994 the WE-177 bomb will be entrusted solely to eight nuclear-capable Tornado squadrons; four based in Britain, four in Germany. WE-177 bombs have already been withdrawn from Britain's aircraft carrier-based forces. These commitments suggest that the number of operationally available WE-177 weapons is in the order of 120-150 bombs (though the number might be as low as 50–75).[5] Britain is presently seeking a replacement for the ageing WE-177 in the form of an air-to-surface stand-off weapon. The US tactical air-to-surface missile (TASM) was regarded for some time as the most likely option, though there was also some thought that a joint Anglo-French venture to produce a successor to the French *air-sol moyenne portée* (ASMP) could be a contender. Both of these possibilities must now be doubted for a number of reasons, although the government officially remains committed to the procurement of a replacement for the WE-177.

French nuclear forces are more diverse, reflecting the more self-sufficient rationale under which they have always been developed and produced. It presently fields a complete triad of land- air- and sea-based systems, ranging across the strategic and sub-strategic categories. At the core of the triad are the main strategic nuclear forces: four nuclear submarines (SSBN) which account for over 90 per cent of strategic French warheads.[6] France possesses six SSBN boats, two of which are presently out of service and probably will remain so. It is still possible (though increasingly unlikely) that one will emerge from its long refit and be loaded with modernized M-4 missiles. The heart of the French SSBN force, however, remains *L'Inflexible* and three *Le Redoutable* class boats each carrying 16 M-4 missiles, plus some Exocet missiles capable of submerged launch. The M-4 carries six warheads, so each submarine is capable of carrying 96 warheads in all – a considerable increase in the previous SSBN capability. In addition, and technically classifiable as 'strategic', France fields 18 intermediate-range ballistic missile (IRBM) launchers in two squadrons (consisting of four silos at the Plateau d'Albion in Haute-Province), each carrying one warhead. These missiles have a range of some 3,000–3,500 km, which makes them strategic in a European context, but leaves their range somewhat short of any of the putative threats to France's east and south.

At the sub-strategic level – though now as 'strategic' as the IRBM force – France deploys 18 Mirage IV aircraft carrying the 300-km range ASMP stand-off missile and around 45 Mirage 2000s, also with ASMP. Until 1991 some 30 Jaguar and 40 carrier-borne Super Etendard aircraft were equipped with AN-52 free-fall bombs. These have now been scrapped. The Jaguars no longer have a nuclear role and it is believed that 20 Super Etendard have been converted to carry one ASMP missile apiece. Finally, France still deploys 30 Pluton short-range missiles (120km), which were due to be replaced in 1993–94 with the 480-km range Hadès. Original plans called for the Hadès forces to be composed of 120 missiles, but current plans are to store rather then deploy the 15 launchers and 30 missiles that have been produced and to suspend any further production.[7]

Nuclear Rationales

The rationales by which Britain and France maintain nuclear forces are inevitably a mixture of military and political motives. More particularly, they can be grouped into two types of rationale, the logic of which has not always moved in the same direction. First, independent nuclear forces are justified on a raft of general East–West deterrent motives; secondly, they have also been justified according to more particular national purposes peculiar to each country.

For Britain, the general 'East–West deterrent' motives underlying its nuclear policy can be stated fairly simply. First, there was the general motive of deterring aggressive action that was believed to be contemplated by Soviet leaders. On the assumption that Western Europe lived under the shadow of putative Soviet aggression, British nuclear forces had an essential purpose in deterring such aggression. Secondly, the nuclear deterrent was assumed to compensate for the weaknesses of British (and allied) conventional forces in relation to those of the Warsaw Pact. Since NATO could not realistically expect to do more than delay a determined Warsaw Pact attack against Western Europe, nuclear weapons provided the essential deterrent and an indispensable element to the strategy of flexible response. Any aggressive action against Western Europe would have to take into account the fact that NATO reserved for itself the right to use nuclear weapons when and how it chose, leaving uncertain the point at which their employment would be deemed necessary. Thirdly, nuclear weapons were justified as an exercise in risk-sharing, since a nuclear war in Europe could not realistically be limited and any war between the Warsaw Pact and NATO would, *ipso facto*, be a general conflict in the most dire of circumstances. This therefore provided a large measure of the collective political cement that was felt necessary for an alliance of sixteen nations. Fourthly, British nuclear weapons were justified on the grounds that their very presence – the existential deterrent – was in itself a stabilizing factor and one that would help prevent the outbreak of conventional war at any level in Europe. This assumption was based upon a reading of the historical record which saw conventional war as endemic to European politics. The nuclear shadow over the continent, therefore, made any war unthinkable and, in effect, outlawed conventional conflicts. Fifthly, British nuclear forces constituted a weapon of last resort. Though they were justified in the four previous rationales as part of the collective defence of NATO, there could be no doubt that an independent deterrent remained the ultimate weapon of last resort, should the survival of Britain be at stake.

Apart from these general East–West deterrent rationales, however,

British nuclear forces have been justified by a number of other more particular reasons. First among them is that of international status. In the 1940s it was regarded as inconceivable that Britain should not be a nuclear weapon state given that it had co-operated so closely in the Manhattan Project and had the capacity to develop not only its own atomic and thermonuclear weapons but its own strategic delivery systems. This argument was later justified as being the entry price to the top table in world politics.[8] More particularly, the nuclear deterrent was justified as providing a 'second centre of decision'. On this argument, the uncertainties posed to a potential aggressor of the existence of more than one centre of nuclear decision-making – other than the major decision-maker in Washington – was regarded as a stabilizing factor. In reality, the second centre of decision argument had two more subtle variations. One was that the second centre of decision provided, in effect, a trigger for a US response. If Britain launched a nuclear attack against Warsaw Pact forces independently, this would trigger a retaliation that would encompass US forces. And if a nuclear attack against Europe was ever initiated by the Soviet Union it would still act as a trigger. For any attack on Europe would have to target Britain, since it was a nuclear power, and given that it was a logistical necessity that US military facilities should be based in Britain, any attack on Europe could not help but be *ipso facto* an attack on US forces. British nuclear weapons therefore made it almost certain that a United States nuclear response would be triggered even if the United States was not the intended target of nuclear aggression in Europe.[9] British strategic weapons, therefore, provided a very tangible device by which the United States was 'entangled' in the defence of Europe.

The second long-standing motive behind the independent British deterrent was that it gave Britain some influence over the United States. In the 1940s this was justified on the grounds that it would be unwise to allow the United States a monopoly in nuclear technology; by the 1960s it had come to be justified as one of the principal vehicles of the 'special relationship' between Britain and the United States.[10] And over the last fifteen years the nuclear relationship has been picked out as one of the main strands in the Anglo-American relationship: it has become relatively more important (along with intelligence-sharing and armed service co-operation) as other aspects of the 'special relationship' have declined.[11] The 'second centre of decision', therefore, is justification for both a triggering mechanism for US nuclear forces and a means of maintaining political influence with the United States.

For France, the general East–West deterrent rationales have been identical to those of Britain; the particular national rationales, however, could hardly be more different. Although France also shares, in much the same terms as Britain, the rationale that the nuclear deterrent is a weapon of last resort, this conviction is held at a much deeper level than is the case in Britain. French nuclear planners have always anticipated – to a far greater extent than their British counterparts – that France might indeed find itself in need of an independent weapon of last resort. This gets to the heart of all the subsidiary national motives for the possession of an independent nuclear deterrent. For France, the humiliations of the Second World War, and not least the ways in which the peace-making process in 1945 was handled by its allies, created a much sharper status motive for the acquisition of nuclear technology. As an extension of this desire for a major status symbol, nuclear weapons were also a means for France to assert its independence from the United States. In contrast to British motives to 'entangle' and 'trigger' the US military through the doctrine of nuclear deterrence, French thinking was predicated precisely on the assumption that a US response could not be guaranteed. In contrast to the British deterrent, which could not be relied on since it was so closely tied to the United States, the very independence of French nuclear forces provided the existential deterrent that worked on behalf of all West European allies.[12]

On this assumption, independent nuclear forces were seen to provide France with leadership in Western Europe, compensating for the conventional military strength of the Federal Republic of Germany. If Britain was a US 'trojan horse' in Europe, and Italy a great power of less than critical significance, then the fact that France was an independent nuclear power gave it some countervailing influence over the FRG, sufficient to bolster the Paris-Bonn axis around which so much else hinged. More particularly, the deterrent was felt to provide France with the prerequisite political weight to engage effectively in its own brand of *Ostpolitik*, and to act as an effective shop window for high-technology exports, both in the military and the civilian fields. In almost every respect, therefore, the particular French reasons for maintaining an independent nuclear deterrent were the precise opposite of those that prevailed in Britain.

Nuclear Strategies

British nuclear doctrine was articulated in some detail from the earliest phase and – though the emphasis has changed from time to time – has remained generally consistent throughout forty years.[13] It rested on two compatible, though exclusive, scenarios. The first was the scenario that Britain was part of a collective alliance that claimed the right to use nuclear weapons first in response to any aggression, nuclear or conventional, against a NATO member. Britain was only likely to be threatened – and in turn to threaten retaliation – as part of a more general threat to the Western allies. In this circumstance, British weapons were part of NATO's 'spectrum of deterrence'. They were part of the Single Integrated Operational Plan (SIOP) run from Omaha in the United States and in this guise they were generally believed to have been allocated to theatre targets in Eastern Europe. They therefore represented a useful addition to NATO's deterrent spectrum which was an essential part of the doctrine of flexible response. The British were great believers in the 'spectrum', for both strategic and political reasons. This had justified the deployment of battlefield nuclear weapons in the early days; it had backed up the British view of flexible response in the fierce debates within NATO between 1964 and 1967, where the European interpretation of the doctrine – smaller nuclear weapons rather than more conventional ones – had prevailed over the American interpretation.[14] And it was the strategic justification behind Britain's support of intermediate-range nuclear force (INF) modernization in the 1980s. This strategy preserved for the Alliance the greatest number of strategic options in response to any aggression.

In the second scenario, British nuclear strategy is based upon the premise that the country may find itself having to face the potential aggressor alone. In this case, the strategy has been far simpler. It was one merely of decapitation; in particular of the leadership of the country assumed to be behind the threat. The 'British' target set, therefore, was always assumed to be Moscow, and British Polaris missiles could be retargeted from their SIOP assignments towards Moscow in a matter of hours (though opinions vary as to whether this was a matter of a few, or many hours). The whole of the available strategic force, a minimum of one Polaris boat's missiles, and an absolute and lucky maximum of three, would then be targeted against Moscow. It was always assumed that the available forces would be sufficient to penetrate any defences around Moscow, but in the event of Britain acting alone in this way, there was never any question of British nuclear forces covering tactical targets as well.

In the NATO context, therefore, British forces were predicated on a doctrine of flexible nuclear deterrence where the numbers of weapons, and the potential targets, were necessarily high and where the object of the exercise was to preserve the option of a nuclear exchange that was not automatically a resort to all-out nuclear war (even if that remained the most likely outcome). In the independent context, however, the deterrent was 'minimum' in that it could only be used in a single retaliatory strike against one strategic target: there was no other relevant calculation and no graduation; just simply a weapon of last resort. The contradiction between the nuclear doctrines that addressed these two different contexts was more apparent than real, for if an East–West nuclear war was generally unlikely, then a Soviet–British one was extraordinarily unlikely. In reality, therefore, Britain's claim to the right to use its deterrent forces independently could sit comfortably with the prevailing facts of the East–West balance, which made it inconceivable that it would ever have to.

French nuclear strategy, on the other hand, was never so in tune with the direction of events in the European continent. Since France has maintained a complete triad of nuclear forces and has insisted on deploying them in an entirely independent mode, it has encountered both the political and technical limitations that a middle-ranking nuclear power must suffer if it assumes (at least in Europe) superpower strategic responsibilities. From a political point of view, France has not been entirely consistent about the direction of the threat it anticipated. It has moved from the collective NATO view that the Soviet Union was the defining strategic threat, briefly to the doctrine of *tous azimuts* (defence in all directions), and then virtually back again to the accepted version of the threat. In the same way, it has varied from a doctrine of massive retaliation, towards a concept of 'pre-strategic' nuclear use (which in effect would be little different from the reality of NATO's flexible response, though it arises from different motives), and more recently has veered back towards massive retaliation, standing now somewhat imprecisely between the two.[15] On this latter issue, a degree of ambiguity is entirely predictable, since it mirrors the debates within the United States as technological advances opened up nuclear 'war-fighting' doctrines in the late 1960s.

On technical grounds, however, France also suffered from ambiguities that did not affect the superpower. The range of some French nuclear systems meant that they would land in West Germany; not necessarily a problem within a collective NATO framework, but a considerable shadow over Franco-German relations where France remains an independent nuclear player. Similarly, notions of 'pre-strategic' use and 'warning shots' outside the collective decision-making of the Alliance could not but make France's European partners nervous, since independent action could accidentally trigger a nuclear exchange to which the allies had not resolved. This was not the case for Britain, since its 'triggering' capacity was solely in relation to its strategic weapons. Its tactical nuclear weapons were all under NATO's collective decision-making procedures. It would be inconceivable that a strategic exchange could be used ambiguously in any 'warning' or 'pre-strategic' capacity. With independent French nuclear weapons at the tactical level, however, this remained a realistic fear for the allies.

Though none of these problems has been resolved in French nuclear debates since 1989, it would be fair to summarize present trends in thinking around three principles: first, that a secure retaliatory capacity must be maintained, based on the SSBN force; second, that this should be backed up by at least one other leg of the traditional triad of nuclear forces, even if one leg of the triad has to be abandoned; and third, France must still be capable of delivering a final, highly precise, nuclear warning shot, probably with some version of the air-delivered stand-off missile. Taken together, these principles are designed to preserve the independence of French nuclear strategy, a crucial consideration to retain political support.

In the French context, the very existence of an independent strategy and of indigenous weapons systems, however, is more important than the logical consistency with which its strategy accords with a European reality created by an alliance structure from which France deliberately stands apart. Both British and French policy-makers have generally believed that nuclear weapons are a stabilizing factor in any situation and that 'existential' deterrence is particularly potent in Europe. For the British, this provides a powerful rationale to tie the United States into the deterrent umbrella, and to do this, a logical doctrine of graduated deterrence is desirable to keep the allies united. For France, only a national internal logic need apply and the inconsistencies in this are irrelevant in the face of the overwhelming reality of existential deterrence in Europe. In French thinking, its own nuclear forces are not only capable of providing the existential deterrent for Europe, but are also more credible since they are operated by a power that would have no option of withdrawal.

Post-Cold War Deterrence

Independent Nuclear Forces

In the present international situation, both British and French force structures, and the strategies that back them up, have become more convergent. Both find themselves moving towards a doctrine, and a force structure, of minimal (if not quite minimum) deterrence based on the threat of strategic retaliation rather than any ability to 'fight' a nuclear war.

British nuclear forces for the 1990s are presently planned to be the Trident SSBN force, and the air-delivered WE-177 bomb, due to be replaced by a stand-off missile. In reality, the prospects of a stand-off replacement are very low. The US TASM is no longer a realistic option and the prospects of collaboration with France on a second generation of the ASMP that would serve both air forces is technically questionable. The first generation ASMP is so far from the technical requirements necessary for an effective second generation that an Anglo-French project would, in effect, be starting from scratch. Certainly, there was no specific mention of the TASM in the 1992 Statement on the Defence Estimates; a sign for most analysts that 'the Government was quietly "airbrushing" it out of the picture'.[16] In the present political and financial climate, this is highly likely. For Britain, therefore, the nuclear deterrent will come down to the Trident force.

In the case of France, its forces, too, will rely to a far greater extent than before on its SSBN force. It is entirely likely that the IRBM force at the Plâteau d'Albion will be abandoned, on the grounds of its strategic obsolescence.[17] Its nuclear-capable aircraft will need replacement by the turn of the century and will, in any case, be carrying a small number of the present ASMP which is of limited range and capability. A French strategic dyad is emerging, therefore, in which one of the legs will be extremely weak. Whether France will maintain a credible 'pre-strategic' ability – to strike at highly significant, but not 'strategic' targets – has now to be doubted. As in the British case, however, the SSBN forces that form the unambiguously strategic component of the force, will not only be modernized but will also represent a warhead delivery capacity greatly in excess of the systems they are designed to replace.

On the issue of SSBN warhead numbers, it is possible that both British and French capabilities have been overestimated, and that it has suited both governments to allow this to be so. Like Britain, it may be that France has only three sets of M-4 missiles for its four SSBN, and that it will retain this total loading, each missile carrying six warheads. The French strategic warhead total may therefore be as low as 288; and the British 192.[18] If this is the case, it may be in the interests of both powers to announce this fact to the world and allow it to be verified, rather than maintain their right to warhead loadings up to the full theoretical capacities of their strategic systems. Unless such an announcement is made, however, other powers in the world would be prudent to assume that relatively high numbers of British and French warheads are deployed.

Finally, this SSBN capacity is to be backed up with a very big French investment in command, control, communication and intelligence (C^3I). Learning from their salutary experiences in the Gulf War, where French forces found themselves reliant on US intelligence assets, the government increased the space budget by 17.5 per cent in 1992 and France's four main intelligence services are being reorganized into a single unit, the *Direction du Renseignement Militaire*.

Significant though such changes in force structures are, constituting as they do a *de facto* move towards minimum deterrence doctrines, this evolution pales beside the revolution in the strategic environment they are designed to address.

Nuclear Rationales

Much of the nuclear rationale that has underpinned British and French forces has now either been undermined or else remains valid only in a sense that is wide open to question in the light of current world events. For the purposes of analysis, the two types of rationale outlined earlier should now be extended to three, namely independent deterrence as a factor in East–West stability, as a device to pursue specifically national interests, and as a general deterrent against security threats from any quarter.

East-West Deterrence. The relevance of any nuclear forces in this context has radically changed. The 'Soviet threat' has, quite literally, disappeared, along with the prospect of a total war between East and West in which physical survival was at stake. For the same reason, Western nuclear forces cannot now be justified as compensating for conventional weakness. Following the break up of the Warsaw Pact and the Soviet Union, together with the ratification of the Treaty on Conventional Armed Forces in Europe, NATO is now infinitely stronger in conventional forces than any of its neighbours. Russia itself is in a position of conventional inferiority in some important respects against the combined armed forces of all its immediate neighbours. Similarly, nuclear weapons no longer perform the same role in risk-sharing among the NATO allies. The logic of risk-sharing depended on the assumption that *any* war in Europe would be a general East–West conflict in which the nuclear shadow would loom large. This is no longer the case. Local wars in Europe are already a fact and may indeed become a phenomenon of the 1990s. The nuclear shadow neither shares the risks (Germany, Italy, Greece and Turkey bear significantly greater direct risks in conflicts in Eastern and Southern Europe than Britain and the United States), nor moderates the motives to conflict (certainly not in the Balkans, for example). The Western world's nuclear forces remain essentially intact, configured more or less as they were during the Cold War, and yet European peace and stability are now greatly at risk and it is difficult to think of any ways in which NATO's nuclear doctrines can make a contribution to our attempts to promote stability across the continent. The logic of deterrence in the Cold War, in other words, rested on the facts of European bipolarity. Since this has collapsed, most of the subtleties of the West's deterrent position – compensating for conventional weakness, risk-sharing, outlawing conventional wars and so on – have become irrelevant.

What is left in the East–West deterrent rationale is the much less subtle notion of existential deterrence against any European nuclear power – in practice, Russia.[19] It is not realistic to believe that Russia presently poses any strategic threat to Western nations. Nor would it be realistic to envisage such a threat even in the event of an anti-democratic Russia emerging from its present domestic crisis. A future Russia at war with some of its neighbours in Europe is always conceivable, of course, but this is a quite different proposition from Russia as a strategic threat to the survival of Western societies. In the short to medium term, a Russian attack on NATO must be ruled out altogether; in the long term, it remains an outside but still very unlikely possibility. In other words, it is impossible to characterize an East–West (Russia–NATO) deterrent relationship in the highly applied way in which it was characterized before 1989, where force structures and doctrines were well-known, warning times were based on known standard operating procedures in the adversary, where opposing military scenarios were understood, and so on. In the present world, the 'East–West existential deterrent' is simply an assurance that in the medium to long term future, Russian leaders must take account of the fact that other nuclear powers will also exist in Europe.

Specific National Purposes. In the case of Britain's own national purposes for being an independent nuclear power, the changed circumstances are more matters of opinion than strategic logic. The possession of independent weapons as a trigger for a US nuclear response has been crucially undermined in two respects. One is that this was only credible when the US assumed that it was facing, in Europe, only one front in a multi-front attack on the United States. Nothing less would be worth the price of a US nuclear response. For this still to be the case it would be necessary to believe that a future Russia would choose to make total war not only against the whole of Europe but against the US as well; a reckless bid, in other words, for world domination. A second reason is that with the progressive US withdrawal from Europe and from bases in Britain – and the scrapping of short- and intermediate-range nuclear systems – there is considerably less to act as a trigger. It will increasingly be conceivable (if barely imaginable) that a Russian nuclear attack on Britain could be carried out in such a way as to exempt US forces.

Whether or not British nuclear weapons still provide some influence with the United States must also be doubted. This rationale was most prevalent in the 1940s when there was some equality between the embryonic nuclear capabilities of both states. It is difficult to imagine that in the 1990s there is much US awareness of Britain having a special place in its decision-making *because* of its nuclear weapons. There is certainly no evidence since the Cuban missile crisis of 1962 that Britain was specially consulted by the United States before it made some of its more crucial national nuclear decisions: in the US nuclear alert during the 1973 Middle East crisis; in its decision to press ahead with developments of MIRV technology; in its negotiating positions in the strategic arms limitation talks; in the decision to initiate the Strategic Defense Initiative in 1983; in its willingness to move to a denuclearized Europe during the Reykjavik summit of 1986; in the Congressional decision of 1992 to suspend all nuclear testing (which after 1996 is due to deprive Britain of its one test a year in the United States). One searches in vain for any genuine British influence in any of these – and other – cases.

On the other hand, it is true to say that nuclear co-operation between Britain and the United States has remained close even after the end of the Cold War. Britain will be operating missiles purchased from the United States; it will be having them serviced at the US facility at Kings Bay rather than in Scotland; and it still has its weapons locked into the US SIOP (though this may change as the SIOP is radically revised and in light of NATO's new strategic concept).[20] Nuclear co-operation, therefore, will probably remain one of the tangible aspects of the Anglo-American relationship. But this should not be confused with influence over the United States. Britain derives cheapness and convenience from joint nuclear arrangements, not access to US decision-making. This, moreover, has to be set in a more general political context. There are other elements in the Anglo-American relationship, arguably more important than nuclear co-operation, and at a time when the United States military commitment to Europe is set to decline even further, the non-military aspects of the relationship are likely to be more important in the future.

For the French independent deterrent, much the same applies, though for different reasons. The applied East–West deterrent has disappeared for the French exactly as it has for the British. They, too, are left with the deterrent merely in its existential capacity, though to be fair to Paris, this has always loomed larger in French thinking than in British. French national motives for nuclear weapons are affected in different ways. The alleged ability they provided France to conduct its own *Ostpolitik* has disappeared with the collapse of the bipolar structure. This rationale would only stand up if there was evidence that French bilateral relations with the new democracies of Eastern Europe, the Commonwealth of Independent States, and with Russia itself, were critically influenced by the fact that France was perceived as a nuclear power. Similarly, the view that the French deterrent was an advertisement for French nuclear technological exports also runs against the grain of post-Cold War realities. Nuclear proliferation has become a much more prominent international issue as the world faces the prospect of the former Soviet stockpile of nuclear weapons and technology leeching away into the wider international community. Civil nuclear power, too, may not recover from the shock of Chernobyl – and other future eventualities like it. Though it is possible to argue that the French nuclear 'shop window' still applies despite all this, it is clear that it will increasingly conflict with the rationale which maintains that nuclear deterrence is, in itself, a factor for international stability.

The two domestic rationales that may still stand for French nuclear weapons are the arguments that they provide a measure of independence from the US and that they serve to emphasize the leadership role of France within Europe. Since these are essentially matters not only of perception but of *self*-perception, they remain valid as long as they are believed. And the level of French investment in the modernized SSBN force and in space-based C^3I assets indicates that this self-perception remains very prevalent in France. As long as the Mitterrand administration endures, there is no expectation that the policy of fierce nuclear independence from the United States will change. Certainly, it has been a French belief for some years that as the Cold War declined, so too would NATO and the trans-atlantic Alliance, and that its maverick stance of independence within a more assertive Western Europe would be vindicated by events. President Mitterrand has already spoken of the desirability of establishing a nuclear doctrine among the Europeans, as a logical development in the trend of events on the continent. Indeed, since this is an ongoing political argument of some ferocity, it is possible that the future direction of events in Europe could prove French politicians right. It is conceivable that the US military commitment to Europe might quickly collapse, along with NATO, and that there would be no alternative for the Western Europeans but to co-ordinate their defence policies, in effect, within the European Community by means of the full integration into the EC of the Western European Union (WEU). In these circumstances, French independence from NATO and the United States would provide the model, and the organizing framework, for a new European approach to defence.

Nevertheless, such beliefs also have to be set in the known political context of Europe in 1993. European security is challenged not by the players in the nuclear deterrent game, but rather by the fragmentation of political order throughout Europe – particularly in the East and South. If the French claim to a leadership role in European security is to be sustained, it seems likely that political, economic and conventional military action will be at a premium. Certainly, it is not obvious how being a nuclear power – independent or otherwise – will buy influence in European security matters when the nature of the problems are intra-state, ethnic, economic and cultural. And in addressing immediate security problems in the Balkans through contributions to United Nations efforts in the former Yugoslavia, independence from the United States becomes even more difficult to achieve. European conventional military operations of any size depend on US political and financial backing in the United Nations and on various forms of US and NATO logistical aid, whether or not US personnel are involved. It was no coincidence, for example, that the headquarters of the second UN Protection Force (UNPROFOR 2) in Zagreb and Kiseljak – commanded by a French General – was nevertheless provided by NATO, transplanting large elements of NATO's Northern Army Group headquarters as a functioning unit to the operational theatre, and including in its number some 15 US officers.[21] In other words, to maintain a leadership role in the crises of European security likely to occur in the foreseeable future, will require France to put more stress on conventional rather than nuclear capabilities and on gradual *de facto* reintegration into the military structure of NATO. There is a good deal of evidence that such a reintegration in the conventional sphere is already underway, though it is unlikely to be a declared policy under the present administration. On 29 September 1992 French Defence Minister Pierre Joxe spoke explicitly in these terms, arguing that France 'must be present in the various decision-making or discussion bodies, where the management of present crises is being organized and where our future security is being planned'.[22] Since at least November 1991 both Joxe and the Elysée Palace have maintained such a line, though NATO is never mentioned by name. French agreement that the proposed Franco-German corps would be integrated with NATO in the event of a crisis within the NATO area moves in the same logical direction.[23] But all of this conflicts ever more sharply with the logic – and the battle for scarce defence expenditure – of a policy of nuclear independence.

On the basis of the first two types of rationale for British and French nuclear forces – rationales based on East–West deterrence, and those based on specific national purposes – some residual elements still stand up in the new Europe. On the first type of rationale it is possible to argue that what remains is existential deterrence. British and French policy-makers have always assumed that nuclear weapons constitute a stabilizing factor in an inherently unstable world. Existential deterrence, it may be argued, however difficult it is to apply to any emerging scenario, may be preferable to no deterrence. On the second type of rationale there are less logical, but probably more persistent, residual arguments that have to be given some weight. For Britain there remains a somewhat perverse negative reasoning which states that though we cannot expect nuclear weapons to give Britain much leverage over the United States, either politically or operationally, to abandon them now would damage Anglo-American relations since it would come to symbolize a lack of collective commitment on Britain's part. It is not at all clear that this is shared in Washington, but on this particularly British conception, the heavy symbolic value of nuclear weapons, in this argument, condemns Britain to remain a nuclear power.[24] If the monetary price of staying in the nuclear club is high, the political price of exit is even greater. For France, the symbolic value of remaining an independent nuclear power is still great. Whether or not this goes against the grain of European trends, it remains a self belief both of present French leaders and within most sections of the public and will continue to drive the force structure and defence spending of France for some time to come.

General Deterrence against Threats from any Quarter. Facing the post-Cold War world with a modernized configuration of nuclear forces, both Britain and France have fallen back on what might be termed the 'general deterrent' scenario: that as weapons of last resort, they are to protect the homeland against aggression from any quarter. This is existential deterrence in a global context. The implication, left unstated in official pronouncements, is that future threats to the homeland could come from third world countries, including from unstable leaderships who have nuclear weapons and delivery systems, state-sponsored terrorism, and perhaps even from terrorist groups themselves. Independent nuclear forces, modernized to last well into the next century, remain the ultimate guarantee of national security in a world that shows every sign of becoming increasingly disordered. This broad proposition is underpinned by three more detailed assumptions.

First, it is assumed that nuclear proliferation will inexorably increase. Sooner or later, many states will be nuclear powers. Even if this does not raise the realistic spectre of a strategic attack on the homeland in the way it was assumed to exist in the days of the Cold War (why would a South Asian or a Southern African state attack the British or French homeland for purposes of conquest?), it does raise the possibility of nuclear blackmail either against the homeland or perhaps against British or French forces operating away from the homeland. Secondly, it is assumed that Britain and France will be involved in more *ad hoc* alliances in the future. French planners have always maintained this. Now they believe it more strongly, while British planners have officially conceded the point.[25] If alliances are likely to be more *ad hoc*, then a premium is placed on the independence of British and French nuclear forces in any situation where nuclear deterrence is relevant. Thirdly, there remains the assumption of independent nuclear capability as a symbol of international status. It may be thought that such symbolism remains part of the entry price for a seat on the United Nations Security Council, which both London and Paris will fight fiercely to maintain in the face of German and Japanese pressure to be admitted to permanent member status. It may also be felt that in the context of relations between European powers and other states in the world – in the Middle East, Asia, sub-saharan Africa – the international status that nuclear weapons confer counts as a greater foreign policy asset than it did in the East–West context where there were a number of such players producing, operating, or hosting nuclear capabilities.

Such assumptions are seldom spelt out in any detail, except in private. As an official policy position, it is sufficient for governments to assert that their nuclear deterrent forces are a good insurance policy for the unforeseeable future, on which the main premiums have already been paid. If it is not clear that deterrence has a central place in East–West politics, then it may still have one in the future of politics between North and South.

The Logic of Disarmament

The analysis so far indicates that the end of the Cold War leaves British and French independent nuclear forces standing on some thin strategic rationales. Put simply they amount to: (i) residual national political motives, including independence for the French, Anglo-Americanism for the British, and status in Europe – and in the wider world – for them both; (ii) existential deterrence in Europe against, in practice, the hypothetical long-term re-emergence of a nuclear threat from Moscow; and (iii) existential deterrence in the wider world (possibly including successor states in Asia of the former Soviet Union) with no specific focus for the hypothetical threat.

The logic of nuclear disarmament for Britain and France attacks these existing rationales head on. Residual national political motives are already running against the trend of events, as indicated earlier. The logic of disarmament is that their political and economic costs now outweigh the advantages. At a time when both Britain and France are finding their conventional forces severely stretched, the continuation of expenditures on nuclear systems to address hypothetical threats, when so much more resources are manifestly required to address the tangible immediate security problems of Europe, may be regarded as an excessive opportunity cost. If the nuclear forces are an 'insurance policy', then some high premiums have still to be paid, both in monetary terms and in respect to equipment choices for the conventional forces. This is particularly the case for France. More to the point, if French and British national objectives remain largely 'independence' and 'Anglo-Americanism' respectively, and 'status and leadership in Europe' for them both, then in a non-bipolar environment – where nuclear threats are at most long-term hypothetical scenarios – the question arises whether the provision of independent nuclear forces is the most efficient way to pursue them. Gestures that address actual security problems will presumably carry far greater political weight than those which remain hypothetical.

More important, however, is the logic of disarmament on the existential deterrent assumptions that Britain and France make in relation to Europe and now, with considerably greater emphasis, in respect of the wider world. The existential deterrent argument – particularly in its 'North–South' application – is open to fundamental logical criticisms. When deterrent logic was thought through in the 1950s, though it was articulated as a series of general propositions about the behaviour of any two actors, the reality was that the theorists had the United States and the Soviet Union firmly in mind. What was being thought through was, from the very first, a highly applied version of nuclear deterrence. The sort of general deterrence that could apply to *any* two or more, actors was never properly addressed. Therefore, when current nuclear planners provide a general (that is, world-wide) deterrent rationale for British and French nuclear forces, they are also making a number of assumptions that appear highly questionable in any context other than that of NATO and the Warsaw Pact. They assume, for example, that the actors with whom they might enter into a nuclear deterrent relationship share roughly the same logic system; that nuclear war would remain for these actors the ultimate catastrophe; that these are countries where population densities and high levels of physical infrastructure would make a first strike equally disastrous for both; where leaders are in control of their nuclear forces and failsafe routines are generally good; where strategic decision-making is not entirely at the mercy of the temperament of a single leader; where political elites understand the general rules of deterrence; where adversaries have the technical capacity to interpret deterrent signals accurately, and so on. There are any number of reasons to argue that the moral, intellectual and technical basis of North–South deterrence is somewhat different to the deterrence the West has come to see as 'existential', as if it was a simple fact of life.[26]

There is a more fundamental problem of logic against existential deterrence arguments, however. Firstly, both Britain and France have taken a view that deterrence is an essentially stabilizing force in world politics. They also have taken the view that nuclear proliferation is inevitable; indeed, the new emphasis on North–South concepts of deterrence is based upon this argument.[27]

In the post-Cold War world, however, these two propositions cannot be simultaneously upheld. If proliferation is inevitable, then it can only be a matter of time before many states are forced into multiple deterrent relationships. These will not all be two-actor relationships; rather they will tend to be multiple deterrent games, between nuclear forces of different sizes, technical capabilities, different degrees of extended deterrence, and perhaps between very different cultures. In general, it is difficult to believe that a world of many nuclear powers will be safer – and safer for the promotion of European interests – than the present one. In particular, a world of highly complex deterrence will not be able to draw on the reassuring logic of simple deterrence that we all grew up on. Deterrence loses its natural tendency towards stability once it becomes too complex for humans to comprehend in total: when it becomes, in other words, the stuff of normal politics. Unless one is prepared to sign up to the logic of Kenneth Waltz's provocative concept of a world structured by a 'unit veto system' whereby nuclear proliferation effectively outlaws war between the vast majority of the world's 180–200 states, precisely because a high proportion of them are nuclear, then a world structured by extensive deterrence can hardly be more stable.[28]

Secondly, there is the problem that the expectation of inevitable nuclear proliferation becomes a self-fulfilling prophecy. The British and American governments, in particular, have led the international community in an increasing concern about nuclear proliferation since 1989, with the prospect not only that Iraq was further along the road to a bomb-making capacity than was generally believed, but also because so much former Soviet nuclear technology will probably leak into the Third World. The French government has traditionally taken a less cautious attitude to proliferation in favour of an aggressive export policy. Even France, however, has taken the test ban and the non-proliferation regimes more seriously during the last year, sharing the general concern.[29]

But all this is an attempt merely to slow down the process rather than reverse it, since neither government believes that it is generally reversible. Deprived of the useful shadow of Cold War deterrence, which offered an immediate imperative for British and French nuclear forces, the contradictions in their own positions are now seen in a much harsher light. Britain and France no longer face any credible threats to their homelands. Yet they maintain that nuclear deterrent forces are essential to their security and are a non-negotiable element in their defence. There is an illogicality – to put it politely – in Britain (and to a lesser extent France) lecturing the near-nuclear states – many of whom face considerable threats to their homelands – on the disutility and even the ethics of possessing nuclear weapons. In December 1992, for example, a Ukrainian delegation to Britain received such a lecture from the government and wondered aloud why the logic did not apply to their hosts.[30] British objections to the US test moratorium imposed in 1992 pose a similar contradiction. Britain claims to aspire to a comprehensive test ban as an effective measure of non-proliferation (which it would be), but not while it conducts its own single test every year.[31] The effort to sell either nuclear technology directly or dual-use civil technology, has also fuelled this contradiction in policy. Clearly, the competition between French, American, German and British companies to sell dual-use technologies to Iraq prior to 1990, took precedence over the commitment of their governments to effective non-proliferation.

The expectation that non-proliferation policies will ultimately fail is a particularly powerful form of self-fulfilling prophecy when it is held by those states who possess nuclear weapons. For they are the states whose example, whose technology, and whose efforts to safeguard their exclusive status does most damage to the non-proliferation concept. This is particularly the case for middle-ranking powers, since arguments that would have been valid in the 1940s that the 'pinnacle' countries in the system should be allowed to retain weapons in a world otherwise denuclearized, to establish a stable and benevolent hierarchy of military power, cannot be maintained when other middle powers are now more significant actors in the system.

Finally, there is a timing problem in hanging on to the concept of existential deterrence because of the likely sequence of developments in the next 20 to 30 years. The problem of nuclear proliferation presently appears intractable, but it is not as immediate as had previously been thought. Under present pessimistic assumptions and contradictory policies we will face a world of many nuclear powers in the future; but perhaps not until after 2020. Certainly, proliferation has not proceeded at the pace that was envisaged in the 1960s. We have underestimated the problems in assembling technologies that are comparatively simple to the West in countries that lack a more general technical infrastructure. We overestimated the ability of developing countries to pay for the technologies necessary to create effective delivery systems. And we did not foresee the long-term economic decline of most Third World countries after the mid-1970s, which has so restricted their ability to import technology of any sort. The case of Iraq is instructive in this respect. Saddam Hussein was further down the nuclear road than had been anticipated, but further away from a usable, and deliverable, capacity against the West, than was feared in 1990–91. The same is true of Libya and its potential threat to the countries of the Northern Mediterranean.[32]

Against this background, present non-proliferation policies may appear to be working. Certainly, it is possible to tighten the noose around particular nuclear aspirants quite tightly and slow the process a little further in some key cases. There is a breathing space of perhaps 20 to 30 years, therefore, before global nuclearization crosses a new threshold after which it will almost certainly be impossible to reverse. During the lifetime of the new generation of British and French SSBN systems, as it happens, neither country is likely to face a nuclear challenge of any credibility from a Third World country. The problem inherent in the timing of all this is that the contradiction in pursuing both pessimistic non-proliferation alongside minimum deterrence may stand out with greater clarity than ever before, but it is unlikely to carry any short-term political penalties. It will be a two-handed policy that will not seem to be failing, until the inevitable happens, and it will already have failed.

The 1990s may represent the last good opportunity to denuclearize the world. Certainly, the breathing space allows Britain and France – more so than the United States or Russia – to undertake a disarmament operation in greater physical safety than ever before in their histories. It gives them a cushion to graduate their disarmament and combine it with a determined effort to promote optimistic non-proliferation. It gives them some considerable time to assess in safety the effects of any disarmament and, if necessary, even to reverse it. The incentives for Britain and France to do this, however, are all abstractions – logically overwhelming and morally powerful abstractions – but abstractions nevertheless. The monetary and political costs of maintaining independent forces will only be felt as opportunity costs. London and Paris will be under only moral and intellectual pressures to disarm; at present there is little prospect that acute political dilemmas will make disarmament appear as a lesser evil. Once the world has passed the proliferation threshold of many and various nuclear states, however, the disarmament option may not then even be a lesser evil for Britain and France; and we will have condemned ourselves to a world of complex, multiple deterrence.

Mechanisms of British and French Disarmament

Complete nuclear disarmament on the part of Britain and France has to be regarded as highly unlikely, however desirable and logical it may appear to an observer of the post-Cold War world.[33] Nuclear arms reductions are still conceivable, however. Furthermore, it is possible – though not likely – that further arms reductions could create a downward spiral and break through the taboos against the concept of complete nuclear disarmament that were fuelled by 40 years of Cold War thinking. Four types of mechanism are conceivable, ranging from the promotion of marginal reductions in numbers and systems, to a fundamental rethinking of the strategy of deterrence as a device to promote security for European states.

Further Unilateral Pressures. Both Britain and France are under technical and economic pressures to dispense with their sub-strategic nuclear weapons, the role of which is now very much in doubt. They could simply make a virtue of necessity and abandon all but their SSBN forces. This would be a relatively easy but significant act of political will on the part of London and Paris. It should not be confused with anything more courageous, but neither should its usefulness be dismissed.

There would also be some scope for Britain and France to make unilateral gestures in reducing the warhead numbers carried by each SSBN. This has the attraction that it could be easily reversible. To be a credible reduction, however, removing some nuclear warheads from their SLBMs would have to be carefully and intrusively verified – a requirement that, in itself, would be a useful confidence-building measure.

Pressures Arising from Progress in US-Russian Arms Control. The START-II Treaty puts British and French nuclear forces under some interesting potential pressures. With US and Russian warhead numbers due to be reduced to a maximum of 3,500 each by 2003, Paris and London cannot go on arguing that their potential warhead numbers (896 between them) are insignificant. Of course, if the lower numbers postulated are correct, the joint total would only be 480 – still a not insignificant proportion of 7,000, however (and possibly a good deal less than 7,000 if there is a START III). Moreover, if the US Strategic Defense Initiative is reined in under the Clinton administration, particularly the further development of GPALS, it will be impossible to argue that such significant warhead numbers are still required by Britain and France to maintain a minimum deterrent, since extra penetration will not be necessary.

In these circumstances the best way for Britain and France to keep their SSBN forces as genuinely minimum deterrents, respond positively to START pressures, and act in a clearly stabilizing way would be to de-MIRV their missiles. This would bring the numbers down dramatically, would be a technically attractive option if Britain and France are having as much difficulty producing sufficient warheads as is constantly rumoured, and would require intrusive on-site verification that would be a useful confidence-building measure in itself. Such low numbers – 16 or perhaps 32 warheads available at any one time – would keep the two allies more in line with the trend of superpower strategic developments and reinforce the general move away from destabilizing MIRV technologies.

Co-operative Nuclear Arrangements among the European Allies. On the assumption that British and French nuclear forces come down in essence to their respective SSBN forces, there are a number of motives and mechanisms that might lead to co-operation between their strategic forces that would permit some further reductions. Given that defence budgets in both countries are likely to be severely stretched in the near future, the prospects of savings on the building or the running costs of a fourth submarine in each force may come to seem more attractive. If patrol schedules were co-ordinated between British and French SSBNs then an effective joint force of six submarines would be more than adequate to maintain constant coverage. In a period of great international tension akin to that of the Cold War, defence ministries would have been very reluctant to allow 'their' deterrent to rest on the patrol of the other. In the present climate, however, not only is threat of a bolt-from-the-blue nuclear attack barely conceivable, but it is a safe planning assumption that a long period of warning would be available if such a threat ever began to materialize, thus allowing procedures to be reviewed.

National pride apart, very little indeed would now be at risk in such an arrangement and the advantages could be considerable. It would establish the fact that – at least at the strategic level – British and French security interests are virtually identical. It is difficult to imagine an attack on the one alone, and impossible to imagine that if an attack did occur, it would not have deleterious effects on its neighbour. It would provide a framework in which further reductions could take place, since a force of six SSBNs could be reduced to four. Other submarines could be mothballed as a hedge against a need to change the policy within, say, a two-year period. It would allow both powers to demonstrate a commitment to further reductions in warhead numbers, and might constitute a way of preserving a genuinely minimum deterrent in the face of international pressures to enter a third START round or make proportionate reductions to the United States and Russia.

Nuclear co-operation of this sort has the initial advantage in that it would be minimal: it would not require any compromises in boat design or basic operational procedures, it would not demolish the technical capacity to produce SSBNs; and it need not be regarded as diminishing either national independence or the US military commitment to Europe. Finally, such an arrangement would provide a useful transitional stage to the deepest form of plausible medium-term transformation in nuclear forces, the institutionalization of European nuclear forces. It would therefore be consistent with recent British and French aspirations for much closer defence co-operation.[34] In particular, French statements have discussed possible nuclear co-operation between London and Paris as part of an initiative to use it as a building block towards a 'Europeanization of France's nuclear arsenal'.[35] And at a symposium in Paris on 30 September 1992 the British Defence Secretary spoke of opportunities for Europe to support more fully what was termed 'collective deterrence', through closer co-operation between the two West European nuclear powers and through a 'clearer perception' and 'an interpretation of "vital national interest" that took account of the fact that we are nation states within a community of allied states and within a framework of European Union, to whose destiny we are vitally linked.'[36] In the world of national deterrent statements this may be seen as a big shift in emphasis.

Institutionalizing a European Nuclear Force. An extension of this logic would be for Britain and France to place their co-operating SSBN forces at the service of their European allies. In such an arrangement both forces would be assigned a European, rather than a national, function.[37]

In present circumstances, the realist is tempted to offer both countries an opt-out clause from this arrangement along the lines of the present British position in relation to the SIOP: 'these British forces will be used for the purposes of international defence of the Western Alliance in all circumstances . . . [e]xcept where Her Majesty's Government may decide that supreme national interests are at stake'.[38] Since, as discussed, the strategic need for such an opt out is highly academic, it perhaps could be conceded without difficulty as a harmless placebo to help a couple of badly addicted patients get themselves off the drug of deterrence thinking. On further reflection, however, it should not be conceded, since it would prevent both countries from making the clear commitment that would be necessary to evolve away from the concept of independent nuclear deterrence. More importantly, to maintain the opt-out clause, even as a placebo, would severely weaken the effect of internationalization on potential proliferators. Opt-outs would simply appear to confirm the motives to proliferate in the first place.

At a practical level, planning for this SSBN force could be carried out in a European Nuclear Planning Group (NPG) in which other allies would have a right to be consulted in advance, though no absolute right of veto. Britain and France could have a right of veto over each other, since this would merely be a recognition of the real situation in which they would continue to control their own submarines. The advantages of this arrangement for the national interests of Britain and France would be that it preserves a form of independence for them both, and is in fact reversible, but will evolve towards greater *de facto* co-operation in the very likely event that independent nuclear actions on the part of Britain and France come to seem incredible. For France, it would represent a tangible sense in which the French deterrent plays a real role in European security; for Britain, it would represent a dramatic integration of French forces into the allied context. This would be a considerable benefit for the United States. There is no reason, in principle, why both forces should not be built into a new SIOP, if there is to be one, worked out with the European NPG. This might satisfy both European allies and be a small price for the United States to pay to engineer a reintegration of French forces – one that would make conventional force integration a good deal more politically palatable in France. It would not force Britain to choose between the Anglo-American relationship and a more European role.[39] The nuclear elements of co-operation with Washington – such as they are – could remain, though they might have to be handled more sensitively in relation to reactions in Paris.[40]

The strategic advantages of this arrangement would be to encourage stability in Europe's relations with other actors in the world. It would link the national deterrents explicitly to the security of the continent *vis-à-vis* non-Europe, embedding potentially dangerous technologies firmly in the political and economic weight of Europe. Deterrence was relatively safe in the Cold War because of the sheer weight of bipolarity which ensured that *any* war between East and West in Europe was unthinkable – nuclear weapons simply made it even more unthinkable. In this situation, something similar would be created. It is difficult to imagine any actor attempting to go to war with the combined powers of Europe. An institutionalized deterrent would both bolster this sense of invulnerability and also be protected by it. The deterrent would exist in a politically stable situation. This is not to say that politics within Europe are going to be stable, but nuclear deterrence within Europe is now all but irrelevant.[41]

The disarmament advantages of this arrangement is that it would allow the nuclear powers a cheap and safe experiment with deterrence. In essence, British and French deterrents would be claiming to perform the 'extended deterrence' trick for their European partners. This would be a burden-sharing operation among the allies that would compensate for the fact that the US extended deterrent is likely to lose all credibility in the post-Cold War environment. If the institutionalized deterrent were ever called on to perform an extended deterrence role, it would at least be more credible than the present alternative. And in the much more likely event that it is never invoked, this institutional arrangement would help to establish the present superfluousness of deterrent strategies. It would be very difficult for Britain or France to claim that their essential national interests were at stake – sufficient to make their single-warhead minimum deterrents relevant – in any North–South confrontation in which they became involved, since this would almost certainly not be a matter of national survival for them. The pressure from other allies would be considerable at any suggestion that the deterrent force was performing any other role than intra-war nuclear deterrence for Europe as a whole against an external threat. And the knowledge that this would be the case should reassure other actors in the world that British and French nuclear forces existed in a context where their protestations of 'minimum deterrence only for last resort defence' could be taken at face value. In the words of Ivo Daalder, the purpose of this sort of internationalization 'is not deterrence of aggression but rather deterrence of nuclear acquisition and use'.[42]

The ultimate disarmament objective in this situation, of course, would be to wean Paris and London off the notion of deterrence. If I am wrong in my analysis of the redundancy of British and French nuclear forces in the contemporary world, then both of them could revert to the position they are presently in, or will be in by the mid-1990s. If I am right, however, then they will retain the form both of national strategic independence and of nuclear deterrence while the reality of both concepts fades away. If we cannot think ourselves into abolishing something, then the best way to give history the chance to abolish it for us is to institutionalize the problem where it can be allowed to become superfluous without creating political crises. Similarly, if it is not possible to envisage the world making a self-conscious move away from the notion of deterrence, then at least deterrence operated in a series of international institutional contexts suggests greater stability, more political and practical vetoes on its use, an opportunity to set a co-operative example to near-nuclear states, and more chances to integrate confidence-building measures into the proliferation process.

Having established the principle, the question of which European international institution could be the framework for such an arrangement cannot be dodged. It is not impossible that it could be done within an amended NATO framework. There is now a French debate on the possibility of a European deterrent[43] and other moves towards a reintegration with NATO forces are not now taboo within French intellectual circles. A new type of European NPG is also possible within the Western European Union, which would be much more to the taste of French politicians and could be presented as a decisive move towards a common European defence policy.[44] This could be palatable to Britain as long as the WEU was not integrated into the European Community, and remained a bridge between NATO and the EC.

There could also be considerable advantages in establishing a European NPG outside existing institutions. This would allow it to have a wider consultative membership than the European NATO allies, and could include Russia itself in an experiment in highly co-operative security in Europe. It could, perhaps be established among the states of the North Atlantic Cooperation Council (NACC), though not formally within that institution. Numbers here might be regarded as too high, but it should be possible to devise a system in which the three effective European nuclear powers become permanent members, while a rotation of, say, 10-12 other members maintain a representative spread of other members of the NACC. The same arrangement could, in principle, operate in a CSCE grouping, though in this case the geographical spread and sheer numbers involved (52), would not be conducive to constructive discussions.

Conclusion

The end of the Cold War has opened up a number of windows of opportunity for British and French nuclear forces. There is an opportunity to reappraise the hierarchy of nuclear rationales that have applied for more than 40 years and now look so different in the absence of an apparent Soviet threat. There is an opportunity to rationalize nuclear forces without being accused of undermining East–West deterrence. There is an opportunity to save money by reducing forces and cancelling programmes that are superfluous to a minimum deterrent. Specifically, there is an opportunity to de-MIRV British and French strategic forces. There is then an opportunity to rationalize nuclear forces further downward and gain political impetus for a stronger European security pillar in an Atlantic relationship that is in any case changing.

Above all, there is a window of opportunity to decide whether British and French independent deterrents are worth the political cost, when compared to the nuclear proliferation they serve to encourage. A decision to abandon nuclear weapons will not alone serve to reverse nuclear proliferation in the rest of the world. It is a necessary but not sufficient condition. Without it, however, a world of many nuclear states is guaranteed. The only questions are how long it takes to evolve and to which generation of our successors we bequeath it.

NOTES

1. International Institute for Strategic Studies, *The Military Balance 1991–1992* (London: IISS, 1991), p. 223.
2. Stockholm International Peace Research Institute (SIPRI), *SIPRI Yearbook 1986* (London: Taylor & Francis, 1986), p. 61. More recent material is contained in John Ainslie, *Cracking Under Pressure: The Response to Defects in British Nuclear Submarines* (Glasgow: Scottish Campaign for Nuclear Disarmament and Faslane Peace Camp, June 1992).
3. SIPRI, *SIPRI Yearbook 1992* (Oxford: Oxford University Press, 1992), p. 80.
4. *Statement on the Defence Estimates 1992*, Cm 1981 (London: HMSO, 1992), p. 28.
5. SIPRI, *SIPRI Yearbook* 1992, p. 83.
6. See Bruce George and James Piriou, 'France', in *Jane's NATO Handbook, 1991–92* (Coulsdon: Jane's Information Group, 1992), p. 278.
7. SIPRI, *SIPRI Yearbook 1992*, p. 81.
8. See Lawrence Freedman, *The Evolution of Nuclear Strategy* (New York: St. Martin's Press, 1981), p. 311.
9. Stuart Croft and Phil Williams, 'The United Kingdom', in Regina Cowen Karp (ed.), *Security With Nuclear Weapons?: Different Perspectives on National Security* (Oxford: Oxford University Press, 1991), p. 160.
10. Lawrence Freedman, *Britain and Nuclear Weapons* (London: Macmillan for the Royal Institute of International Affairs, 1980).
11. See Michael Clarke 'The Europeanization of NATO and the Problem of Anglo-American Relations', in Michael Clarke and Rod Hague (eds.), *European Defence Cooperation: America, Britain and NATO* (Manchester: Manchester University Press, 1990), pp. 28–44. See also, John Baylis, *Anglo-American Defence Relations 1939–1980: The Special Relationship*, 2nd edition (London: Macmillan, 1984).
12. On the general consensus behind French defence thinking see, Diego A. Ruiz Palmer, *French Strategic Options in the 1990s*, Adelphi Paper no. 260 (London: IISS, 1991), pp. 15–18.
13. See Ian Clark and Nicholas Wheeler, *The British Origins of Nuclear Strategy 1945–1955* (Oxford: Clarendon Press, 1989).
14. See Ivo H. Daalder, *The Nature and Practice of Flexible Response: NATO Strategy and Theatre Nuclear Forces Since 1967* (New York, Columbia University Press, 1991), pp. 69–105. See also, David N. Schwartz, *NATO's Nuclear Dilemmas* (Washington, DC: The Brookings Institution, 1983).
15. Klaus Schubert, 'France', in Karp (ed.), *Security with Nuclear Weapons?*, pp. 180–182; and Palmer, *French Strategic Options*, pp. 53–54.
16. 'Defence Strategy Casts Doubts on Tactical Missiles', *The Independent*, 8 July 1992, p. 4.
17. Frederic Bozo, 'France's Nuclear Albatross', *Peace and Security* (Spring 1992), p. 9.
18. See SIPRI, *SIPRI Yearbook 1992*, pp. 80–81.
19. In logic, existential deterrence in Europe should calculate a nuclear threat from other

NATO allies and from Ukraine and Kazakhstan. In reality, however, NATO allies do not plan for nuclear threats from each other, and the strategic threats posed by the retention in Ukraine and Kazakhstan of former Soviet strategic weapons cannot be rated very high for technical reasons. Strategic weapons sitting in silos in Ukraine, for example, remain dependent on navigational and software infrastructures held in Moscow in order to fire.

20. 'The Alliance's New Strategic Concept', *Press Communiqué* s-1 (91) 85, 7 Nov. 1991, paras 55–57.
21. *The Times*, 18 Dec. 1992, p. 1. See also James Gow, 'The Future of Peacekeeping in the Yugoslav Region', *Brassey's Defence Yearbook 1993* (London: Brassey's/Centre for Defence Studies, 1993).
22. 'Joxe in Box', *The Economist*, 3 Oct. 1992, p. 52.
23. See Mark Durman, 'Collective approach key to European task force plans', *Jane's Defence Weekly*, 29 Aug. 1992, p. 22.
24. This negative conception of Britain's nuclear status was particularly prevalent in the arguments of Conservative governments during the 1983 and 1987 general elections, when the unilateralist stance of the Labour Party was cited as evidence that incalculable harm was about to be done to Anglo-American relations, which would leave Britain without either influence or respect.
25. This point is acknowledged in the *Statement on the Defence Estimates, 1992*, p. 9.
26. The best work on this still remains Ken Booth, *Strategy and Ethnocentrism* (London: Croom Helm, 1979), though it does not seem to have had much impact on policymakers.
27. See, Croft and Williams, 'The United Kingdom', pp. 147–51; and Schubert, 'France', pp. 171–174.
28. Kenneth Waltz, *The Spread of Nuclear Weapons: More May Be Better*, Adelphi Paper no. 171 (London: IISS, 1981).
29. On this new concern, see Christopher Smith, 'The Topography of Conflict: Internal and External Security Issues in South Asia', in *Brassey's Defence Yearbook 1993*.
30. Personal interview with one of the officials left trying to square the circle of policy for his highly sceptical visitors.
31. British officials claim that the single test per year is essential for warhead safety. There is great scepticism about this in the scientific community, where it is frankly doubted that British annual tests over recent years have been conducted to derive safety information.
32. See, Martin Navias, *Saddam's Scud War and Ballistic Missile Proliferation*, London Defence Study No. 7 (London: Brassey's/Centre for Defence Studies, 1991).
33. For a good summary of the disarmament argument during the Cold War, see Dan Smith, *The Defence of the Realm in the 1980s* (London: Croom Helm, 1980), pp. 212–25.
34. See, statement of Malcolm Rifkind, British Minister of Defence, in Foreign Broadcasting Information Services, *Daily Report–Western Europe*, 27 Oct. 1992, p.2.
35. 'Nuclear Forces in Focus', *Jane's Defence Weekly*, 20 June 1992, p. 1084. President Mitterrand spoke explicitly of the possibility of developing a unified European nuclear doctrine in January 1992, *Atlantic News*, No. 2387, 14 Jan 1992, p. 4. See also Beatrice Heuser, 'Nuclear Weapons: The Issues and the Options', Paper for Centre for Defence Studies, University of Bradford, and IPPR conference on 'UK Defence Policy for the 1990s', 28 April 1992.
36. Remarks by the British Secretary of State for Defence at an Anglo-French symposium in Paris, 30 Sept. 1992.
37. See Heuser, 'Nuclear Weapons'.
38. Cited in Andrew Pierre, *Nuclear Politics* (Oxford: Oxford University Press, 1972), pp. 346–7.
39. See Stanley R. Sloan, 'The US Nuclear Role in NATO at the End of the Cold War', *CRS Report for Congress*, 92-484 S, 5 June 1992.
40. See the conclusions in Beatrice Heuser, 'Containing Uncertainty: Options for British Nuclear Strategy', *Review of International Studies* (Summer 1993, forthcoming).

41. Except in the scenario that Russia emerges as a long-term nuclear threat. But this is only a realistic planning assumption if we also assume a considerable warning period.
42. Personal communication.
43. Heuser, 'Nuclear Weapons'.
44. See Roberto Zadra, *European Integration and Nuclear Deterrence After the Cold War*, Chaillot Paper No. 5 (Paris: WEU Institute for Security Studies, 1992), pp. 29–34.

From Nuclear Deterrence to Reassurance: The Role of Confidence-Building Measures and Restrictions on Military Development

LISBETH GRONLUND

With the end of the Cold War, new possibilities have opened up for addressing the threat posed by the world's nuclear arsenals. Progress in this direction has been made with the completion of the START-I and START-II treaties, which will reduce US and Russian strategic nuclear warheads by two-thirds from current levels. The focus of these treaties has been on reducing the excessive levels of weapons and eliminating some of the more destabilizing components in the US and Russian nuclear arsenals (for example, multi-warhead land-based missiles). In addition, a fair amount of attention has focused on ensuring that nuclear weapons in the former Soviet Union are under adequate control, and that fissile material, nuclear technology, and human resources do not proliferate out of the newly independent states.

Like their predecessors, however, the START treaties include no requirements for the dismantlement of warheads, the verification of such dismantlement, or the placement of fissile material under safeguards. On the other hand, the US and Russian arms control communities have given these issues serious attention,[1] and there may be hope for implementing such measures under the Clinton administration.[2] By limiting the number of nuclear warheads that could be retained in storage and the amount of fissile material at hand for weapons purposes, these measures would seek to ensure that the quantitative reductions made in the START treaties cannot be reversed in the future.

Although the post-Cold War nuclear arms control efforts have made significant progress in achieving quantitative reductions in nuclear weapons, qualitative restrictions and openness measures have so far been largely ignored. They cannot for long if further progress in limiting nuclear weapons is sought. Greater openness and transparency regarding the development of nuclear weapons-related technologies would result in a more stable deterrent posture at START-II force levels and will most likely be a prerequisite for building sufficient confidence to embark on further and deeper cuts in nuclear forces. In addition, reducing US and Russian forces to minimum deterrence levels of some hundreds of weapons may require constraints on the development of offensive and defensive military technologies. Any prospect of moving away from a reliance on mutual nuclear deterrence towards mutual nuclear reassurance will most certainly depend on a high degree of transparency and strict and verifiable limitations on certain types of military development. In short, nuclear confidence-building measures (CBMs) and development restrictions will become an increasingly important element on the nuclear arms control agenda.

Confidence-building measures, which mandate a degree of openness about certain military programmes or activities, have already been implemented in several different political contexts, both on their own and as a complement to quantitative arms control measures. For example, since the 1980s CBMs have been applied extensively in Europe to address conventional force deployments. The Vienna accords and the Treaty on Conventional Armed Forces in Europe (CFE) include measures such as on-site inspections and information exchanges to provide increased openness about the military capabilities and intentions of each nation. The Open Skies Treaty provides for surveillance overflights of the entire territory of the signatory states. Restrictions on the development and testing of certain types of military technologies also have precedents. Examples include the nuclear Non-Proliferation Treaty (NPT), which prohibits the non-nuclear weapons states that are signatories from using fissile material to develop nuclear weapons; the Anti-Ballistic Missile (ABM) Treaty, which restricts the development of ABM systems; and the Chemical Weapons Convention (CWC), which prohibits all signatories from developing any chemical weapons.

Now is the ideal time for the United States and Russia to pursue confidence-building measures. As James Macintosh has noted,[3] CBMs are best suited to improving relations between 'suspicious but not belligerent' states. Thus, the best time to apply CBMs is when the relationship between states is at least somewhat co-operative but needs strengthening, as is currently the case with the US-Russian strategic relationship. Moreover, while two or three years ago the US-Soviet relationship was improving so rapidly that it seemed that any attempt at negotiated arms control would be quickly superseded, that process of improvement has slowed, and the break-up of the Soviet Union and the political uncertainty in Russia suggests that arms control and confidence-building measures can play a particularly useful role now.

This paper examines the desirability, feasibility, and possible means of implementing confidence-building measures (CBMs) and restrictions on the development of nuclear weapons, their delivery systems and related military technologies. It focuses mainly on US and Russian capabilities, although in the future it would be important to include all actual and potential nuclear powers in this regime.

In the following section, the possible advantages of applying CBMs and development restrictions to strategic weapons technologies are considered. The next section briefly discusses the broad types of military technologies that would be candidates for CBMs and development restrictions. The third section examines several examples of arms control treaties that include openness measures and restrictions on the development of specific weapons technologies and considers what lessons from these examples may be applied to devising and implementing nuclear CBMs. The final section makes a number of suggestions on the possible structure of CBMs and development restrictions and how these measures might be implemented in the specific case of US and Russian nuclear weapons.

The Benefits of Nuclear CBMs

Transparency measures and restrictions on the development of US and Russian strategic weapons and related technologies could serve several purposes. These include: enhancing security at START-II force levels, enabling deeper cuts in nuclear arsenals, and facilitating a fundamental change in the US-Russian security relationship from mutual deterrence to reassurance. Moreover, each of these developments would of themselves contribute to advancing the acceptability of the international norm of nuclear nonproliferation.

Enhancing Security at START-II Force Levels

Some may argue that Russia's economic difficulties will render any future nuclear arms agreements spurious because the Russians can no longer afford to develop or deploy new strategic weapons or advanced defences. However, Russia still retains a large nuclear arsenal and will remain a threat without any new investments. In order to reduce this threat, and to make further cuts politically acceptable in Russia, it is very likely that the United States will have to offer Russia more security incentives in the form of reciprocal restrictions and transparency measures on the development of new nuclear weaponry and strategic defences. It would therefore be very short-sighted for the United States to take the position that the Russian economy obviates any need for the United States to negotiate measures mandating mutual openness or mutual restraint.

To build on the progress made in the last few years and to enhance security at START-II force levels, it would be desirable to enhance predictability about future nuclear force structures in the qualitative as well as quantitative dimension. Implementing transparency and other confidence-building measures could enhance both predictability and arms race stability. Such measures would eliminate one of the incentives for ongoing research and development (R&D) of advanced offensive and defensive technologies, which is to avoid 'technological surprise'.[4] In the absence of greater openness, engaging in R&D is often deemed necessary in order to gain information about what R&D the other country is capable of doing and, therefore, may actually be doing. For example, the US Department of Energy budget request for fiscal year 1993 stated that one of the major nuclear weapons-related missions of the national laboratories is 'avoiding technological surprise and assessing potential threats'.[5] The need to avoid technological surprise is therefore a continuing motivation (or at least is presented as such) for US nuclear R&D, despite the fact that it is generally assumed that Russia's economic difficulties will severely limit its ability to develop new nuclear weapons in the future.

Research on anti-ballistic missile technologies provides a good example of research being undertaken at least in part to avoid technological surprise. The ABM Treaty, which came into force in 1972, is an example of qualitative arms control in that it prohibits the development, testing (which is an advanced stage of development), and deployment of certain ABM components and systems. The ABM Treaty does not, however, include any restrictions on research, since restrictions on the early stages of R&D could not be verified by national technical means (NTM), and more intrusive inspections were not politically acceptable at that time. Moreover, it was argued that by engaging in ABM research each country would be better able to know what the other was capable of and be better prepared to avoid technological surprise.

In the absence of openness measures, engaging in R&D (in conjunction with applying intelligence methods) may in fact be the best available method of estimating the capabilities of another country. However, this method has clear limitations, since weapons technology is not necessarily developed at the same rate or in the same way in two countries and different countries may make different political decisions about which technologies to pursue. Moreover, relying on this method of prediction tends to encourage worst-case analysis in that absent information to the contrary, one would assume that anything a country is believed capable of doing it will in fact be doing.

Openness measures can supply much more reliable information about the state of development of a given technology in another country. For example, in the late 1980s one of the arguments advanced by Congressional supporters of the Strategic Defense Initiative (SDI) programme was that the Soviet Union had succeeded in developing an advanced ground-based laser that was capable of shooting down satellites and that would be ABM-capable in the future. The United States therefore needed to increase SDI funding to 'catch up'. This laser was purportedly being developed at the main Soviet ABM and air-defence research facility in Sary Shagan. When Moscow then allowed a team of US scientists and Congresspeople to visit Sary Shagan in July 1989, the Americans found that no laser of such capability existed, and that the Soviet ABM laser programme was actually less advanced than the US programme.[6] The visit to Sary Shagan is an example of a transparency measure that was explicitly designed to enhance US confidence about the Soviet ABM programme. As such, it undercut the 'we need to catch up with the Soviets' argument for increased SDI funding.

In order to enhance predictability at START-II force levels, it may not be necessary to restrict R&D more than it is already, but only to make the process more open so each country would have confidence that it knew what the other was doing. Increased openness would then provide a longer time to react if necessary, which would reduce the incentive for ongoing R&D in the first place.

Transparency measures would also enhance crisis stability at START-II force levels. While the risk of a nuclear exchange is currently very small, as long as nuclear weapons exist this risk is not zero. How might a nuclear exchange start? The most plausible scenario involves miscalculations and erroneous assumptions about the other country's first strike capabilities and intentions during a time of increased tension. As James Goodby has noted, confidence-building measures both reduce the chance that a crisis will develop by increasing stability during normal times, and increase stability and reduce pressures on decision-makers during a crises should one develop.[7] There is a strong psychological component to crisis stability, and co-operation in transparency will make worst-case judgements during a time of crisis less likely, as well as reduce the likelihood of crises occurring.

In the absence of development restrictions, however, if either country did continue to pursue certain military technologies, openness measures would provide confidence but not security. Thus, to enhance security as well as predictability at START-II force levels, it may be necessary to negotiate development restrictions in addition to transparency measures. Development restrictions could also be useful in increasing crisis stability. For example, by restricting the development of anti-satellite weapons (ASATs), the future invulnerability of early warning satellites could be ensured, which would enhance crisis stability.

There are several additional reasons why including development restrictions as well as transparency measures may be important to increasing security at START-II force levels. First, transparency measures will be most politically acceptable for those technologies that both countries have agreed not to pursue, and it may be possible to implement intrusive measures only for such restricted technologies.

Second, without restrictions, there exists the danger that decisions about what military technologies should be developed and deployed will be subjugated to the pressures of the weapons labs and other defence industry interest groups. For example, by allowing research and some development on strategic defences to continue, the ABM Treaty may ultimately only postpone rather than cut off this line of weapons development. By the mid-1980s, R&D on ABM systems had put both countries, and particularly the United States, in a position where advances in technology could be used by missile defence proponents to undercut the political and strategic arguments against building strategic defences that were fundamental to the ABM Treaty. Despite the fact that none of the technological advances made any of the strategic arguments less valid, they resulted in calls for abandoning or modifying the treaty. Thus, if it had been possible to include verifiable restrictions on the early development stages of strategic ABM technologies in the ABM Treaty, the decision embodied in the treaty – that US and Soviet security would best be guaranteed if neither country deployed strategically significant ABM systems – would not have been undermined by arguments about the technical feasibility of SDI.

Perhaps the most important reason for incorporating development restrictions in a future nuclear weapons security-building regime is that modernization is often viewed by the other country as an indication of political intent. Thus, during his confirmation hearing to become the next US Secretary of Defense, Les Aspin expressed concern about Russia continuing to modernize its strategic nuclear weapons. Aspin and CIA analysts offered two possible explanations for Russia's ongoing R&D programme: either the programme was continuing largely by inertia or the weapons were being developed by 'people who have a different view of the world' from the Russian leadership.[8] It apparently was not considered possible that the Russian leadership could be deliberately engaged in this work and still have a benign view of the world. Rather, deliberate Russian modernization indicates to US politicians that Russia is potentially hostile to the United States. The fact of Russian modernization is considered something to worry about, notwithstanding that this does not violate any treaty, that no agreement to halt modernization has even been discussed, and that US modernization is continuing as well. In view of these suspicions, a US-Russian agreement to renounce certain new weapons developments could be critical to building confidence between the two countries, even at START-II force levels.

Promoting Deep Cuts in Nuclear Forces to Minimum Deterrent Levels

Russia's warmer relationship with the West opens the possibility of deep reductions in existing arsenals to minimum deterrent levels, which could be an important means of increasing international security.[9] However, in order to make this possible, both nations will want guarantees that new offensive or defensive developments that could undermine their deterrent will not be pursued by the other. In general, there is an inverse relationship between the size of nuclear forces and stability: the smaller a country's nuclear forces are, the more sensitive is its retaliatory capability to new offensive or defensive developments by another country. Moreover, it is likely that this sensitivity will be perceived to be even greater than it actually is. Thus, restrictions on the development of certain technologies as well as openness measures may well be required as part of an agreement to reduce nuclear forces to minimum deterrence levels (hundreds rather than thousands of nuclear weapons).

Restrictions on certain types of military development would establish the longest possible breakout times. In some cases, restricting earlier stages of development would be a complement to restricting testing; in other cases, there may be no visible testing stage and restricting early stages of development would be the only means of control available before manufacture and/or deployment.[10] In fact, if this approach is taken seriously, an assessment of which technologies would be most amenable to verifiable development restrictions should in part determine the optimal composition of a minimum deterrent force. Currently, the United States and Russia guard against vulnerability to potential future developments by maintaining a triad of strategic forces, on the grounds that even if one type of delivery system should become vulnerable, it is unlikely that all three would become vulnerable at the same time.

Even so, despite the deployment of a triad, concern about the reliability of the US deterrent has been raised in the past when just one leg was becoming more vulnerable. For example, in the early 1980s US analysts expressed concern about the 'window of vulnerability', as a result of the purported vulnerability of US ICBMs to a Soviet first strike.[11] At very low numbers of weapons, the potential vulnerability of one type of delivery system may become even less psychologically acceptable. Since deterrence is based as much on perception as reality, it may be preferable for a minimum deterrent force to include only those delivery systems for which openness measures and development restrictions could best ensure invulnerability with high confidence, rather than several types of delivery systems if high-confidence guarantees of invulnerability can not be made for all of these systems. Of course, all delivery systems will have potential vulnerabilities to unforeseen developments, but there may be a difference in the degree to which transparency measures and development restrictions can guarantee invulnerability against foreseeable and possibly expected developments.

Hence, in addition to relying on certain technical features of a delivery system (for example, stealth, mobility or hardness) to ensure future invulnerability in a potentially changing technical environment, invulnerability would be enhanced by controlling the degree to which the technical environment can change. Thus, in guaranteeing the long-term invulnerability of a given delivery system, the ability to restrict verifiably the development of technologies that could be used to defeat that delivery system should be a key criterion by which to judge the adequacy of minimum deterrent forces.

For example, if it is difficult in practice to restrict the continued development of anti-submarine warfare (ASW) capabilities, it may be preferable to have a minimum deterrent force with no SLBMs rather than a dyad or triad (that included SLBMs).[12] This could be true regardless of whether submarines actually could become vulnerable to detection – what matters is the perception that they could. While other views abound,[13] the perception of the growing vulnerability of the US strategic submarine force has increased in recent years. For example, the Senate Armed Services Committee recently stated that the current challenge to SLBM invulnerability is 'truly unprecedented'. Citing recent Russian work that may allow the detection of submerged submarines by non-acoustic imaging of the ocean surface using microwave sensors, the Committee recommended that the United States initiate an 'aggressive' test programme of its own.[14] While current scientific judgement about the long-term invulnerability of SLBMs is important, it should not be the only factor considered in structuring a minimum deterrent force. If there is potential for future scientific disagreement, which there seems to be in this case, then it is possible that doubts will arise about the continued invulnerability of SLBMs in the future.

Facilitating the Transition from Deterrence to Reassurance

While a departure from a policy of nuclear deterrence may be a somewhat distant possibility, it is constructive to think about how the United States, Russia and, indeed, the rest of the world, might move in that direction. Currently, nuclear weapons are deployed to deter both the use of nuclear weapons by other nuclear powers (which is referred to here as 'mutual' deterrence) and the development and use of nuclear weapons by potential new nuclear powers (which is referred to here as 'unilateral' deterrence). Proponents of unilateral deterrence argue that some nuclear powers should maintain their nuclear forces to ensure that no other states will be able to gain a comparative advantage by developing and deploying a small number of nuclear weapons.[15] Of course, while nuclear weapons may deter some non-nuclear states, the deterrent threat may also provide these states with an incentive to acquire their own nuclear weapons.[16]

Eliminating the mutual deterrent function of the existing nuclear arsenals will require the nuclear powers to make the transition from mutual nuclear deterrence to mutual nuclear reassurance. Under a policy of nuclear reassurance, each nuclear power would attempt to reassure the others that its nuclear weapons are irrelevant – in any military or political sense – to their security. Nuclear CBMs and restrictions on military development could have a role to play in effecting such a transition. CBMs and other cooperative arms control measures can reduce 'the salience of military force in interstate relations',[17] and thereby play an integral role in the transition from a relationship between cautious allies to one between security partners.

A regime of nuclear CBMs and development restrictions comprehensive and effective enough to allow such a change could only be brought about in a step-by-step process taking place over a period of many years. Each country would have an opportunity to assess if and how subsequent steps would enhance their security, and whether or not these steps allow them to scale back their military research and development. It is not possible to know with certainty the end result of such a process. However, it is possible to visualize the first few steps and the process can begin with the expectation that the process itself will provide further insights. Deploying minimum deterrent forces would be a logical step towards nuclear reassurance, since doing so requires that each nuclear power reassures the others that it will not attempt to undermine their deterrent. Transparency and other confidence-building measures will necessarily play a large role in the transition from mutual deterrence to reassurance, and development restrictions would become more comprehensive as the transition proceeds.

Advancing the Norm of Non-Proliferation

One of the main benefits of this step-by-step approach is that at each stage there would likely be some non-proliferation value, if only because by implementing transparency measures and development restrictions, the United States and Russia would demonstrate to other countries that they were taking seriously their NPT commitments. Ultimately, non-proliferation and disarmament will require increased transparency and openness on the part of all nations. Implementing nuclear CBMs, especially if it were done with an eye not only toward deep cuts but also toward moving from mutual deterrence to reassurance, would encourage a more equitable world order and discourage further proliferation.

Any hope of dealing effectively with the nuclear proliferation problem in the long term cannot rely exclusively on export controls and technology transfer control regimes.[18] As technology progresses, the capabilities of developing countries (although not necessarily their desire) to develop and deploy nuclear weapons will necessarily become greater. At some point in the future, controlling the transfer of relevant technologies will no longer be possible, because these technologies will be within reach of those countries who may want to develop nuclear weapons. For example, it is generally acknowledged that Japan and Sweden could build a bomb if they decided to do so, and this will be true for more and more countries as the worldwide level of technical development advances.

Export controls can be used to buy time, but stemming proliferation in the long run will require strengthening the international norm against the deployment of nuclear weapons by all countries. It will almost certainly be necessary for the current two-tier system of the nuclear haves and have-nots codified in the NPT to be replaced by something more equitable. However, ultimately the issue of sovereignty may be as important to some countries as having nuclear weapons: to be a have-not means renouncing the 'right' to acquire nuclear weapons and then accepting intrusive verification measures by the International Atomic Energy Agency (IAEA), which monitors compliance with the NPT. If the United States, Russia, and the other nuclear powers were to accept limits on their sovereignty, then it would perhaps be more palatable to other countries to continue to accept such limits. In fact, by adopting the measures outlined below, the nuclear powers would be subject to more verification measures and inspections than would the non-nuclear powers, which is a more appropriate distribution of the verification burden.

Candidate Technologies for CBMs and Development Restrictions

The discussion so far has demonstrated that there are clear benefits to pursuing nuclear CBMs and restrictions on military development. In trying to create a stable and secure environment that would allow deep reductions to minimum deterrent forces, and a move from deterrence to reassurance, several types of technical developments would be candidates for openness measures and restrictions. In particular, these include: new offensive technologies that are designed to increase the capacity to destroy command and control systems or retaliatory forces before they are launched; new warheads, re-entry vehicles (RVs), and delivery systems, especially those that could increase pre-emptive capabilities; and technologies designed to defend against offensive forces and thereby reduce the retaliatory capability of other countries.

There are several factors to consider in deciding which technologies to apply CBMs and development restrictions, and how to do so. First, the specific nature of a given technology will make it more or less difficult to apply CBMs; a more detailed examination will be required for each system in order to determine the degree of difficulty. For example, it will be easier to apply CBMs to missiles, which must undergo flight testing, than to ASW technologies. Second, some military developments will have applications in both the strategic nuclear sphere and in other military areas as well (for example, for use in conventional combat). In such cases, it will be necessary to assess whether distinctions can be made between the various applications and, if so, how transparency measures can be implemented to provide confidence that the strategic nuclear applications are not being pursued. For example, even developing a sophisticated anti-tactical ballistic missile (ATBM) system might interfere with deep cuts since it may not be possible to draw a clear dividing line between the capabilities of strategic and tactical missile defences, and the technologies developed for tactical missile defences will be to at least some extent applicable to strategic defences. If any of the nuclear powers wants to develop tactical missile defences while maintaining missiles for deterrence, then deep cuts will likely require implementing transparency measures between the nuclear powers on all ATBM work done, and perhaps sharing or jointly developing the technology.

There will be other cases where it is not possible to make distinctions between different applications of a given military technology. In such cases the benefits derived in applications for other military purposes (for example, conventional uses) must be weighed against the disadvantages in the strategic nuclear sphere. For example, the development of a real-time satellite surveillance (RTSS) capability would allow real-time tracking of moving objects on the ground, including mobile missiles and tanks. Since it is not technically possible to develop a RTSS system that could track tanks but not mobile missiles, the relative importance of including mobile missiles in a minimum deterrent force and developing RTSS capabilities for conventional warfare purposes must be weighed to determine whether it would be best to restrict the development of RTSS capabilities or eliminate mobile missiles. Thus the technologies and systems discussed below are not necessarily ones that should be included in a CBM regime, but are candidates for further consideration.

Several offensive technologies under development are designed to prevent or limit the launch of a retaliatory strike. These include an enhanced anti-submarine warfare capability based on improved acoustic detection methods and new, non-acoustic means of submarine detection, and a real-time satellite surveillance capability. Both technologies have applications for conventional warfare, so there may be political and military pressures not to restrict their development. In both cases, moreover, much of the development work being done is in advanced computer data processing, which would make such R&D difficult to monitor and verifiably restrict.

Another candidate for inclusion in these measures is anti-satellite weapons (ASATs). Flight tests of kinetic energy ASATs are readily observable and measures to verifiably limit the development of laser ASATs by near-site ground-based monitoring have been proposed.[19]

Potential new delivery systems include long-range, supersonic, stealthy cruise missiles; stealthy strategic aircraft; and new ballistic missiles, especially SLBMs designed for short flight time, depressed trajectories.[20] These systems all feature decreased flight and/or warning times, which make a pre-emptive attack – at least in theory – more possible. On the other hand, the development of these delivery systems could be motivated by ongoing work on ABM or air defence by another country since depressed trajectory SLBMs can be designed to 'underfly' an ABM system, long-range stealthy air-launched cruise missiles (ALCMs) can be used in a stand-off role to overcome air defences, and stealthy aircraft are potential countermeasures to improved air defences. In order to restrict new missile development while allowing the development of space-launch vehicles, on-site inspections of all missile launches would probably be required. Similarly, openness measures on new aircraft could be used to distinguish their features.

New RVs that could potentially be developed include maneuvering RVs (MaRVs), precision-guided RVs (PGRVs),[21] RVs for SLBMs designed specifically to accommodate the extra heating that would be experienced on a depressed trajectory, and RVs for earth-penetrating warheads. In the past, relatively crude MaRVs have been developed (but not deployed) as a countermeasure to missile defences,[22] and if development of ABM systems continues, this might be an incentive to develop new MaRVs. While crude MaRVs would presumably not threaten a minimum deterrent force, PGRVs could. To restrict the development of PGRVs, since flight testing of PGRVs could be disguised as MaRVs, openness measures would be needed to distinguish the two.

New weapons technologies would also include new types of warheads, such as earth-penetrating warheads (EPW)[23] and microwave weapons, and directed energy weapons such as the X-ray laser.[24] A comprehensive test ban (CTB) would remove much of the possibility for developing such new weapons, but both the United States and Russia have been developing inertial confinement fusion (ICF), in part to allow weapons development without warhead testing. ICF would allow weapons designers to achieve the high pressures and temperatures generated by a nuclear explosion without having to detonate a warhead. The other incentive for working on ICF is to develop fusion as a viable energy source. To allow such research to continue, while assuring other countries that this technology is not being used to develop new weapons, transparency measures and joint research projects could be implemented.[25]

Technologies that could defend against the other country's retaliatory forces include ABM systems, such as SDI. It is difficult to envision a scenario in which ongoing development of an ABM system against long-range missiles would not interfere with deep cuts by the nuclear powers as long as they deploy ballistic missiles to maintain deterrence *vis-à-vis* each other. Similarly, advanced air defences could undermine confidence in a minimum deterrence force that relied on nuclear-armed aircraft.

The importance of considering these technologies in an integrated fashion should be apparent from the preceding discussion. For example, if developing ATBM was considered important, then this could be a reason to move to minimum deterrent forces without ballistic missiles. If ballistic missiles are not to be included in minimum deterrent forces, then the development of ASW and RTSS capabilities need not be subject to CBMs and restrictions. On the other hand, if ballistic missiles are thought to be an important component of minimum deterrent forces, then the development of these technologies may interfere with deep cuts.

Feasibility of CBMs and Restrictions on R&D

The underlying premise of all confidence-building measures is that if two or more countries have a genuine desire not to engage in military conflict, their security is better achieved by mutual openness than by mutual secrecy, by measures designed to reassure rather than to deter, by the deployment of military systems that engender mutual security rather than superiority, and by co-operative rather than unilateral defence planning. Since CBMs can only be expected to work if all countries participating want improved relations, it must be assumed that at least a minimal level of trust and goodwill exists.

It follows from this premise that mutual and verified restraint in the application of new technologies to weapons development will result in greater security for all parties than the mutual (or unilateral) pursuit of new, more advanced weapons systems. A clear advantage of a security regime based on such mutual (or, where applicable, universal) restraints is that it reduces the potential for new instabilities and insecurities to develop.[26] However, a comprehensive regime of this sort for nuclear weapons has so far proven infeasible because there have been no practical means of verifying or providing assurance that restraints were mutually adhered to. The verification of such restraints may now be possible, since intrusive on-site inspections are becoming increasingly acceptable and have, in fact, been implemented in recent years.

However, long-held and persistent beliefs stand in the way of implementing nuclear CBMs and restrictions on military development. There has long been a strong belief that R&D, and particularly military R&D, is inherently uncontrollable. This belief has in part been encouraged by scientists who have been involved in the nuclear weapons development process. For example, in his book *Race to Oblivion*, Herbert York, a past director of the US Lawrence Livermore National Laboratory (whose main mission has been to develop nuclear warheads), wrote 'the technological side of the arms race has a life of its own, almost independent of policy and politics'.[27] In fact, the development of nuclear weapons and related technologies did not just 'happen' as if it had 'a life of its own'; it was directed and managed by some of the world's most capable scientists, thousands of individuals worked hard to make it happen, and special facilities and materials, and large amounts of money were required. It is these same features that make it feasible to apply CBMs and restrictions to these activities.

In order to implement CBMs on military R&D, it is useful to consider what aspects of an R&D programme such measures could focus on. In general, CBMs could be applied to five different elements of a research and development programme:

- materials (e.g. fissile material);
- facilities (e.g. uranium enrichment plants, weapons development laboratories);
- activities (e.g. flight testing of missiles);
- budgets; and
- people (e.g. personnel with specific training and/or experience).

The more of these elements the CBMs cover, the higher will be the level of confidence. In fact, the effect will in general be non-linear since it is much more difficult to hide something if the deception has to be consistent in a number of different ways. It can be expected, for example, that if the number of elements included in a CBM regime is doubled, the degree of uncertainty will decrease by more than a factor of two.

But are nuclear CBMs feasible? There are few examples of such measures that apply directly to the nuclear-weapons complexes of the United States and Russia – the narrow limits on nuclear testing contained in the Threshold Test Ban Treaty form the only restrictions on offensive research and development negotiated by the two countries, while nuclear CBMs have so far been confined to the advance notification of ballistic missile flight tests. However, there are a host of relevant experiences in other areas that demonstrate that nuclear CBMs and restrictions on military R&D are not only feasible but also practical. These include the safeguards on nuclear material under the International Atomic Energy Agency (IAEA) regime and the NPT; the verification regime for the Chemical Weapons Convention (CWC); and the confidence-building measures that have been added to the Biological Weapons Convention (BWC) and proposals for a verification regime for the BWC. A review of these examples will not only demonstrate the feasibility of these measures, but also provide valuable insights on how best to apply CBMs to strategic weapons R&D.

Relevant Lessons of IAEA and NPT Safeguards Regime

A principle element of any nuclear CBM regime would be the monitoring of fissile material, which is the key component of a nuclear weapon. Both the United States and Russia currently possess stockpiles of weapons-grade fissile material, which will grow as they dismantle large portions of their tactical and strategic nuclear forces. This material would need to be monitored to ensure that cuts made in nuclear weapons are irreversible and that clandestine weapons construction or transfers of fissile material to other states was not taking place. In addition, a monitoring regime would need to include all nuclear facilities that produce or use fissile material for civilian purposes to insure that this material was not being diverted for weapons purposes. Clearly the experiences of the IAEA regime and the NPT can provide relevant principles and practices that could be adapted for nuclear CBMs to monitor the fissile material stocks and nuclear facilities of the United States and Russia.

The methods used for IAEA and NPT safeguards are very similar, and both are administered by IAEA; for specificity the NPT safeguards will be discussed.[28] There are two categories of NPT signatories: nuclear weapons states and non-nuclear weapons states. The purpose of the NPT is to distinguish between permitted (nuclear power) and prohibited (nuclear weapons) uses of nuclear material on the part of the non-nuclear weapons states that are signatories, and full-scope safeguards – covering all nuclear material – are required for these states. The goal of the NPT safeguards is to detect any diversion of nuclear material, and thus to deter diversion by the possibility of detection. The safeguards are intended to provide 'timely' detection of the diversion of a 'significant' quantity of nuclear material for weapons or unknown purposes. Timely detection refers to the length of time it would take to convert the material into a form suitable for a nuclear weapon; significant quantity refers to the amount of a given material that would be needed to build a weapon.

NPT safeguards are primarily based on material accountancy – keeping track of all nuclear material throughout the fuel cycle. Non-nuclear weapons states that are NPT signatories must declare all fissile material. In addition, to enable the IAEA to determine how best to monitor the fissile material and apply safeguards, design information on any facility that will have fissile material in it must be given to the IAEA before the introduction of the material. In the past, countries were required to notify the IAEA of the existence of any such facility 180 days in advance of the introduction of fissile material, but this has recently been changed in response to the discovery that Iraq, despite being a member of the NPT, was making progress toward building a nuclear bomb. The new rules require IAEA notification as soon as the construction decision is made.[29] Thus, while facilities are only monitored if they have or will have nuclear material in them, these facilities are now a more integral part of the NPT safeguards.

The method used to monitor fissile material is by self-reporting, with verification of these reports conducted by on-site inspections. Each non-nuclear weapons state is required to set up a 'State System of Accounting for and Control of Nuclear Material', which must include a measurement system for the fissile material received, produced, shipped, lost, etc; an evaluation of the precision and accuracy of the measurements taken; and the means for taking a physical inventory. The verification of non-diversion is accomplished primarily by routine inspections, the purpose of which are to verify that the reports submitted by each state to the IAEA are consistent with the state's records, to verify the location, identity, quantity and composition of all safeguarded material, and to verify information on the possible causes of any fissile material that is unaccounted for and of any shipper/receiver differences. Verification methods include examining records, making measurements of all safeguarded material, determining whether the state's instruments and measuring equipment are calibrated and functioning properly, applying surveillance and containment measures (such as closed circuit TV and seals and tags), and taking and analysing material samples at key surveillance points.

There are two types of safeguards agreements, a general agreement that applies to all signatories, and a more specific one that is negotiated for each country. The general safeguards agreement spells out the maximum allowed routine inspection effort in terms of person-days per year for different types of facilities handling certain amounts of material, but the actual intensity of inspections for a given country is related to the quality and effectiveness of its State System of Accounting. The specific agreement covering routine inspections, which specifies such details as which containment and measurement methods are to be used for each declared facility, are negotiated in 'subsidiary arrangements' and 'facility attachments' between the IAEA and each country. These subsidiary agreements are confidential, reflecting the concern about revealing proprietary information that prevailed when the NPT was negotiated. Moreover, while the annual IAEA report is public, the safeguards implementation report – which does not include a country-by-country breakdown – is only available to member states.

The standard procedures for routine inspections, which are considered to work quite well for declared facilities,[30] vary for different types of facilities. For fuel fabrication facilities, the inspectors verify that the material received is the same as that shipped, monitor the fabrication process to ensure the isotopic content of the fuel, and seal the fuel containers when they are shipped to the reactor. At the reactor, the inspectors verify the integrity of the seal on the fuel container, observe the removal of the seal and the placement of the fuel element in the reactor, possibly seal the reactor after loading and possibly install cameras to monitor any places through which a fuel canister might leave the reactor. An inspector is usually present when the reactor is opened for refuelling or maintenance. The spent fuel is moved to a storage pool to cool off, and the racks in the storage pool are sealed and monitored via camera. When the spent fuel is reprocessed, it is sent under seal to the reprocessing plant. When the reprocessing starts, there are usually inspectors at the facility full time to monitor the process of plutonium separation and conversion to plutonium-oxide. The finished product – reactor fuel – is sealed in a container and placed in storage until it is again placed in a reactor.

In addition to routine inspections, the IAEA can conduct two other types of inspections: *ad hoc* inspections and special inspections. *Ad hoc* inspections are used to verify the initial report of a state just joining the NPT, and for identifying nuclear material before transfer into or out of the state. The IAEA can ask for a special inspection if routine inspections are not adequate to verify non-diversion.

The IAEA safeguards have been strengthened rather than undermined as a result of the Iraq episode: in addition to adding the early notification requirement for nuclear facilities, in 1992 the IAEA Board of Governors recently clarified what is authorized by the special inspection provision of the IAEA safeguards document. The board reaffirmed that the right to conduct special inspections includes 'challenge' inspections of undeclared facilities, thus clearly giving the IAEA the right to conduct challenge inspections of suspect sites. However, the director of IAEA, Hans Blix, has said that since the IAEA has no independent intelligence resources, the organization has had no basis for requesting challenge inspections of undeclared facilities.[31] (In fact, in order to carry out the post-Gulf War inspections in Iraq,[32] the IAEA has relied on intelligence information provided by member states and Iraqi defectors.) To address this shortcoming, Blix has now requested member states to provide, in a confidential manner, relevant intelligence information to the IAEA. This information will then be evaluated by Blix and a small number of his staff to determine if this information merits a suspect site inspection. On the basis of such information, the IAEA recently made its first request for a challenge inspection – of two North Korean facilities. If the suspect state refuses to allow an inspection, the IAEA Director will report this to the IAEA Board, and then the matter can ultimately be referred to the UN Security Council, as happened in the case of North Korea.[33]

There are several relevant lessons from the NPT and IAEA safeguards for transparency measures and development restrictions for strategic weapons technologies. First, requiring self-reporting of specific information by each state is a useful way to structure CBMs, and these declarations also provide a concrete set of items to verify. Second, while IAEA routine inspections apparently provide adequate confidence that material is not being diverted from declared facilities, there were some weaknesses in the routine inspection regime, in part because until recently it directly included only one of the five relevant R&D elements, that is, materials. Thus Iraq's development of calutrons for uranium enrichment – the discovery of which caused great concern about Iraq's incipient nuclear weapons capability – was not a violation of the NPT since no nuclear material had been introduced in these facilities. In addition to material, certain facilities (those that will contain nuclear material in the future) must now also be declared once a decision is made to build them. With more R&D elements included in the NPT safeguards, the confidence level of inspections can be expected to increase. However, the NPT could be further strengthened and the efficacy of routine inspections improved, if the types of facilities to be declared were increased. For example, declarations could be required for facilities that will not contain fissile material but are relevant to acquiring a nuclear weapons capability, such as factories that make centrifuges or other nuclear-related equipment. The lesson for US-Russian nuclear CBMs is that it will be important to incorporate several of the five R&D elements in such a regime.

Finally, the recent IAEA clarification of its special inspection rights demonstrate that while it is important to make routine inspections as useful as possible, the right to conduct challenge inspections of non-declared facilities is critical to maintaining international confidence in a verification regime. Moreover, the Iraqi case showed that this right is meaningless without access to intelligence data that could indicate where to conduct such challenge inspections. On the other hand, if intelligence data are available, the IAEA inspections in Iraq demonstrate that challenge inspections can provide a much better means of establishing treaty compliance than intelligence alone.

Relevant Lessons of the Chemical Weapons Convention

Undoubtedly the most problematic element of nuclear CBMs will be implementing transparency measures and development restrictions for strategic weapons facilities. Ensuring transparency and verification of development restrictions will necessarily entail intrusive inspections of facilities used for R&D purposes. Gaining acceptance of such measures may prove politically difficult. Both the United States and Russia are apprehensive that such intrusive inspections will jeopardize state secrets, while civilian companies engaged in defence contracting will have concerns about the security of proprietary information and technologies. The Chemical Weapons Convention, to which both states are signatories, offers insights that may be pertinent to devising transparency measures for application to R&D facilities, and provides guidance for the construction of nuclear CBM regimes more generally.

The Chemical Weapons Convention prohibits the use and development, production, acquisition and stockpiling of chemical weapons.[34] It will be implemented and administered by a body similar to the IAEA – the Organization for the Prohibition of Chemical Weapons (OPCW). Unlike the NPT, which has two categories of membership, the provisions of the CWC will apply to all members equally. All signatories to the CWC must declare all chemical weapons production facilities that have been in use since 1946 and all chemical weapons stocks, and verifiably destroy these facilities and stocks within ten years of the convention entering into force. The declarations will be verified by on-site inspections, the chemical weapons in storage awaiting destruction must be sealed and monitored, and the destruction of chemical weapons stocks and former production plants must be monitored.

Most relevant for the discussion here, however, are the provisions for ongoing monitoring of commercial and government chemical facilities that manufacture or use chemicals that could be used in chemical weapons. As with the IAEA safeguards, the goal of the CWC is to verify that certain materials (in this case, certain chemicals) are not being used for prohibited purposes. Three different categories of chemicals, which are listed in three 'schedules', are covered by the CWC, and there are three corresponding levels of inspections and control. All facilities that produce, process, consume or store more than a specified amount (which varies with the chemical) of any of the chemicals listed on the three schedules must be declared. At slightly higher thresholds of these chemicals, these declared facilities become subject to routine inspections. Other 'relevant' facilities – plants producing more than specified amounts of any other organic compounds – must also be declared; it will be decided in the future if these facilities will also be subject to routine inspections. By some estimates as many as 10,000 chemical plants world-wide could be subject to routine inspections.[35] Schedule-1 chemicals are the chemical weapons agents banned by the CWC.[36] Schedule-2 chemicals are key chemical weapons precursors that have significant commercial applications, whereas Schedule-3 chemicals are commercial chemicals produced on a large scale that have the potential to be used as chemical weapons or have been used in the past for chemical weapons (for example, phosgene in World War I) but are less effective than Schedule-1 chemicals.

Since most of the facilities that will be monitored are commercial, an important consideration in designing the verification measures was to protect proprietary information. Chemical manufacturers associations in the United States, Canada, Australia, Europe and Japan were closely consulted during the negotiation process, and in fact proposed an inspection plan that included 'anywhere, anytime' challenge inspections.[37] One of the few conditions these groups insisted upon was that any analysis of samples be conducted on site to protect proprietary information from leakage.[38]

The non-production of Schedule-1 chemicals will be verified at all declared facilities by sampling; modern equipment can detect materials at concentrations of up to one part per trillion,[39] and therefore allows easy determination of the presence or absence of any banned chemical. Samples may be taken from storage tanks, nearby soil, the waste stream, and production batches. The operations of the facilities that are allowed to produce Schedule-1 materials will be monitored through both on-site inspections and on-site instrumentation. Routine inspections of declared Schedule-2 facilities will verify the absence of Schedule-1 chemicals and the consistency of the declarations of Schedule-2 chemicals. These inspections will rely heavily on in-plant examinations and sampling. A subsidiary facilities agreement (similar to IAEA subsidiary agreements) must be negotiated for routine inspections of each such facility. Advance notification of 48 hours is required for these routine inspections, but this should not present a problem since the detection equipment is very sensitive, making it extremely difficult to hide the presence or previous presence of prohibited chemicals. The routine inspections for Schedule-3 chemical facilities (and for other relevant facilities subject to inspection) are less intrusive, and require 120 hours advance notice. In this case, the degree of access that the inspectors will have is not guaranteed, but will depend in part of the consent of the inspected state. No facilities agreements are required. These inspections are intended to be qualitative in nature, with their purpose being to verify that scheduled chemicals are not present, but not to determine what chemicals are present. With the exception of Schedule-1 facilities, the facilities to be inspected will be selected randomly from those declared, with no state subject to more than 20 routine inspections annually, and no facility subject to more than two inspections annually.

Challenge inspections are an explicit and central feature of the CWC. Since the number of declared commercial chemical facilities in a state can be very large compared to the annual quota of routine inspections of those facilities,[40] provision was made to inspect any of these facilities about which suspicions arise. Moreover, the production capabilities in facilities that either do not produce any of the listed chemicals, or do so under threshold for declaration, will be undeclared and will not be subject to routine inspections. In theory, at least, these production facilities might have the equipment and capability needed to produce chemical weapons. Challenge inspections can also be used to inspect any of these facilities. Finally, challenge inspections will allow the OPCW to determine whether clandestine chemical weapons activities are occurring at any facility.

Challenge inspections of any suspect facility will be conducted by OPCW at the request of any one of the member states, although the request can be denied if 75 per cent of the Executive Council, voting within 12 hours of the request, determines that it is frivolous or otherwise inappropriate. While the inspection will be conducted by the international inspectorate, the requesting state has the right to send an observer. Member states cannot refuse a challenge inspection of any site. Access to the challenged site must be granted, but the challenged state has the right to negotiate the degree of access with the inspectors. The challenged state also has the right to propose alternative means of demonstrating its compliance.

A major feature of challenge inspections is the right of the inspected party to manage access to the inspected site. The concept of 'managed access' was developed by Britain, which conducted numerous trial inspections in some of their most sensitive military and commercial facilities and found that sensitive information could be adequately protected. Under managed access, the challenged country can protect sensitive information by, for example, shrouding equipment, turning off computers, and providing access to only a percentage of the buildings or rooms within the perimeter of the inspected site, with the proviso that the specific buildings or rooms that the inspection team will have access to are selected by the inspection team itself. By having only selective access, the inspectors will presumably not be able to get a full picture of the activities taking place, but since they choose the sites randomly, they can have confidence that if they find no prohibited materials or activities this is not the result of manipulation.[41]

Another quite important provision of the CWC is that member states are required to pass 'national implementation measures', which is national legislation supporting the CWC. In this way, another layer of insurance will be added to the verification provisions, since any treaty violations will be violations of both international and domestic law.

The CWC contains important lessons for transparency measures and development restrictions for strategic weapons technologies. First, the concept of managed access embodied in the CWC is broadly applicable to a variety of facilities, and could be an important feature of any on-site inspection regime concerned with the development of nuclear weapons and related technologies. Second, it will undoubtedly be useful in a nuclear CBM regime to establish different levels of routine inspections for facilities that are of varying degrees of concern, similar to the different types of routine inspections that are applied to the three different classes of chemical facilities in the CWC. Third, from the experience with the CWC, the importance of involving relevant industry representatives in designing the inspection regime is clear. The fact that the proprietary concerns of the chemical industry were satisfactorily addressed is encouraging; these concerns may be even more sensitive for the chemical industry than for the arms industry, because even the existence of a certain chemical may be considered to be sensitive information. Fourth, the CWC requires the passage of national legislation implementing the provisions of the treaty. This would be an important measure to include in a nuclear CBM regime, because it backs up international law with domestic law. Finally, by resting the right to request a challenge inspection in member states, the CWC circumvented the problem the IAEA has had in not having access to intelligence information that would enable it to request a challenge inspection of an undeclared site. Since the United States and Russia have extensive intelligence resources, it would be reasonable for such an arrangement to be included in any US-Russian regime as well.

Relevant Lessons of the Biological Weapons Convention

The signatories to the Biological Weapons Convention (BWC) are prohibited from developing, producing, stockpiling or acquiring biological agents or toxins for weapons purposes. The convention does not contain any verification provisions, although there have been a number of proposals to add these.[42] Instead, periodic review conferences of the states parties have been used to add politically binding (but not legally binding) confidence-building measures to the convention in order to increase confidence in the regime.[43] This experience offers certain lessons for designing and implementing transparency measures and development restrictions on nuclear weapons and related technologies.

At the second review conference of the BWC, held in September 1986, several confidence-building measures were adopted. The final declaration provided for the right of any party to request a consultative meeting to resolve compliance concerns. The declaration also provided for the voluntary exchange of information, including the name, location, source of funding, scope and general description of activities of all research centers and laboratories that have high-containment (P4) facilities for handling dangerous biological materials for permitted biological activities. It also requested that information on all outbreaks of infectious diseases relevant to the BWC be exchanged. Member states were further encouraged to publish in scientific journals the results of any research on defensive applications, and actively to promote contacts between scientists engaged in permitted biological research, including joint research and exchanges. Although fewer than half of the BWC signatories have submitted declarations (possibly because they had nothing to declare), both the United States and the USSR have done so. These declarations are publicly available, but they are not published.

The third review conference, held in September 1991, included several additional confidence-building measures in its final declaration. The number of categories on which information was requested was increased to include four of the five R&D elements – facilities, activities, budgets and people. States were asked to declare all current R&D programmes in biological and toxin weapons defence and, for each such programme, were requested to specify its objectives, summarize the main R&D activities, and indicate its sources and level of funding. The same reporting requirements apply to any R&D that is conducted under contract at an industry facility, university, or other institution. In addition, the requested information includes a diagram of the organizational structureof each programme and the reporting relationships. For each facility, states are requested to declare the following: its name and location; the floor area devoted to laboratories of different containment levels; the number of personnel broken down into several categories (military and civilian, scientists, engineers, technicians, administrative staff and support staff, and for the scientists and engineers, their scientific disciplines); funding levels for all research, development, testing and evaluation programmes; and all publicly available reports and publications.

In addition, states were asked to provide historical information on all offensive and defensive biological R&D programmes from 1946 onwards. States were also asked to provide details on all vaccine production facilities, and to report on any domestic legislation that had been enacted in support of the BWC. The reporting requirements for high containment (P4) research labs and disease outbreaks were clarified and details added; a state should now explicitly declare that it has nothing to declare, or nothing new to declare. The procedures for calling a consultative meeting were also elaborated. Most significantly, a group of governmental experts was established to examine verification measures from a scientific and technical standpoint. This group aims to finish its work by the end of 1993. In the past, US administrations have opposed adding verification provisions to the BWC, partly because they believed that the convention's provisions could not be adequately verified, and that any reliance on these measures could therefore give a false sense of security.[44]

A more recent development has important implications for the question of whether adequate verification of the BWC is possible, and for assessing the role of on-site inspections in providing confidence in treaty compliance. Russian President Yeltsin acknowledged in February 1992 that the Soviet Union had been carrying out research on biological weapons for several decades, in violation of the BWC. While Yeltsin ordered all such work stopped in April 1992, the United States and Britain remained concerned that the Russian military was not complying with this order. To address these concerns the three countries reached an agreement on 11 September 1992 that will allow 'any time' on-site inspections of civilian biological research facilities that will include 'unrestricted access, sampling, interviews with personnel, and audio and video taping'.[45] After initial inspections of Russian facilities there will be reciprocal visits to US and British facilities. In addition, working groups will be established to address several further issues: to consider visits to military biological facilities on the same 'anytime, anywhere' basis; to review potential measures to monitor compliance with the BWC and means of testing such measures; to determine jointly whether any of the physical features of the biological facilities (for example, their capacity or any specific equipment) in the three countries are inconsistent with their stated purpose; to consider co-operation in the development of defences against biological weapons; to provide periodic reports to the public and legislative bodies detailing biological R&D activities; and to encourage long-term exchanges of scientists at biological research facilities.

US State Department spokesperson Richard Boucher stated that through these inspections 'we expect to be able to demonstrate to the satisfaction of ourselves as well as to anybody else who's worried about this kind of thing that the Soviet programme to develop offensive biological weapons is effectively ended'.[46] In fact, the desire of the United States to conclude this agreement undermines its past contention that adequate verification of the BWC is not possible. Moreover, US willingness to allow reciprocal inspections indicates that the United States finds such CBMs extremely valuable.

Despite the absence of any verification provision, the BWC contains a number of useful lessons for designing openness measures and development restrictions on nuclear weapons and related technologies. The experience of the second and third review conferences indicates that if verification provisions are considered undesirable, it may still be possible to move in a positive direction by requesting that states declare certain information. The BWC also demonstrates that there is some value in a step-by-step process; measures adopted at the third review conference are much more comprehensive than those adopted at the second conference, giving some indication that most states had become comfortable with the measures adopted at the second conference during the intervening five years and were willing to go further. This step-by-step process could be sped up if there was an opportunity for more frequent review, as there would be for an agreement involving CBMs on nuclear weapons and related technologies because there would be many fewer signatories, at least initially. Indeed, the US-UK-Russian agreement indicates that if there is a desire to demonstrate compliance there are ways of doing so, and that it is possible to come to quick agreement on how to do so when there are only three parties involved. Finally, the measures adopted at the third review conference help to increase confidence by expanding the scope of the requested declarations to include many of the five main R&D elements.

Structure and Implementation of Nuclear CBMs and Development Restrictions

Past experience suggests that the best way to implement CBMs for the development of strategic weapons would be in stages, starting with the least intrusive measures. Over time, CBMs could become more intrusive and evolve into verification provisions for restrictions on weapons development. As their scope is expanded, their application could be as well. Thus, while initially nuclear CBMs could be confined to the United States and Russia, the other nuclear powers could be included next. Finally, all countries with relevant capabilities could join the regime.

Any nuclear CBM regime should at least contain the following elements. First, participants should be required to exchange information on treaty-relevant facilities, material and activities. Such self-declarations would provide the basis for both confidence-building measures and any future verification regime. Second, a verification regime should contain two types of inspections: routine inspections designed to verify each party's declarations, and challenge inspections designed to verify compliance at both undeclared sites and declared sites about which suspicions arise. The less comprehensive the declarations and routine inspections are, the more important will be the challenge inspections. For example, challenge inspections are central to the CWC both because the routine inspections are only statistical in nature (the annual quota for routine inspections can be much less than the number of declared sites in a country) and because all the sites that may be treaty-relevant are not subject to routine inspections (plants producing less than a specified amount of some scheduled chemicals are not subject to routine inspections). On the other hand, the IAEA routine inspections are comprehensive rather than statistical in nature (in theory, all declared fissile material is tracked and accounted for), therefore limiting the need for challenge inspections. As the Iraqi case illustrates, however, even if all declarations are verified, challenge inspections provide a mechanism to inspect activities that were not declared but should have been.

Third, as the Iraqi case demonstrated and the CWC reflects, intelligence assets, both technical and human, are vital to an effective verification regime, because they provide a means of detecting activities, sites or material that have not been declared. Much of the information that the UN Special Commission used in its inspections of Iraq's nuclear facilities came from Iraqi informers. In the United States, the Federal Drug Administration, which is responsible for inspecting all facilities that produce drugs for human consumption, gets most of its information on violations from tips, many unsolicited.[47] Making provisions to protect (and possibly reward) individuals who provide information about possible treaty violations would therefore be useful.

Fourth, requiring all states that are signatory to the treaty to implement national legislation provides an additional layer of assurance. In this case, any person violating the treaty would be violating domestic as well as international law. Any such person would then be under the jurisdiction of their domestic legal system, which might produce an added deterrent, and would give support to whistle blowers and others who would be in the position to expose a secret programme. Finally, at the lowest level of intrusiveness, countries could report all past offensive and defensive R&D programmes, as is required for parties to the CWC and requested of parties to the BWC. These reports could be used in part to assess national intelligence-gathering capabilities. They would also serve as a baseline for future declarations.

As noted above, there are five basic elements of an R&D programme: materials, facilities, activities, funds, and trained and skilled people. Each of these elements is a potential focal point of CBMs, and the more that are covered, the higher will be the level of confidence. In a step-by-step approach, it may be easiest to begin by requiring declarations about funding. First, the United States and Russian budgets should be declassified and made public. In the US, a significant portion of the military budget is 'black', meaning that the amount of funding for a programme, the programme description, and sometimes even the title of the programme are classified.[48] Passing national legislation requiring a declassified budget would add a measure of confidence by adding another layer of legal restraint to that provided by an international agreement. In addition, detailed declarations of budgets for strategic weapons-related programmes could be required.

Next, it will be necessary to obtain information about and gain access to certain facilities. Since government laboratories and defence industries engaged in strategic weapons development may also conduct R&D on other types of weapons whose development may not be restricted, the challenge will be to design measures that provide confidence that any R&D being conducted is permitted and not restricted. For practical purposes, it will be very difficult to restrict basic research into new technologies, both because it is intrinsically difficult to monitor and because in the early stages it often is generally applicable to many purposes. It may therefore be impossible to make a reasonable distinction between what should be permitted and what should be restricted. However, later stages of the development process, when new technologies are applied to weapons systems, would be easier to monitor and more clearly distinguishable from permitted development.

Relevant US facilities for which declarations would be required could be defined as those receiving Defense Department R&D or certain types of Energy Department funding, with a comparable definition for Russian facilities. Initially, declarations of all such facilities could be required, and at a later stage, on-site inspections to verify these declarations could be added. Only some of these facilities would be conducting strategic weapons development, but declarations of all military R&D facilities would be desirable because these would be the most likely candidates for hidden programmes. For any inspections of these facilities, especially those not engaged in strategic weapons R&D, the concept of 'managed access' could be employed.

Activities about which declarations could be required include development testing of certain weapons systems or their components, such as flight tests of missiles or space launch vehicles, flight tests of new re-entry vehicles, and field tests of any components for strategic or tactical missile defence systems. Advance notification of such tests and invitations to observers from other countries or an international inspectorate could be required. Nuclear weapons testing, or a nuclear test ban, could also be monitored by on-site instrumentation and inspections.

The principal material to be monitored would be fissile material, which is an essential component of a nuclear weapon. This will be particularly important if deep cuts in nuclear weapons were made. However, current US and Russian fissile material stockpiles are so large and the amounts of material relatively uncertain that monitoring all material with a high degree of confidence would be infeasible. This is complicated by the fact that the fissile material in use in US and Russian commercial power reactors is not currently monitored either. A first step would be to put all commercial fissile material under IAEA safeguards, as is done in other countries that are NPT signatories. The fissile material from all US and Russian warheads that are dismantled under the START treaties could also be verifiably monitored, and put under IAEA or other international safeguards. At the same time, a ban on the production of plutonium, tritium and highly enriched uranium for weapons purposes could be instituted.

Finally, people with certain kinds of training and experience are an essential component of any development programme, and if a country were engaged in clandestine activities it would need trained and experienced people. To increase confidence that no covert development programmes exist, people with security clearances and a certain level of technical training or experience could be required to enter a registry. This could be a condition of getting a security clearance, and would in fact be less intrusive than some of the conditions individuals getting a security clearance in the United States must currently accept.

A potential US-Russian CBM regime on nuclear weapons and related technologies could in some respects be easier to negotiate and implement than the NPT and CWC. At a basic level, the number of parties involved would be much smaller. There would also be fewer relevant facilities than there are for the CWC. Moreover, the concern about proprietary material and information leaking out during inspections may not be as great as in controlling chemical and biological weapons, since there is no comparable commercial sector. All of the R&D on nuclear weapons and defences is sponsored either directly or indirectly by governments. In the United States, R&D on nuclear warheads is conducted at a few government laboratories and R&D on missiles and other delivery systems is performed at a relatively small number of defence industries, all with government funding. Similarly, R&D on ABM and anti-satellite technologies is conducted at a limited number of Defence Department research labs and private defence industries. Moreover, since the United States and Russia have substantial intelligence-gathering capabilities, CBMs and on-site inspections would be a supplement to rather than a substitute for conventional intelligence-gathering. The problems faced by the IAEA in not knowing where to demand suspect site inspections, would to a great extent be alleviated by an extensive satellite network and other intelligence methods.

Conclusion

This paper has discussed some of the benefits that might be derived from implementing transparency measures and restrictions on the development of nuclear weapons, their delivery systems, and related technologies. These benefits include enhancing security at START-II force levels by increasing predictability and decreasing the incentive for continuing R&D on relevant military technologies, allowing deep cuts in nuclear forces to minimum deterrent levels by reducing the possibility that a nuclear deterrent force could become vulnerable to potential future qualitative developments, and eventually facilitating a transition in the US-Russian nuclear relationship from one of deterrence to reassurance.

While these measures are not without risk, neither is the alternative. Moreover, by implementing nuclear CBMs and development restrictions in a step-by-step process, the benefits of the approach will become apparent before the potential costs become too great. It should be evident, however, that the time has arrived to move beyond negotiating reductions in deployed weapon systems and to begin negotiating transparency measures and restrictions on the development of nuclear offensive and defensive systems and associated technologies, both to enhance US and Russian security and that of the rest of the world,

ACKNOWLEDGEMENTS

The author would like to thank George Lewis and David Wright for useful comments and suggestions, and the editors of this volume, Ivo Daalder and Terry Terriff, for their very helpful editorial assistance. Research for this paper was assisted by an award from the Social Science Research Council of an SSRC-MacArthur Foundation Fellowship in International Peace and Security.

NOTES

1. In the past few years, two private US arms control groups – the Federation of American Scientists (FAS) and the Natural Resources Defence Council (NRDC) – have sponsored five international workshops on the subjects of the verified elimination of nuclear warheads and fissile material controls. These meetings, held in Moscow, Washington, and Kiev, have brought together US and Russian scientists and weapons designers, and Soviet officials to discuss the practical problems of how co-operatively and verifiably to dismantle nuclear weapons and dispose of the fissile material. See Federation of American Scientists, 'Ending the production of fissile material for weapons, Verifying the dismantlement of nuclear warheads' (Washington DC: Federation of American Scientists, June 1991); Christopher Paine and Thomas B. Cochran, 'A How-to Session on Warhead Destruction', *Bulletin of the Atomic Scientists*, Vol. 48, No. 1 (Jan./Feb. 1992); William J. Broad, 'Nuclear Bomb Designers from East and West Plan Bomb Disposal', *New York Times*, 17 Dec. 1991, p. C1; Federation of American Scientists and Natural Resources Defence Council, 'Report on the Fourth International Workshop on Nuclear Warhead Elimination and Nonproliferation held in Washington, DC, February 26-27, 1992', (Washington, DC: FAS/NRDC, March 1992); and Thomas Cochran, Christopher Paine, and Frank von Hippel, 'Report on an International Workshop on the Future of Reprocessing and Arrangements for the Storage and Disposition of Already Separated Plutonium (Moscow, 14-16 December 1992), and an International Workshop on Nuclear Security Problems (Kiev, 17 December 1992)', unpublished.
2. Ashton B. Carter, the new Assistant Defence Secretary for Nuclear Security and Counter Proliferation, and Graham Allison, the new Assistant Defence Secretary for Plans and Policy, can both be expected to push for dismantlement of the warheads eliminated by START I and II and placement of the resulting fissile material into safeguarded secure storage under international custody. See Graham Allison, Ashton B. Carter, Steven E. Miller, and Philip Zelikow (eds.), *Cooperative Denuclearization: From Pledges to Deeds*, CSIA Studies in International Security No. 2, (Cambridge, MA: Center for Science and International Affairs, Jan. 1993). It is important to note, however, that this study makes no mention of verified dismantlement and endorses only selective reciprocity on the part of the United States (see p. 287).
3. James Macintosh, 'Containing the Introduction of Destabilizing Military Technologies: The Confidence-Building Approach', in James Goodby (ed.), *Bipolarity Revisited: North-South Security Issues After the Cold War* (Oxford: Oxford University Press, 1993, forthcoming).
4. A 'technological surprise' is a military technology developed by a country in secret that could be exploited to give that country a military advantage.

5. United States Department of Energy FY 1993 Congressional Budget Request Atomic Energy Defence Activities, Vol. 1 (Jan. 1992), pp. 23–4. The budget request also maintained that new weapons concepts and continued testing were needed to 'avoid technological surprise by exploring new weapons concepts which could constitute potential new threats *or could provide significant enhancements to our own deterrent*' (emphasis added) ibid., p. 67. This statement illustrates the confused and close relationship between avoiding technological surprise and improving national capabilities. Thus, even when the development of a certain technology to enhance US capabilities is rejected, it is still possible for research to continue under the guise of avoiding technological surprise. A good example is research on nuclear directed energy, including the X-ray laser programme, supporting the Strategic Defence Initiative, which, according to the Energy Department, 'has evolved into a threat assessment effort', ibid., p. 24.
6. See Frank von Hippel, 'Visit to a Laser Facility at the Soviet ABM Test Site', *Physics Today* (November 1989), p. 34; and von Hippel, 'Sary Shagan and Kyshtym: A Visit to Soviet Nuclear Facilities', *Science and Global Security*, Vol. 1, Nos. 1–2 (1989), p. 165. Of course, it is possible that the US government was not surprised by the findings at Sary Shagan, but was instead interested in promoting the myth of Soviet superiority to gain Congressional support for increased SDI funding. In this case, it would have been important that the information gathered was made public rather than being made available only to the US government. Given that the Soviet government chose to invite independent scientists and members of Congress rather than administration officials to take part in the visit, it seems likely that it was trying to provide confidence of its behaviour not just to the US government but to Congressional opponents of SDI as well.
7. James E. Goodby, 'Transparency in the Middle East', *Arms Control Today*, Vol. 21, No. 4 (May 1991), pp. 8–11.
8. Paul Quinn-Judge, 'Russia is Upgrading Arms, Aspin Reports at Hearings', *Boston Globe*, 8 Jan./Feb. 1993, p. A8.
9. Creating small, secure nuclear forces could in itself reduce the risk of accidental use, and if the cuts were deep enough, the consequences could be limited in event of their use – accidental or otherwise. There may also be some non-proliferation value to the existing nuclear powers making deep cuts in their arsenals. See Ivo H. Daalder, 'Stepping Down the Thermonuclear Ladder: How Low Can We Go?', in this volume.
10. In order to make deep cuts in nuclear weapons possible, effective controls on fissile material would be most likely needed in addition to controls on the development of certain technologies. There have been numerous suggestions as to how this should be done, including verifying the dismantlement of the warheads to be removed from service under the START treaties, applying international safeguards to the fissile material extracted from these warheads, extending IAEA safeguards to all fissile material in the weapons states with the exception of that in deployed nuclear warheads, instituting a world wide cut-off of the production of fissile material for weapons purposes and eventually banning the production of all weapons-grade fissile material for civilian purposes. See, for example, Theodore B. Taylor, 'Verified Elimination of Nuclear Warheads', *Science and Global Security*, Vol. 1, Nos. 1–2 (1989), p.1; FAS, 'Ending the Production of Fissile Material for Weapons'; Spurgeon M. Keeny and Wolfgang K. H. Panofsky, 'Controlling Nuclear Warheads and Materials: Steps Toward a Comprehensive Regime', *Arms Control Today*, Vol. 22, No. 1 (Jan./Feb. 1992), p. 3.; Jonathan Dean and Kurt Gottfried, A Programme for World Nuclear Security, (Cambridge, MA: Union of Concerned Scientists, February 1992); and Daniel Ellsberg, 'Manhattan Project II', *Bulletin of Atomic Scientists*, Vol. 48, No. 4 (May 1992).
11. See, for example, Paul H. Nitze, 'Deterring Our Deterrent', *Foreign Policy*, No. 25 (Winter 1976-77); and Paul H. Nitze, 'Assuring Strategic Stability in an Era of Detente', *Foreign Affairs*, Vol. 54, No. 2 (Jan. 1976).

12. No opinion on the future vulnerability of SLBMs is implied, or should be inferred, from this discussion.
13. For a sanguine view of SLBM survivability, see US General Accounting Office, 'Unclassified Summary Statement on the GAO Triad Project', inserted in *Congressional Record–House*, 29 Sept. 1992, p. H9862.
14. US Congress, Senate, *Military Implications of the START I Treaty and the June 17, 1992 US/Russian Joint Understanding on Further Reductions in Strategic Offensive Arms*, Report of the Committee on Armed Services, 102d Cong., 2nd Sess., 18 Sept. 1992, p. 18. See also 'Vulnerable Subs?', *Aviation Week and Space Technology*, 28 Sept. 1992, p. 19.
15. See, for example, George H. Quester and Victor A. Utgoff, 'US Arms Reductions and Nuclear Nonproliferation: The Counterproductive Possibilities', *The Washington Quarterly*, Vol. 16, No. 1 (Winter 1993), p. 129.
16. An alternative way to maintain this unilateral deterrent function without at the same time legitimating the possession of nuclear weapons by states would be for all nations to relinquish their nuclear weapons and an international body to retain control over a small residual nuclear force.
17. Ivo H. Daalder, *Cooperative Arms Control: A New Agenda for the Post-Cold War Era*, CISSM Paper 1 (College Park, MD: Center for International and Security Studies at Maryland, Oct. 1992), p. 11.
18. Cf. John Hawes, 'Nuclear Non-Proliferation: New Energy, New Direction', in this volume.
19. 'Laser ASAT Test Verification', Report of the Federation of American Scientists Study Group on Laser ASAT Verification, (Washington, DC: Federation of American Scientists, 20 Feb. 1991).
20. Currently deployed SLBMs are capable of flying on depressed trajectories that result in significantly shorter flight times than SLBMs flown on standard, minimum energy trajectories. However, SLBMs have never been flight tested on such depressed trajectories, and apogee restrictions on flight testing of existing SLBMs could be used to enhance confidence. A short time-of-flight capability could also be enhanced by designing a new booster and re-entry vehicle, so restrictions on such developments would also be useful. Of course, eliminating SLBMs from a minimum deterrent force would eliminate the DT problem. For more details, see Lisbeth Gronlund and David C. Wright, 'Depressed Trajectory SLBMs: A Technical Assessment and Arms Control Possibilities', *Science and Global Security*, Vol. 3, Nos. 1–2 (1992).
21. In my notation, MaRVs are designed to manoeuvre during re-entry but have no terminal guidance, so can be very inaccurate compared to a standard RV. PGRVs also manoeuvre, but for the purpose of improving accuracy; they are equipped with terminal guidance.
22. See, for example, Matthew Bunn, 'The Next Nuclear Offensive', *Technology Review* (Jan. 1988), p. 28.
23. EPWs are designed to burrow into the ground before exploding, thereby increasing the coupling of the explosive energy to the earth. Development of these weapons has been championed as a means of targeting deeply buried underground targets such as command bunkers.
24. Dan Fenstermacher, 'Arms Race: the Next Generation', *Bulletin of the Atomic Scientists*, Vol. 47, No. 2 (March 1991).
25. Annette Schaper, 'Arms Control at the Stage of Research and Development: The Case of Inertial Confinement Fusion', *Science and Global Security*, Vol. 2, No. 4 (1991).
26. For this reason, mutual openness and restraint is also preferable to unilateral openness and restraint on the part of one's potential military adversaries.
27. Herbert York, *Race to Oblivion: A Participant's View of the Arms Race* (New York: Simon and Schuster, 1970), p. 180.
28. The material in this section is based on *The Structure and Content of Agreements Between the Agency and States Required in Connection with the Treaty on the*

Non-Proliferation of Nuclear Weapons in International Treaties Relating to Nuclear Control and Disarmament, (Vienna: International Atomic Energy Agency, 1971); Lawrence Scheinman, *The IAEA and World Nuclear Order*, (Washington DC: Resources for the Future, 1987); Ronald Sutherland, 'General Introduction to the IAEA Safeguards', Walter W. Rehak, 'The State System of Accounting for and Controlling Nuclear Material in the German Democratic Republic', and Eric Payne, 'Canadian Implementation of IAEA Safeguards System: an Evaluation of the Interplay Between the National Board and the International Organization', in Thomas Stock and Ronald Sutherland (eds.), *National Implementation of the Future Chemical Weapons Convention*, SIPRI Chemical and Biological Warfare Studies No. 11, (New York: Oxford University Press, 1990); Ben Sanders, 'IAEA Safeguards: A Short Historical Background', in David Fischer *et al., A New Nuclear Triad: the Non-Proliferation of Nuclear Weapons, International Verification and the International Atomic Energy Agency* (Southampton, England: Programme for Promoting Nuclear Non-Proliferation, September 1992); and Archelaus R. Turrentine, 'Lessons of the IAEA Safeguards Experience for On-Site Inspection in Future Arms Control Regimes', in Lewis Dunn with Amy Gordon (eds.), *Arms Control Verification and the New Role of On-Site Inspection*, (Lexington, MA: Lexington Books, 1990).

29. Jon Wolfsthal, 'IAEA to Implement "Suspect Site" Inspection Powers', *Arms Control Today*, Vol. 22, No. 2 (March 1992), p. 27.
30. The possible exception is for large plutonium bulk handling facilities, for which the measurement error is probably greater than a significant quantity. Plutonium bulk handling facilities are located only in developed countries such as Japan and Canada, so the inability to detect reliably diversion at such facilities has not been regarded as a serious problem.
31. See, for example, Wolfsthal, 'IAEA To Implement "Suspect Site" Inspection Powers', p. 27.
32. The IAEA inspections of Iraqi nuclear facilities are authorized under UN Security Council Resolution 687 (1991), which declared the cease-fire to the Gulf war.
33. Private communication with David Kyd, Director of Public Information, IAEA, Vienna, 21 Jan. 1993. Mr Kyd indicated that since the request has been made, member states have provided intelligence information to the IAEA on states other than Iraq, but that this information had not led to a request for a special inspection. He also noted that although there have been recent media claims that Iran is developing a nuclear military capability, no country had provided any information on Iran to the IAEA that might indicate such claims are justified.
34. The Geneva Protocol of 1925 prohibits the use of chemical and biological weapons, but not their development or production. Information on the CWC is based on *The Convention on the Prohibition of the Development, Production, Stockpiling and Use of Chemical Weapons and on Their Destruction* (United Nations, Conference on Disarmament, 3 Sept. 1992); Lee Feinstein, 'CWC Executive Summary', *Arms Control Today*, Vol. 22, No. 8 (Oct. 1992); and *Chemical Weapons Convention Bulletin*, (Washington DC: Federation of American Scientists, quarterly).
35. George Leopold, 'Civilian Facilities Could Overwhelm Arms Inspectors', *Defence News*, 11–17 May 1992, p. 20.
36. Exceptions are made for research using Schedule-1 chemicals at one small-scale government laboratory that has less than 1 metric ton annual capacity and aggregate amount, the production of less than 10 kg of chemicals per year per facility for medical or research purposes, and the production of less than 10 kg of agent per year at one facility for protective purposes.
37. Apparently, one reason for their strong support of the CWC is that it was good for public relations. See Lee Feinstein, 'Government-Industry Cooperation in Canberra', *Arms Control Today*, Vol. 19, No. 10 (Nov. 1989), p. 25.
38. Amy Smithson, 'Chemical Inspectors: On the Outside Looking In?' *Bulletin of Atomic Scientists*, Vol. 47, No. 8 (Oct. 1991), p. 23.
39. Kyle B. Olson, 'The US Chemical Industry Can Live with a Chemical Weapons Convention', *Arms Control Today*, Vol. 19, No. 10 (Nov. 1989), p. 21.

40. By contrast, the number of facilities containing fissile material is much smaller and under the NPT, all such facilities are monitored through routine inspections.
41. For example, in a trial challenge inspection of a British nuclear weapons storage site, the inspectors were allowed to choose which 20 per cent of the visible storage bunkers to enter. At another site where components for nuclear weapons were designed and produced, one sensitive building was divided into 40 zones, and inspectors chose 20 percent of those zones. Shrouding was used to cover objects too small to be of concern to the inspection. In this case, managed access prevented inspectors from piecing together the purpose of the building or the types and quantities of material used. See Graham Cooper, 'Inspections on Request: Coming to Terms with Their Scope', *Chemical Weapons Convention Bulletin*, No. 10 (Dec. 1990), p. 1.
42. See, for example, Matthew Meselson, Martin M. Kaplan, and Mark A. Mokulsky, 'Verification of Biological and Toxin Weapons Disarmament', *Science and Global Security*, Vol. 2, Nos. 2–3 (1991), pp. 235–52; Barbara Hatch Rosenberg and Gordon Burck, 'Verification of Compliance with the Biological Weapons Convention', in Susan Wright (ed.), *Preventing a Biological Arms Race* (Cambridge, MA: MIT Press, 1990); S.J. Lundin (ed.), *Views on Possible Verification Measures for the Biological Weapons Convention* (New York: Oxford University Press, 1991); Federation of American Scientists (FAS) Working Group on Biological and Toxin Weapons Verification, 'Proposals for the Third Review Conference of the Biological Weapons Convention', Oct. 1990; and FAS Working Group on Biological and Toxin Weapons Verification, 'Implementation of the Proposals for a Verification Protocol to the Biological Weapons Convention', Feb. 1991. The FAS proposals are reprinted in *Arms Control*, Vol. 12, No. 2 (Sept. 1991), pp. 240–78.
43. Information presented here on the BWC is based on *Convention on the Prohibition and Stockpiling of Bacteriological (Biological) and Toxin Weapons and on Their Destruction; Final Declaration of the Second Review Conference of the BW Convention* (United Nations Document BWC/CONF.II/13); *Final Declaration of the Third Review Conference of the BW Convention* (United Nations Document BWC/CONF.III/22); Erhard Geissler (ed.), *Strengthening the Biological Weapons Convention by Confidence-Building Measures* (New York: Oxford University Press, 1990); Nicholas A. Sims, 'The Second Review Conference on the Biological Weapons Convention', in Susan Wright (ed.), *Preventing a Biological Arms Race*, (Cambridge, Massachusetts: The MIT Press, 1990); and Marie Isabelle Chevrier, 'The Biological Weapons Convention: the Third Review Conference', *Politics and Life Sciences* (Feb. 1992), p. 5.
44. Chevrier, 'The Biological Weapons Convention: the Third Review Conference', p. 9.
45. 'Joint Statement on Biological Weapons by the Governments of the United Kingdom, the United States and the Russian Federation', issued 11 Sept. 1992. See also R. Jeffrey Smith, 'Russia Agrees to Inspection of Its Biological Research Facilities', *Washington Post*, 15 Sept. 1992, p. A14.
46. Smith, 'Russia Agrees to Inspection of Its Biological Research Facilities', p. A14.
47. Private communication with Tom Bozzo and other staff from the Division of Compliance of the FDA Center for Biologics, Evaluation and Review in Rockville, Maryland, 7 Jan. 1992.
48. For example, over the past eight years, roughly 20 per cent of the Defence Department R&D budget has been black. See Stephen Alexis Cain, *Analysis of the FY 1992–93 Defence Budget Request* (Washington, DC: Defence Budget Project: 7 February 1991), Table 14.

Rethinking Strategic Ballistic Missile Defences

WILLIAM J. DURCH

In 1972 the United States and the Soviet Union agreed to limit their respective deployments of strategic ballistic missile defences in a treaty of indefinite duration. The Anti-Ballistic Missile (ABM) Treaty, as amended, allows the two countries just one ballistic missile defence site containing a treaty-defined mix of radars and no more than 100 interceptor launchers. Both the radars and the launchers must be fixed in place; they may not roll or crawl about, fly through the air, or go into orbit. For all intents and purposes, excepting the case of a small attack on Grand Forks, in North Dakota, or on Moscow, in the Russian Federation, the two countries have intentionally left themselves defenceless against nuclear ballistic missile attack.

This paper takes a fresh look at the ABM Treaty and the issue of ballistic missile defence (BMD) in light of the end of the Cold War, the dissolution of the Soviet Union and, with it, the demise of the Soviet threat. The remaining threats to American security in this context appear to be political disorder and Murphy's Law. The former may at some point allow unauthorized access to a nuclear missile; the latter suggests that anything that could contribute to a future nuclear missile accident eventually will do so. A modest amount of BMD could be viewed as prudent insurance against the actual occurrence of such disastrous events. However, deployment of limited BMD should take place only within a framework of Russian-American political-military co-operation, including a modified but still active ABM Treaty. Co-operation is necessary for three related reasons: first, to preserve both the perception and the reality of mutual nuclear deterrence for the time being; second, to maintain that deterrent relationship at the lowest feasible force levels; and third, to lay the groundwork for the eventual elimination of strategic ballistic missile forces and the destruction-in-30-minutes threat they pose, and further still, the elimination of nuclear threats even as a 'hip pocket' national option.

The first reason for co-operation acknowledges that both the United States and the Russian Federation would consider a unilateral effort by the other party to make itself invulnerable to nuclear attack to be a threat to its own security. The second suggests that any such effort would be met by a countervailing offensive arms build-up that would wreck arms reduction agreements like START and destroy current progress toward offensive postures consistent with 'minimum deterrence'. And the third looks toward a more distant future in which defensive systems could be used to avoid the instabilities of a Schellingesque 'disarmed world.' In short, because of the historical intermingling of strategic offence and defence in politics and strategy on both sides of the Cold War, and because of the very newness and uncertainty of only recent friendly relations, deployment of missile defences beyond what is currently allowed by the ABM Treaty must be the subject of negotiation and agreement between Washington and Moscow. Asymmetries in politics, in security situations and in technology will make such negotiations difficult. But the United States has no realistic alternative to engaging in such talks if it wishes to give itself, within the next decade, a system to protect its citizens against accidental or unauthorized nuclear missile attack that does not also sabotage arms control at the moment that the endeavor is finally paying dividends on more than twenty years' investment.

This paper concludes that the United States should pursue with the Russian Federation a proposal to deploy between 250 and 300 long-range, ground-based, non-nuclear ballistic missile interceptors within the continental United States. It should abandon efforts to place interceptors in space, but continue to pursue improved space-based sensors that could help fewer ground-based interceptors do a better job. It should continue negotiations toward a joint missile early warning system to which any country could belong. Finally, it should negotiate testing and performance limits on theatre missile defences (TMD) so that systems and technologies for TMD can be clearly distinguished from strategic BMD, be developed and deployed without constraint, and not, at the same time, be a way seriously to undermine the ABM Treaty. Somewhere early in the next century, minimum deterrence would be joined by minimum defence, to produce a transitional strategic arrangement that might be dubbed 'managed vulnerability'.[1]

Post-Cold War Offence and Defence

The two principal alternatives for protecting US territory from nuclear war are deterrence and defence: preventing war by threatening to unleash it, and limiting damage once war breaks out. In a hostile or uncertain political environment, both can generate ongoing arms acquisition, modernization and expansion: deterrence because it proliferates targets and defence because it undercuts deterrence. Defences alone would not be a problem, but defences appear in response to specific threats. They exist in the shadow of the offence and function as close substitutes for it, as Thomas Schelling argued, when they defend against retaliation.[2] Retaliation is what nuclear weapons are good for.

Nonetheless, the American defence community spent the better part of 40 years denying and trying to escape these attributes of nuclear weapons, casting them as both warfighting tools and military equalizers, and distributing short-range weapons throughout the general-purpose force structure as the Soviet Union did the same. Although no one knew how to fight on a nuclear battlefield, policy and forces evolved as though they did. Decision-makers, who felt keenly the danger and futility of relying on nuclear weapons, also felt, if anything more keenly, the need to deliver to Soviet leaders in as stark a fashion as possible the message that the West really would rather be dead than Red, and that if war came it would take them down as well. American leaders periodically recoiled from this formula and set about looking for ways to contain nuclear war if it broke out. This search always tended to upset our allies, since the containment vessel was usually some large fraction of Europe.[3]

'Assured destruction', the ability to destroy a designated fraction of Soviet industry and populace, became the minimum retaliatory planning objective of US strategic forces in the 1960s. 'Damage limitation' became the corollary wartime requirement: that retaliating US forces reduce as far as possible the Soviet Union's remaining capacity for war (and thus its capacity to damage the United States any further). Requirements for offence-based damage limitation are far broader and more exacting than the requirements of assured destruction, which have not changed in decades. Moreover, they evolve with the other side's forces and efforts to protect itself. A damage-limiting offensive doctrine stalks its quarry and works best if employed pre-emptively, when offensive forces haven't suffered attrition from being attacked, and when their command and control system is intact.[4]

These decades-long struggles over how to use nuclear weapons have been a dance of the politically trapped with the morally numbed. American political leaders, who set the nuclear age in motion during World War II and subsequently funded US weapon systems, have had little choice heretofore (beyond personal political oblivion) in the matter of building the arsenal and keeping it on the cutting edge of technology.[5] Until Soviet policy and doctrine changed, neither could US policy.

Soviet foreign policy changed under Gorbachev, but the West remained sceptical that the change was either deep enough or indelible until the coup attempt of August 1991. Thereafter, US policy and behaviour began to change abruptly. President Bush pulled tactical nuclear weapons from the Navy, withdrew Army nuclear weapons, and cancelled most US strategic modernization programmes. Half of the Minuteman ICBM force and all of the bomber force were taken off alert, demobilization of older missile submarines was accelerated, and both sides offered deeper cuts in strategic forces than contemplated during years of START negotiations. US back-up command and control aircraft, airborne constantly in relays for decades, returned to base.[6] In short, when political leaders were no longer stuck in the *pas de deux* of the Cold War, they rapidly shed systems, programmes, and policies that had been dictated by the politics of fear and a narrow strategic logic that bears only passing resemblance to the common sense that guides most human affairs.

Despite declining reliance on nuclear weapons to support US foreign policy objectives, there may yet be future circumstances in which war cannot be deterred or contained by means other than the threat or use of retaliation in kind.[7] Knowledge of how to make fission weapons will never be eliminated, and acquiring the means to make a bomb will not become significantly harder until the industrial world's nuclear allergy is universal, affecting the private sector as well as government. Thus, the world's status quo powers will want to retain some nuclear capability for the indefinite future, if only to be able to face the next Saddam Hussein who builds a nuclear arsenal first before committing aggression or blackmail.[8] And they will want to do more than just retaliate; they will want to defend themselves and whatever expeditionary forces fight the next 'Desert Storm'.

The ABM Treaty and American Politics

The ABM Treaty, signed by Presidents Nixon and Brezhnev in May 1972, was originally intended to be half of an offence-defence bargain. The treaty was designed so that neither side could quickly develop and deploy a defence at the other's expense. It was also designed to facilitate limitation of offensive armaments by stabilizing the requirements for deterrence and helping the two sides avoid an offence-defence arms race. Treaty supporters view it as the long pole in the tent of strategic arms control; since 1977 (when the SALT I interim accord on offensive missiles officially lapsed), it has been the only pole (at least until Ukraine has ratified START). To its critics, however, the ABM Treaty is an instrument for keeping US security in the hands of the adversary and for preventing US achievement of necessary, defence-backed nuclear superiority.

Whereas supporters are guilty of wishful thinking about the meaning and the power of arms control, the critics' charges, while superficially appealing, overlook or deny certain facts about the nuclear age. The first is that insecurity is both mutual and unavoidable at high levels of strategic armament. The second is that meaningful nuclear superiority over the USSR was achievable only if the United States had been willing to engage in all-out weapons competition in perpetuity, or until one side collapsed. The presumed Soviet collapse under desperate competitive conditions might not have been as cost-free for the United States as the actual one was under conditions of growing co-operation, that is, instead of reaching out, Moscow might have lashed out. Although the ABM Treaty did not leave the US in a particularly comfortable position, neither did it rob the country of achievable security in anything but myth.

The agreement came under increasing pressure as the years passed without a complementary limit on offensive weapons (the SALT I Interim Agreement of 1972 limited launchers but not warheads, at a time when both sides were adding multiple warheads to their missiles; SALT II was not ratified but both countries observed most of its provisions in principle). At the same time, however, the task of missile defence was becoming more difficult. Not only were warhead numbers growing, but technologies to penetrate defences were becoming more sophisticated. Decoys, chaff and booster debris coasting along in space with the warheads made it hard for the defence to discriminate true from false targets before the attacking warheads re-entered the atmosphere. In the early 1980s, moreover, the United States shifted BMD research away from nuclear-armed interceptors, making warhead discrimination even more important, since non-nuclear interceptors would need to approach close to their quarry or even hit it head-on to destroy it.[9]

'Point' defences were suggested at various times in the past fifteen years as a possible solution to the predicted vulnerability of land-based missiles to nuclear attack. Able to protect hardened military targets but not society at large, point defences would reduce ICBM vulnerability without contributing to either side's ability to shoot first and fend off retaliation, that is, without undermining the stark threat of destruction thought to underpin deterrence. The catch was that for this to be the case, both Moscow and Washington had to agree to deploy *only* point defences. At the time, Moscow was not interested; its missiles were probably primed for launch when under attack, in accord with a strategic doctrine that called for infliction of maximum damage on the enemy. If that were the case, then in the event of war there would be nothing in the silos to defend.[10] Neither was Washington particulary interested. Pure point defence is the ABM equivalent of the neutron bomb: it saves weapons and lets people die. Both weapons have their military utility, but both are now equally hard sells, politically.[11]

American BMD research returned to its original focus on defence of national territory after Ronald Reagan's speech of March 1983. For its first seven years, the Strategic Defense Initiative (SDI) struggled to find technologies and to design a deployment that could plausibly implement the President's vision. But ambitious vision proved unable to overcome either physics or politics, and the supporting metaphysics also proved somewhat shaky.[12]

On the political front, in the mid-1980s the Reagan administration argued that the ABM Treaty permitted tests of 'exotic' anti-missile weapons in space, where exotic could mean anything not deployed when the treaty was signed in 1972. The traditional interpretation of the treaty held that only immobile, ground-based weapons could legally be developed and tested for strategic ballistic missile defence. This and other development constraints were devised to prevent circumvention of the agreement, for example, by replicating aboard aircraft or in space what was forbidden to deploy on the ground. The Reagan administration argued, however, that the treaty had nothing to say about exotic missile defence technology, thus testing of such technology should be considered unconstrained. The Soviet Union objected to this interpretation; most members of the US delegation that negotiated the treaty objected to it; and congressional Democrats objected. Once the Democrats regained control of the Senate in 1987, a few months after the 'reinterpretation debate' began, Congress inserted language in the DoD authorization requiring that SDI development and testing conform to the traditional reading of the treaty. That language has been reinserted annually ever since.[13]

When President Reagan launched what became SDI, he emphasized the moral superiority of his concept of assured survival over present, mutual vulnerability. The difficulty lay in the transition from one operational reality to the other, especially under conditions of political-military competition. Until a defence becomes good enough to destroy all but a handful of the warheads in an all-out attack, it can break up closely-timed counterforce attacks but cannot do much for society at large. Cities and industry are harder to protect than sheltered nuclear forces, so as defences improve, they would tend to drive a power bent on maintaining its deterrent threat to target cities and industry by default. Deterrence depends, after all, on the capacity to do the damage that one has threatened to do. Imperfect defences in a competitive environment not only would fail to overcome the condition of mutual vulnerability, they would place a premium on non-combatant targeting and drive war planning toward very large attacks.[14]

SDI no longer labours under this difficult charge. It was redirected in early 1991 to protect the country against limited (especially accidental or unauthorized) missile attacks. The system of Global Protection Against Limited Strikes (GPALS) now on the drawing boards would be sized to absorb 200 warheads, the number carried by a fully-loaded Soviet Typhoon-class ballistic missile submarine.[15] The struggle to design a leak-proof missile shield in the 1980s highlighted the problems of defenders who face a determined nuclear competitor. It became increasingly clear that a near-perfect missile defence would be achievable and affordable only if the threats against which it was built were not open-ended.[16] That is, the success of a programme predicated on competition actually depended on some large degree of co-operation between the competitors. Where the arms control equation of the early 1970s restrained defence to encourage restraints on offence, the new equation called for restrained offence to facilitate defence. The path from an offence-based strategic policy to one that is defence-based can be trickier than might be supposed, however, because deterrence is by now a conditioned reflex, and while Russia and the United States are on friendly terms at present, the future is uncertain. Thus the two countries' militaries will wish to maintain robust (that is, relatively large and secure) nuclear strike capabilities, and will track carefully the anticipated ability of any new missile defence system to absorb incoming warheads. Moreover, the policy of Britain, France and China is unclear. Their nuclear forces are not treaty-constrained and presumably they would prefer not to have them devalued by Russian missile defence.

Missile Defences and Russian Politics

Russian opinion appears seriously split on the question of deploying additional ballistic missile defences. In early 1992 President Boris Yeltsin proposed a co-operative Global Protection System against limited missile attack, but it is not clear how much political or bureaucratic backing the proposal had, or has, in Moscow. Some Russian analysts favour defences as a way to keep weapon design bureaux and manufacturing plants operational. Others (for example, elements of the Strategic Rocket Forces) view defences as obstacles to their mission. Some point out that Russia simply cannot afford a programme that would match GPALS, while others note that, for Russia, a missile defence would be of little use without a substantially upgraded air defence system, given the number of potential intruders around its new borders. Russian commentators are more united, however, in their opposition to space-based interceptors, mirroring a long-standing Soviet concern that space-based ABM and anti-satellite (ASAT) capabilities would give the United States an undesirably dominant position in space and, *mutatis mutandis*, on earth.[17]

Russia also reserves the right to withdraw from START should the United States deploy strategic defences in excess of what is allowed by the ABM Treaty. There is not yet sufficient trust of the West, or perhaps more to the point, there are simply no other symbols of great power status sufficiently compelling that the Russian military and the country's political hardliners would be willing to forgo the power to hold US territory at risk. GPALS, as currently planned, is not intended to take the US out of risk, but its backers point to its ready expandability as a hedge against an uncertain future, including 'resurgent militarism' in Russia.[18] Russian critics of GPALS point to the same expandible capability with the opposite concern. So if the US hopes to deploy defensive capabilities much beyond those specified by the ABM Treaty, and to do so with Russian co-operation, it faces a potentially difficult negotiation. But if it tries to do so without Russian co-operation, it could trigger unpleasant Russian countermoves.

The cheapest of these countermoves would be to halt ballistic missile reductions under the START accords. Should US defence deployments take place after the latest round of reductions is completed (as is likely, given current development timelines), the cheapest countermove would be to restore warheads to land-based missiles, then to submarine-launched missiles, and then to build more single-warhead SS-25s and deploy them in existing missile silos. An anticipated need to re-use some silos in that fashion could lead Moscow to slow the destruction of ICBM launchers in the latter 1990s or to keep the SS-25 production line warm longer than would otherwise be the case.

On the other hand, if Russian and American strategic forces are reduced to 3,000–3,500 warheads apiece as envisaged in START II, if Russian politics do not destabilize, and if the West's relations with Moscow remain friendly, then Russian attitudes toward strategic missile defence and its ability to afford it may both improve. Initial co-operative efforts in shared early warning might spread to co-operative efforts in defensive operations. Although trust might never be so great as to permit sharing of weapons technology, increased interoperability of command and communications, officer exchange programmes, and some joint planning could become the norm. (This might be done at first with respect to projection forces and their tactical ballistic missile defence components.)

Moreover, the decreasing size of the two sides' nuclear arsenals makes it possible to contemplate a co-operative, phased transition to a more defence-dominant strategic posture. Fifteen to twenty years of good relations, a stable, democratic political system and a recovering economy would make Russia the functional equivalent of the European Community, and the US does not target the EC, or feel the need to do so, despite the fact that two of its members are nuclear-armed. In such a context, limited missile defences (and limited defences against nuclear weapons delivered by other means), could add to, rather than detract from, international stability. The capacity to deflect a limited nuclear attack would help to ease concerns about possible covert weapons capabilities that might be retained or created in the future. By reducing incentives to hedge in that fashion, defences would help to avoid the Schellingesque instabilities of a disarmed world.[19]

Strategic Force Alternatives for 2010

Offensive Forces

The military logic that drove the size and configuration of strategic forces during the Cold War, and particularly the counterforce logic that produced the gargantuan arsenals of the 1980s, has lost much of its power to persuade political leaders and legislatures. Modernization of US strategic weapons is an all but dead issue in the Congress. The B-2 programme has been capped at 20 aircraft, production of the advanced air-launched cruise missile has been halted, and the small ICBM and mobile MX ICBM programmes have been cancelled. The Trident submarine building programme will end when boats currently under construction are commissioned, rounding out the force at 18. Although production of Trident II (D5) sea-launched ballistic missiles continues for the time being to fill out the launch tubes of the Trident force, no more high-yield W88 warheads will be built for them. Most D5s will use smaller W76 warheads recycled from Trident I missiles that are retired as older missile submarines are withdrawn from service.

Russian cutbacks in offensive nuclear forces have been equally severe. When the US took its heavy bombers off alert status, then-Soviet president Gorbachev took a comparable number of ICBM warheads off alert; their SS-11, SS-13, and SS-17 missiles were slated for retirement. Non-strategic naval nuclear weapons are said to have been withdrawn from the fleet, mirroring US actions. Production of strategic ballistic missile submarines has ceased and no follow-ons to the latest Typhoon and Delta IV classes are in evidence. Remaining submarine production in the Russian Far East is to be halted and all future production is to be concentrated in naval yards in Russia's northwest. Production of large SS-18 and SS-24 ICBMs (both built in the Ukraine)

FIGURE 1
US AND RUSSIAN STRATEGIC WARHEADS
START AND POST-START DRAWDOWN OPTIONS

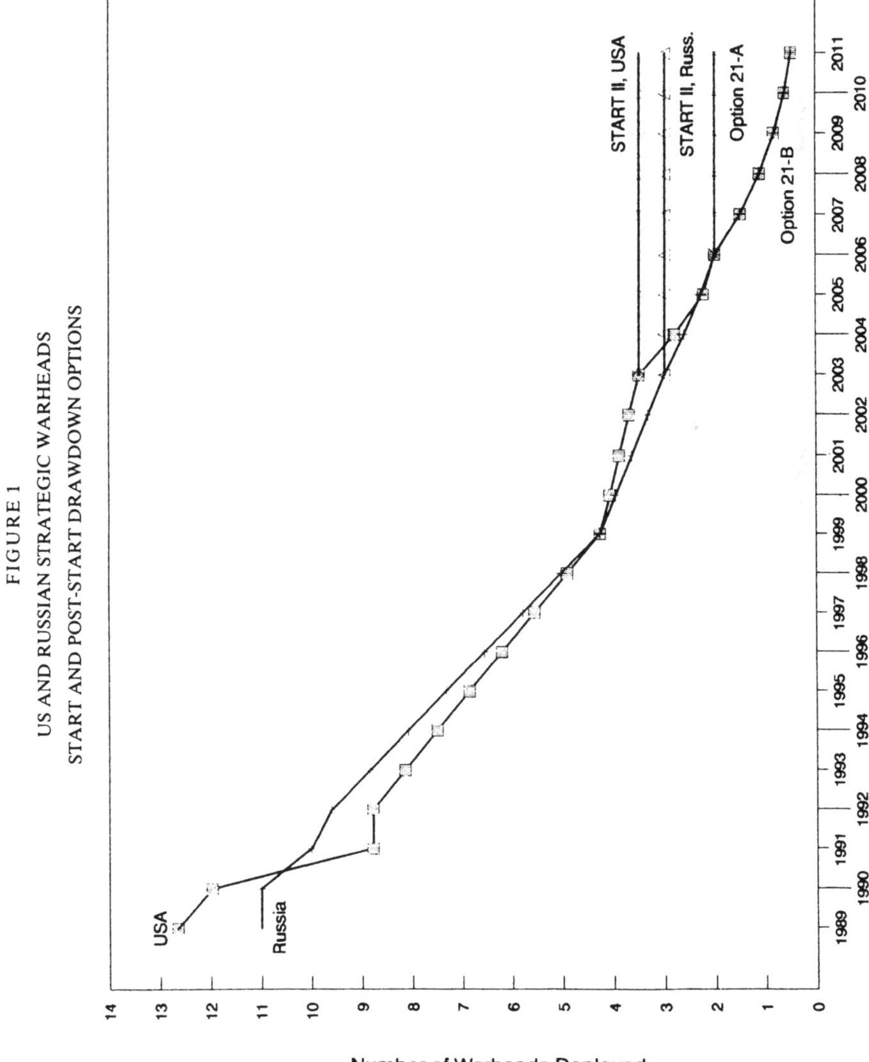

has ceased, and development of follow-on missiles appears to have slowed down or stopped for the moment. Production of Blackjack strategic bombers has also been halted. Two supersonic cruise missile programmes (the AS-X-19 air-launched and SS-NX-24 sea-launched missiles) have been cancelled. All non-strategic nuclear warheads have been removed from the now-independent states of Kazakhstan, Ukraine and Belarus, and sources suggest that a good number of warheads have been removed from strategic missiles still deployed in those countries.[20]

Figure 1 plots the declining size of US and Russian strategic nuclear arsenals, assuming that START II is fully implemented by 2003. Remarkably quick to be negotiated and representing substantially deeper cuts in strategic forces than achieved by any other arms accords, the new agreement really represents a kind of return to normalcy, namely the substantial reduction of US armed forces when a war is finished. Now that the Cold War is over, strategic forces are no longer needed in the quantities or configurations to which their handlers have become accustomed.

US strategic planners argue that the warhead levels of START II represent a 'rock bottom' number for executing US targeting plans.[21] But what is 'rock bottom' depends precisely on strategy; on what the offensive forces are supposed to accomplish by way of peacetime deterrence and wartime tasks. If strategy were to change and particularly if conventional forces were to assume responsibility for a large measure of extended deterrence US and Russian central strategic forces could be taken down to the lower levels sketched in Figure 1 by 2003–2010, by sticking to the glide slope for implementing the terms of START II. Whether these further steps prove feasible depends, of course, on the conditions of co-operation outlined earlier. But anticipating levels to which the two arsenals might ultimately be reduced is necessary to determine a ceiling on strategic defence capability that could facilitate, rather than prevent, such reductions.

START II will leave the United States 432 sea-launched ballistic missile launchers, carrying missiles with four warheads apiece, aboard 18 SSBNs; 500 single-warhead ICBMs; and 100 accountable heavy bombers (Table 1). Comparable Russian forces are likely to include 456 sea-launched missiles aboard 27 SSBNs, just under 500 single-warhead ICBMs, and 100 bombers (Table 2).

Some argue that implementing START II alone will prove difficult, and that further reductions are fanciful. But economics has a way of tickling strategy and causing it to adapt in unpredicted ways. The world is likely to remain an unsettled place, but the causes of most trouble are

TABLE 1

US STRATEGIC FORCES

Launcher Type	Remaining Launchers			Warheads on Launchers		
	Pre-START 1990	START I 1999	START II 2003	Pre-START 1990	START I 1999	START II 2003
Heavy Bombers	(276)	(208)	(100)	(4436)	(3700)	(1272)
B-52	181	93	80	2916	1860	1018
B-1B	95	95	0	1520	1520	0
B-2	0	20	20	0	320	254
Land-based Missiles	(1000)	(550)	(500)	(2450)	(1400)	(500)
Minuteman	950	500	500	1950	900	500
MX	50	50	0	500	500	0
Sea-based Missiles	(672)	(432)	(432)	(5760)	(3456)	(1728)
C3, C4/W76	576	192	192	4992	1536	768
D5/W-76	0	144	144	384	1152	576
D5/W-88	96	96	96	384	768	384
Totals:	**1948**	**1190**	**1032**	**12646**	**8556**	**3500**

TABLE 2

RUSSIAN STRATEGIC FORCES

Launcher Type	Remaining Launchers			Warheads on Launchers		
	Pre-START 1990	START I 1999	START II 2003	Pre-START 1990	START I 1999	START II 2003
Heavy Bombers	100	100	100	1600	1600	665
Land-based Missiles	1398	850	495	6612	3060	495
Sea-based Missiles	944	456	456	2804	1840	1840
Totals:	2442	1406	1051	11016	6500	3000

Note: Russian START I & II allocations are author's estimates.

likely to reside at fairly low levels of the international food chain. Both powers may find that they need to apply greater resources to conventional forces, and those resources may have to be generated within defence establishments. Given a choice of cutting Marines and cutting ICBMs, what would Washington prefer to do? Given a choice between cutting airborne divisions and cutting strategic missile submarines, which would Moscow cut? To leave room for such reductions, that is, to leave room for deterrence at levels as low as 500 warheads apiece, strategic defences should be limited to levels that can reliably absorb far fewer than that many warheads using highly *optimistic* assumptions about the performance of the defence.

Ballistic Missile Defences

If the National Missile Defence Act of 1991 continues to define US policy toward ballistic missile defence, then by 2004 the United States will have deployed a ground-based, 100-interceptor force as permitted under the ABM Treaty. If the Russians agree, the US may deploy more than that. The SDI Organization's plan for a thin defence of US territory against accidental or unauthorized attack contemplates four or five ground-based defence sites within the Lower 48 states, one site in Alaska and one in Hawaii.

Any co-operative agreement to deploy additional BMD should include substantial provisions for verification to ensure that the system deployed does not grow beyond agreed limits. This may entail direct inspection of deployment sites, monitoring of radar and interceptor production, and agreement on terms to differentiate theatre from strategic missile defences. The latter definition is perhaps the most pressing agreement to reach whatever else is decided about strategic BMD, as TMD systems are in an advanced state of development in both countries.

The ABM Treaty prohibits giving such technologies the ability to intercept strategic ballistic missiles, prohibits testing them 'in an ABM mode', and establishes a 'power-aperture product' threshold above which a radar counts as a treaty-constrained ABM radar unless it is dedicated to providing early warning of attack, or to arms control verification. These strictures were designed to prevent circumvention of the treaty. Until recently, no TMD interceptor or radar looked like a serious contender for ABM capability. But the Russian SA-12B 'Giant' seems to blur the distinction and American systems like THAAD (for Theater High-Altitude Area Defense) will blur it further. If the difference between constrained and unconstrained systems is not clarified, then the ABM Treaty soon will be fatally undermined in perception if not performance. What impact that may have on either side's willingness to reduce offensive forces further is anyone's guess; if neither side considers deterrence important anymore, then the impact will be marginal, and the effectiveness of the ABM Treaty can be allowed to fade away as 'theatre' defences proliferate.

If, however, the Russians are serious about linking offence and defence, a fading ABM Treaty means fading prospects for reduced reliance on nuclear threat and counterthreat. The question of a TMD/ABM boundary has been explored by several authors. One definition of 'testing in an ABM mode' would define it as a test conducted against a target moving at least three kilometres per second (thereby allowing TMD tests against missiles of up to 1,000 kilometres range) or a test against a target at more than 70 kilometres in altitude (thereby permitting very high altitude air defence). The speed and range constraints are both necessary because an interceptor tested against slow targets at extreme altitude 'could well have capabilities against faster targets at lower altitudes'.[22] Any intercept technology tested against higher or faster targets would fall under the writ of the treaty, and its development, testing, and deployment would be limited. Herbert Lin has suggested that ABM interceptors also be distinguished by their size, which implicitly defines their fuel capacity and the combination of range and speed of which they are capable. After reviewing figures for a number of US and Soviet/Russian air defence and missile interceptors, he proposed that those greater than eight metres in length or two and one-half cubic metres in volume be considered ABM-capable. Such a definition would define a Sprint (the hypervelocity missile developed for the US Safeguard system) as ABM-capable but not a Patriot or an SA-12.[23] More exotic technologies such as lasers could eventually pose a definitional problem as well if they are tested in other than a fixed, ground-based configuration. The two parties to the treaty could either try to define testing thresholds for such devices as well, or, as long as no development of a workable weapon appeared imminent, they might choose merely to watch.

Assuming that appropriate definitions of terms make continued limits on missile interceptors meaningful, what levels of deployment would likely provide what level of protection against what level of threat(s)? Tables 3 and 4 suggest a range of answers. They do not include an exhaustive set of scenarios, or an exhaustive range of defence configurations; rather, they extrapolate from capabilities that the SDI programme has projected for a defence using the long-range ground based interceptor, the ground based radar, upgraded ground-based early warning radars and perhaps additional sensors in orbit.[24] The simulations evaluated ground-based BMD systems with 100 to 2,000 ground-based interceptors of varying capability. Because the task was area defence, the BMD system used 'random subtractive' intercepts, not protecting any location more or less than any other. The simulation tested both a single-layer defence, one that shoots everything it has at incoming warheads, and a two-layer, 'shoot-look-shoot' defence, the second wave firing only at warheads that the first wave has missed. Interceptors of different ranges were simulated by varying the fraction of the defensive force available for a given intercept, from 100 per cent to 25 per cent. Finally, defences of 'high', 'medium', and 'low' capability were simulated by varying the 'single-shot kill probability' (SSPK, the probability of one interceptor successfully destroying one attacking warhead). A low-capability defence had an SSPK of 25 per cent (a one-in-four chance of destroying its target; still historically high for surface-to-air missiles). A medium-capability defence was given an SSPK of 50 per cent, while a high SSPK was 75 per cent.[25] In simulating a two-layer defence strategy, a higher SSPK was assigned to the second wave of defence interceptors to account for the more accurate warhead tracking information likely to be available from ground-based radars, and to account for the separation of warheads from decoys by atmospheric drag. Second-layer SSPKs rose to 50, 75 and 90 per cent for the low, medium and high capability defences, respectively.

The effect of interceptor range on system requirements was simulated by equating a single category in the tables (say, 500 effective interceptors) with several different-sized BMD systems. That is, all of the following produce the same results in the simulation: a system with 500 interceptors, all of which have the range to engage attacking warheads; a system with 1,000 interceptors, half of which are within range; and a system with 2,000 interceptors, one-fourth of which are within range. Thus, depending on what one believes to be a reasonable maximum intercept range, and a reasonable intercept geometry, the number of effective interceptors that produce a given result in Tables 3 and 4 might represent a total deployment that is two to four times larger.

Simulations of strategic missile defences vary greatly in their sophistication, and the one conducted here is relatively simple and favourable to the defence. I have not degraded SSPKs specifically to account for defence suppression measures that might be taken by the offence. In the smaller attacks that are the principal concern of this analysis, the attacker would not have a large number of warheads with which to saturate or blind the defence, as could readily be done in a full-scale attack. Moreover, an accidental missile attack would tend, by definition, to be less than fully co-ordinated.[26]

TABLE 3

MISSILE DEFENCE PERFORMANCE AGAINST 2000, 1500 AND 300 RE-ENTRY VEHICLES

Defence Characteristics		*Raid Size*							
		2000 (START II Level)		1500 (Option A)		300 (Option B)			
		One-layer defence		One-layer defence		One-layer defence		Two-layer defence	
Effective Number of Interceptors	Interceptor SSPK	RVs Missed	P(perf. defence)	RVs Missed	P(perf. defence)	RVs Missed	P(perf. defence)	RVs Missed	P(perf. defence)
2000	High	725	0	428	0	<<1	0.68	0	>0.99
	Med	1150	0	740	0	8	0	0	0.99
	Low	1575	0	1098	0	62	0	an3	.09
1000 (=2000*0.5)	High	1363	0	862	0	11	0	0.99	
	Med	1575	0	10745	0	49	0	<2	0.18
	Low	1788	0	1288	0	136	0	46	0
500 (=1000*0.5) (=2000*0.25)	High	1681	0	1181	0	63	0	10	0
	Med	1788	0	1288	0	124	0	56	0
250 (=500*0.5) (=1000*0.25)	High	1841	0	1341	0	141	0	109	0
	Med	1894	0	1394	0	194	0	141	0

The task of these simulations was to gauge the size and capability of ground-based defences needed to stop *all* of the missile warheads that might be launched against the United States by accident or by low-level circumvention of the normal chains of command, while at the same time remaining *insufficient* to neutralize the respective deterrent capacities of the Russian and American nuclear arsenals.[27] First, I tested alternative defences against raid sizes ranging from 2,000 re-entry vehicles (a maximum strike by a force the size of that permitted by START II), through 1,500 (the number of ballistic warheads contemplated by twenty-first century option A), and 300 (twenty-first century option B). The results of these simulated attacks are presented in Table 3, against missile defences with as many as 2,000 and as few as 100 effective interceptors.[28] Against the two larger raids, none of the postulated defences staved off total devastation; at least 725 warheads penetrated the defence. In short, a ground-based defence with as many as 2,000 effective interceptors would not, by any objective measure, eliminate either Russian or American capacity to destroy the other country so long as arsenals remained as high as 2,000 warheads apiece. If, on the other hand, the two arsenals were reduced to 500 warheads apiece, of which perhaps 300 would continue to ride on ballistic missiles, then the number of missile interceptors deployed would begin to matter more. The simulations suggest that 1,000 effective, high-capability interceptors might be able to nullify a 300-warhead missile attack. On the other hand, such a concerted attack might be heavily orchestrated and accompanied by sophisticated counter-measures to fool the defence, suggesting that, to be assured of having 1,000 effective interceptors, the country might need to deploy 2,000, 4,000, or more.

An offensive planner charged with keeping targets under threat despite such a defence could not view such deployments with equanimity, nor could they be considered in any sense 'limited'. If political leaders have any notion of reducing the Russian and American strategic arsenals to very low levels (say, 500 or less) over the long run, they should be most reluctant to deploy *in advance of such agreements on offence* a defensive force that appeared capable of neutralizing offensive arsenals, however improbable such capability may appear from the perspective of a conservative defensive systems planner. To keep the door open to reductions, defensive deployments ought perhaps to be limited to fewer than 500 interceptors. In making that judgement, one ought to consider the attacker's worst case analysis: the 500 might have high SSPKs, and they might have sufficient range to make all 500 effective. Under such circumstances, 500 interceptors might destroy all but about 10 incoming warheads, still an unmitigated disaster for those on the receiving end, but a potentially recoverable disaster for their country.

In the case of a 200-warhead attack, the largest of the apologies-over-the-Hotline scenarios depicted in Table 4, the results were similar. Five hundred effective interceptors would have as much as an 88 per cent chance of absorbing such an attack if they were highly capable and could be used in two waves. One thousand effective interceptors would have a more than 99 per cent probability of destroying every incoming warhead under similar circumstances. (By the same token, a lower probability of intercept, or a lower effective number of interceptors, would virtually guarantee severe societal damage.)

Table 4 also looks at prospects for defending against a smaller accidental or unauthorized launch by the equivalent of one squadron of single-warhead ICBMs (estimated here to involve 50 warheads). If at least half of the deployed interceptors could be counted on as effective against this size attack, then actual deployment of 250–500 medium-capability interceptors may be adequate to give a reasonably high degree of protection. Such a defensive system should have a better-than-70 per cent to a better-than-99 per cent chance of destroying all of the incoming warheads if interceptors were of at least medium capability. More than 500 effective interceptors would be needed, however, if the expected SSPK of the defence were low (that is, of the order of 25 per cent).[29]

A Suggested Offence-Defence Mix

The trick is to arrange the security environment to allow for defence as well as deterrent capabilities, monitoring both in a manner that increases the transparency of their operational characteristics (their size, readiness and operational strategy) so as to give countries early indications of changes in status, to do what can be done to secure these systems against mishap, and to go on to deal with other, more pressing matters, like the volatility of the rest of the world. This suggests a twenty-first century security strategy for the United States that includes the following. First, it should retain for the foreseeable future a strategy of assured nuclear retaliation for direct nuclear attacks on the homeland, but orient its deterrent threats primarily to that scenario. To this end, it should maintain a force structure that can survive nuclear attacks to implement retaliation at leisure (giving it deterrent value without contributing to crisis instability). Second, the United States should deploy long-range, ground-based missile defences sufficient to absorb small missile attacks (where 'small' means 50 or fewer warheads), negotiating its deployment with the Russian Federation. Third, it should strongly emphasize three elements of strategic arms control: for offensive weapons, for defensive weapons, and for operations. Limitations

TABLE 4

MISSILE DEFENCE PERFORMANCE AGAINST 200 AND 50 RE-ENTRY VEHICLES

Defence Characteristics		*Raid Size*							
		200 (One Typhoon submarine)				50 (One ICBM Squadron)			
		One-layer defence		Two-layer defence		One-layer defence		Two-layer defence	
Effective Number of Interceptors	Inter-ceptor SSPK	RVs Missed	P(perf. defence)	RVs Missed	P(perf. defence)	RVs Missed	P(perf. defence)	RVs Missed	P(perf. defence)
2000	High	0	<0.99	0	>0.99				
	Med	<1	0.45	0	0.99				
	Low	18	0	<<1	0.84				
1000 (=1000*0.5)	High	<	0.29	0	>0.99				
	Med	13	0	0	>0.99				
	Low	61	0	11	0				
500 (=1000*0.5) (=2000*0.25)	High	18	0	>>1	0.88	0	>0.99	0	>0.99
	Med	52	0	>9	0	<<1	0.82	0	>0.99
	Low	111	0	52	0	5	0.01	<<1	0.96
250 (=500*0.5) (=1000*0.25)	High	61	0	34	0	<<1	0.73	0	>0.99
	Med	103	0	61	0	3	0.04	0	>0.99
	Low	149	0	102	0	15	0	>2	0.10
100	High					>6	0	<1	0.64
	Med					<17	0	6	0

on the offence might extend the START-II accord indefinitely, leaving both the United States and Russia with a triad of long-range nuclear systems and 3,000–3,500 weapons in a reasonably survivable configuration. If further reductions prove politically feasible, they should be pursued. Even 500-warhead arsenals would let the two countries keep enough weapons on hand to destroy the other's civilization. However, that capability could recede to the background of the relationship, and the probability of it ever being used would be further reduced by the other two elements of arms control.

On the defensive side, the ABM Treaty should be revised to permit constrained deployments of ground-based interceptors. Setting permissible limits would first require defining the boundary between strategic ballistic missile defence and defences against theatre/tactical range missiles. That boundary should be defined, as suggested earlier, in terms of size and testing limits so that any weapon that exceeds them becomes, by definition, an ABM interceptor subject to constraint. With that distinction made, the number of ABM interceptors allowed each side could increase. Since the capabilities of ground-based radars and interceptors would evolve over time, the numerical limits built into the revised ABM Treaty should be calibrated to a system with *highly* capable, long-range performance against a threat of 50 warheads. Such a defence could grow into its role (that is, its intercept probabilities could be improved over time) without undermining deterrence, as part of an evolving system of 'managed vulnerability'.

Interceptors and their associated battle management radars should continue to be ground-based on national territory, consistent with the notion of a limited defence. To make it easier to verify the new capabilities, and to make breakout from the expanded limits somewhat more difficult, both interceptors and radars should continue to be confined to fixed sites. (Mobile units require no fixed sites, so when produced, they are also 'deployed'. Fixed units require additional field construction, which tends to be visible to overhead sensors.) Nuclear-armed ABM interceptors might require special treatment, since, with the right guidance software, they might be directed to fly ballistic trajectories and thus to function as surface-to-surface missiles (as could the old US Nike-Hercules SAM, widely deployed at one time by NATO). A long-range, nuclear-armed ABM interceptor might even be construed to violate the 1988 Intermediate-range Nuclear Forces (or INF) Treaty, a US-Russian agreement that bans ground-based missiles of 500–5,500 kilometres' range.[30] Relaxed ABM Treaty limits on numbers of ABM interceptors and their associated radars would need to be matched by the sorts of on-site inspection regimes negotiated for the INF and START agreements, to assure adherence to the new limits. The parties would need to be able to monitor one another's production facilities as well as their operational units and depot maintenance facilities, for an indefinite period.

Sensors, especially long-range ground-based radars, have traditionally been the long pole in the tent for ABM systems, playing a crucial role in battle management and requiring a long time to build. Placing tight constraints on them in the ABM Treaty was an effective way to prevent either side laying a 'base' for a rapid expansion of missile defence capabilities that might then be used in a grab for political dominance.[31] The views of Russian analysts on GPALS, noted earlier, reflect a similar concern about 'breakout'. As Robert Jervis's spiral model suggests, it is hard to hedge one's security bets without generating perceptions of threat. Closely monitored production and deployment of ABM components should help to allay fears of pre-planned breakout, but the greater deterrent to such behaviour is always going to lie in the quality of the overall political relationship and, to be blunt, in the availability of alternative nuclear threats (stealth bombers, cruise missiles) not affected by BMD and not entirely neutralized by air defence.

Care should be taken when modifying the ABM Treaty that the results do not undermine prospects for later co-operative security arrangements. The first stage of co-operation toward what President Yeltsin dubbed a 'global protection system', for example, would involve sharing early warning data. Early warning should be interpreted to include data on the alerting status of all nuclear-capable systems owned by either side. Once those systems are taken off alert, they could not be surreptitiously returned to rapid-fire status if such a transparency system were in place. They could not, in other words, be used for surprise nuclear attack. Although this system might start out bilateral, all nuclear powers could be encouraged to join. In exchange for joining the early warning net, they should agree to abide by the terms of the modified ABM Treaty, which would be opened to multilateral signature, and not to undermine offensive limitations by increasing the size of their strategic forces.[32]

Joint early warning would ensure that all participating parties had full information about any subsequent launch of space launch vehicles and ballistic missiles, nuclear-armed or otherwise. All parties would know the point of origin of the launch within the same brief period of time. Opportunities for blame arising from misperception or bad data in the event of nuclear attack would be reduced.[33] To facilitate timely and accurate information on global missile launches, such a system would need good sensors, whether ground or space-based. It should have access to data from American Defense Support Program satellites in equatorial orbits, from Russian warning satellites in Molniya orbits, and American and Russian ground-based missile warning radars (BMEWS, PAVE PAWS and Pechora).[34]

Because a joint system would provide common warning of accidental, unauthorized, or other 'rogue' missile launches, it should be able to assist the defences of any threatened participant to intercept such missiles. This would argue for allowing the deployment of sensors in space, such as SDIO's proposed 'Brilliant Eyes', provided there was equal access to the satellites' information and equal ability to make use of it. This could require, in turn, sharing of communications and data standards and protocols, if not sharing of ground terminals and software. Co-operation might actually be enhanced in some cases by not sharing such hardware and software directly, since it may be difficult to allay recipient suspicions about software, in particular, being doctored to alter or degrade its performance, as is often the case with exported arms. In that case, the joint system would evolve only as fast as the technology of its slowest independence-minded participant.

Although sensors may well be based in space, interceptors should not be so based. A malfunctioning space-based weapon system could pose a threat to other space users in low earth orbit. These would include space stations *Mir* and *Freedom*, space shuttle missions, other space launches, military weather and reconnaissance satellites, and the multiple constellations of low-altitude cellular communications satellites likely to be in orbit by early in the next decade. Orbital weapons would have the theoretical ability to attack all of these space objects with little warning, on a broad scale, and with higher effectiveness than they would display against rising ballistic missiles. An ASAT attack could be planned and co-ordinated months in advance because satellites follow fairly predictable paths, and it could be executed in rapid-fire fashion against these relatively soft targets. In short, space-based weapons would contribute a capability for surprise attack in space that is at variance with, and could place at risk the objectives of, the rest of the proposed offence-defence-early warning edifice. The United States is the only power able at present to contemplate building such a system. Its unilateral deployment, whatever the rhetorical justification, would be seen outside this country as a bid for domination of near-earth space that is incompatible with a structure of shared risk and co-operative security. Prospects of such deployment could only worsen Russian concerns about the evolution of 'space-strike complexes' that they cannot replicate.

Of course, all deployments of long-range ABM interceptors would give their owners some ASAT capability, and non-nuclear ABMs would be more useable in this role than their nuclear-armed cousins. But ground-based ASATs that ascend directly to their target like an ABM interceptor would have to wait for their targets to pass over an ABM launch site (about four to six times every 24 hours for a satellite in near-polar orbit, assuming that interceptors are spread across Russian and American territory). Thus an ASAT engagement conducted from the ground might be stretched out long enough to permit diplomacy to play a role in containing conflict. Diplomacy might have no chance to do so in the case of a space-based engagement.

Conclusions

Strategic defence has something to offer in the twenty-first century, but that something is relatively modest levels of protection from ballistic missile threats that are tiny by comparison with the full capacities of the superpowers (or former superpowers), even at the force level objectives contemplated in START II. Moreover, defences are expensive and there are many other pressing needs.[35] Yet, with the passing of the ideological confrontation of the Cold War, it seems reasonable to reassess our approach to strategic ballistic missile defence, if only because intercontinental missiles will be in existence for a good long while, and we have an opportunity to avert the potential consequences of tragedy or insanity. An American president would be hard-pressed to explain, after the fact, why he or she did not avail the country of such limited nuclear disaster insurance.

The future shape of international politics is uncertain, and the defensive system suggested here would be consistent with a number of alternative configurations of strategic forces and political relations, provided only that relations with Russia remain basically co-operative for the next few years, that is, long enough to renegotiate the ABM Treaty. A ground-based BMD system of 250 to 500 interceptors would be consistent with START I and II; consistent with the maintenance of basic nuclear deterrence even if US and Russian offensive arsenals decline to as few as 500 warheads apiece; and insufficient to block a concerted British-French retaliatory attack. Being able to defend against small numbers of ballistic missile re-entry vehicles will not take us out from under the threat of nuclear destruction, and is not meant to, but it may be sufficient to provide a hedge in support of an eventual move away from long-range ballistic missiles altogether. And that might also be worthwhile.

ACKNOWLEDGEMENT

This article draws upon work done for the Henry L. Stimson Center's Project on the Roles and Missions of the US Armed Forces in the 21st Century, funded by the Carnegie Corporation of New York. The views expressed are those of the author alone.

NOTES

1. I am grateful to Stephen Flanagan for suggesting this descriptor.
2. Thomas Schelling, *Arms and Influence* (New Haven, CT: Yale University Press, 1966), p. 248.
3. Lawrence Freedman, *The Evolution of Nuclear Strategy* (New York: St. Martin's Press, 1983), pp. 43–4, 155–72. Lt. Gen. Arthur S. Collins, Jr. (USA-ret'd), 'Theater Nuclear Warfare: The Battlefield', in John F. Reichart and Steven R. Sturm (eds.), *American Defense Policy*, 5th edn. (Baltimore, MD: The Johns Hopkins University Press, 1982), pp. 356–65. Ivo Daalder, *The SDI Challenge to Europe* (Cambridge, MA: Ballinger, 1987), p. 40.
4. Alain Enthoven and K. Wayne Smith, *How Much Is Enough?* (New York: Harper & Row, 1971), 174–5, 207. The assured destruction threat is spelled out succinctly in Schelling, *Arms and Influence*, pp. 22 ff.
5. Soviet weapons tended to trail US innovations by about five years (examples include multiple independently targetable re-entry vehicles [MIRVs] and long-range sea-based ballistic missiles). This was enough of a lag that maintaining an edge seemed feasible if the United States kept the pressure on and the budgets up, but not so great a lag as to give Congress an excuse to postpone modernization. Soviet design bureaux obligingly pumped out a full panoply of competitive weapon system designs at regular intervals, although a lot of what they developed was not produced in significant quantities. On threat inflation and 'gamesmanship', see Michael Salman, Kevin J. Sullivan, and Stephen Van Evera, 'Analysis or Propaganda? Measuring American Strategic Nuclear Capability, 1969-88', in Lynn Eden and Steven E. Miller, (eds.), *Nuclear Arguments* (Ithaca, NY: Cornell University Press, 1989), pp. 172–245.
6. For a summary of US proposals, see *Testimony of Secretary of Defense Cheney before the Senate Armed Services Committee on the Strategic Arms Reduction Treaty* (Washington, DC: Department of Defense, mimeograph, 28 July 1992). See also, 'Nuclear Notebook', *Bulletin of the Atomic Scientists*, Vol. 48, No. 4 (May 1992), p. 49; and Neil Munro, 'DoD Reviews Nuclear C^3 System', *Defense News*, 20 May 1991, pp. 3, 36.
7. Gary Guertner, for example, believes that the United States should retain some strategic nuclear forces for retaliation against direct attacks on US territory, and may also need to retain a distinct theatre nuclear capability, lest use of strategic forces for local deterrence encourage regional nuclear 'balancing', that is, nuclear proliferation. See his *Deterrence and Conventional Military Forces* (Carlisle, Penna.: US Army War College, Strategic Studies Institute, 1992), pp. 9–10. Why proliferation should be less likely in response to a nuclear retaliatory threat posed by shorter-range weapon systems is not clear, however; the strongest incentive for proliferation is a nearby threat, especially a nuclear threat.
8. A harder case would be one of severe domestic repression, verging on genocide, conducted by a nuclear-armed regime that threatens to use its weapons against any state

or coalition that 'interferes' in its affairs, or to use them against segments of its own populace. Should the international community choose to intervene nonetheless, it may wish to assign the job to special forces. The intelligence requirements for successful operations under such circumstances would be extremely demanding, and their backers would have to be prepared to move quickly and in force should the operation fail – yet another reason why prevention of nuclear proliferation must be a high priority.

9. American BMD work moved away from nuclear-armed interceptors for a number of reasons, some of them technical (interceptor detonations could flash-blind defence radars, for example), while others were political. Since President Reagan had called upon science, in March 1983, to make nuclear weapons 'impotent and obsolete', a nuclear-armed defence was effectively ruled out (although a notional 'X-ray laser' received substantial funding for several years).
10. Stephen Meyer, 'Soviet Nuclear Operations', in Ashton Carter, John Steinbruner, and Charles Zracket, (eds.), *Managing Nuclear Operations* (Washington, DC: Brookings Institution, 1987), p. 490, 503, 529–31. See also V.Z. Dvorkin and V.M. Surikov, 'Strategic Offensive Forces and Ballistic Missile Defense', in Alexei Arbatov (ed.), *Implications of Strategic Defense Deployments for US-Russian Relations*, A Stimson Center Report (Washington, DC: The Henry L. Stimson Center, June 1992), p. 28.
11. Congress did orient BMD toward point defence in the mid-1970s as a way to keep research and development alive without threatening the ABM Treaty or continuing SALT talks.
12. An initial emphasis on space-based directed-energy weapons prompted severe technical criticism from the American Physical Society, and directed-energy soon was eclipsed in SDI's architecture by kinetic-energy interceptors (rockets). See American Physical Society Study Group, *Science and Technology for Directed Energy* (April 1987).
13. William J. Durch, *The ABM Treaty and Western Security* (Cambridge, MA: Ballinger Publishing Co., 1987), pp. 58–68. US House of Representatives, Committee on Armed Services, *National Defense Authorization Act for Fiscal Year 1993*, Conference Report (H.Rpt.102-966), 102d Cong., 2nd sess., pp. 46, 643–4. The broad interpretation had the great advantage, from the Reagan administration's perspective, of opening paths for development of SDI while continuing to constrain the deployment of the older-style ABM equipment still being produced and fielded by the USSR.
14. Durch, *The ABM Treaty and Western Security*, p. 37.
15. In light of this chosen benchmark, it should be noted that Russian submarine-launched ballistic missiles have electronic locks on their weapons that American sea-based missiles lack. Computer validation of an encoded message from higher authority is required to unlock nuclear weapons. Bruce Blair, testimony before the House Committee on Armed Services, US Congress, 31 July 1991.
16. Charles L. Glaser, *Analyzing Strategic Nuclear Policy* (Princeton, NJ: Princeton University Press, 1990), esp. pp. 107–11. Glaser notes that in a competitive political environment, very good defences would not be 'perfect' but just 'temporarily impenetrable' until the next swing of the technical pendulum.
17. For a good review of Russian statements on missile defence, see *The Emerging Russian View of Missile Defense: Implications for GPALS* (Washington, DC: SDIO Countermeasures Integration Programme, April 1992). For analyses that demonstrate graphically the divergent opinions on BMD among Russian academics, diplomats, and military analysts, see Arbatov (ed.), *Implications of Strategic Defense Deployments for US-Russian Relations*.
18. Briefing slide, 'Dealing with Uncertain Futures', Strategic Defense Initiative Organization, April 1992.
19. Schelling, *Arms and Influence*, pp. 248–51, 259.
20. Balancing these cutbacks, *Russia* has begun a serious push to sell conventional

variants of missile systems previously thought to be only nuclear capable. Examples include the AS-16 short-range attack missile, the SS-N-21 long-range sea-launched cruise missile, and the AS-15 long-range air-launched cruise missile. If estimates are correct that these missiles carry relatively small (less than 500-pound) warheads, it is likely that the conventional capability has been created simply by filling the space reserved for the nuclear warhead and fuzing with a comparably-sized non-nuclear substitute. Conventional variants of dual-capable US missiles typically devote much more of the missile volume to the warhead at the expense of fuel, and thus range. See Robert S. Norris and William M. Arkin, 'Nuclear Notebook', *Bulletin of the Atomic Scientists*, Vol 48, No. 1 (Jan.–Feb. 1992), p. 48; Vol. 48, No. 2 (March 1992), p. 49; and Vol. 49, No. 1 (Jan.–Feb. 1993), p. 50.

21. David A. Fulghum, 'SAC Chief Says US to Maintain At Least 2,000-Warhead Nuclear Arsenal', *Aviation Week & Space Technology*, 13 April 1992.
22. Herbert Lin, *New Weapon Technologies and the ABM Treaty* (Washington, DC: Pergamon-Brassey's, 1987), pp. 39–40. Lin notes that DoD's compliance guidelines are apparently 2–4 km/sec and 40 km altitude. These are similar to the parameters suggested by Alexei Arbatov and G. K. Lednev, who reason that ICBM re-entry speeds range upward from 5 km/sec, and that terminal defence of non-hardened targets needs to take place at least 50 km overhead (reflecting continued Russian deployment of nuclear-armed interceptors and/or concern about 'salvage fusing' of incoming warheads). A. Arbatov and G. K. Lednev, 'Limited Anti-Missile Systems and International Security', in Arbatov (ed.), *Implications of Strategic Defensce Deployments for US-Russian Relations*, p. 23.
23. Lin, *New Weapon Technologies*, pp. 45–6. ABM interceptors could also be defined by weight if on-site inspections were available.
24. US Department of Defense, Strategic Defense Initiative Organization, *1992 Report to the Congress on the Strategic Defense Initiative* (Washington, DC: SDIO, July 1992), pp. 2-9 to 2-15. Also *Report to Congress: Plan for Deployment of Theater and National Ballistic Missile Defenses* (Washington, DC: SDIO, June 1992). Neither report indicates the number of interceptors to be deployed at defence sites, other than the 100 that are Treaty-permitted. Sensors in space would be 'Brilliant Eyes' passive infrared satellites in relatively low earth orbit.
25. More than one interceptor was launched at each incoming warhead, as numbers allowed. The formula for calculating their joint probability of destroying the warhead is $1\text{-}(1\text{-}SSPK)^n$, where 'n' is the number of interceptors assigned to the task. The lowest BMD kill probability used in these simulations is equivalent to the highest SSPK for a surface-to-air missile used in combat against manned aircraft, attributed to Israeli HAWK interceptors during the October 1973 Middle East War, with kill probabilities ranging from 20 to 33 per cent. See Kenneth N. Freeman, *The Combat Effectiveness of Guided Weapons in the Battle for Air Superiority: Perceptions versus Performance* (doctoral dissertation, King's College, University of London, Sept. 1989), p. 509.
26. For a discussion of defence vulnerabilities, see US Congress, Office of Technology Assessment, *Ballistic Missile Defence Technologies* (Washington, DC: US Government Printing Office, Sept. 1985), pp. 170–77.
27. The probability that no warheads penetrate the defence (assuming that all intercepts are statistically independent and that all warheads are engaged by interceptors) is given by $\pi(PKn_k)^{wk}$, or the probability that 'n' interceptors will destroy one warhead raised to the number of warheads engaged by that combination of interceptors ('w_k') these joint probabilities for each combination of interceptors are then multiplied together. The assumption that intercepts are statistically independent makes this final probability higher than it would be if discounted for interceptors' actual common dependencies (for example, shared ground-based radars, or shared early warning facilities whose failure or destruction would affect the performance of many interceptors). Because it gives a best case for the defence, this measure is best used to illustrate conditions under which the defence *cannot* fully protect society.

28. The term 'effective' interceptors refers to the number of deployed interceptors that are able to engage attacking reentry vehicles. An effective deployment of 500 interceptors is equivalent in the simulation to an actual deployment of 1,000 interceptors if only half of those can bear on an attack (they might be based near the West Coast and unable to counter an attack concentrated on New York, for example). Likewise, if just one-fourth of the 1,000 interceptors deployed are within range of an attack, then it has an effective force size of 250. In evaluating tables 5.5 and 5.6, readers can make their own assumptions about likely SSPKs and effective fractions in deciding what size of defensive deployments would be desirable to counter what size of attack.
29. Though not depicted in Table 4, some 25 to 50 effective interceptors of high capability, or 50 to 100 of low to medium capability, would be able to absorb a 10-warhead attack. That is equivalent to the payload of a single MIRVed ICBM or the sort of attack that a rogue power might be capable of some years hence. Depending on the fraction assumed to be effective, that translates into a system of perhaps 50 to 200 deployed interceptors.
30. The long-range modified-Galosh interceptors now deployed around Moscow would have to be grandfathered into the new agreement, but perhaps with a clause requiring that they be retired or replaced by non-nuclear interceptors within a fixed period of time. However, the Russian military research and development establishment may or may not be capable of making such a transition. If not, Russia may seek to deploy more nuclear-armed missile interceptors under a modified ABM Treaty. To defend locations on the country's borders (for example, Murmansk, St. Petersburg, or Vladivostok) they would need to be able to conduct high-altitude intercepts well beyond the border. Therefore, before embarking on amendments to the ABM Treaty, it would be important to determine whether missile interceptor warheads could be rendered verifiably incapable of surviving atmospheric re-entry (for example, by disabling the warhead fuzing and requiring nose cone heat shielding to be jettisoned automatically once interceptors climb above, say, 150 kilometres altitude). If so, the 'INF' problem might be resolved by excepting such specially-engineered missiles.
31. This was one reason why the Reagan administration and many outside arms control experts jointly objected to Soviet construction of an early warning radar at Krasnoyarsk, in south-central Siberia, in the 1980s, in violation of the ABM Treaty's radar siting provisions.
32. Although opening the ABM Treaty to multilateral signature could be construed as giving signatories the 'right' to deploy up to so-many-hundred interceptors, they already have that right at present. But most countries do not have the capability to develop their own BMD systems and the treaty's Article IX prohibits the transfer of ABM systems or components to third countries. Thus the more ABM-capable countries that sign the treaty, the less potential proliferation of BMD systems.
33. But they would not be eliminated. In the case of a sea-launched ballistic missile attack, countries operating ballistic missile submarines might be required to reveal their locations briefly in a verifiable manner, something counter to normal practice, and potentially risky to individual boats, but preferable to nuclear war by mistake. Sufficient technical attention to the problem ought to be able to devise a small marker buoy that could be released in such a situation to transmit a tight, encrypted navigation signal to a designated relay satellite. The final signal on the warning net could merely confirm that submarines A, B, and C of country X were *not* within N-miles radius of the launch point when launch occurred.
34. As of late 1992, US and Russian negotiators were reportedly close to agreement on sharing 'processed' early warning data from their respective warning networks.
35. SDIO director Henry Cooper estimated in May 1992 that a ground-based, six-site national limited defence system (LDS), involving perhaps 1,200 interceptors, would cost about $35 billion 1992 dollars to deploy through the year 2012. Deployment of a national system with 250–500 interceptors spread among three or four sites would probably cost about $21-24 billion 1992 dollars. See US Department of Defense,

Strategic Defense Initiative Organization, *Strategic Defense Initiative*, briefing slide package (Washington, DC: SDIO, 11 Dec. 1992). See also US Congress, General Accounting Office, *Strategic Defense Initiative: 15-Year Funding Requirements*, GAO/NSIAD-92-92FS (Feb. 1992), p. 3.

Zero Ballistic Missiles and the Third World

LORA LUMPE

Following the Iraqi Scud attacks against Israel and Saudi Arabia during the 1991 Gulf War, ballistic missile proliferation – particularly in conjunction with actual or potential nuclear weapons capabilities – has emerged as a central US security concern. Some commentators suggest that developing countries may soon be able to strike the continental United States,[1] and such fears have become the primary public justification for the development of strategic anti-missile systems.

Testifying before the Senate in January 1992, however, the Director of Central Intelligence, Robert Gates, stated that 'only China and the Commonwealth of Independent States have the missile capability to reach US territory directly'. (Although unlikely, French and British SLBMs could strike the continental US, too.) 'We do not expect increased risk to US territory from the special weapons of other countries – in a conventional military sense – for at least another decade', he continued.[2] Gordon Oehler, the director of the CIA's new non-proliferation centre, added that those countries thought most likely to develop ICBMs in the next decade are 'not any of the major Third World countries that we're interested in' for political reasons. Without naming names, he went on to say that these are the 'countries with the more advanced space-launch vehicle programmes'[3] – that is, Israel, India and Brazil, none of which the United States considers particularly worrisome politically.

In fact, the threat to the continental United States from a ballistic missile attack originating in the Third World has been vastly overstated. Virtually all ballistic missile capabilities in developing countries consist of short-range Scud missiles. Of the 27 current or recent ballistic missile states in the world,[4] ten deploy only Scud range and quality missiles: that is, a 300 km range, single stage, liquid-fuelled rocket with a circular error probable of 900–1,000 metres. Some Third World countries have embarked on missile upgrade or development programmes, and are working on advances such as inertial guidance, solid fuel and multi-staging. The CIA testimony indicates, however, that it will take at least a decade before a politically hostile state may develop an ICBM capability.

The response to the current ballistic missile threat to US security is an export control/proliferation management regime, along with a search for a 'technical fix' in the form of anti-missile systems. This article suggests why this response is inadequate to the task. Instead, I advocate a novel and non-discriminatory approach: a complete, world-wide ban on ballistic missiles of all ranges. This approach has many benefits, not the least of which is an effective response to the threat posed by existing and future ballistic missile capabilities in the Third World that meets not just US security concerns but also those of countries that are now directly exposed to the possibility of missile attack.

The Management Approach

The Missile Technology Control Regime (MTCR), initiated in 1987 with seven members, has grown to include 23 Western industrialized countries.[5] Several additional countries – including Russia, China and Israel – have pledged to abide by MTCR export guidelines, but for various reasons (including reportedly concerns about the inadequacy of their export controls and the sensitivity of sharing intelligence with them) have not been invited to become formal members.[6]

MTCR members and adherents pledge to abide by common export guidelines on missile-relevant technologies and missiles themselves. MTCR 'Category I' covers 'Complete rocket systems (including ballistic missiles, space-launch vehicles, sounding rockets) and unmanned air vehicle systems (including cruise missile systems, target drones and reconnaissance drones) capable of delivering at least a 500 kg payload to a range of at least 300 km',[7] as well as complete sub-systems usable in those weapons and production facilities for them. Adherents to the MTCR are to attach a 'strong presumption to deny' such exports; however, if a binding government-to-government assurance is obtained that the technology will not be used in a military ballistic missile, transfers of these items are permitted. 'Category II' items, export of which are to be considered on the basis of proliferation concerns, include propulsion components, propellants, structural materials, flight instruments and flight control systems, among others.

While the MTCR has gone a long way toward creating a norm against ballistic missile proliferation among suppliers, and has been effective in slowing and reportedly even in ending some missile programmes[8], it has several shortcomings. First, the goal of the regime is ambiguous: as first articulated the intention was to prevent the development and deployment of nuclear-capable missiles, determined to be those capable of delivering a 500 kg payload to a distance of 300 km. However, as the regime has evolved, its goal has seemingly grown to one of preventing the spread of *all* ballistic missiles. At the same time, the regime seems to have acquired the goal of preventing developing countries from gaining access to space through independent space-launch programmes. A fact sheet on the MTCR issued by the US government in 1987 states that the guidelines 'are not designed to impede national space programs or international cooperation in such programs as long as such programs could not contribute to nuclear weapons delivery systems'.[9] The problem is that any space-launch vehicle (SLV) programme could by definition contribute to the development of a ballistic missile that could conceivably deliver a nuclear payload.

This ambiguity is compounded by the fact that the agreement is not a treaty, but rather a set of guidelines that are implemented by each member/adherent through national legislation. Thus the regime is subject to differing interpretations of its restrictions and varying levels of compliance. For example, the legislation implementing the regime in the US export control system draws no distinction between space-launch vehicles and weapons payload launchers. This was evident in the case of the Russian space agency's sale of a cryogenic rocket booster to the Indian Space Research Organization in May 1992. The United States considered the export of this technology to be prohibited under the terms of the MTCR, although India had provided necessary assurances to Russia that the booster was for use in its space programme. Nevertheless, the State Department termed the sale a clear violation of the MTCR, and US export law necessitated that sanctions against the two countries be invoked.[10] No other MTCR member or adherent has denounced this transaction as a violation or applied sanctions.

The imposition of sanctions against Russia for the cryogenic booster sale angered Russian military hard-liners, who already complained that Russia was deferring too much to American arms control policy. If cash-starved Russia cannot make sales of legitimate civilian space technology, it may be propelled to make less discriminate and more covert sales of surplus weaponry. The sanctions are also costly to US commercial aerospace and electronics industries. The Indian Space Research Organization and Glavkosmos, the Russian space agency, are both ineligible to buy space-related technology from US industry for two years, costing US industry at least $50 million annually. While this is a small portion of the $5 billion in space-related commerce expected for American industry in 1992,[11] the chilling effect on the market for US industry could prove a much greater loss. Such loose application of sanctions may also undercut necessary industry support for the goal of containing ballistic missile proliferation.[12]

A third problem with the MTCR is its restriction on membership. All countries are free to implement the MTCR export controls,[13] but not all are able to become members of the regime. Although the guidelines do not explicitly say so, transfers of the listed, restricted technologies are permitted to MTCR members and adherents. Theoretically, then, any country could claim to be an adherent to the regime and restrict its exports of missile technologies, in order to be eligible to *import* missile technologies from other countries. But, under the State Department's interpretation of the US implementing law, only countries that sign a bilateral agreement with the United States are considered 'adherents'. Thus only developing countries that the US decides may become an adherent (like Israel) – and therefore eligible to make missiles – may import relevant technologies for space-launch programmes. This discrimination within the Third World between 'good proliferators' and 'bad proliferators' does little to help make the MTCR and its goals acceptable among the 'bad proliferators'.

Fourth, the MTCR fails to take into account the particular industrial capabilities of recipient countries. In the case of the cryogenic booster sale from Russia, India was not gaining any new, militarily significant capability. The booster employs liquid hydrogen fuel, which is non-storable and must be loaded at super-cool temperatures, making it extremely difficult and expensive to maintain ready for launch. Because of this difficulty, no nation has ever used a hydrogen-fuelled rocket engine in a ballistic missile. Liquid oxygen was used in early US and Soviet ICBMs, and it would be reasonable to oppose this transfer if it was feared that India could obtain some significant technical advantage due to the similarity of the two types of engine. But India already has experience with hypergolic fuels from previous work with France on liquid-fuelled Viking rockets.[14] The French Minister for Research and Technology reportedly defended past proposed sales of cryogenic SLV technology to India, as well as Brazil, by saying the two countries already have 'the necessary expertise to develop these on their own. It is only a problem of time and money'.[15]

Fifth, given the short distances separating borders and cities in the Middle East, South Asia and East Asia, the MTCR parameters limiting missiles of 500 kg/300 km or more are not inclusive enough to provide real security benefits to countries in these regions. This threshold omits the 120 km range SS-21 in the Syrian arsenal and the 110 km range Lance in the Israeli arsenal.[16] In recognition of this, lowering the threshold was discussed but not agreed to at a plenary meeting of the MTCR in Washington in November 1991. In January 1993, the members revised the MTCR guidelines, extending the scope of the regime to 'control of all delivery systems (other than manned aircraft) capable of of delivering weapons of mass destruction'[17] – effectively missiles, rockets or artillery of any range. Furthermore, the Bush administration sought agreement by the five permanent members of the UN Security Council to forgo sales of missiles below the MTCR ranges to the Middle East.[18] Sixth, the MTCR also fails address the already existing ballistic missile arsenals in Third World countries. Although the regime may be successful in forestalling development of missiles that can strike the United States directly, missiles already in place can strike US allies and overseas bases and, indeed, this is one of the major arguments for deployment of space-based weapons in a global anti-missile system.

Probably the greatest weakness of the MTCR is that it is only a suppliers' cartel and does nothing to address the demand for missiles, born of regional political tension and local arms races. The developing world views the effort with suspicion and hostility; many see an attempt by the developed countries to hinder their entry into peaceful space activities. Like the nuclear Non-Proliferation Treaty (NPT), the MTCR is seen as another discriminatory regime in which the North is allowed a certain category of weaponry and the South is not.

Given the weaknesses of the current approach, the rising concern about missile proliferation and the opportunities afforded by end of the Cold War, what other measures could be taken to prevent the further development and deployment of ballistic missiles?

A Global INF Regime?

One idea, first suggested by Kenneth Adelman and Kathleen Bailey, would be to open up the bilateral US-Soviet Treaty on Intermediate-range Nuclear Forces (INF) for signature by other countries.[19] The internationalization of the INF Treaty, which bans ground-based missiles with ranges between 500 and 5,500 km, would offer a non-discriminatory approach to ballistic missile proliferation in the narrow sense that everyone would give up missiles of this class. However, nearly all of the systems currently deployed by developing countries would fall below the 500 km limit covered by the treaty. The ubiquitous Scud-B, for example, would not be included, nor would the SS-21, Lance, Israeli Jericho I, or Chinese M-9 or M-11 systems. In the Middle East, only the Israeli Jericho II, the Saudi CSS-2, the Indian Agni (under development), and Iraqi missiles (which are now being destroyed in any case) would be covered. A regime that left their adversaries' missiles in place would most likely be unacceptable to the Israelis and Saudis.

In September 1991 President Bush unilaterally pledged to eliminate the US world-wide arsenal of short-range nuclear ballistic missiles, a pledge since reciprocated by Russia, which now controls the entire stock of Soviet non-strategic nuclear forces. Agreement by Russia and former Warsaw Pact as well as NATO countries also to eliminate their short range missiles (110-500 km), and inclusion of developing countries in a short-range plus intermediate-range missile ban agreement, could produce a more palatable and certainly a more meaningful regime. But such a regime would still leave open the possibility, however slim, of Third World countries developing and deploying missiles above the 5,500 km INF ceiling, approaching ranges that could strike the continental United States.[20] Also, some ballistic missile programmes are driven, in part, by arms races or tension with countries that possess ICBMs, as in India's concern with China.

Finally, there are both costs and questions associated with verifying an international INF (or an expanded-range INF) agreement. Unlike the bilateral agreement, an international agreement would require an international and impartial inspectorate to oversee implementation and verification. This would not be a cheap or easy proposition. A similar international verification agency would also be needed to implement a Zero Ballistic Missiles agreement, but the greater benefits of such a regime would better justify the cost. There would also be significant questions about whether the agreement could be verified, since some testing (for strategic-range missiles) would still be allowed.

Going to Zero

Continued maintenance of missiles by the five declared nuclear powers, while attempting to deny them to developing countries, simply makes missiles appear all that much more valuable in terms of international prestige, if not actual military utility. According to a study by Stanford University's Center for International Security and Arms Control, demand for ballistic missiles appears in many cases to be driven more by prestige considerations than by military capabilities (which are fairly limited). 'Such motives may be strongly enhanced by the simplistic, albeit compelling, view of ballistic missiles as the visible symbol of superpower might and, thus, the object of emulation'.[21] As with the multilateral, non-discriminatory Chemical Weapons Convention just completed, total disavowal of ballistic missiles by the major powers is most likely a necessary precondition for renunciation of missiles by regional powers such as India, Israel, and Iran.

At the October 1986 Reykjavik summit, President Reagan proposed the complete elimination of US and Soviet ballistic missiles – the 'fast fliers', as he called them. Reagan's plan called for a fifty per cent reduction in strategic nuclear arsenals within five years and complete elimination of strategic missiles (ICBMs and SLBMs) within ten years, returning the two superpowers to a bomber-based nuclear deterrent. The idea – known as 'zero ballistic missiles' or ZBM – was greeted enthusiastically by First Secretary Gorbachev, and was also supported by such notable hard-liners as Paul Nitze, Fred Ikl, Richard Perle and Kenneth Adelman. However, differences on research and development of strategic defences derailed the proposal at that time.[22]

The Reykjavik proposition was put forward without reference to Britain, France and China, nor to incipient missile states. Indeed, in 1986, the spread of ballistic missile capabilities to more countries was just emerging as a serious security concern to the West. Seven years later, with the Cold War ended, the strategic benefits of ZBM are still compelling: decreasing the possibility of accidental nuclear warfare, reducing fears of pre-emption and pressures for escalation of any hostilities.[23] Equally important, a global ban on all ballistic missiles down to a very short range (e.g. 100 km), that permitted the unimpeded but verified development of indigenous space-launch capabilities by members to the regime, could be the best way to stop the proliferation of long-range missiles. Such a regime would not equalize the global military imbalance; the United States and Russia, in particular, would retain massive conventional superiority as well as still sizeable nuclear capabilities. But the developing world would gain some palpable security benefits through ZBM. While ballistic missiles have been thought of primarily as deterrents in the superpower context, in the developing world they have a recent history of extensive counter-city use, mainly as weapons of terror and attrition.[24] ZBM would immediately improve the security environment of many countries by eliminating costly and destabilizing regional missile races. If the ban extended down to missiles with a range of 100 km/500 kg payload, the benefits would be even greater, as deployed short-range (yet often 'strategic') systems would be eliminated. Certain developing countries would also be relieved of anxiety about US and Russian ICBMs being re-targeted on them.[25] The entire world would benefit by decreasing the chance of accidental or intentional nuclear war. A ZBM regime would also alleviate the perceived need for space-based anti-missile systems, lessening global tensions and freeing up vast resources that would be spent to develop and deploy such systems.

A regime that permits the development and maintenance of independent space-launch capabilities while banning globally the possession of military ballistic missiles poses some verification challenges (further discussed below). However, overcoming these challenges would likely be easier than convincing countries that they have no legitimate space aspirations. Moreover, if affordable launch services, unimpeded access to satellite imagery, and other forms of co-operation were available, most developing countries undoubtedly would forgo the expense of developing an indigenous launch capability. The international commercial space-launch industry is extremely competitive. Currently only seven countries and one European consortium have operational space-launch capabilities.[26] To avoid waste and redundancy, these countries should actively explore among themselves and with non-SLV countries alternatives for international space co-operation, including an international launch service.

However, it is doubtful whether the countries currently possessing SLVs are prepared to satisfy the space needs of all developing countries. Internationalization of space-launches and the formation of a world space agency may be desirable but may not yet be politically feasible. When asked in September 1992 if he saw a need for a world space organization, Nandasiri Jasentuliyana, the Director of the office of Outer Space Affairs at the UN, said 'No. . . . this is very far down the line'.[27] Development of space technology also provides an avenue for achieving the sort of political, economic, technological and military prestige that is usually only gained through the development of high-tech weaponry. Thus while it might be preferable for resource-poor developing countries to forgo development of an independent space-launch capability, a few are unlikely to do so.

Gaining access to dual-use materials for SLV programmes from the developed world would be an incentive for these few developing countries to sign on to a zero ballistic missile regime. Co-ordinated export restrictions like those of the MTCR would at some point be phased out against countries abiding by a ZBM regime.[28] This would be especially beneficial to India and Brazil, both of whom have been denied technology for their space programmes because of fears about ballistic missile proliferation. Removal of MTCR export controls would not mean that any country would be compelled to sell technology to an SLV programme, but it would mean that treaty signatories would not be able to punish other signatories for transferring space-relevant technology to third-party signatories.

Verification Issues

Verifying compliance with a ballistic missile ban, while politically challenging, would be no less feasible than verifying compliance with the Chemical Weapons Convention or with NPT obligations. Satellite and aircraft reconnaissance could be used to verify that no missiles are deployed at fixed-site launch pads. Verifying the absence of mobile missiles would be more difficult; however, it is probable that the permanent five members of the UN Security Council who have in the past sold missiles to Third World countries maintain accurate records of the number of launchers and missiles sold. Some base-line figures of missiles and launchers liable for dismantlement should therefore exist.

Development of a new missile cannot be kept secret. As then CIA Director William Webster acknowledged in May 1989 that 'the status of missile development programs is less difficult to track than nuclear weapons development. New missile systems must be tested thoroughly and in the open'.[29] Flight testing is essential and is unavoidably observable – and becomes more easily observable the longer the range of the missile. US early warning satellites, which reportedly tracked all of the Iraqi Scud launches during the Gulf War, could reliably determine whether missiles were or were not being flight tested.

But ballistic missiles and space-launchers are nearly identical.[30] It is therefore possible that testing could be conducted under the guise of an SLV programme, with the intention later to produce and deploy missiles. However, SLVs and ballistic missiles can be distinguished by differences in trajectory, rocket size, guidance, propulsion, launch facilities and infrastructure and, of course, payload.[31] Warhead technology – and especially the presence of ablative or other heat shielding materials – is probably the most obvious discrepancy between the two vehicles. SLVs, except for a few specific missions, such as manned flights, do not have heat protected nose cones, as their payload is not re-entering the earth's atmosphere with the expended launcher.[32] Distinguishing between SLVs and missiles would be simplest if the regime provided for pre-launch inspection, yet detection of a covert missile programme should be possible even without such provisions.[33]

For verifying destruction of missiles, safeguarding dual use materials, and inspecting and observing space-launches, an international inspectorate would most likely have to be created. This body could also promote regional missile disarmament in pursuit of ZBM and explore verification options for all aspects of a ZBM regime. For instance, this body could decide whether conversion of decommissioned ICBMs to SLVs would be permitted and how this would be verified.[34]

Getting to Zero

At their June 1992 summit, Presidents Yeltsin and Bush agreed to START-II cuts that addressed both the Russians' desire to cut submarine-based ballistic missile weapons and the US desire to cut multiple-warhead land-based weapons to an interim ceiling of around 4,000 warheads. The cuts are to be accomplished within the seven-year

START implementation period, and by 2003 both sides are to have reduced to a total of 3,000-3,500 warheads each, with all MIRVed ICBMs to be eliminated and SLBM warheads to be reduced to no more than 1,750 on each side.

These reductions bring the two countries down to levels where reciprocity from the other nuclear powers can begin to be expected.[35] A ZBM approach would reorient future superpower strategic cuts away from counting warheads and toward counting missiles and launchers. To initiate such a regime, the US and Russia might announce further (perhaps 50 per cent) 'post-START-II' strategic cuts and invite the other three declared nuclear powers to join them. Ballistic missiles of each type deployed and stockpiled could be halved, with the warheads dismantled and the launchers and missiles destroyed (unless agreement was reached that they could be converted to SLVs). Of course, other forms of delivery, including cruise missiles and bombers, must be subject to ceilings to prevent their being built up in place of the ballistic missiles that are eliminated.

The 50 per cent reduction need not take long; when President Reagan put forward the idea at Reykjavik in 1986, his proposal called for a 50 per cent reduction within five years and total elimination of the US and Soviet missile stockpiles within ten years. While these cuts are being realized (concomitant with START and START-II cuts), the US and Russia should promote a global consensus banning ballistic missiles as weapons delivery vehicles. They could make their further reduction, and eventual elimination of all ballistic missiles, contingent on missile reductions from other states with ballistic missiles and pledges of ballistic missile non-proliferation from countries that do not possess them. Regional missile disarmament negotiations could be facilitated by Russia and the United States. The first steps would be to take a sounding of which countries in principle are willing to disavow ballistic missiles, to discover their concerns about the proposal, and to address those concerns. Janne Nolan has suggested an 'International Missile Conference', analogous to the Paris Conference on Chemical Weapons held in January 1989, where countries could air their views on missile proliferation restrictions and international space co-operation schemes.[36] Such a forum would provide an excellent opportunity for the superpowers to propose the elimination of all ballistic missiles.

Over 160 countries today do not deploy ballistic missiles, and could be expected to sign a missile ban right away. Entire regions of the world currently remain free of deployed ballistic missiles and apparently free of intentions to deploy them. These regions include South and Central America, sub-Saharan Africa (with the possible exception of South

Africa), Australasia and Antarctica.[37] Third World missile proliferation is fairly well localized on the Korean peninsula, on the Indian subcontinent and, most intractably, in the Middle East. It is in these regions that ZBM is most needed, and perhaps most difficult to envision. In each of the regions where proliferation is occurring, confidence building measures on route to ZBM agreement could first implemented. Such measures might include pre-notification of missile flight tests and inspection of missile production or deployment facilities. There follows a brief examination of the three regional missile races, and an examination of the feasibility of missile disarmament in each case.

Middle East Missile Roll-Back

In late 1988 the State Department began exploring missile control in the Middle East through separate talks with the Egyptian and Israeli governments. Under discussion, reportedly, were small confidence-building steps such as advance notice of missile flight tests and possibly 'no first use' pledges that could lay the groundwork for farther-reaching steps in the future.[38] Nothing more was reported of these efforts until 1991. In his policy pronouncement on Mideast arms control on 29 May of that year, President Bush called for a halt to further acquisition, production and testing of ballistic missiles of any range by states in the region, leading to 'the ultimate elimination of such missiles from their arsenals'.[39] At a subsequent meeting of the permanent five UN Security Council members in Paris, the world's other major military powers endorsed this proposal. Principally, their support will take the form of increased vigilance on export controls of related technologies and, presumably, a reaffirmed pledge by all five not to sell any further missiles to the region.

Whether there is any support from within the region for the plan remains uncertain. No country has yet specifically embraced this one component of the President's arms control package, but many states have endorsed other, related measures. In general, Israel advocates limits on conventional arms transfers to the region, while the Arab states prefer to deal with unconventional weapons (notably nuclear) first. Because of their historical use as delivery vehicles for nuclear payloads, and because of their relationship to conventional air force capabilities, ballistic missiles fall into a grey area and so missile disarmament might be acceptable to both sides as a first step. Indeed, Egyptian President Hosni Mubarak has vigorously endorsed a plan for a zone free of weapons of mass destruction in the Middle East, which calls on all Middle Eastern countries to announce their commitment to 'deal effectively and honestly with matters involving the delivery systems of various weapons of mass destruction'.[40]

During a background press briefing on the President's Mideast arms control plan, an unnamed 'senior official' explained why the administration was optimistic about the possibility of a missile roll-back in the region: 'We've got an environment where you've just had an awful war; where you've had an awful image of the future; where you've got a lot of proposals out there; where you've got a coalition of potential suppliers that have shown an ability to work together; where you had countries in the region working together in unprecedented ways. It seems to all of us [in the administration] that this is certainly a situation worth exploring'.[41] Furthermore, the official said that the countries of the region with whom the administration consulted after the war were encouraging on the prospects of such a plan.

Israeli acceptance of such a plan would be a mandatory first step. Having endured 39 missile launches during the 1991 Gulf War, the Israeli public would likely be supportive of a missile disarmament regime. Israel has been, and remains, very worried about the delivery of unconventional – especially chemical – payloads via Arab missiles, and, as the Gulf War demonstrated, ATBM systems cannot provide complete protection.[42] Missiles are part of Israel's deterrence structure, and the Jericho I is believed to be a delivery means for at least some of Israel's nuclear weapons.[43] But Israel also has a potent air force and would not need ballistic missiles to provide a credible means of delivery for its nuclear weapons. Given that Israel also possesses a highly effective air defence system, a move away from ballistic missiles toward air-breathing threats only should be comforting to Israel.

A negotiated ban on missiles would seem to serve the Arab states' and Iran's security interests as well. Many of the non-Israeli missiles in the Middle East threaten not just Israel, but other Islamic states as well, and the inaccuracy of most of the deployed missiles means that they primarily threaten civilian population centres. Iranian, Iraqi and Saudi, as well as Israeli, civilians have all come under indiscriminate attack by 'Muslim missiles' in the past decade. The Middle East peace talks, initiated in Madrid in October 1991, have established a multilateral arms control working group. Regional ZBM could be discussed in this forum and might provide an issue where all sides' interests converge. Even if some countries in the region might not accept such an agreement, regional missile disarmament could still be effective. For example, if Libya refused to join the regime, this decision would immediately affect only Algeria and Egypt, since Libya currently only has 300 km range Scud missiles. Political and military assurances could be pledged in support of Algeria and Egypt (or any country against whom missiles are used or threatened), including perhaps the provision ATBMs.

Averting an Indian-Pakistani Missile Race

India began pursuing a civilian space-launch capability in the mid-1970s and has used some of its space-launch vehicle technology in a military missile programme. The two-stage, 2,400 km range Agni – first tested in May 1989 – uses, as its first stage, the solid-fuel booster motor of the SLV-3 satellite launch vehicle.[44] India first tested the 240 km range Prithvi in 1989, and has tested this system several times since. This short-range system was expected to be deployed by now, but, testifying in January 1992, the Director of the Defense Intelligence Agency said that both Pakistan and India 'may deploy short-range ballistic missiles by the end of the decade',[45] making it seem unlikely that the longer-range Agni will be deployed for quite some time, if at all. In fact, it has been described by Indian officials as a 'technology demonstrator', a demonstration undoubtedly aimed at Beijing as much as Islamabad. With the Agni launch, India joined the ranks of the US, CIS, UK, France, China and Israel, as the only countries to have built a missile of such long range.

In early 1989 Pakistan reportedly tested two short range missile systems, Hatf-I and Hatf-II. Pakistan claimed at the time that these were indigenously developed with some Chinese assistance, but it is now believed that they were French-supplied rockets.[46] Pakistan does have some indigenous missile activity, and its space agency, SUPARCO, is working toward a space-launch vehicle. In mid-1991 some missile technology controlled under the MTCR was transferred from China to Pakistan, resulting in the imposition of sanctions by the United States against the Chinese and Pakistani companies and government agencies involved.[47] In November 1992 China reportedly transferred 24 M-11 missiles to Pakistan.[48] As of May 1993, however, the State Department refused to validate the allegations, saying no determination of whether a transfer in violation of the MTCR, US law, or Chinese obligations had yet been made.

Both Pakistan and India are believed to be 'nuclear capable' on short notice. Robert Gates testified in January 1992 that the CIA has 'no reason to believe that either India or Pakistan maintains assembled or deployed nuclear bombs'. He said that both countries have all of the parts or can make the parts on very short notice. 'But we believe that they would not want to assemble them for safety reasons'.[49] It has been reported that Pakistan has converted some of its F-16s for nuclear-weapons delivery; on this, Gates testified that the CIA has 'information that suggests that they're clearly interested in enhancing the ability of the F-16 to deliver [nuclear] weapons safely'.[50] India, too, has dozens of aircraft suitable for nuclear bomb delivery.

The main source of tension between Pakistan and India is the disputed territory of Kashmir. Aligned with India after the break-up of the two countries, Pakistan and India have fought three wars over the state, which is 64 per cent Muslim. A major recent flare-up occurred in April 1992, almost leading to war. Negotiations over the issue are ongoing, but it remains a volatile situation. Nevertheless, some progress has recently been made. In December 1990, the two agreed to resume high-level weekly contacts between their militaries and to finalize an agreement on pre-notification of military exercises.[51] In January 1991 they ratified a treaty banning attacks on both countries' nuclear installations.[52] Further, in August 1992, India and Pakistan signed a bilateral treaty forswearing the development, production, acquisition or use of chemical weapons.

An agreement to forgo a costly ballistic missile race would seem to be in the interests of both India and Pakistan; both countries have per capita GNPs of under $350. Pakistan has been seeking bilateral discussions with India to address missile proliferation in South Asia,[53] and it has proposed a meeting on regional arms control, especially nuclear arms control, to include India, Pakistan, China, the US and Russia. All have agreed to attend such a meeting but India, which claims that given the global reach of nuclear weapons, they should be discussed only in a global context.[54]

India and China have recently improved relations as well. The two countries recently agreed to establish confidence-building and crisis-response measures, such as hot-line communication links between their militaries and greater openness in military operations.[55] India's acceptance of a ZBM regime would clearly be linked to Chinese acceptance. Since the majority of China's strategic nuclear deterrent is missile-based, Chinese acceptance might be difficult to obtain initially. But, as Alton Frye put it: 'China would face a clear choice: either accept the advantages to its own security of the Russo-American initiative and join the process, or keep its missiles and continue to face two vastly superior missile forces'.[56] In addition, Beijing would have to factor in a likely near-term ballistic missile threat from India.

Ballistic Missile Disarmament on the Korean Peninsula

Currently North Korea most likely deploys only the 300 km range Scud missiles which it received from Egypt, as well as some slightly extended-range Scud clones which it now produces. According to a number of sources, North Korea is refining the Scud to increase its range to about 600 kilometres and to improve its guidance system, although no technical details are available.[57] In its first flight test, in May 1990, the extended-range missile blew up on the launch pad.[58] It has apparently not yet been successfully flight tested. In December 1992 Robert Gates stated that 'Pyongyang is not far from having a much larger missile for sale – one with a range of at least 1,000 km. We also believe that North Korea may be developing an even longer range missile'.[59] However, no flight tests of a missile anywhere near this range have been reported in the press.

North Korea's currently deployed Scud missiles already permit strikes on most of South Korea. Joseph Bermudez writes that 'of the 109 active air fields/bases within the ROK, 48 are within the operational range of FROG-5 [50 km range artillery rocket] and 91 are within operational Scud-B range' of the forward-based missiles.[60] An enhanced-range Scud might be able to hit the remaining strategic rear area military targets in the southern end of the peninsula, while a 1,000 km North Korean missile would put Japan, China and part of Siberia within striking distance. Reports of North Korea's nuclear programme make such missile developments highly worrisome to those countries. Allegations that North Korea is selling its Scud missiles to countries in the Middle East, as well as helping some countries establish their own production facilities, add to the desirability of obtaining North Korean agreement to missile disarmament.

Through reverse-engineering of US-supplied Nike-Hercules surface-to-air missiles, South Korea produced the 240 km 'Korean SSM', a two-stage, solid fuel, surface-to-surface missile. Seoul has also announced plans for an ambitious space-launch programme. The Congressional Research Service reported in 1988 that a launch vehicle was to be tested by 1991 (it never was), with the launch of a 1,100 lb. satellite by 1996.[61] While this early date is unlikely, South Korea is a technically advanced industrializing country and is developing a military aerospace industry through licensed production of the American F-16. It had a GNP of over $210 billion last year (compared to an estimated $30 billion for North Korea), and could likely produce fairly sophisticated ballistic missiles if it chose to do so.

Until recently, relations between the two Koreas had been improving markedly. In December 1991 they signed both an agreement on 'Reconciliation, Non-aggression and Exchanges and Cooperation', and a 'Joint Declaration of the Denuclearization of the Korean Peninsula'. Under the agreements, each side commits not to 'test, manufacture, produce, receive, possess, store, deploy or use' nuclear weapons.[62] These agreements entered into force on 19 February 1992, but the verification mechanisms were not worked out. The two sides also agreed to establish a North–South Joint Military Commission to 'discuss and carry out steps to build military confidence and realize arms reductions . . . including the elimination of weapons of mass destruction and attack capabilities, and vertification thereof'.[63] They also agreed to hold further talks aimed at national reconciliation, and are carrying out exchanges in the sciences, sports and art. The Agreement also calls on the two sides to 'permit free correspondence, reunions and visits between dispersed family members and other relatives and . . . promote the voluntary reunion of divided families'. In a lengthy interview, out-going South Korean President Roh Tae Woo said in September 1992 that tensions on the peninsula were greatly reduced, and that South Korea's recent normalization of relations with China and Russia (further isolating North Korea) imnproved prospects for unification.[64]

Ties between the two countries, however, took a sudden turn for the worse in late 1992 over the alleged North Korean nuclear weapons programme. In early May 1992 Pyongyang made a declaration of its nuclear materials holdings and nuclear facilities to the International Atomic Energy Agency (IAEA), in order to negotiate an effective safeguards agreement under the nuclear Non-Proliferation Treaty. In November technicians discovered discrepancies which indicated that the North had actually separated more plutonium than it had declared. Although the IAEA has thus far uncovered no evidence to indicate that North Korea possesses a nuclear weapon, some experts fear that the North may have separated the five to ten kilograms necessary for the construction of an atomic bomb. Because of these fears and discrepancies, as well as intelligence information provided by the CIA, the IAEA now wants to inspect two undeclared sites which are suspected of being covert waste storage facilities. Pyongyang refused to allow the inspections and instead, in early March, opted to withdraw from the NPT, a process which takes six months to effect. At the time of writing, representatives from the United States are meeting with officials from North Korea in Beijing, attempting to persuade the North to reverse its decision to withdraw, and to allow full IAEA inspections. Obviously the establishment of a ballistic missile-free peninsula hinges on a satisfactory resolution of this ongoing crisis.

Conclusion

Given this regional progress, one may question whether a global ZBM regime is needed. But because certain of the regional ballistic missile aspirants are engaged in arms races with the declared nuclear powers, a purely regional approach would probably not work. India is not likely to agree to ZBM unless China is involved, and Pakistan would not likely agree if India did not. And if Pakistan did not agree, Israel (in light of Pakistan's alleged 'Islamic bomb') might not join a Mideast ZBM. And so on.

By itself, a ballistic missile capability is far less dangerous than a nuclear weapons capability. Ballistic missiles do, however, heighten the danger by radically reducing decision-making time and increasing fears of a sudden attack. Currently, few countries in the world deploy nuclear-tipped ballistic missiles, and only a handful have intercontinental range missiles. But more ICBM countries can be expected to emerge in the coming decades, and the Third World countries closest to developing long-range missiles and SLVs also have nuclear weapons. While these countries (Israel and India) may not be politically very worrisome to the United States, deployment of long-range nuclear missiles by them is bound to increase the anxiety and insecurity of many other countries.

Currently, the preferred strategy of the US government to prevent or at least forestall this eventuality is a missile technology export control regime and research and development of anti-missile systems. Such a system, rather than providing global security, may actually increase global anxiety and tension. A global ballistic missile disarmament regime, co-operatively engaging the developing world in the disarmament process, providing demonstrable security benefits, and not seeking to obstruct legitimate civilian space efforts, provides a more promising solution to the missile proliferation threat posed to those countries and to the United States.

To achieve ZBM, the United States and Russia must restructure future strategic cuts away from warhead reductions and toward missile reductions. They must announce a substantial bilateral missile force cut beyond the recent 'START-II' agreement, while making the complete elimination of their ballistic missiles contingent on agreement by the other missile states to join in going to zero. The superpowers could jump-start the process by initiating a treaty of declared intent and opening it for signature, or by holding a global conference in which participants engaged in regional missile races would be asked to declare that if their adversary (or adversaries) would get rid of its (their) missiles, they would do likewise.

Elimination of ballistic missiles, while not a solution to all of the world's security problems, provides a good interim goal for further nuclear reductions. Dismantlement of all the five declared nuclear powers' nuclear missiles would constitute large-scale nuclear disarmament and a clear demonstration of good faith. At the 1995 Non-Proliferation Treaty review conference, where the signatories will decide whether to extend the treaty, and beyond, such measures will be needed to persuade today's non-nuclear states that their long-term goal should be to live in a nuclear-free world, not to join the club.

NOTES

1. For example, the Chairman of the Senate Armed Services Committee, Sam Nunn, has argued in favour of developing an anti-ballistic missile (ABM) system, claiming that the US will not 'remain safe from long-range ballistic missiles launched . . . deliberately by a third world country'. Sam Nunn, 'Needed: An ABM Defence', *New York Times*, 31 July 1991, p. A19.
2. Prepared testimony of Robert Gates, before the Senate Governmental Affairs Committee, 15 Jan. 1992, p. 3
3. Testimony of Gordon Oehler before the Senate Governmental Affairs Committee (Washington: Federal News Services, 15 Jan. 1992).
4. Of the approximately 180 nation-states in the world today, only eight – the United States, France, Britain, China, Russia, Kazakhstan, Belarus and Ukraine – deploy inter-continental range ballistic missiles or submarine-launched ballistic missiles. Of these, three (Belarus, Kazakhstan and Ukraine) have pledged to eliminate or transfer these missiles.

   Four additional countries deploy or have until recently deployed intermediate range (500–5,500 km) ballistic missiles: Bulgaria (500 km), Czechoslovakia (500 km), Israel (1,450 km), and Saudi Arabia (1,850 km). North Korea is reported to be working on a 600–1,000 km range missile, but no successful flight tests of it have been reported. India has twice flight tested a 2,400 km range missile, the Agni. Iraq previously deployed 600 km and possibly 800 km extended-range Scud missiles. These missiles have now been destroyed by the UN Special Commission implementing the Gulf War cease-fire agreement.

   Fifteen other countries deploy or have until recently deployed short range ballistic missiles (110–500 km). These are: Afghanistan, Pakistan, North Korea, South Korea, Egypt, Iran, Libya, Syria, Yemen, Germany, Italy, the Netherlands, Hungary, Poland and Romania. Of these fifteen, six are European countries that have already demobilized their short-range Lance, Scud, SS-21 and SS-23 missiles. Of the remaining nine – all of which are developing countries – four deploy only Scud missiles transferred from the Soviet Union in the 1970s and 1980s and have no known indigenous missile production capability or intent. The remaining five countries also imported Scud or other short-range missiles and are now producing them or attempting to do so. See Lora Lumpe, Lisbeth Gronlund and David C. Wright, 'Third World Missiles Fall Short', *Bulletin of the Atomic Scientists*, Vol. 48, No. 2 (March 1992), p. 32.
5. Australia, Austria, Belgium, Canada, Denmark, Finland, France, Germany, Greece, Iceland, Ireland, Italy, Japan, Luxembourg, the Netherlands, New Zealand, Norway, Portugal, Spain, Sweden, Switzerland, the United Kingdom and the United States.
6. In 1990 the Soviet Union agreed to abide by the MTCR export guidelines. At least four of the former Soviet republics – including Russia – are interested in becoming formal members of the MTCR, and 'have asked [the US] to send out a team to tell them what they have to do to qualify' for membership. Transcript of remarks by Richard Clarke, Assistant Secretary of State for Politico-Military Affairs, to the Washington Institute for Near East Policy, 4 Dec. 1991, pp. 5-2 and 6-1. As of December 1992, none had become members.

   The Chinese are apparently not slated to become full members of the MTCR either, although during former Secretary of State James Baker's trip to China in

November 1991 the Chinese Foreign Ministry spokesman reportedly said that 'China intends to abide by the standards and interpretations of the Missile Technology Control Regime when making technological transfers, on the condition that the United States lift the three sanctions it placed on China on 16 June 1991'. *Zhongguo Xinwen She*, 21 Nov. 91, reprinted in Foreign Information Broadcasting Service (FBIS), *China: Daily Report*, No. 91-225, p. 1. This condition was met by the Bush administration in February 1992 after the Chinese government put its pledge down in writing. In September 1992, in waiving further satellite export sanctions as part of this agreement, the State Department reported: 'The Administration has carefully monitored Chinese compliance [with its missile export control pledge] and concludes that Chinese behavior is consistent with its obligations'. Statement by State Department Spokesman Richard Boucher, 11 Sept. 1992.

Israel announced in the autumn of 1991 that it would adhere to the MTCR export guidelines beginning on 1 January 1992. This adherence was urged by Washington in exchange for the US not applying sanctions against Israel for missile proliferation activities involving South Africa. The Foreign Affairs and Defence Committee of the Knesset approved amendments to Israel's relevant legislation (the Control of Commodities and Services Order) to implement Israel's adherence to MTCR export guidelines on 24 December 1991. No other approval is required to make the decision effective. See *Davar* 25 Dec. 1991, reprinted in FBIS, Near East: Daily Report, No. 91–251, p. 19; and *Wall Street Journal*, 26 Dec. 91, p. 4.

According to State Department testimony before Congress in March 1992, a dialogue with East European countries, South Africa, Argentina and Brazil about membership to the regime has begun. State Department testimony the following month stated that Argentina now observes 'MTCR-equivalent controls'. Testimony of Richard Clarke before the Joint Economic Committee, 13 March 1992.

At the last meeting of the MTCR, on 8 March in Canberra, Australia, both Argentina and Hungary were invited to become members. US Department of State, Office of the Assistant Secretary/Spokesman, 25 March 1993.

7. Office of the Press Secretary, White House, 'Summary of the Equipment and Technology Annex', 16 April 1987, p. 3.
8. For example, the joint Argentine-Egyptian-Iraqi Condor missile programme.
9. 'Missile Technology Control Regime: Fact Sheet to Accompany Public Announcement', White House Office of the Press Secretary, 16 April 1987, p.1
10. *Federal Register*, 18 May 1992, pp. 21143–4 and *Federal Register*, 19 May 1992, p. 21319.
11. *Aviation Week & Space Technology*, 29 June 1992, p. 68.
12. A better approach for controlling exports of missile- or space-launch relevant technology was outlined in a major study of export controls released by the National Academy of Sciences in 1991. The report recommended that the US avoid unilateral application of export controls and focus on destinations of the greatest proliferation concern – countries that violate some norms of conduct. 'In order to be effective, proliferation controls must be focused only on narrowly proscribed military activities or items that are required *directly* for weapons systems and must include, to the extent practicable, verifiable end-use assurances. Lacking such specificity, efforts to control exports of proliferation-related technologies create a risk . . . [of] imposing significant economic costs that may be disproportionate to their effectiveness'. Panel on the Future Design and Implementation of US National Security Export Controls, Committee on Science, Engineering and Public Policy, *Executive Summary: Finding Common Ground*, Washington DC: National Academy Press, 1991, pp. 23–4.
13. The 'Missile Technology Control Regime (MTCR) Fact Sheet', undated, but released by the State Department following the November 1991 MTCR plenary meeting in Washington DC, notes that 'the Guidelines are open to all nations to implement, and all governments are encouraged to do so'.
14. Dan Revelle, 'US Muscle Misses the Mark', *Bulletin of the Atomic Scientists*, Nov. 1992, pp. 10–11, 44.

15. 'French Cryogenic Technology for GSLV', *The Hindu*, 30 Oct. 1989 cited in Center for International Security and Arms Control, *Assessing Ballistic Missile Proliferation* (Stanford: Center for International Security and Arms Control, 1991), p. 127.
16. A better standard might be any projectile following a ballistic trajectory for the majority of its flight with a range of 100 km or greater with a 500 kg payload.
17. 'Revisions to MTCR Guidelines', released on 7 January 1993 by US Department of State.
18. Prepared testimony of Undersecretary of State Reginald Bartholomew, before the House Foreign Affairs Committee, Subcommittees on Arms Control and Europe/ Middle East, 24 March 1992.
19. Kenneth Adelman, 'Curing Missile Measles', *Washington Times*, 17 April 1989, p. D1 and 'How to Limit Everybody's Missiles', *New York Times*, 7 April 1991; Kathleen C. Bailey, 'Rushing to Build Missiles', *Washington Post*, 6 April 1990, p. A15 and 'Can Missile Proliferation be Reversed?', *Orbis*, Vol. 35 No. 1 (Winter 1991), pp. 5–14.
20. The continental United States is roughly 8,000–10,000 km from the Middle East and 8,000 km from the Korean peninsula.
21. Center for International Security and Arms Control, *Assessing Ballistic Missile Proliferation*, p. 162
22. For more on the proposal at Reykjavik, see Don Oberdorfer, *The Turn: From the Cold War to a New Era* (New York: Touchstone, 1992, pp. 155–209. For analyses of the proposal at the time, see Richard Perle, 'Reykjavik as a Watershed in US-Soviet Arms Control', Thomas C. Schelling, 'Abolition of Ballistic Missiles', Leon Sloss, 'A World Without Ballistic Missiles', and Randall Forsberg, 'Abolishing Ballistic Missiles', in *International Security*, Vol. 12, No. 1 (Summer 1987), pp. 175–96.
23. See Sidney D. Drell, 'Science and National Security', *Occasional Paper*, American Association for the Advancement of Science, 1992; *F.A.S. Public Interest Report*, May/June 1992; Sidney D. Drell, 'Abolishing Long-range Nuclear Missiles', *Issues in Science and Technology*, (Spring 1992), pp. 34–5; and Alton Frye, 'Zero Ballistic Missiles', *Foreign Policy*, No. 88 (Fall 1992), pp. 3–20.
24. The presence of hundreds of ballistic missiles in the Middle East has not deterred war or the use of these missiles. In fact, only Afghanistan and the Middle East have seen ballistic missile warfare since Germany fired V-2 missiles in World War II. Over a thousand Scud missiles have been fired in the 1973 October War, the intense missile warfare in the Iran-Iraq War, the Afghan civil war and the recent war over Kuwait. This pattern of missile use is especially ominous when considering the possible proliferation of mass destruction payloads. It is not clear that such unconventionally armed missiles will be effective as deterrents, and not be used, eventually.
25. A report leaked to the press in January suggested that in the post Cold War, 'every reasonable adversary' – some presumably in the developing world – should be targeted with nuclear and non-nuclear weapons. R. Jeffrey Smith, 'US Urged to Cut 50% of A-Arms', *Washington Post*, 6 Jan. 1992, p. A1.
26. The United States, CIS, Italy, China, Japan, Israel, India and the European Space Agency. Brazil is working to attain such a capability but is not projected to do so for several years.
27. *Space News*, 7–13 Sept. 1992, p. 22.
28. In the multilateral Chemical Weapons Convention, just completed, the 'Australia Group' chemical weapon-relevant export controls will initially be left in place, but their continued application will be reviewed as the treaty is implemented. Some provision would have to be made under ZBM to maintain the MTCR export controls that restrict the transfer of cruise missiles and related technologies to developing countries.
29. Prepared testimony of William Webster, before the Senate Governmental Affairs Committee, 18 May 1989.
30. A recent paper prepared for the SDI Organization notes the potential ballistic missile threats to the US posed by these launch vehicles: 'Those nations with access to space

launch vehicles can readily convert the vehicles into ICBMs. Certain countries may be willing to sell or transfer their space launch vehicles to other states for legitimate space purposes, such as communications, surveillance and scientific exploration; once sold, these vehicles may be used for weapons purposes . . . The increasing availability of space launch vehicles and space launch services could result in the ability of certain Third World countries to threaten the continental United States with ICBMs carrying nuclear, chemical or biological payloads in the mid to late 1900s [*sic*]. Although these threats will be limited to a few ICBMs – probably 10 or less – with very poor accuracies, they could be an effective deterrent to desired US actions or they could be used as terrorist weapons. These potential threats should be taken into account in GPALS planning. Sidney Graybeal and Patricia McFate, 'GPALS and Foreign Space Launch Vehicle Capabilities', Science Applications International Corporation, prepared under SDIO contract no. 84-91-C-0012, p. 18.

31. See Jürgen Scheffran, 'Dual Use of Missiles and Space Technologies', in Götz Neuneck and Otfried Ischebeck (eds.), *Missile Technologies, Proliferation, and Concepts for Arms Control* (Baden-Baden: Nomos Verlag, 1993).
32. Dr Phillip Morrison, in *F.A.S. Public Interest Report* (May/June 1992), p. 12.
33. For more on verification issues, see Frye, 'Zero Ballistic Missiles', pp. 12–17.
34. Russia is currently proposing to convert SS-25 and SS-18s into SLVs. Ironically, the SDIO has even suggested that Russian SS-18s might be used to launch 'Brilliant Pebbles' – part of GPALS – into orbit. Conversion in the US space industry is highly controversial. Most companies, fearing lost revenues (and jobs and industrial base capacity) oppose the idea; however, Martin Marietta currently has a £660 million contract to refurbish 14 US Titan II to SLVs. This work includes modifying the forward end of the second stage to accommodate 10 foot fairings of varying lengths; refurbishing the liquid fuel engines; upgrading the inertial guidance and developing new command, destruct and telemetry systems. One reworked Titan has already flown. The cost per missile is $47 million. *Aerospace America*, May 1992, pp. 15–16.
35. In the past, Britain, France and China have each said that they would reduce their nuclear weapons forces only after Washington and Moscow reduced their nuclear forces by some substantial, but unspecified, amount. In response to cuts announced in 1991 and 1992, however, China declared that before it will join them, the US and Russia must first 'cut their nuclear arsenal to China's level'. Zhang Ping, 'State lauds disarming proposals', cited in John Wilson Lewis and Hua Di, 'China's Ballistic Missile Programmes', *International Security*, Vol. 17, No. 2 (Fall 1992), p. 39.

    Britain and France currently deploy all of their strategic nuclear forces on ballistic missiles. ZBM would therefore imply renunciation of their strategic nuclear deterrents or a reconfiguration of their forces. Currently Britain plans to continue with the procurement of US Trident nuclear submarines, having ordered its fourth in July 1992. Under pressure from the United States, it is likely that Britain would reconsider its position. France has canceled its short-range Hads nuclear missile and will eliminate its Pluton missiles, and further evolution of the French position is not inconceivable.

    China is believed to have eight nuclear ICBMs, 12 nuclear SLBMs, about 60 nuclear IRBMs and 120 H-6 medium-range strategic bombers with about 240 nuclear bombs. See IISS, *The Military Balance 1992–1993* (London: Brassey's for IISS, 1992), p. 236. As part of a ZBM arrangement, China could be permitted to acquire a more credible strategic bomber force, perhaps by buying Russian bombers.
36. Janne Nolan, *Trappings of Power* (Washington, DC: The Brookings Institution, 1991), p. 165
37. A ban on the deployment of ballistic missiles in South America was recently proposed by Peru. (UN General Assembly A/46/397)
38. 'US Presses Mideast Missile Talks', *Washington Post*, 28 Dec. 1988, p. 15.
39. White House, Office of the Press Secretary, 'Fact Sheet on Middle East Arms Control Initiative', 29 May 1991, p.2
40. MENA (Cairo), 5 Aug. 1991, reprinted in FBIS, *Near East: Daily Report*, No. 91–151, p. 20.

41. White House background briefing on President Bush's Middle East Arms Control Initiative, Released by the Office of the Press Secretary, Colorado Springs, Colorado, 29 May 1991.
42. Some have questioned whether Patriot provided any protection from Scud launches, or even increased the danger and physical damage. See Theodore A. Postal, 'Lessons of the Gulf War Experience with Patriot', *International Security*, Vol. 16, No. 3 (Winter 1991/92), pp. 119–71.
43. 'Surface-to-Surface Missile Systems Handbook – Free World', DST-100H-283-89, July 1989, p. 20
44. Gary Milhollin, 'India's Missiles – With a Little Help from Our Friends', *Bulletin of the Atomic Scientists*, Vol. 45, No. 9 (Nov. 1989), p. 35
45. Prepared testimony of Lt. Gen. James Clapper before the Senate Armed Services Committee, 22 Jan. 1992, p. 13.
46. Aaron Karp, 'Ballistic Missile Proliferation', in *SIPRI Yearbook 1991* (Oxford: Oxford University Press, 1991), p. 341.
47. *Federal Register*, 17 July 91, p. 32601.
48. Jim Mann, 'China Said to Sell Pakistan New Missiles', *Los Angeles Times*, 4 Dec. 1991; R. Jeffrey Smith, 'China Said to Sell Arms To Pakistan', *Washington Post*, 4 Dec. 91, p. A10.
49. Testimony of Robert Gates, before the Senate Governmental Affairs Committee, 15 Jan. 1992.
50. Ibid.
51. Steve Coll, 'India, Pakistan Agree on Treaty', *Washington Post*, 21 Dec. 1990.
52. Although it had been signed in 1988, lists of protected sites – nuclear power and research facilities, uranium enrichment plants and other related facilities – were first exchanged in Jan. 1992.
53. FBIS, *Near East: Daily Report*, no. 92–108, pp. 42–3.
54. 'We don't want a meeting in which three powers outside the region tell us what to do', the Indian Foreign Secretary said in March 1992. Gus Constantine, 'India Ready to Discuss Nuclear Arms Control with US', *Washington Times*, 11 March 1992.
55. Brahma Chellaney, 'India-China Border Tensions Easing', *Washington Times*, 11 August 1992, p. A8.
56. Frye, 'Zero Ballistic Missiles', p. 9.
57. Karp, 'Ballistic Missile Proliferation', p. 319; Joseph S. Bermudez, Jr., 'New Developments in North Korean Missile Programme', *Jane's Soviet Intelligence Review*, August 1990, p. 343.
58. Bill Gertz, 'North Korean Missile Apparently Blows Up', *Washington Times*, 5 July 1990.
59. Robert Gates, 'Weapons Proliferation: The Most Dangerous Challenge for American Intelligence', prepared remarks for the Costmock Club, Sacramento, 15 Dec. 1992, p. 16.
60. Joseph S. Bermudez, Jr., 'Korean People's Army NBC Capabilities', Statement for the Record before the Senate Permanent Subcommittee on Investigations, 9 Feb. 1989, p. 16.
61. Shuey *et al.*, *Missile Proliferation: Survey of Emerging Missile Forces*, CRS Report for Congress, Oct. 1988, p. 82.
62. 'Joint Declaration of the Denuclearization of the Korean Peninsula', CD/1147, 25 March 92.
63. 'Agreement on Reconciliation, Non-aggression and Exchanges and Cooperation between the South and the North', CD/1147, 25 March 1992.
64. David E. Sanger, 'North Korea's A-Bomb Plans Seem Less Certain', *New York Times*, 18 Sept. 1992; Don Oberdorfer, 'S. Korean Sees Better Chance at Unification', *Washington Post*, 22 Sept. 1992 p. A16.

Multilateral Management of International Security: The Non-Proliferation Model

GEORGE H. QUESTER

The end of the Cold War has had many positive consequences, but many new security problems have also emerged in its wake. The good news is a lowered likelihood of war, nuclear or conventional, between East and West. Ideological issues have receded as a cause of military tension. The prospect that a single power can or will dominate the Eurasian continent has effectively disappeared. As the chance of a major war recedes, the world has come to anticipate substantial disarmament.

But as a part of the 'peace dividend', we have seen Saddam Hussein challenge the world community, daring peace-loving states to go to war in response to his 'unification' of Kuwait with Iraq.[1] Additionally, the termination of the Cold War has uncorked virulent ethnic disputes that liberals and Marxists alike dismissed as outmoded after 1945.[2] Moreover, the break-up of the Soviet Union raises new concerns about nuclear command and control arrangements. More generally, the technology for nuclear and other weapons of mass destruction continues to spread. Yet new problems sometimes create new solutions. With the demise of the Warsaw Pact in 1990 and the break-up of the Soviet Union in 1991, we can anticipate major new multilateral approaches to managing issues of war and peace. We may even come closer to realizing the vision of Woodrow Wilson and his colleagues for the League of Nations – a more effective system of collective security and a stronger and more authoritative multinational consensus on all the arms procurement and use issues that together constitute the international security problem.[3]

This paper examines both the new demands and the new opportunities for the multilateral management of international security. I focus on several new security problems – including the spread of deadly technologies, the break-up of the Soviet Union, and ethnic disputes – whose effective management demands multilateral co-operation. I also suggest what factors will tend to favour a new multilateral approach to these problems, including the role of the United States therein. I contend that past co-operation on nuclear proliferation provides a valuable and encouraging model of new multilateral approaches to international security.[4] Of course, the collective management of international security will confront some inherent logical paradoxes, but these are similar to the paradoxes already encountered and successfully managed in past efforts to deal with the proliferation issue. This suggests that the prospects for collective security may in fact be brighter than many currently suspect.[5]

The Spread of Deadly Technologies

The cliche of the 1990s is that the proliferation of nuclear, chemical and biological weapons, as well as their means of delivery, may be getting out of control. Recent Western concern about this threat is due partly to the fading of Cold War anxieties, allowing previously subordinated threats to receive greater attention. This shift is also attributable, however, to recent revelations about the nuclear capabilities of Iraq and North Korea, as well as to continued concerns about the capabilities of Israel, Pakistan and India. Although there has been some good news as well (with Brazil, Argentina, and South Africa agreeing not to join the nuclear club), pessimism has always characterized discussions of nuclear proliferation. Unfortunately, this continues to be the norm today.[6] The imminence of the 1995 Review Conference of the nuclear Non-Proliferation Treaty (NPT) – a special event in the series of these Review Conferences in that a vote must be taken on whether to continue the treaty – has reinforced a general sense that time is running short to stem the tide of nuclear proliferation.[7]

There was a time when the principal source of all nuclear technology was the United States, and when the United States and the Soviet Union were the main suppliers of conventional weapons. This time has long passed. Since the 1970s, many countries have entered the nuclear technology export and conventional weapons transfer markets, partly to recoup mounting development costs at home. There now is a widespread consensus that a multilateral forum is not only the best, but the only way to manage this set of problems. The London Nuclear Suppliers' Group has set a precedent of support for the NPT and other barriers to nuclear proliferation. Similarly, the Missile Technology Control Regime (MTCR) has sought to halt the spread of ballistic missiles, and the Australia Group has attempted to prevent the proliferation of chemical and biological warfare technology.

Nuclear proliferation is the single issue on which Soviet-American cooperation, continuing since the mid-1960s, has been well established. In negotiations of the nuclear Non-Proliferation Treaty, the NPT Review Conferences and IAEA conferences, and in all of the related dealings since then, the Soviet and American delegations have been repeatedly perceived as close conspirators. A prominent Frenchman who attended most of these conferences once complained that when listening to the proceedings in the French translation, he could never tell whether the Soviet or the American delegate was speaking, since they always said exactly the same thing!

Despite Indian and Brazilian propaganda efforts to paint the NPT as a superpower 'condominium' dictation by the 'haves' to the 'have-nots', the vast majority of nations around the world have steadily and quietly co-operated with the NPT effort. Most nations have abstained from acquiring nuclear weapons, believing this to be in their own national interests. Moreover, most sense a broad international interest in preventing the further spread of nuclear weapons. With very few exceptions, the collective wisdom is that the nuclear weapon is not just another weapon, but inherently different. And, while many nations appear to believe that it might be nice to be the only nuclear weapons state in a region, most agree that it would be very dangerous to be one of a pair of nations in a region facing one another with such weapons. The predominant logic of the nuclear age has become one of 'we won't get nuclear weapons, as long as you don't'.

Nuclear weapons have indeed been 'used' since Nagasaki – to deter others from using these weapons against military or civilian targets and to deter the use of conventional forces. But there is little evidence that such 'use' has led others to acquire a similar capability. What we have seen, rather, is that the capacity of manufacturing the bomb can also be so 'used', in this special sense of mutual deterrence, to encourage mutual abstention.

The Paradoxical Need for Collective Security in a Peace-Oriented World

Perhaps the most difficult test of collective military restraint (a restraint that hopefully will extend beyond nuclear proliferation) comes when dealing with aggression. Clausewitz, astute and subtle on so many matters, captured this paradox well in his comment that the 'aggressor is always peace-loving'.[8] In effect, it is the side that resists aggression that causes a war to begin, rather than the side that first embarks upon it. We remember World War II as having begun in September 1939 when Hitler invaded Poland (and when the Poles resisted), rather than having begun in March 1939 when the Germans entered Prague (and when the Czechs chose not to resist). The Gulf War is remembered as having begun on 16 January 1992 (when the US-led coalition launched its air offensive), rather than on 2 August 1990 (when Iraqi forces overran Kuwait virtually unopposed). Therefore, wars start when there is resistance, not necessarily when there is aggression.

The paradox of the use of military force parallels the paradox of proliferation. If all countries were to forswear the acquisition of nuclear weapons – especially if the existing nuclear powers were to divest themselves of all such weapons – this may set an example of restraint. But there would be a great temptation for some country to acquire such weapons, thereby becoming the only nuclear power, with all of the political and economic leverage this monopoly would provide. A single nuclear power in the world would make for a very unsafe world indeed. Those who believe that nuclear non-proliferation logically and morally requires a commitment to global nuclear disarmament argue the fewer nuclear powers, the better. Five nuclear weapons states are presumably better than six, and four better than five. Two may even be preferable to three. But is one preferable to two? It is precisely this fear of what the world would be like if only one nation again possessed nuclear weapons that makes it so difficult to move to zero. A world with no nuclear powers would abound with rumours of nations sneaking back to being the one and only nuclear power. The paradoxical logic of fewer would be better suggests that two nuclear powers would be better than zero or one. The world therefore should probably resign itself to the existence of at least two nuclear powers – the United States and, probably, Russia.

Some may view such a conclusion as Pentagon propaganda to justify maintaining a US nuclear arsenal, or even as an argument for a special US role as 'world policeman'. The very real paradoxes and logical inconsistencies of world politics are never welcome to those who would apply strict moral standards. Advocates of peace and disarmament are too prone to reject underlying realities of human nature and to dismiss the Roman dictum, 'Si vis pacem, pare bellum'. Conversely, the hard-headed realist may see this fundamental paradox as proof that there can be no permanent world peace, or even an enduring world order. Believers in the inevitability of armed conflict also tend to see proliferation as inevitable, arguing that sovereign nations will seek to acquire nuclear and other weapons of mass destruction as a natural assertion of their sovereignty.

The thrust of my analysis so far is that the paradoxes and nuclear power asymmetries outlined above are quite real, and must be accommodated. But something better than unchecked weapons proliferation and use is nevertheless within reach. Surprisingly, the nuclear powers have maintained nuclear weapons for four decades without ever using them in anger. It is now possible that countries will acquire nuclear weapons production capabilities without actually constructing a weapon. An asymmetry in national nuclear capabilities may strain one's sense of fairness, but accommodating the resulting disparities will be easier if they are managed collectively. The critical mechanism of accommodation, made more likely by the end of the Cold War and the collective response to the Iraqi aggression in Kuwait, is the institutionalization of multinational responses to the use of weapons (in the hope of preventing it), as well as to the problem of weapons proliferation more generally.

The precedent set by the US/UN collective response to Iraqi aggression is highly significant. There could hardly have emerged a more perfect test case for collective security than Saddam Hussein's attack on Kuwait. It blended a blatant aggression across internationally recognized borders, in which an odious dictator threatened the use of chemical, biological, and even nuclear, weapons with the capture of one of the world's most sensitive energy resources. Most countries already were moving toward a collective delegitimization of further nuclear weapons proliferation by their endorsement of the NPT, and the general belief that non-proliferation was an obligation even for non-signatories. As in the recent case of Iraq, the international community now insists on inhibiting access to the crucial ingredients and components of a national nuclear weapons programme. Some would go further and support military intervention to pre-empt the spread of weapons of mass destruction.

The question before us now is how the international community will organize itself to reinforce the precedent of its collective response to Saddam Hussein. If the United States substantially reduces the conventional military capabilities employed in 'Desert Storm', other dictators could find it easier to challenge the international order. Those who would rely on economic sanctions instead of military force must confront at least two concerns: sanctions may not topple the aggressor regime, but they might impose even more suffering on civilians than a military intervention. Maintaining the ability to undertake a military intervention with some hope for a quick success therefore may be desirable. Similarly, if the United States and Russia substantially reduce their nuclear arsenals, will this action discourage or embolden other states to reach for nuclear weapons? The latter, more depressing possibility cannot be ruled out.

The 'Internationalization' of the Soviet Union

Quite apart from Iraq's exploitation of the peace dividend and continuing concerns about nuclear proliferation, the sudden collapse of the Soviet Union has also been a very mixed blessing for arms control. Although it quells most of the concerns of the NATO countries about a massive, Moscow-directed conventional armored attack from the East, the collapse creates major problems in controlling the Soviet nuclear arsenal, which is now spread around several newly independent states.[9]

Unlike the American constitution, the constitution of the 'federal' USSR provided that each of its constituent republics could secede, though many regarded this as a prerogative for which there was no basis in reality. One of the startling facts of 1991 was that the secession option was exercised. Only eleven of the fifteen Republics of the former Soviet Union joined the new Commonwealth of Independent States (CIS), which is expected to gain little power and be of short duration. But while the world need no longer fear a powerful USSR, it must now deal with a host of new international rivalries and disputes. The most worrisome consequence of this development, of course, has been the thousands of strategic and tactical nuclear weapons deployed across the former Soviet Union. If nothing else could make the outside world care about what Ukrainians and Russians, or Azeris and Armenians, do to each other, the fact that a Soviet missile takes only 30 minutes to reach other continents would suffice. (And if nothing else were to make the outside world regret the break-up of the 'evil empire', the nuclear factor might work in this direction.) The United States and others have cited Soviet treaty obligations under the NPT and the INF and START agreements to insist that these commit the republics to completing the reductions that Soviet negotiators agreed to, and that all remaining nuclear warheads be consolidated in a single successor state: Russia.[10] International legal commitments are not a negligible factor in power politics, but they also rarely suffice to force a decision. To maximize their leverage, the outside powers will have to co-ordinate their efforts, using economic assistance as a bargaining chip.

Without the nuclear factor, it might have been easier for Europeans to welcome the break-up of the Soviet Union. If there were no nuclear risk, the most hard-headed realist might have seen a clear-cut strategic advantage in such a break-up. But many nuclear weapons do exist in the former Soviet Union, posing enormous dangers of unintended use in or outside the territory of the former USSR. Therefore, when these weapons are not under safe, secure and, above all, central control, they constitute a major threat to world security.

Some analysts, including former American Secretary of State James Baker, now refer to the former Soviet Union as a 'Yugoslavia with nukes', suggesting that the world would be essentially indifferent to the fate of Russia and the CIS if the nuclear factor were absent from the equation. Yet there has been a serious multilateral effort to curb Serbian military aggressions.[11] In an age of live television coverage, even the most selfish countries have difficulty shrugging off massacres, famines and other forms of human misery. One does not need to have been a recent tourist in Dubrovnik or Sarajevo to sense that something internationally intolerable is underway there.

While it is clear that the international community cannot stand still in these instances, it is equally clear that the response cannot be purely national. Neither the means nor the will for unilateral action exists any longer.

Ethnic Disputes

Analysts who predicted the course of events after 1989 might have been accused of an excessively optimistic outlook on international politics. The view that religious, cultural and racial issues would again become preponderant contradicted conventional expectations. Socialists firmly believed that economic relationships were the basis for most conflicts. Decades of Marxist indoctrination, which taught rival groups that 'all men are brothers' and that workers of the world should unite against capitalist oppression, seemed to have produced fundamental changes in ethnic attitudes in Marxist states.

Woodrow Wilson and his colleagues were determined that, above all, ethnic strife should not be allowed to lead to war. They proposed involving outside powers in adjudicating and arbitrating ethnic disputes. The idea was strikingly similar to a jury in a domestic conflict in which the jurors, having no personal interest in the issue in dispute, can be counted upon to hear the evidence fairly. Such a multilateral approach would be an appropriate means of resolving ethnic conflict in the post-Cold War world. However, if one country persists in trying to have its way by using military force, the international community will have to relinquish the role of jury and become policeman. It must be ready to intervene to separate combatants and relocate populations unable to live together in reasonable civility. To maintain peace, therefore, the international community must be willing to engage in war.

Conventional Weapons: The 'Rich Man's H-Bomb'

If the peace-loving nations of the world are collectively to ensure peace, they must have the economic and military power to maintain and uphold peace. What kind of military power is most effective for this purpose? A fundamental worry is that leaders like Saddam Hussein or Muammar Ghadaffi will come into control of nuclear weapons, though their possession of chemical or biological weapons, often referred to as the 'poor man's H-bomb', is of equal concern.

Yet many would avoid using either nuclear or CB weapons to respond to their threatened or actual use by regional powers. This is partly because the collateral damage of such weapons could be so severe that the winners would suffer almost as much as the losers. But it may now be in larger part because conventional weapons, as graphically demonstrated in 'Desert Storm', have become so supremely effective in defeating and disarming an enemy.

Conventional weapons have never been cheap. Indeed, one attraction of nuclear weapons has been their ability to cut the total economic burden of defence. Superior conventional weapons also require that a nation maintain extensive and sustained defence research and development efforts. The decisive military advantage demonstrated by the United States in 'Desert Storm' amounts to making conventional firepower 'the rich man's H-bomb' – an 'ultimate weapon' that depends on microchips rather than nuclear physics or toxic chemistry to have its desired effect. Economies of scale are likely to give the United States a decisive edge over Japan, Germany, France, or Russia, and of course far ahead of the Irans and Iraqs of the world.[12]

Further Grounds for Multinational Approaches

The role of 'policeman of the world' is fraught with perils for the United States, not the least of which is the possibility that Americans will not support it. However, the United States is probably the only nation with the conventional military capability necessary to play that role. This fact supports the development of multilateral mechanisms for the use and management of such power. The international community will only accept the American 'cop on the beat' if he can be trusted to consult other countries before taking action.

The manner in which the United States consulted with other members of the United Nations when responding to the Iraqi aggression and, more recently, to help feed starving Somalis, should reassure the international community that the United States will use its military power wisely.[13] For example, while Beijing's official statements sometimes warn of US 'hegemony', the Chinese privately say they welcome a continued US naval presence in the Far East, preferring this to the alternatives of a more powerful Japanese naval Self-Defence Force, a Russian or Indian Navy, or a power vacuum in the area.

Other countries in the region have the same preference. For example, Singaporean diplomats lobbied the Philippine government not to drive too hard a bargain on the continued presence of American naval and air forces at Clark Field and Subic Bay (before the eruption of Mt. Pinatubo settled the issue). Since 1975 the US presence in the Far East has been seen as an antidote to, rather than a harbinger of, violent conflict.

This role is not unlike that of the British navy in the nineteenth century which, though denounced by other nations, was also quietly welcomed as it stamped out piracy and the slave trade and kept warfare on the high seas to a minimum.

There are at least two ways in which American action could spoil this picture. First, Washington could avoid consulting other nations, and embark on actions of which most of the world disapproved. Second, the United States could decide that a global military presence was too expensive, too unrewarding, or too likely to get young American men and women killed. Taking steps to strengthen the multilateral management of international conventional military operations may therefore be an important way to avoid either of these pitfalls. Regular consultation, on the pattern established by the Bush administration, will reassure other nations. And the co-ordinated participation of the military forces of US allies (perhaps even the participation of the under-employed Russian navy) might leave American taxpayers feeling that they were not being exploited in the process. Additionally, it will be important to share the financial burden, which means assuring that the United States is reimbursed for its leading role in military interventions. If the United States is to play the role of 'world policeman', it must be paid.

The Nuclear Bottom Line

This paper has detailed why collective approaches may be more workable and more necessary for the entire range of international security issues facing the post-Cold War world. Nuclear proliferation issues are the model for these multilateral approaches because they are among the most consequential and enduring of our concerns. The optimistic idealist position is that all weapons must be banned or sharply reduced, so that war and arms races can be put behind us. The pessimistic realist position is that if weapons can be built, they will be built; and that any weapons that are built will be used. Our experience with nuclear weapons so far contradicts both these positions. A more vigorous effort to strengthen collective co-operation and control could produce more effective barriers against international instability and war.

NOTES

1. On the broader implications of the Iraqi aggression, see John D. Steinbruner, 'The Consequences of the Gulf War', *The Brookings Review*, Vol. 9, No. 2 (Spring 1991), pp. 6–13.
2. The ramifications of these uncorked ethnic tensions are discussed in Gil Loescher,

Refugee Movements and International Security, Adelphi Papers No. 268 (London: Brassey's for the IISS, 1992); and Martin O. Heisler, 'Migration, International Relations and the New Europe', *International Migration Review*, Vol. 2 (Summer 1992), pp. 596–622.

3. For a somewhat optimistic assessment of this collective security mechanism, see Gregory Flynn and David Scheffer, 'Limited Collective Security', *Foreign Policy*, No. 80 (Fall 1990), pp. 77–101.
4. The broad base of opposition to nuclear proliferation is discussed in Joseph C. Nye, Jr., 'Maintaining a Nuclear Non-Proliferation Regime', *International Organization*, Vol. 35, No. 1 (Winter 1981), pp. 15–30.
5. On the inherent difficulties of collective security systems, see Richard K. Betts, 'Systems for Peace or Causes for War? Collective Security, Arms Control, and the New Europe', *International Security*, Vol. 17, No. 1 (Summer 1992), pp. 5–43.
6. An example of a more pessimistic analysis is to be found in Leonard Spector, *Nuclear Ambitions* (Boulder, CO: Westview Press, 1990).
7. On the 1995 NPT Review Conference, see George Bunn, Charles Van Doren and David Fischer, *Options and Opportunities: The NPT Extension Conference* (Southampton, UK: Programme for Promoting Nuclear Non-Proliferation, 1991).
8. Carl Von Clausewitz, *On War* (Princeton, NJ: Princeton University Press, 1976), p. 370.
9. On the control over what had been Soviet strategic nuclear weapons, see 'Soviet Strategic Nuclear Weapons Outside the Russian Republic', *Arms Control Today*, Vol. 21, No. 10 (Dec. 1991), p. 29.
10. The track record of Western negotiations with the former Soviet Union on this issue can be found in Steven E. Miller, 'Western Diplomacy and the Soviet Nuclear Legacy', *Survival*, Vol. 34, No. 3 (Autumn 1992), pp. 3–27.
11. On the implications of the Yugoslav example, see John Zametica, *The Yugoslav Conflict*, Adelphi Paper No. 270 (London: Brassey's for the IISS, 1992).
12. On the possible power advantages of the United States, see Charles Krauthammer, 'The Unipolar Moment', *Foreign Affairs*, Vol. 70, No. 1 (America and the World 1990/1991), pp. 23–33.
13. The Bush administration's handling of the anti-Iraq coalition is discussed in Peter W. Rodman, 'Middle East Diplomacy', *Foreign Affairs*, Vol. 70, No. 2 (Spring 1991), pp. 1–18.

Comprehensive Control over Nuclear Weapons

JONATHAN DEAN

The times are auspicious for getting an enduring grip on the entire nuclear weapons issue, for instituting a world-wide programme of irreversible build-down of nuclear weapons capability, and for achieving results quite soon. We face a unique constellation of circumstances: the Cold War nuclear confrontation has been dismantled; control over the bulk of Soviet nuclear weapons has been transferred to a Russian government striving to institute a democratic form of government and highly dependent on Western countries for economic help; and a new American administration with a chief executive whose outlook was not forged in the Cold War nuclear stand-off has come to power. These circumstances create a highly favourable opening for a multilateral programme to end the production of nuclear weapons materials by both declared and undeclared nuclear weapons states, to cut the arsenals of the nuclear powers to residual levels, and to end any practical risk of independent development of nuclear weapons capability. This programme, moreover, could be implemented within a decade. But the opportunity will not last indefinitely; the opening is already closing slowly as Russia moves closer to authoritarian, nationalist rule.

Nuclear Arms Control and the Bush Administration

The Bush administration performed a brilliant diplomatic feat in persuading the Soviet government to sign the START-I Treaty in July 1991 and to engage in parallel withdrawal of tactical nuclear weapons to central sites. It also succeeded in averting nuclear weapons chaos after the collapse of the Soviet Union by persuading the Soviet successor states with strategic nuclear weapons on their territory to sign on to the START-I Treaty in May 1992, and committing Belarus, Ukraine and Kazakhstan to sign the nuclear Non-Proliferation Treaty (NPT) as non-nuclear weapons states. The administration also performed brilliantly in persuading Russia to sign the Bush-Yeltsin understanding of June 1992 to eliminate multiple warheads on land-based missiles and to reduce strategic-range nuclear warheads to an overall level of about 3,000. The administration provided valuable help in persuading Belarus, Ukraine, and Kazakhstan to allow withdrawal of tactical weapons and reduced strategic warheads to Russia for custody and dismantling.

Urged by Congress, the administration has given Russia and other successor states help in transporting and safeguarding withdrawn warheads, in planning the storage of fissile material recovered from these weapons, and in instituting export controls. Finally, it arranged to purchase from Russia up to 500 tons of highly enriched uranium for conversion to nuclear fuel, thus limiting the possibility of its reuse, diversion, or sale. Most of these actions were packed into the first six months of 1992 after the sudden collapse of the old Soviet Union in December 1991. The Bush administration's actions were based on realistic analysis, rapid timing and astute use of political and economic pressures. They saved the United States and the world from the consequences of immediate nuclear proliferation in the Soviet successor states and were a fitting finale to the equally brilliant administration performance in helping to ease the Soviet Union out of domination of Eastern Europe and in bringing about the unification of Germany in an almost completely peaceful manner.

The Bush administration made another key contribution to control over nuclear weapons capability. In a short, well-planned and executed military campaign, it defeated Iraq, drove its forces from Kuwait, and instituted a control regime under the auspices of the UN Security Council that eliminated Iraq's secretly developed programme to achieve nuclear weapons capability, as well as its capability to produce other weapons of mass destruction.

Together, these actions represent the most important moves toward control over nuclear weapons since the onset of the Cold War.

Shortcomings of the Bush Administration's Approach

At the same time, the Bush administration approach had some serious shortcomings. Some of these were not of the administration's making; others flowed from the design of administration policy.

The weakness of governments in the Soviet successor states, rising nationalism and friction between Russia and Ukraine impeded implementation of the administration's plans and designs. As a result, there were delays and uncertainty over the final ratification of the START-I Treaty, and signature of the Non-Proliferation Treaty by Belarus, Ukraine, and Kazakhstan. In a worst case situation, the three non-Russian republics could become nuclear powers, with devastating effect on efforts to extend the NPT in 1995. Although it is probable that continued efforts by the Western countries will ultimately bring these new states into the NPT regime, each of them may have a large stock of nuclear weapons deployed on its territory for quite some time. For its part, the Russian government encountered nationalist opposition to the START-II agreement and US and Russian efforts to translate the agreement into treaty form, although a breakthrough on this was achieved in early January 1993 with the signing of the START-II Treaty. Critics claimed that the United States would gain too much advantage, given Yeltsin's agreement to eliminate all land-based MIRVed warheads and the retention by the US of a large number of submarine-deployed MIRVs. These are all danger signs for future dealings on nuclear weapons.

Also not of the Bush administration's making is the slow movement of Russia toward more authoritarian government as it staggers under the weight of political and economic reform. Western countries have every reason to hope that all the Soviet successor states, and especially Russia as the most powerful among them, ultimately make decisive progress toward a functioning democracy; its achievement would be the most effective safeguard for Western security. But such an outcome is highly uncertain and its achievement will take many decades. In the interim, factors making for authoritarian development in Russia and other nuclear-armed successor states are numerous: low understanding of democratic procedures and values; weak democratic institutions; large groups of increasingly disaffected citizens, including former party officials and military officers; coalescence of extreme nationalist and former communists into more effective political groups; continuing economic deprivation; and the destructive effects of ethnic violence.

In late 1992 President Yeltsin, with full support from only about a third of the members of the Congress of Peoples Deputies, was obliged in a stand-off with conservative elements of the Congress to drop economic reformer Yegor Gaidar as Prime Minister and to accept one of their representatives as Gaidar's replacement. This development was not of itself a conclusive step toward less democratic government, but it was evidence of a continuing process.

The prospect for Russia is indefinite continuation of political turbulence together with possession of strategic arsenals large enough to launch a devastating attack on the United States and its allies. If an overtly right-wing government does emerge in Russia, it is unlikely at the outset to have hostile intentions toward the West. But the government is likely to be nationalistic, jingoistic and to frighten people inside and outside Russia by recalling the Soviet totalitarian past. In these circumstances, there could be rapid alienation and estrangement between Western governments and Russia or other successor state governments. Finding the right balance of support and admonition would become much harder for Western governments, and Western economic help would probably decrease. An unstable Russia veering toward autocratic government and disposing indefinitely over a large stock of strategic nuclear weapons would create an epicentre of nuclear instability in the world. The answer is to get as much of this nuclear capability as feasible out of Russia, even at the cost of further sharp reciprocal reduction of the US nuclear arsenal.

The Bush administration has not helped matters in this regard. One major shortcoming of its approach is the fact that the START treaties provide for withdrawing nuclear warheads and missiles from field deployment, rather than providing for their irreversible destruction. The treaties do not obligate Russia or the United States to destroy nuclear warheads or strategic-range ballistic missiles, with the significant exception of SS-18 missiles, which must be destroyed under START II. Other than that, warheads and missiles can be retained and stored without limit. Redeployment would breach the treaty, but could be done rapidly. There is also no mutual obligation to account for or dismantle the tactical warheads withdrawn in parallel unilateral action from deployment outside national territory, although in practice each government has stated it would destroy a considerable number. Russia is prepared to dismantle strategic warheads withdrawn from the other republics under START I, but there is no mutual US-Russian obligation to destroy warheads, no provision for full accountability, and no mutual obligation to place the fissile material recovered from these weapons in monitored storage. For Russia, these omissions may mean the indefinite continuation of very large nuclear arsenals in unstable political circumstances.

The stumbling block to changing this dangerous situation has been the Bush administration's unwillingness to engage in reciprocal commitments on this subject with Russia. The main justification for this refusal – up to a point it is a strong justification – is that the administration has been able to bring about a great deal of rapid unilateral Russian action through persuasion backed by the inducement of economic help and that this progress would have been impossible or at least much delayed if the administration had taken the laborious route of treaty negotiation and parliamentary ratification. Bush administration officials have also argued that mutual verification of this process would put at risk details of US weapons design. This argument is less persuasive. It was advanced in a post-Cold War situation, one in which the administration has found acceptable ways to enable mutual verification in START I of the number of warheads mounted on strategic-range missiles and where a number of procedures have been suggested for verifying dismantling of warheads without close examination of the individual warheads.

The administration approach on this subject has created the impression that it would rather have a free hand on US warheads reduced under START, that it prefers to rely on traditional deterrence, thus taking its chances with future developments in Russia, over engaging in irreversible and monitored build-down of the Russian nuclear arsenal at the cost of American reciprocity. As corroborated by President Bush's statements in June 1992 that the US would continue to rely on a policy of nuclear deterrence, the administration appeared to envision the indefinite continuation of a nuclear stand-off of the classic type, although on a much reduced scale. There has been no indication of interest on its part in making the US-Russian nuclear build-down irreversible. There also has been no inclination to use the co-operative attitude of the Russian government to make a major breakthrough on nuclear weapons world-wide by reaching out and bringing the other nuclear powers under a multilateral control regime. This was so even though the government of one of the other nuclear powers, China, was simultaneously increasing its nuclear arsenal and undergoing a succession crisis of its own which could result in regional dispersal of control over nuclear weapons and proliferation on the Soviet pattern.

Finally, the Bush administration did not move to exploit fully the willingness of the non-nuclear states to take decisive steps to tighten the non-proliferation regime after the shocking revelation of Iraq's progress toward nuclear weapons capability without the knowledge of world governments, or of the International Atomic Energy Agency (IAEA), established to warn of just such a development. Strengthening procedures of the IAEA to permit inspection of undeclared sites, improving the flow of information to the IAEA from national intelligence agencies, tightening controls of the Nuclear Suppliers Group and the Missile Technology Control Regime (MTCR), and revising the Cocom controls on transfer of dual-use technology – these are all useful steps, but they are not sufficient.

It is true that, despite some continuing weaknesses of the non-proliferation regime, the balance of developments during the 1990s in the non-proliferation field has been favourable. Iraqi nuclear intentions were after all discovered and blocked. If the members of the Security Council show common sense, these efforts will continue to be blocked for an indefinite period, whatever the intentions of the Iraqi regime. In recent years, moreover, South Africa, which was well on the way to nuclear weapons capability, and two nuclear weapons states, France and

China, have signed the NPT. Brazil and Argentina gave up their weapons development programmes and established a system of mutual inspection implemented by the IAEA. North Korea has at long last signed a safeguards agreement with the IAEA and permitted inspections. These indicated that the North Korean government still had a considerable way to go before achieving a nuclear weapons capability (although it remained possible that it had secretly produced and concealed enough fissile material to make a few weapons). These developments reinforce the conclusion that the international community is now prepared to go still further in controlling nuclear weapons potential.

On the other hand, successful proliferation, for example through a decision by one or more of the Soviet successor states to retain some nuclear weapons, would have severe consequences. Widespread possession of nuclear weapons in various regions of the world would of course decrease the relative military and political power of the United States and other nuclear powers. It could frustrate UN peacemaking operations and the emergence of a world security system capable of keeping organized violence to a minimum. Above all, it could discourage the many non-nuclear industrial states that at this time prefer to trust their security to multilateral security systems from continuing to do so. These countries – states like Sweden, Belgium, Italy, Germany, Japan, Taiwan and South Korea – all have strong military potential, including the capacity to produce nuclear weapons rapidly. In practical terms, these countries are the world's biggest proliferation threat, far more so than the Irans or Iraqs of the world. If they perceive that the non-proliferation regime is not being operated efficiently in a way that will protect them, some may ultimately move toward developing their own nuclear capability.

The combination of large nuclear arsenals and political instability in Russia or in Kazakhstan, Belarus or Ukraine even if they sign the NPT can have a similar effect on these non-nuclear but nuclear-capable governments. These circumstances entail the risk of accidents in weapons handling, of struggles for physical control over the weapons, of nuclear terrorism, or of nuclear threats and intimidation of neighbouring states. If this situation continues, it too will make the states capable of building nuclear weapons more doubtful about the effectiveness of a multilateral approach to controlling nuclear weapons and make them think seriously about ensuring their security by their own means.

Needed: A Comprehensive Approach

These circumstances call for a comprehensive approach which tackles all the major problems of nuclear weapons capability in an integrated and mutually reinforcing way. Up to now, these problems have been handled both by governments and arms control groups in a compartmented way – US-Soviet nuclear arms control, nuclear testing, deterrence strategies, controlling production of fissile materials, and export of components for weapons development have all been dealt with separately. But what is involved is after all one single subject – nuclear weapons capability. It should be addressed in a comprehensive rather than compartmentalized manner.

The central organizing element of a comprehensive approach is to eliminate production of fissile material for nuclear weapons, placing all nuclear installations of all UN member states under strengthened IAEA safeguards. This action alone, carried out by agreement among the five declared nuclear powers and backed by a Security Council resolution requiring all UN members to do likewise, would freeze the arsenals of nuclear weapons powers, both declared and undeclared, and in practical terms end the possibility of independent development of nuclear weapons capability. Without nuclear explosives, there can be no nuclear weapons. This programme is not technically complicated, and it is straightforward. It is a programme the American and the world public will understand and support. It could be achieved within the decade and probably more rapidly.

The central component of this approach is US-Russian agreement to dismantle reduced warheads, place the fissile material in monitored storage, and to end the production of fissile material for weapons, subjecting *all* their nuclear installations to IAEA safeguards. This action would be complemented by parallel actions to reduce US and Russian weapons to residual levels, end testing for nuclear weapons and restrict the production of strategic-range missiles. Acting together, Russia and the United States would then move to persuade the remaining declared nuclear weapons states to end production of fissile material for weapons purposes. Parallel to this, action would be undertaken by the UN Security Council to induce the handful of states which are not members of the NPT to enter a regime of multilateral controls, which would end their capability, present or future, to produce weapons-grade fissile materials.

The comprehensive programme proposed here requires the following steps:

1. Ensure that the START build-down is irreversible

The highest potential risk to Western security is posed by the large Russian strategic nuclear arsenal, especially if it falls into the hands of an authoritarian Russian government. (During the next decade, while Belarus, Ukraine and Kazakhstan continue to have strategic nuclear arms on their territory, this point also applies to them.) This risk is not negligible and needs to be counteracted vigorously.

Arrangements like the US agreement to buy Russian weapons-grade uranium and convert it to fuel for civilian reactors are useful. But they are partial at best and cannot take the place of verifiable formal agreements, for which reciprocity by the United States is necessary. Reductions in US-Soviet nuclear arsenals must be made permanent and not consist merely of withdrawal of nuclear warheads from field deployment and storing them, while retaining the capability to produce new warheads without limit. Therefore, the United States and Russia should negotiate a verified, bilateral agreement to dismantle all strategic warheads reduced under the START and subsequent agreements or negotiations. They would agree not to reuse the fissile material recovered from these warheads for other weapons and to place their fissile material under IAEA-monitored storage, preferably at locations outside the territories of the two countries.

Such a US-Russian agreement would not have great value unless it were accompanied by bilateral agreement to stop production of fissile material for weapons. Agreement to stop production of fissile material for weapons purposes would make it possible for both countries to place all their nuclear installations under IAEA safeguards to ensure that production of fissile material for weapons is not taking place. Technically, this action would be relatively simple. No formal treaty is needed to begin the process; parallel unilateral declarations ending the production of fissile material for weapons and placing all nuclear installations under IAEA safeguards would suffice. The IAEA would monitor cessation of production, but it could be reinforced by bilateral monitoring. The use of plutonium, a fissile material usable for weapons, in civilian power reactors would be closely checked by the IAEA and phased out in a later stage.

The United States and Russia would also agree on verified destruction of the strategic-range missiles cut back under the START and under subsequent reduction agreements, except for a specified number for space use. They would also restrict missile production to replacements and a specified number for space use. The INF Treaty established that verification of missile production could be carried out by monitoring plants producing engines for missiles. Finally, the two countries would agree to phase out testing of nuclear warheads on the terms signed into US law by President Bush in October 1992 – in practice a short period of restricted testing, followed by a complete cessation of tests.

This programme would much reduce the dangers associated with a continuing deployment of a large Russian arsenal, although it would not completely eliminate them. Tagging individual warheads, dismantling reduced warheads and placing fissile material in monitored storage, or even inspecting records of past production of weapons-grade fissile material would not eliminate the possibility that some fissile material (or even finished warheads or missiles) was being concealed. Remaining risks would be decreased through restricting deployed land-based strategic missiles to single warhead systems, destroying missiles and launchers reduced by agreement, and restricting missile production, as well as by the retention of significant strategic-range arsenals, with the bulk of US forces deployed on submarines not vulnerable to surprise attack.

This bilateral nuclear control programme is feasible. The United States will stop nuclear testing under the new 1992 law if other nuclear powers do. It has stopped production of fissile materials and new warheads. Russia is ready to stop testing and producing fissile material. What is required is to formalize these actions in a bilateral agreement to ensure that commitments will in fact be implemented.

2. Expand Nuclear Arms Control to Other Nuclear-Weapons States

The second greatest potential nuclear weapons threat to Western security is from a collapse of central authority in China and loss of effective control over Chinese nuclear weapons. This too is not a negligible risk. Bringing China into an international system of controls would mitigate that risk. Consequently, full implementation of the proposed US-Russian actions could be made dependent on the agreement of the other declared nuclear-weapons states – Britain, France and China – to follow suit by freezing the level of their warheads, restricting missile production, phasing out warhead testing, ending production of fissile material for weapons and placing all their nuclear facilities under IAEA supervision. To induce acceptance of this proposal in Paris, London and Beijing, the United States and Russia could agree to reduce their own arsenals of nuclear weapons to a level of 1,000 warheads each. The central component of this approach, five-power agreement to cease production of fissile material, could be carried out through a declaration of intent from each and a change in the safeguards agreement each has signed with the IAEA. At a later stage, these declarations could be formalized in a five-power treaty or as a protocol to the Non-Proliferation Treaty, whichever is simpler.

This programme also appears feasible. France has declared a moratorium on testing and has repeatedly suggested five-power talks on the future of nuclear weapons. Though Britain opposes an end to nuclear testing, once the United States decides on this course Britain will be under considerable pressure to follow suit, given its reliance on the Nevada site for its nuclear testing programme. China will be the difficult partner, but the suggested approach corresponds to China's position of principle, and China is ultimately likely to go along if the others join in.

The five powers could in turn make implementation of these agreed steps dependent on a positive decision at the review conference for the Non-Proliferation Treaty to be held in 1995 to continue the treaty for an indefinite period. They could also make implementation of these steps dependent on agreement of NPT signatory states to the large increases in the IAEA safeguards budget and staff that the steps would require, and on adoption of the Security Council actions described below. The IAEA is severely underfunded. A 400 per cent increase in the agency's safeguards budget would cost under $400 million a year, of which the United States would pay $100 million, a small fraction of the nearly $4 billion spent annually on the Strategic Defense Initiative (SDI) programme. The agreement of the five declared nuclear powers to stop testing could be incorporated in a comprehensive test ban treaty. Their agreement to cut missile production would at the least result in tightening the MTCR and might form the basis of a worldwide treaty restricting missile production.

3. Cover the Undeclared Weapons States

To pursue non-proliferation more effectively, the five powers would together seek UN Security Council assurances for non-nuclear states stronger than those issued by the Council in 1968 in connection with the signing of the NPT. To facilitate such a statement, they would themselves pledge not to make first-use of nuclear weapons and would support a Security Council decision committing the Council to take joint action against states or terrorist groups that initiate the use of nuclear weapons. This action would respond to demands by states like Ukraine and Nigeria for stronger protection to non-nuclear NPT signatories than is currently the case.

To increase pressure on non-signatories of the NPT to sign the treaty, the Security Council would decide to take joint action under ChapterVII of the Charter, including economic sanctions, against any UN member state that refused to place all its nuclear installations either under IAEA safeguards or under some multilateral equivalent, like the Brazil-Argentina agreement of 1991. States that had not yet taken these steps would be given a grace period of two years or so to make their decision. The Council would justify this action on the grounds that, given the dangers to international peace and security from uncontrolled development of nuclear weapons and the fact that all NPT signatory states had relinquished production of fissile material for weapons purposes and placed all their nuclear installations under IAEA safeguards, it would be an unacceptable threat to international security to permit any UN member state to abstain from multilateral inspection and to conduct untrammelled nuclear weapons development.

This action would bring pressure on the three undeclared nuclear powers – India, Pakistan and Israel – to end their production of fissile material, placing a cap on their nuclear weapons capability. The Bush administration has already suggested that these countries end their production of fissile materials in separate regional agreements. If these countries do not wish to sign the NPT as non-nuclear weapons states (India has indicated that it wishes to be accepted by the international community as a nuclear weapons state), they can conclude multilateral regional agreements providing for safeguards over their nuclear installations to be monitored by IAEA, as Argentina and Brazil have done. Other NPT non-signatories like Algeria would be obliged to do the same.

This action would leave India, Pakistan and Israel with an undisclosed number of nuclear weapons. Whether this situation could be improved by subsequent international understanding would have to be reviewed. But the nuclear weapons holdings of these states could not be expanded. The Security Council approach would close off the open-ended character of the NPT regime which permits states to evade international control by not signing the treaty or by withdrawing from it. This loophole should not be permitted to continue.

Toward a Working System of Collective Security

Given the reductions and restrictions on their own nuclear capabilities to which they would have agreed, the five declared nuclear powers, who are also the permanent members of the Security Council, would have a strong corporate interest in ensuring continued stringent Security Council supervision of this broader system for control over nuclear weapons. They would systematically use Security Council decisions to complement IAEA controls and those of the Nuclear Suppliers Group. For example, the Council could decide to obligate supplier countries to report to the IAEA sales or transfers of all components and items on a list prepared by the Suppliers Group. This action is now carried out on a voluntary and incomplete basis.

Co-operation of the five permanent members of the Security Council on controlling nuclear weapons capability generally and their interaction in operating the systems of mutual controls over their own nuclear arsenals should intensify practical co-operation among them and other Security Council members on peacekeeping and peacemaking, as has already taken place in cases like Cambodia and Somalia.

World-wide elimination of testing and of the production of fissile material for weapons monitored by the Security Council itself and by a strengthened IAEA would for practical purposes end the possibility of independent development of nuclear weapons capability. Reduced nuclear arsenals and greater accountability through verification would reduce the risk of unauthorized transfer of nuclear weapons by a nuclear weapons state. There would be much tighter control of long-range missile capabilities. Thus the proposed programme should in practical terms eliminate the threat of attack on any country with nuclear-armed long-range missiles, making superfluous expensive programmes of defence against long-range ballistic missiles like the SDI programme of the United States and smaller programmes in Russia and elsewhere.

Under this approach, there would still be about 3,000 nuclear warheads in the arsenals of the declared nuclear powers, plus a small number, undisclosed at this stage, of Indian, Pakistani and Israeli weapons. It would not yet be possible to reach a reasoned decision on whether nuclear weapons should be eliminated completely because the prerequisite for such a decision – a functioning system of world security with a proven track record of effectiveness – would not yet exist. But ending the production of nuclear weapons worldwide and capping existing nuclear arsenals at low levels would be a watershed event that would make it possible to relegate remaining nuclear weapons to a residual role of deterring the use of nuclear weapons and of helping to inhibit major war. With nuclear weapons reduced to a secondary role, international attention could focus on moving toward an effective multilateral system of international security relying at the outset on increased voluntary co-operation among the larger countries.

ACKNOWLEDGEMENT

This article draws on a forthcoming book on European security, written with support from the Twentieth Century Fund, the Ford Foundation, and the US Institute of Peace.

Non-Proliferation: New Energy, New Direction

JOHN HAWES

The nuclear non-proliferation campaign has been far more successful than was anticipated when the nuclear Non-Proliferation Treaty (NPT) was concluded in 1968. At the time it was feared that as many as twenty countries might join the United States, the USSR, Britain, China and France in the nuclear 'club'. Instead, no additional state has openly declared a nuclear weapons capability since the NPT was concluded, although three – India, Israel, and Pakistan – have achieved a tacit nuclear capability. Of the other so-called threshold countries, Argentina and Brazil have renounced their nuclear development programmes, South Africa appears to have made the same decision, and North Korea has hosted IAEA inspectors in an apparent effort to demonstrate that it has ended its nuclear programme.

The surprising success of the non-proliferation effort has not, however, brought general satisfaction. On the contrary, in public discussion there is a widespread view that the issue has become more urgent and challenging than ever. This seeming paradox reflects the fact that recent non-proliferation successes have unavoidably focused primary attention on the most difficult regions: the Middle East and South Asia. Both regions already have *de facto* nuclear capable states. Both also have deep political tensions and a long history of conflict. It is therefore hardly surprising that the major remaining nuclear issues are concentrated in these regions. Nor is it surprising that they appear to be harder to resolve than those that have been successfully dealt with elsewhere.

The end of the Cold War has also given new impetus to the non-proliferation effort. The United States and Russia have agreed to radical nuclear reductions in START II, which provides a positive framework for the reduction of all nuclear forces. Implementation of the START-I and START-II agreements will require dealing with 'involuntary proliferation' resulting from the dispersal of nuclear weapons within the former Soviet Union, something that is likely to succeed, however. The first summit meeting of the UN Security Council, in January 1992, pronounced proliferation a threat to international peace. China and France, having rejected the NPT during the Cold War as an artifact of US-Soviet hegemony, have found the regime acceptable in the new context. The end of the East–West confrontation has made it possible to convert the Coordinating Committee for Multilateral Export Controls (COCOM), which had served as the mechanism for co-ordinating the denial of strategic technology to the Soviet Union and its allies, into a broader co-operative arrangement bringing together East and West to limit the spread of technology for weapons of mass destruction.

Finally, concern has been heightened by the revelation of the scope of the Iraqi nuclear programme. United Nations investigations have raised doubts about the effectiveness of existing international control practices to preclude a determined country from developing a nuclear capability. This, in turn, has spurred thinking about a variety of approaches to deal with the perceived inadequacy of the traditional policies. Some have advocated tightening technology control, although the effectiveness of any such measures will be progressively undermined by the continuing global diffusion of technology. Others, hedging against the possibility of additional nuclear-capable countries, have promoted the development of ballistic missile defences. However, even if effective systems can be designed and deployed, they could only handle one of the potential means of delivery of nuclear weapons. Still others have examined the requirements for US nuclear weapons to counterbalance anticipated proliferation. It is prudent to ensure a capability for deterrence, but this, like defences, is of course not a means of restraining proliferation as such. Renewed attention has been given to possible pre-emptive military action to destroy nuclear development programmes, although the Iraqi experience in 1981 and 1991 is likely to make any future proliferator extremely careful in dispersing and protecting its programme. And some have taken a new look at global and regional arms control approaches, although these face major political and psychological hurdles in the two regions of most concern.

No single technological or legal strategem will suffice to deal with the remaining proliferation challenges and to minimize the risk that nuclear weapons may be used. Rather, broader strategies need to be tailored to the particular circumstances of each region and the individual countries concerned. These strategies need to integrate global and regional arms control, confidence-building, political and technological elements. Specific steps include:

- Negotiation of a comprehensive test ban and an agreement to cut off production of fissile material for weapons purposes in order to cap the nuclear programmes of both declared and non-declared nuclear powers;

- Extension of strategic arms control negotiations beyond the United States and Russia, to encompass the forces of all declared nuclear powers;
- Negotiation of new and expanded confidence-building measures on a regional and sub-regional basis, to lessen tension, increase openness, and reduce the risk of war;
- Establishment of regional and sub-regional arms control negotiating frameworks, to develop stabilizing agreements affecting both conventional forces and weapons of mass destruction; and
- Sharpening the focus of technological and material controls, to deal more effectively with genuine threats to international peace while avoiding sterile conflict where such threats do not exist or where the issue has already moved beyond technology control, as in the case of the three *de facto* nuclear-capable states.

Down to the Hard Cases

Because of success in other regions, and the difficulty of the security and political issues in the Middle East and South Asia, the proliferation question has come to be focused largely on these two regions. Now that it is so focused, the relevance of any suggested approach or combination of approaches must be judged in terms of the situation in those regions. What, for example, does a proposed strategy have to say about the existing *de facto* capabilities? How does it propose to address the development of further capabilities? How does it deal with the security interests of the nuclear-capable and non-nuclear-capable states in the region? How does it propose to deal with the security interests of the outside world?

The existence of nuclear capabilities sets the Middle East and South Asia apart from any other area where proliferation problems have been addressed. It is not an accident that, beyond the initial proliferation to five declared nuclear powers, only three additional states situated in these regions have acquired nuclear capabilities. All three believed they had major security concerns that were not effectively covered by Cold War arrangements. All three rejected the NPT. All three chose to pursue a nuclear capability, although all three also chose to do so tacitly rather than explicitly. And none is likely to retreat from present capabilities, absent fundamental changes in their security situation.

Beyond these similarities, however, there are also significant differences in the strategic situations of the Middle East and South Asia that affect the nature of the nuclear issue in the two regions. In South Asia there is a bipolar nuclear relationship, albeit at a much different level than the US-Soviet nuclear stand-off during the Cold War. India and Pakistan are simultaneously historical opponents and nuclear-capable states. There is, moreover, no likelihood that other states in the region will emulate their nuclear ambitions. Finally, despite the bipolar regional relationship, the original impetus for South Asian nuclear capabilities lies outside the region. India's nuclear capability was not stimulated by any threat from Pakistan, but by India's defeat by China in 1962 and the Chinese nuclear test of 1964. The Indian programme, however, led directly to the Pakistani nuclear development effort – stimulated by Pakistan's defeat by India in 1971 and the Indian nuclear test of 1974. In dealing with the South Asian nuclear question, therefore, both its extra-regional and regional aspects need to be kept constantly in mind.

In contrast to South Asia, there is no existing bipolar nuclear confrontation in the Middle East. Israel is the only nuclear-capable state in the region. Also in contrast to the situation in South Asia, other states in the Middle East have both the motivation and the ability to mount nuclear development programmes – as demonstrated by the Iraqi programme which the United Nations has dismantled. Further, unlike South Asia, the original impetus for the Israeli nuclear programme came from perceived security challenges within the region, rather than from threats outside the Middle East. The impetus to develop further nuclear capabilities also relates primarily to internal regional considerations, including but not limited to competition with Israel, the existing *de facto* nuclear capable state.

The US approach to the nuclear issue in these two regions has also been different. In South Asia, the United States has taken the position that the acquisition of nuclear capabilities by India and Pakistan was a mistake that should be rectified. Washington has not questioned the fact of those capabilities – indeed in the Pakistani case their existence has been formally confirmed in response to US law. Rather, it has denied that these capabilities have any legitimacy in terms of the strategic and political requirements of the two countries. Most importantly, the United States has insisted that the American model of global non-proliferation must take precedence over the perceived interests of these two states. This American position has been neither malevolent nor capricious, as is sometimes alleged. It has not reflected any sense of direct threat from either India or Pakistan, but derived from direct experience with the dangers of the US-Soviet nuclear competition, in particular the difficulty of ensuring stability. It also derived from the painfully acquired recognition that these weapons cannot be used but that they can absorb significant resources in an endless quest to stay one step ahead of an opponent. Finally, the US position *vis-à-vis* proliferation in South Asia derived from concern that the emergence of additional nuclear powers anywhere, for whatever reason, could create precedents that could be exploited to justify proliferation elsewhere, where it might pose a significant threat to international order.

Unfortunately, this position has been disconnected from the real situation in South Asia. Not surprisingly, it has therefore failed to attain its presumed objectives, neither reversing Indian nor stopping Pakistani acquisition of nuclear capability. Cynics have even suggested that the policy was never intended to have any real effect, but was designed essentially as a public affirmation of concern in a region where the United States did not believe it was crucial to affect proliferation decisions.

Whatever the intent, the US insistence on a narrow legalistic approach to the nuclear issue has for many years made it suspect in both New Delhi and Islamabad. As a result, Washington has been less able to engage India and Pakistan in serious discussion of regional and global security questions, and less able to help them in minimizing the risks of nuclear competition and nuclear use.

In the Middle East, by contrast, the United States has said as little as possible about the Israeli nuclear capability. Washington has largely accepted Israel's political and strategic rationale for the programme. Realistically, no one expects that capability to be renounced so long as Israel believes it is required for national security. Tactically, the United States has not wanted to focus attention on a capability that could be deemed inconsistent with the formal objectives of the non-proliferation regime. Rather, Washington has concentrated public attention and non-proliferation policy efforts on the nuclear programmes of other states in the region.

Unlike US policy in South Asia, this approach has the virtue of targeting future rather than past proliferation. At the same time, because the dividing line between nuclear have and have nots parallels one of the region's major political divisions, any approach to the proliferation question will inevitably be seen in the context of the underlying political issues of the region. Long-term success will require broad efforts to create a regional environment that will provide lasting security for all states in the area. The rapid evolution of political, religious, economic, military and technical factors in the region has shown the inadequacy of narrow defensive policies. The future requires dynamic, inclusive approaches, such as the United States has already sketched out for part of the region in its vigorous efforts to stimulate a Middle East peace process.

Prospects in South Asia

Now that both India and Pakistan have nuclear weapons, the first operative issue is how to reduce the danger of their use. The second is how to diminish pressures for an expensive nuclear arms race. The leadership in Islamabad and New Delhi has been mindful of these two requirements. The continuing crisis over Kashmir only serves as a reminder of the long history of military conflict and political tension and the inherent potential for escalation. Moreover, although both have invested heavily in their nuclear capabilities and in military forces generally, both countries also have far better things to do with the scientific and financial resources.

India and Pakistan have preferred to keep their nuclear capability somewhat ambiguous, avoiding the all-out public arms race that the United States and the former USSR engaged in. Doctrinal restraint may be helpful in managing bilateral politics. It may also be helpful internally in limiting programmatic competition, to the degree that the programmes are subject to resource reviews and constraints. Both countries, moreover, have pursued a dialogue aimed at developing confidence-building measures. These include agreements not to attack nuclear facilities, the designation of those facilities, pre-notication of exercises, limits on flight of aircraft near borders, hot lines between military commanders and simultaneous accession to the Chemical Weapons Convention. These measures suggest a serious desire to deal with the consequences of the nuclear posture that has developed. They may reflect leadership concern at the volatility of their own societies and the dangers of unrestrained competition. Given the intensity and violence of domestic politics in both countries, including most ominously the deliberate exacerbation of religious divisions for partisan purposes, it is understandable that leaderships would want to find ways of hedging against nuclear risks. Outside powers might have a positive impact on the situation. The international community must be concerned at the potential for a nuclear arms race, or the actual use of nuclear weapons, in South Asia. And it must be concerned that the violent political passions within each country could overwhelm even the most intelligent and well-intentioned leaders. In these circumstances, the availability of unbiased international advice, conciliation and encouragement may be particularly valuable.

A serious strategy for dealing with the nuclear issue in South Asia needs to combine global and regional elements that: (a) minimize the risk of use of nuclear weapons in the region, or between the countries of that region and neighbours like China; (b) reduce the desire of countries in the region to proliferate the technology and capabilities to other regions, most importantly the Middle East; (c) lessen the risk of war generally, and (d) focus more energies on peaceful development and co-operation.

At the global level, the elements of such a strategy would include:

Early negotiation of a comprehensive test ban and a halt to the production of fissile material for weapons purposes.
During the Cold War it was impossible to move forward on either of these measures, for reasons unrelated to South Asia. Now, however, negotiations on both steps are ripe at the global level. Their implementation can fill an important role in South Asia, which could not be achieved by purely regional agreements, given at a minimum Indian concerns about China. Both India and Pakistan have already said that they favour a comprehensive test ban. Agreeing to halt their production of fissile material for weapons purposes could be more problematic, in that it would freeze stockpiles at a relatively low level, but it would not be inconsistent with their security requirements and would permit the maintenance of *de facto* nuclear capabilities.

Extension of nuclear arms control negotiations to include all five declared nuclear powers.
While the absolute numbers of British, Chinese and French forces are still much smaller than Russian and US forces, the principle of their involvement in arms control has always been important to New Delhi. This is another issue that was effectively off the table during the Cold War. It should be more feasible to address it in the post-Cold War environment, and with attention more sharply focused on limiting the nuclear weapons race in South Asia there is now a greater incentive to try to do so.

Extend the NPT indefinitely, without amendment.
India and Pakistan would neither participate in nor oppose the treaty. Everyone understands that neither party will join the NPT as a non-nuclear power. No one wants to admit them as nuclear powers. Nor does anyone want to amend the treaty to create some intermediate category of 'nuclear-capable' powers. The obvious answer is to extend the regime unchanged when the issue comes up at the 1995 review conference. At the same time, sterile arguments over the fact or terms of potential Indian and Pakistani membership should now cease.

At the regional level, elements of a comprehensive strategy dealing with nuclear issues in South Asia should include:

Intensification of the existing bilateral dialogue on confidence building and arms control.
This process already includes measures relating to both nuclear and conventional forces. Continued momentum is essential, however, if it is to avoid being swamped by internal politics in both countries. Additional measures of information exchange, observation, and operations could contribute to military stability, help to contain the growth of defence requirements, and reinforce responsible political efforts to reduce tensions.

Involvement of India and Pakistan in confidence building and arms control affecting broader areas.
This can be achieved either through the extension of bilateral measures to other countries in South Asia and neighbouring regions, or through accession by India and Pakistan to wider-ranging regimes, such as Open Skies. The objective would be to stretch security horizons and to begin to build frameworks to manage issues in a portion of the world that has up until now been largely outside of arms control and confidence-building efforts.

Conversion of both India and Pakistan from targets of international non-proliferation efforts into fully responsible, participating members of the international community.
The former members of the Warsaw Pact and the Soviet Union have been invited to share in the enforcement of nuclear and other proliferation restraint efforts in return for access to technology and material. This reverses the old Cold War structure of technology control, for good reasons. The same logic should apply to India and Pakistan. As a counterpart for responsible Indian and Pakistani international performance, they should be freed of outdated nuclear controls that were designed to prevent them from doing things it is universally agreed they have already done. Moreover, to the degree that concern with South Asian nuclear capabilities has focused on the potential for the spread of technology from there to other regions, the only way to deal with this threat is to strengthen control measures in South Asia itself. There is a lot of work to be done to ensure an effective Indian and Pakistani ability to control the export of technologies. But that is where energies can be most productively employed.

The primary objection to this course of action has been that it could appear to condone proliferation by India and Pakistan, creating a breach in the NPT regime and a potential invitation to other potential proliferators. This is not a black and white matter. Rather, it gets down to balancing anomalies. There are obvious legal, rhetorical and political advantages to sustaining a virgin regime. To protect those advantages, some people are willing to blink at the facts, including in this case the existence of two *de facto* nuclear capable states. Non-proliferation is hardly the only issue on which governments have deliberately sustained non-factual perceptions over decades for alleged reasons of precedent. Other people, however, believe that this kind of anomaly actually weakens the very concept of virginity and undermines the credibility of the states defending it. They note that other states which might wish to acquire nuclear weapons in the future have not failed to point out the gaps in the concept of an immaculate non-proliferation regime. They assume, moreover, that the motivations of any future proliferators have their own roots and would not be greatly increased by the United States and others building a closer working relationship with India and Pakistan on nuclear issues.

There is, perhaps, a way of having your anomaly and eating it too. The real interest in South Asia is in performance. The primary concern is that nuclear weapons should not be used, that India and Pakistan should not engage in a nuclear arms race and that nuclear technology and material should not flow from the area to other regions. These three objectives could be a common goal, significantly ignoring the sensitive issue of capabilities. All parties can and will maintain their known views on that point. The United States, for example, will reassert the objectives of non-proliferation at the NPT review conference in 1995.

What parties will have in common, however, is the objective of co-operation for regional and global security. They will point to the new opportunities that have been opened up by the end of the Cold War. And they will make clear that the measures included in the package approach outlined above could only have been undertaken on the basis of post-Cold War reassessments in all capitals, that is, this is a mutual, not a unilateral reassessment. Such a common statement of co-operation for security will be a strong positive message to project toward other regions. For those concerned about precedents, it might even outweigh the question of balancing anomalies. The message is that co-operation is possible, but that it is only available on the basis of mutual reassessments, that all parties have to make contributions and that its elements are interrelated. This could be instructive to states in other regions, which would not yet have undertaken, or even considered, their own reassessments, and whose relations with the developed world were still confrontational and sterile.

Prospects in the Middle East

With only one nuclear-capable state, the Middle East is now where the United States and the former Soviet Union were after World War II, where the USSR and China were in the 1950s, and where India and Pakistan were in much of the 1970s and 1980s. If such situations were enduring they would offer a high degree of nuclear stability, which would not be the worst of all possible worlds for all parties concerned. However, both the historical examples and the political conditions of the region suggest that it is more likely to be transient.

Despite the difficulty of the challenge, there is widespread agreement that the operational objective in the Middle East should be to contain nuclear proliferation at its present level. First, it is clear that the nuclear situation in the Middle East is not about to go backward. Israel will not reverse its acquisition of nuclear weapons and delivery systems at least until durable peace is achieved in the region, and could well envision an enduring nuclear weapons capability as part of the system sustaining an eventual peace. Second, there is little disagreement that the introduction of additional nuclear capabilities would be destablizing, given the level of hostility in the region, the multiple lines of fracture, and the existence of state-sponsored terrorist groups.

The goal of limiting nuclear weapons in the Middle East to only one state is recognized by both advocates and opponents as discriminating in favour of Israel. Advocates, including the United States and its allies, tend to accept that as a simple matter of fact and would argue that any real or perceived diminution of the security of other parties is more than offset by the greater instabilities that would ensue from the diffusion of nuclear capabilities to additional regional states. They would further argue that the presence of state-sponsored terrorist groups increases the security risks and puts an even greater premium on preventing further proliferation. In contrast, opponents, arguing more from the point of view of the Third World, would contend that the monopoly is inherently unstable and that, as in the case of earlier US, Soviet and Indian monopolies, it will itself stimulate continuing efforts to overturn it and neutralize whatever political or strategic advantage it may be perceived to provide.

It is, unfortunately, possible that both of these points of view are correct: further proliferation would diminish the security of all countries in the region, but it may nevertheless be strongly sought by countries with a credible chance of carrying it off. The real issue then becomes not the defence of one or the other argument, but rather how to deal most effectively with the implications of both truths. The nuclear issue in the Middle East can only be successfully addressed by a combination of measures adapted to the region's highly conflicted political terrain. As in the case of South Asia, those measures will include both global and regional elements. Given the greater complexity of the region, however, many of the measures will have to be tailored to the sub-regional level.

The global measures discussed above in the South Asian context will also help with the Middle East. A CTB and a cut-off of the production of fissile material for weapons purposes would strengthen the framework of non-proliferation, creating a verifiable cap on Israel's capabilities. The verification measures needed to implement a cut-off would themselves help greatly to build confidence. It may not be easy to reach agreement on such a regime, but Israel's willingness to accept the stringent verification provisions of the Chemical Weapons Convention suggests that intrusive verification in the nuclear area cannot be excluded. The reaffirmation of the NPT without amendment in 1995 would also help, although Israel, like India and Pakistan, would not be expected to participate.

Unlike South Asia, there is no single Middle East confrontation around which regional confidence-building and arms control efforts could be organized. Given the range and complexity of conflicts, it may be easiest to attack the problem of confidence building and arms control in three separate but parallel groupings: the 'peace process' context; the Gulf; and the Mahgreb. These rough geographic groupings have a certain logic, which makes it possible to address issues of security and stability, without ignoring the important intersections between these sub-regions.

The Peace Process Context

The Arab–Israeli conflict has been and remains one of the most divisive issues of the second half of the twentieth century. The states involved have experienced intense international and domestic conflict, social change, ideological and religious tension, and arms races involving both conventional forces and weapons of mass destruction. It includes the region's one nuclear power. The other states actively involved in the peace process do not appear to have serious nuclear programmes, but many have justified the construction of ballistic missiles, chemical and biological weapons as ways to offset Israel's nuclear capability.

Despite or because of all this, the states most actively involved in the peace process are also those in the region with the greatest history of discussion, negotiation, and actual agreements. This includes the participants in the present talks – Israel, Jordan, Lebanon and Syria – as well as Egypt, which negotiated a settlement in the 1970s. After two generations of regional conflict, it is apparent that the underlying issues between Israel and its neighbours will not be solved by military force. The end of the Cold War, moreover, has removed the illusion that outside intervention would somehow resolve the issue. The fact that the parties are now at the table owes much to the efforts of the United

States. But it would not have happened at all had there not also been a recognition in the area that the situation had changed and that the future requires new approaches by all of the concerned parties.

It is in the context of the regional peace negotiations that the United States has also stimulated a discussion of arms control and confidence-building. Participation in these arms control discussions is broader than in the peace process talks, in recognition of the broad regional nature of security concerns. There are many precedents for such a discussion, going back to the disengagement provisions in the Sinai and Golan, for example. With the prospect of further political agreements, the requirement for arms control and confidence-building measures will grow. Indeed, the precedent of the 1970s suggests that arms control and confidence-building arrangements may be required even from the beginning to make political settlements possible.

The question for nuclear policy is whether measures can be devised that are acceptable to all the parties involved in the peace process, without challenging Israel's *de facto* nuclear capability at least in the near and medium term. This poses a number of challenges. There has been, for example, reluctance on the part of Israel's neighbours to give up other weapons of mass destruction while Israeli nuclear weapons are retained. Yet many of the states of the region, including Algeria, Israel, Iran, Morocco and Tunisia, have already signed or indicated they are prepared to sign the Chemical Weapons Convention, which will impose stringent verification provisions. Most of the states in the region, except Israel, are parties to the Biological Weapons Convention, which is likely to be significantly strengthened in the wake of the Russian acknowledgement that the former Soviet Union had conducted an illegal offensive biological weapons programme.

In another area, the United States and others will continue to press for effective implementation of the Missile Technology Control Regime, though some of Israel's neighbours perceive that the MTCR's restrictions on international transfers of missile technology and equipment work in favour of the demonstrated Israeli missile capability, supplemented by more sophisticated Israeli industrial and scientific infrastructure and Israeli access to restricted technology through its adherance to the guidelines of the MTCR. In this connection, it is worth noting that the Israeli Foreign Minister has recently called for the negotiation of a verifiable regional ban on surface-to-surface ballistic missiles in the region, as part of an overall ban on weapons weapons of mass destruction. Finally, both Israel and its immediate neighbours will be concerned that any limitations undertaken in the peace process context not expose them to greater threats from other states not party to the process, for example Iran.

These are not easy questions. But they are surmountable in the context of a sub-regional discussion that assumes that peace and security are the only acceptable objectives. That discussion will start from the conservative military requirements of all parties, including the retention of Israel's nuclear capability. But it will aim to enhance the security of all by limiting the risk of conflict, enhancing confidence and openness, and regulating force deployments in particular areas. There will be outspoken opponents of such a course throughout the region. That is hardly surprising; passionate debates took place during the Cold War, which in some ways was less divisive. But the opponents ultimately have the more difficult case. Endless confrontation is a dead end, and a dangerous one at that.

The Persian Gulf

In the aftermath of two recent wars, there has been an effort to strengthen political and military defences in the Gulf against either a resurgent Iraq or Iranian ambitions for regional hegemony. However, there is as yet no framework or concept that might supercede these confrontations. On the contrary, thinking both in the region and outside seems dominated by the assumption that progress requires the overthrow of one or more regimes – the only issue being which regimes must go first. That may or may not be a correct assumption, but if it is there will be little or no near-term prospect of building co-operative security structures that would bolster other efforts to restrain arms races, including the nuclear arms race. There will, instead, be an acceleration of the present arms build-up, paralleled and rationalized by ideological competition, including the further politicization of religion.

In this competitive context, the non-proliferation effort in the Gulf is dependent almost exclusively on the international control of technology and materials. Iraq remains subject to special United Nations monitoring in addition to trade controls. In the case of Iran, which is believed to be pursuing a nuclear capability, the United States has sought an intensification of control measures by all exporting states. The limits to the effectiveness of trade controls are likely to be felt in the Iranian case, as they were in the case of Iraq. Even under the best of circumstances, technology denial is a delaying strategy. It is intended to win time to prepare new defences, move on to new offensive technologies, or develop new political alliances. It cannot block acquisition of a given capability for all time. This is true even if, as expected, international trade controls are further tightened in the aftermath of the Iraqi example. The problem is not simply a matter of corruption or inattention, although both play important roles. It also reflects the constant movement of the international economy, which makes nuclear technology progressively older, more diffused, more accessible and more difficult to distinguish from legitimate civilian technologies. Gaining the co-operation of the South Asian states will help to make controls more effective than they would otherwise be. But broader approaches will eventually be required.

One potential supplement to technology control is pre-emption. The idea has a history in non-proliferation. The Chinese feared it from the Soviets; and the Pakistanis from the Indians. The Israelis practised it against the Iraqis. In the follow-up to the Gulf War, the United Nations is now pre-empting the Iraqi nuclear capability. Sometimes the approach works. Physical facilities are vulnerable. It is not certain, however, that pre-emptive strikes could cover all the bases, over a long period of time. The scope of the Iraqi programme suggests that Baghdad made major efforts to lessen its vulnerability to a single bolt from the blue on the order of the 1981 Israeli strike against the Osirak reactor. Other potential proliferators can presumably follow similar strategies. And some of them might be smart enough not to engage in a war with a coalition led by the United States acting with the authority of the UN Security Council. If this is so, pre-emption, like trade control, can only postpone the issue, and may intensify countervailing efforts. Another potential supplement to technology control is the development of ballistic missile defences. This may be a prudent investment in some circumstances. However, it does not really respond to the proliferation problem as such. Even if defences could handle all ballistic missiles – which none can – there would be a remaining nuclear threat from aircraft or from surface transportation, which would be next to impossible to rule out by technical means.

The most difficult supplement to technology control would be be an effort to construct the sub-regional political and security framework that is now so obviously lacking. The primary responsibility for this effort must rest with the United States, partly because of the assets it can bring to the task, but more so because of the absence of any other credible actors. No outside power is now capable of pulling together the kind of discussion between the Gulf states that has been generated in the Middle East peace process. No concept exists for such a discussion. But just as the United States has found it desirable to project a future-oriented negotiation in the peace process context, so too in the Gulf it can best protect important economic, political and strategic interests by stimulating an effort to look beyond present confrontations. Neither the United States nor the countries of the sub-region will ultimately benefit from the prolongation and intensification of the existing national, religious and ideological hostility.

The Mahgreb

No state in this part of the Middle East has a nuclear capability, nor are there at this point any credible nuclear development programmes. Despite this, Algeria and Libya have recently been thrown into journalistic lists of potential proliferators. Such lists could create misimpressions and cause unnecessary confusion for the non-proliferation effort.

The real concerns in the Mahgreb are not with nuclear weapons. The United States and others have been concerned at Libyan state-supported terrorism and its aggressive efforts to acquire a broad range of sophisticated weaponry. There has also been a more generalized fear that the continuing social and political revolution in the region, exemplified by the competition between the government and the Islamic opposition in Algeria, could eventually lead to international confrontation. It is important not to confuse these two concerns. Countering Libya's support for terrorism and its weapons ambitions have long been high priorities. There has been growing acceptance of the international norm against rogue activity outside the bounds of responsible state conduct. So long as Libya continues its policies, it needs to be the object of increasingly stringent international controls aimed at both the issue of terrorism and acquisition of weapons of mass destruction. Social and political revolution poses a fundamentally different set of issues. As in many other parts of the developing world, including much of the rest of the Middle East, the first question in North Africa concerns the domestic failures of post-colonial governments. The current struggles, and the answers they will produce, are oriented to those domestic concerns. Not surprisingly, the competition has led to efforts by both regimes and oppositions to mobilize religious identity for political purposes. This is, after all, part of the recent experience of US elections. The regimes, and their outside supporters, however, have attempted to generate international sympathy by attempting to equate their domestic opponents with Iranian extremists, spreading fear that governmental change in North Africa could lead to sharpened North–South confrontation and suggesting that this could lead to further nuclear proliferation.

Geography, history, culture, economics and population movements all give Europe tremendous interest and potential influence in these countries. The relationship, however, has weakened over time, and is further threatened by nervousness about how to manage relations during the present political struggles. The West, and primarily the European states, needs to move beyond existing economic ties to develop a framework of political, human rights, arms control and confidence-building measures to structure long-term security relations between the two sides of the Mediterranean. The United States must encourage this process. Too often in the past the United States has been a restraining influence, fearful that European-North African contact would undermine its military position in the Mediterranean, or would politically outflank the conduct of the Middle East peace process. With the Cold War over and the peace process launched again, it should be possible to move beyond these exaggerated fears.

The Need for a Focused Approach

The non-proliferation effort has been successful to date. Nuclear capabilities have not spread nearly as far as anticipated and nuclear weapons have not been used since 1945. The remaining proliferation questions may be more difficult than earlier ones, however, and dealing with them may require going beyond the application of controls on technology and materials. Specifically, now that START I and START II are completed, the United States should move beyond the Cold War nuclear arms control agenda to negotiate a global CTB and an agreement to a verifiable halt to the production of fissile material for weapons purposes, capping all nuclear programmes, declared or undeclared. Neither step should pose any difficulty for the United States now that the Cold War is over. Both steps should receive broad international support and pressure for accession by all states of concern. At the same time, the United States should seek to extend nuclear arms control to all five declared nuclear powers, ending the situation where relatively small forces run free. While this will encounter resistance in all three of the capitals that have not participated to date, this is another issue that should be easier to address with the end of the Cold War.

The United States should overcome its legalistic fear of precedents and recognize that the three tacit nuclear-capable states do not pose a threat to international stability and that overall non-proliferation efforts will gain in strength to the degree they can be adapted to this reality rather than pretending to ignore it. Finally, and most difficult, the United States needs to apply all available energy to the construction of regional frameworks of confidence building and arms control, to lessen tensions and reduce the risk of conflict. This is being actively pursued between India and Pakistan, but much more is needed and political pressures are mounting. The requirement is clearly understood in the context of the Arab-Israeli peace process, but discussions are only at the beginning, and the entire process faces serious hurdles. The question has not begun to be addressed in the Gulf, where the most serious proliferation issues have arisen.

The years since the end of the Cold War have seen a great unleashing of energies. Some of that has seemed threatening, as in the eruption of primitive ethnic nationalism in the former Yugoslavia. Much of it, however, has been positive, as in the global response to the Iraqi invasion of Kuwait, the defusing of long-standing conflicts from Central America to Afghanistan, and the rapid expansion of the concept of peacekeeping and peacemaking, from Cambodia to Somalia. It is in this positive sense that the new energy for non-proliferation can find its most productive focus, bolstering its fundamental objectives and its traditional technical and legal tools by building essential political and security frameworks in the most troubled regions of the world.

Notes on Contributors

Alexei G. Arbatov is Director of the Center for Arms Control and Strategic Stability in Moscow. His writings on strategic nuclear weapons policy have appeared in numerous publications. He is the editor and co-author of a recent Stimson Center Report, *Implications of Strategic Defense Deployments for US–Russian Relations.*

Michael E. Brown is a senior fellow at the International Institute for Strategic Studies in London and editor of the Institute's quarterly journal, *Survival.* He has published extensively on strategic nuclear policy. His articles have appeared in *International Security, Orbis* and *Survival* amongst other places. He is the author, most recently, of *Flying Blind: Decision Making in the U.S. Strategic Bomber Program* (Cornell University Press, 1992).

Michael Clarke is Executive Director of the Centre for Defence Studies at King's College in London. He has previously held posts at the University of Newcastle-upon-Tyne, the University of Manchester and the University of Wales, Aberystwyth. He has been a guest fellow at the Brookings Institution, Washington, DC and at the Royal Institute of International Affairs. His most recent book is *British External Relations in the 1990s*, published by Macmillan in 1992.

Ivo H. Daalder is Director of Research at the Center for International and Security Studies at Maryland, where he directs the Center's Project on Rethinking Arms Control. He is also a visiting assistant professor at the University of Maryland's School of Public Affairs. He has published extensively on arms control and European security issues, including most recently *The Nature and Practice of Flexible Response: NATO Strategy and Theater Nuclear Forces since 1967* (Columbia University Press, 1991) and *Cooperative Arms Control: A New Agenda for the Post-Cold War Era* (CISSM, 1992).

Jonathan Dean is senior arms control adviser to the Union of Concerned Scientists. He has a long experience in US arms control policy, including as ambassador to the Mutual and Balanced Force Reduction negotiations. He has written extensively on European security and arms control issues, including *Watershed in Europe* (Lexington Books, 1987) and *Meeting Gorbachev's Challenge* (St. Martin's Press, 1991).

William J. Durch is a senior associate at the Henry L. Stimson Center. He is a former assistant director of the Defense and Arms Control

Studies programme at MIT and served in government at the US Arms Control and Disarmament Agency. He is the author of *The ABM Treaty and Western Security* (Ballinger, 1988), and co-author of studies on conventional forces in Europe, naval arms control, and United Nations peacekeeping, including *The Evolution of UN Peacekeeping: Case Studies and Comparative Analysis* (St. Martin's Press, 1993).

Lisbeth Gronlund is senior staff scientist at the Union of Concerned Scientists and a visiting fellow at the Defense and Arms Control Studies programme at MIT. She received her doctorate in theoretical physics from Cornell University in 1988 and has been a recipient of a Social Science Research Council-MacArthur Foundation post-doctoral fellowship in international peace and security. Her research has focused on technical aspects of arms control, which has appeared among other places in the *Bulletin of the Atomic Scientists* and *Global Science and Security*.

John Hawes is diplomat-in-residence and a distinguished international executive at the Center for International and Security Studies at Maryland. He is a career foreign service officer with extensive experience in arms control and security policy, including most recently as the head of the US delegation to the Open Skies Treaty negotiations. His most recent publication is *Arms Control: A New Style for a New Agenda* (CISSM, 1993).

Lora Lumpe is a senior research analyst at the Federation of American Scientists, where she directs the Arms Sales Monitoring Project and co-directs the Zero Ballistic Missile Project. She also administers the Federation's work on chemical and biological arms control and produces the quarterly *Chemical Weapons Convention Bulletin*. She also compiles and edits the monthly *Arms Sales Monitor*, which reports on and analyses US arms sales and arms sales policies.

George H. Quester is a professor in the Government and Politics Department at the University of Maryland. He has analysed the impact of nuclear weapons on international politics for decades. His publications on the subject include *Nuclear Diplomacy, The Politics of Nuclear Proliferation*, and *The Future of Nuclear Deterrence*.

Terry Terriff is a senior research fellow with the Strategic Studies Program at the University of Calgary and North American editor of *Arms Control: Contemporary Security Policy*. He has written widely on NATO strategy and European security policy. His book, *The Innovation of U.S. Nuclear Strategy in the Nixon Administration*, will be published by Cornell University Press in 1994.

For Product Safety Concerns and Information please contact our EU representative GPSR@taylorandfrancis.com Taylor & Francis Verlag GmbH, Kaufingerstraße 24, 80331 München, Germany

Printed and bound by CPI Group (UK) Ltd, Croydon, CR0 4YY
11/04/2025
01844008-0011